HIGHER EDUCATION

HIGHER EDUCATION

Between Quality and Reservation

Editors
Dinesha P.T.
Ramesh

KALPAZ

ISBN : 978-93-5128-050-7

Price: ₹ 1450

First Published 2014

Published by

Kalpaz Publications
C-30, Satyawati Nagar,
Delhi-110052
Ph. : 9212142040
E-mail: kalpaz@hotmail.com

Laser Typesetting : Sanya Computers, Delhi
Printed at : G. Print Process, Delhi

Cataloging in Publication Data—DK
Courtesy: D.K. Agencies (P) Ltd. <docinfo@dkagencies.com>

"Inclusive Higher Education and Marginalised Sections: Dynamics and Discourses" (Conference) (2013 : University of Mysore)
Higher education : between quality and reservation / Dinesha P.T., Ramesh.
p. cm.
Includes bibliographical references and index.
ISBN 9789351280507

1. Education, Higher—India—Congresses. 2. People with social disabilities—Education (Higher)—Government policy—India—Congresses. 3. Higher education and state—India—Congresses. I. Dinesha, P. T. II. Ramesh (Reader in law) III. Title.

DDC 378.54 23

Contents

Foreword

The growth of any nation is measured by the quality and quantity of educated people in that nation. The Developed Nations have Gross Enrollment Ratio GER of 58 per cent in higher education, whereas the developing nations have a GER of 24 per cent, India today has a GER of around 17 per cent as of 2011. Hence, to become a super power India must increase its GER to a significant level. In the coming decades, India is set to reap the benefits of demographic dividend with its huge working age population. International Labour Organisation (ILO) has predicted that by 2020, India will have 116 million workers in the age bracket of 20 to 24 years, as compared to China's 94 million. India has a very favourable dependency ratio and it is estimated that the average age in India by the year 2020 will be 29 years as against 40 years in USA, 46 years in Japan and 47 years in Europe. In fact, we have more than 60 per cent of our population in the age group of 15 to 59 years. This trend is very significant on the grounds of what matters is not the size of the population, but its age structure. It would be a lost opportunity if this dividend is not converted into an advantage. Here lies the significance of higher education. An educated and productive workforce is what we must strive to achieve through a concerted effort to improve quality and relevance of higher education.

Globally, the literacy rate has increased from 56 per cent in 1950 to 82 per cent during 2000–04 (UNESCO, 2006). However, despite considerable improvement in the literacy status, India is home to the largest number of illiterate people in the world. According to UNESCO's *Global Monitoring Report 2006*, out of 771 million illiterate people in the world, 268 million (nearly one-third) were estimated to be in India. According to Census 2011, literacy rate in India has increased to 74 per cent in 2011. Overall, female literacy rate in India is 65 per cent and male literacy rate is 82 per cent in the year 2011. The general literacy rate among Muslims in 2001 was 59.1 per cent and for SC 54.69 per cent and for ST it was 47.10 per cent. This is far below the national average (65.1 per cent) (*As per Census 2001).*

The focus of the Twelfth Five Year as well as the preceding Eleventh Five Year Plan is on, inclusive growth of education. Number of schemes was launched for reducing regional/disciplinary and gender imbalances.

Despite these efforts and regulatory norms of reservation, focus on rural areas etc., we haven't made even a reasonable progress in this regard. Studies reveal that the higher education system in India today suffers from many challenges. The Scheduled Castes (SCs) and Scheduled Tribes (STs) and Minorities especially Muslims are among the most socially and educationally disadvantaged groups in India. The low enrollment ratio of these marginalised groups is well documented in research studies. The 11th Five Year Plan recognised the problem of multiple natures of disparities in enrollment rate and proposed policy measures to enhance their access to higher education. It brought the inclusiveness in higher education at the centre of our higher education policy. Inclusive education essentially requires an increased access to higher education to those multiple groups who suffers from lower access to higher education. The approach and strategy thus, formulates policies and schemes for the STs, the SCs, the OBCs, girls, minorities particularly the Muslims, physically challenged persons, semi-nomadic and denotified and the poor. Hence, it could be said the increasing rate of higher education is essential for the sustainable development of India.

The task therefore before the planners and policy makers is to create enabling conditions so that historically deprived social groups, religious and linguistic minorities, the landless and poor wage earners could be brought within the ambit of education in general and higher education in particular, which singularly may create strong and sound bases for socio-economic change and upward mobility. Inclusiveness, in this context, refers to application of the principles and instruments of equity, which could benefit groups that have so far either remained untouched or excluded from the processes of socio-economic and political development. I am sure the issues raised by the paper writers of this book will evoke genuine interest for further analyses and take on to a few policy leads. In this connection this edited volume will serve the purpose intended.

PROFESSOR K.S. RANGAPPA
Vice Chancellor
University of Mysore, Mysore

Preface

Education is universally recognised as an investment in human capital. It is the basic requirement and the most effective instrument of social empowerment and can contribute to socio-economic development by endowing individuals with the means of improving their health, skill, knowledge, and capability for productive work. The success of *Sarva Shiksha Abhiyan* (*SSA*) and *Rashtriya Madhyamik Shiksha Abhiyan* (*RMSA*) has laid a strong foundation for primary and secondary education in India. However, the sphere of higher education still has not seen any concerted efforts for improvement in its access or quality. Hence, in India, a significant proportion of the relevant population still remains deprived of the benefits of higher education and the Scheduled Castes and Scheduled Tribes, Women and Minorities comprise important categories of the deprived communities. Hence, ensuring access to quality higher education for these marginalised sections of India has been the greatest challenge for the Indian government.

The participation and representation of marginalised sections like SC/ST and Minorities in education especially in higher education has alarmingly remained low. Various governments both state and central have made several efforts to uplift these marginalised sections through several innovative programmes including educational programmes, reservations etc. However, it has not succeeded up to a satisfactory level due to many confronting issues and inhibitions in the society. Studies show that structural hindrances still exist for these marginalised sections to attain quality higher education. Also it is found that unless the state makes a significant evaluation of their strategies in promoting higher education among them, their best efforts may not prove sufficient for overcoming various problems being faced by them today. The problems of ST's, Minority women in rural areas are still worse and needs an urgent attention towards their policies. Given these myriad of challenges, a drastic change is required in the approach that has traditionally been adopted for the development of higher education in the country.

Against this background the core rationale of the proposed book is an attempt to have a solid discourse on the various problems being faced by the marginalised sections in attaining higher education and also to discuss suitable policy measures to be implemented soon. Alongside the book also throws light on the different constraints faced by the educationally marginalised sections and suggests some suitable policy prescriptions. The book is expected to give a solid platform on theoretical and empirical approach thereby diluting the magnitude of the problem of perpetuation from the benefit of the higher education for the marginalised sections especially for Scheduled Castes, Tribals and Minorities. The book will also facilitate to develop some information and analysis on the theoretical understanding and practical implications of various inclusive higher education programme initiatives. Besides this, a bunch of recommendations was given by various authors to both Government and NGOs regarding improvement of the existing interventions and will form the basis for necessary reorientation to the implementing agencies in line with the established recommendations and agreed changes for future action.

This is a collection of research papers presented in the national level conference entitled "Inclusive Higher Education and Marginalised Sections: Dynamics and Discourses" conducted by the Centre for Study of Social Exclusion and Inclusive Policy (CSSEIP), University of Mysore, Karnataka held on August, 1st and 2nd, 2013. The Centre would like to thank the Indian Council of Social Science (ICSSR), New Delhi for its funding support for its national conference and all its contributors in this conference. We also thank our Hon. Vice Chancellor Professor K.S. Rangappa for his never ending encouragement and support. We also gratified to our beloved Registrar Professor C. Basavarajau for his logistic prop up. I take this opportunity to express my heartfelt thanks to all the authors, who have enriched the book by contributing their learned papers. We thank to Dr Siddaraju V.G. and Dr Nanjunda, faculty members of CSSEIP, University of Mysore for their support. We acknowledge all others who have supported and assisted directly and indirectly for the completion of this work. We are also indebted to the Kalpaz Publications, Delhi for publishing this edited version.

Dinesha P.T.

Ramesh

List of Contributors

Dr. Jinusha Panigrahi, Assistant Professor, Institute for Studies in Industrial Development (ISID), 4, Institutional Area, Vasant Kunj, New Delhi- 110070.

Amit A. Joshi, (Asst. Prof.), Department of Economics, Swami Vivekanand Night College of Arts and Commerce, Dombivli, Affiliated to Mumbai University.

Latha M.T., Junior Research Fellow, Department of Studies in Economics and Co-operation, University of Mysore, Karnataka.

Dr. Shivanand Nari, Assistant Professor, Maharaja's College, Mysore, Karnataka.

Manjunatha G., Research Scholar, DoS in Economics and Co-operation, Manasagangothri, Mysore.

Dr. M. Mahesha, Associate Professor, DoS in Economics and Co-operation, Manasagangothri, Mysore, Karnataka.

Chetan B. Singai, National Institute of Advanced Studies, Bangalore, Karnataka.

Reetika Syal, Assistant Professor, Jain University, Bangalore, Karnataka.

Manisha M., Associate Professor Jain University, Bangalore, Karnataka.

Dr. Vishwanath M., Associate Professor, P.G. Department of Studies in Law, Karnataka University, Dharwad, Karnataka.

Dr. B.P. Mahesh Chandra Guru, Professor and Chairman, Department of Studies in Communication and Journalism, University of Mysore, Manasagangotri, Karnataka.

Dr. N. Sanjeevaraja, Assistant Professor, Department of Communication, Central College, Bangalore University, Bangalore, Karnataka.

D. Srinivasa, Project Fellow, UPA, University of Mysore, Manasagangotri, Mysore, Karnataka.

Mohammed Ashfaq Ahamed, ICSSR Doctoral Fellow, Department of Economics, Karnatak University, Dharwad, Karnataka.

Dr. P.M. Honakeri, Professor, Department of Economics, Karnatak University, Dharwad, Karnataka.

Dr. Nagaraj. M. Muggur, Assistant Professor-cum-Assistant Director, Centre for Study of Social Exclusion and Inclusive Policy (CSEIP) Mangalore University, Mangalagangothri, Mangalore, Karnataka.

Dr. V. Sudesh, Associate Professor, P.G. Department of Studies and Research in Law, University Law College, Bangalore University, Bangalore.

Dr. Shriprasad H., Joint Director, Population Research Centre (Ministry of Health and Family Welfare GOI), Dharwad, Karnataka.

Mr. Jnaneshwar Pai Maroor, Assistant Professor, Justice K.S. Hegde Institute of Management NMAMIT, Nitte, Karnataka.

Dr. Ashalatha K., Associate Professor, Justice K.S. Hegde Institute of Management, NMAMIT, Nitte, Karnataka.

Dr. B. Vamana Baliga, Associate Professor Department of Commerce, Sri Mahaveera College, Moodbidri, Karnataka.

Dr. K.K. Murugan, Guidance Counsellor, Regional Institute of Education (NCERT), Mysore. Karnataka.

Mr. C. Radha Krishnan, Ph.D. Scholar, Bhatrathiar University, Coimbatore, Tamil Nadu.

Prof. Mallika Krishnaswami, Dean of Humanities and Social Sciences, Christ University, Bangalore, Karnataka.

Dr. Indira. M., Professor, Department of Studies in Economics and Co-operation University of Mysore, Mysore.

Prabhavathi P.O., Research Scholar, Department of Studies in Economics, Dr. M.G. Co-operation, University of Mysore.

Basava Raja, Professor, Department of Economics, Sir M. Visveshvaraya P.G. Centre, Mandya, University of Mysore, Mysore.

Dr. Santhosh Areekkuzhiyil, Assistant Professor, Government Brennen College of Teacher Education, Thalassery, (Research Centre in Education), Kannur, Kerala.

Dr. Huchhe Gowda, Assistant Professor, Department of Studies in Economics, Rani Channamma University, Vidyasangama, PBNH-4, Belagavi, Karnataka.

Dr. S.V. Girikumar, Project Fellow, University Law College, Bangalore University, Bangalore, Karnataka.

Kaikashna Begum, Ph.D Research Scholar, Department of Political Science, Ravenshaw University, Cuttack, Odisha.

Dr. Siddaraju V.G., Associate Professor *cum* Deputy Director, Centre for study of Social Exclusion and Inclusive Policy University of Mysore, Manasagangothri, Mysore, Karnataka.

Dr. H.K. Mariswamy, Professor and Chairman, Department of Studies in Communication and Journalism, University of Mysore, Manasagangotri.

Dr. C.K. Puttaswamy, Assistant Professor, Department of Communication, Central College, Bangalore University, Bangalore.

Dr. Gopala, Project Fellow, UPA, University of Mysore, Manasagangotri, Mysore.

Vidhya, V., Junior Research Fellow, Department of Education, University of Calicut, Kerala.

Dr. Baiju. K. Nath, Assistant Professor, Department of Education, University of Calicut, Kerala.

K.R. Bommarayanayaka, Associate Professor and Research Scholar, Department of Sociology. Government First Grade College. Krishnaraja Nagara. Mysore, Karnataka.

Dr. Gopalaraju. R., Associate Professor, Department of Sociology, Maharaja College, University of Mysore, Mysore, Karnataka.

Nagma Sona, Research Scholar, DoS and Research in Commerce, Gulbarga University, Gulbarga, Karnataka.

Harish D.N., Assistant Professor of Commerce, Government First Grade College, Hukkeri, Belgaum, Karnataka.

Chandan D.N., Research Scholar, DoS and Research in Commerce, Dr. C.V. Raman University, Kota, Bilaspur, Chhattisgarh.

Suresh Kumar M.B., Research Scholar, DoS and Research in Commerce, Dr. C.V. Raman University, Kota, Bilaspur, Chhattisgarh.

V. Rama Krishna, Assistant Professor, Department of Political Science, Tumkur University, Tumkur, Karnataka.

R. Shashidhar, Assistant Professor, Department of Studies and Research in Business Administration, Tumkur University, Tumkur, Karnataka.

Dr. Shweta Deshpande, Lecturer, K.P.E.S. Dr. G.M. Patil Law College, D.C. Compound, Dharwad, Karnataka.

Mrs. P. Shailaja, Assistant Professor, Department of Public Administration, Osmania University, Hyderabad, Andhra Pradesh.

Kiran Kumar P., Assistant Professor, Department of Economics, Rani Channamma University, Vidya Sangama, Belagavi, Karnataka.

Sivakumar, I, PhD Research Scholar, Centre for Women's Studies, Pondicherry University, Puducherry, Karnataka.

Usha V.T., Associate Professor, Centre for Women's Studies, Pondicherry University, Puducherry, Karnataka.

Vidya S. Shettemmanavar, Lecturer, KPES's Dr. G.M. Patil Law College, Dharwad, KSLU Dharwad, Karnataka.

Usharani B., Research Scholar, Department of Sociology, Mangalore University, Mangalagangothri, Karnataka.

Hanumantha. G.H., Dos in Law, University of Mysore, Mysore, Karnataka.

K. Vinutha Somanna, Guest Faculty, Government Law College, Hassan, Karnataka.

Lohith. R., Dos in Law, University of Mysore, Mysore, Karnataka.

Sri. Nandeesh C., Assistant professor, J.S.S Institute of Education, P.G. Center in Education, Sutturu, Mysore, Karnataka.

Dr. Kotreshwaraswamy A. Surapuramath, Assistant professor, J.S.S Institute of Education, P.G. Center in Education, Suttur, Najangudu, Mysore, Karnataka.

Archana M., Research Scholar, DoS in Economics and Co-operation, Manasagangotri, University of Mysore, Karnataka.

Ravi. P., Research Scholar, DoS in Sociology, Manasagangotri, University of Mysore, Mysore, Karnataka

Dr. R. Gopalaraju, Associate Professor, Maharaja College, University of Mysore, Mysore, Karnataka.

Dr. H.R. Uma, Professor DoS in Economics Mysore University, Karnataka.

Madhu. G.R., Research Scholar, DoS in Economics Mysore University, Karnataka.

Pushpa Nanaiah K., Research Scholar, DoS in Economics Mysore University, Karnataka.

Dr. N. Mudduraju, Lecturer in Law, DBHPS Law College, Koppal, Karnataka.

Dr. H.H. Bharadi, Assistant Professor, Department of Studies in Economics, Rani Channamma University, Belagavi, Karnataka.

Ramesha, K., Project Fellow, Centre for the Study of Social Exclusion and Inclusive Policy, University of Mysore, Mysore.

Prakruthi, A.R., Research Scholar, DoS in Law, University of Mysore, Mysore.

Dr. Nanjunda, UGC-CSSEIP, University of Mysore, Karnataka.

S. Jyothi Lakshmi, Dept of Economics, KSOU, Mysore, Karnataka.

Mr. Harisha N., Assistant Professor, Department of Economics, Karnataka State Open University, Mysore Karnataka.

Dr. Jayasheela, Professor, Department of Economics, Tumkur University, Tumkur-572103, Karnataka.

1 Inclusive Higher Education and its Access by the Underprivileged

Dr. Jinusha Panigrahi

Abstract

The world economy is experiencing unprecedented and irreversible changes. One of the major challenges in the context of rapid changes in the higher education sector in globalising India is to make it socially relevant and equitable without compromising in its role in skill formation and innovation. The question of access to higher education (HE) is a global concern that is strongly associated with the ethical principle of justice and equity and creation of a knowledge-based society. While the term equity is defined in multiple ways in literature, the concern for access to education to achieve this specific equity aspect is universal. But, with the gradual transformation in the nature of higher education due to the forced intrusion of neo-liberal market principles into the sector, access has suffered. Though, the operation of market forces gives enormous scope to the consumers' of higher education (i.e., the students) in terms of diversified choices and preferences of educational products and services, it further aggravates the inequality in the society basically due to financial constraints faced by the underprivileged section of population.

Introduction

To cope with the rapid changes in the Higher Education sector in the globalising India the government programmes and policies have emphasised on making higher education sector socially relevant and equitable (CABE committee report, p. 8, 2005). The eleventh FYP has the mandate of an inclusive growth that has given greater importance to the growth in higher education enrollments, i.e., to raise the GER from around 11 per cent to 15 per cent by the end of 2012 (NUEPA, 2008). But, various government reports show the unequal picture of access to education and particularly higher education by the different underprivileged sections of the society characterised in terms of region, gender, and socio-economic class.

The unequal access is more acute in the low and middle income States, as argued in the literature. 'Odisha', one of the poorest Indian States has been chosen as the study area and has been compared with States such as Kerala and Tamil Nadu, which have an overall higher attendance ratio in higher education in comparison to the other States of the country. Many inherent characteristics such as low per capita income (PCI) and per capita expenditure, high illiteracy, lesser percentage of urban population, high density of population of scheduled tribes (ST's) who mostly have low PCI, less developed general/non-technical (G/NT) institutes, growing demand for professional courses, concentration of growing private institutes in developed areas, lack of job opportunities, declining public expenditure towards higher education due to heavy fiscal burden, add to the miseries of the State that are reflected in its low attendance/enrollment ratio in higher education.

Background

An increased access to education to achieve an equitable society is a major challenge before the policy makers. The ultimate objective of increasing access to education, in particular Higher Education is an achievement of an inclusive society where every individual would have an equal access to societal resources to foster pro-equity growth. The term equity is defined as a psychological concept (Secada, 1989; Sen, 1992) created and formulated by different social institutions through various kinds of redistributions of social benefits (Alexander, 1982) for the achievement of certain predetermined ethical standards of fairness (McMahon, p. 16, 1982).

While the achievement of equity is the ultimate objective for any society, the current state of equality (or inequality) determines the society's capability towards the achievement of this future objective. The state of equality is judged upon the availability of the resources, the individuals' requirements and thus, their preferences, which differs among the societies (Atkinson, 1975). And, the state of inequality prevalent in any society is argued to be due to dissimilarities among the individuals arising out of their different abilities and aptitudes that are inherited and are inevitable in the future life of the individuals concerned (Béteille, p. 12, 2002 and 2010). But, it is education, particularly, higher education, which is argued to work as a panacea to such intergenerational inequality. Both higher education and higher income are argued to be interrelated. All those individuals who have highly educated parents and high income families are argued to have a prosperous future than their counterparts (Tresch, 1995). Various principles and policies guide towards the improvement in access to higher education by the underprivileged sections of population in any kind of society and therefore, achieving equality in opportunity in the concerned society.

Tresch (p. 12, 1995), distinguished between *"process equity"*, that maintains an equal access to various opportunities available in the society by the individuals who are willing and able to pursue them irrespective of their caste/race, religion, or gender and the *"end-results equity"* that maintains that, individuals with equal ability and productivity (case for horizontal equity) or unequal ability or productivity (case for vertical equity) must be treated in respective ways. The *"principle of level the playing field"* and the *"principle of non-discrimination or merit principle"* follow the same suite in this respect as suggested by Roemer (p. 17, 2001). The affirmative action policy or the positive discrimination policy (in Indian context) is very much influenced by the above mentioned principles of Roemer. It is a moral obligation on the part of the government to support the underprivileged sections of the society.

Apart from the positive discrimination policies, some, policies of restitution, in terms of fiscal policies by the government is also suggested by Alexander (1982), for a just distribution of socio-economic advantages available in the society. And, along with progressive taxation policies, Moore (1978) suggests for selective public support to the needy and deserving students through comprehensive student assistance programmes to improve their access to higher education. Such funding programmes by the government, as pointed out by Geske (1982) and others would improve the intergenerational equity (through social mobility) of such weaker sections in the society (particularly, the students belonging to the less educated parents and low income families).

Expansion in educational institutions is advocated by many theories and approaches (Tyler, 1977; Hannum and Buchmann, 2005 and others) to improve access to education. But, higher education being a positional good (Marginson, 2007), the students from middle and high income families acquire more education compared to the students from low income families (who enter higher education by virtue of positive discrimination policies and other government policies) and the pre-existing deprivations continue in future (Mare, 1981; Raftery and Hout, 1993; Walters, 2000). And, among the underprivileged group of population [particularly, scheduled castes (SC's) and scheduled tribes ST's], it is the students from well-off families who are argued to be generally benefited from the positive discrimination policies (Patwardhan and Palshikar, 1992; Rao, 2001; Weisskopf, 2004). As pointed out in the Indian context, by the eleventh FYP document, it is a balanced inclusive expansion in higher education that improves access and reduces inequalities in the long run. Thus, expansion of higher education without adequate government policies on improving access to it by the potential individuals of weaker sections will further widen the gap between the privileged and under privileged. It is, not only the creation of the opportunities, rather, how those created opportunities are reaching the masses is an important factor. Take for example, according to the study by Halsey (1993) the current transition of higher education in Britain from a elite system to mass system of education has not been successful in reducing the continuing class inequalities prevalent in Britain's higher education sector.

Besides, expansion of higher education, the quality of education imparted in the higher educational institutions (HEI's) as well as at the school level matters a lot in the achievement of equality in educational opportunities. Quality is the cognitive achievement of pupils or efficiency of output compared to inputs (Psacharopoulos, 1989; Heynemann and Loxley, 1983). In Indian context there are instances when students suffer due to the lack of quality education at the school level due to regional barriers, gender barriers and other societal obstructions (Chanana, 1993; Chowdhury, 1998; Rao, 2002; Weisskopf, 2004). Though the positive discrimination policies have improved access to the general or non-technical courses (G/NT) by the underprivileged sections of population (HRD report, 1997) that too in the less prestigious courses and institutes (Chitnis, 1988; Chanana, 1993 and 2000, and others) but, they lag behind in the technical or professional (T/P) courses due to their poor quality schooling (Rao, 2002 and others). Thus, an integration of all the segments of education system is suggested in the literature (Barr, 1993 and others) to improve access to education and achieve long term objective of equality in accessing educational opportunities. But, ultimately, the achievement of an equitable society is dependent upon the potential of the deprived sections of population in reaping the benefits out of the provided opportunities by the government concerned (Sen, 1992).

Odisha as the Study Area

Per Capita Income and Sector-wise Net State Domestic Product in Odisha

Odisha's PCI compared to other low income States of the country such as Bihar, MP, and Rajasthan, etc., shows its backwardness in many aspects. The relative PCI of Odisha has declined compared to these States in the second half of the 1990s and it is declined to the half of the all India level PCI (OHDR, 2004).

The fluctuations in the gross state domestic product (GSDP) and per capita net state domestic product (NSDP) show the fluctuations in the production level and thus income level of the general population.

The GSDP at constant prices (1999-2000) has increased from rupees 425.2707 billion in 1999-2000 to rupees 637.7471 billion as per the advanced estimates in 2006-07 registering an annual compound growth rate of 5.96 per cent over the period (Odisha economic survey, 2007-08). The trends of the fluctuations in the NSDP and per capita NSDP (PCNSDP) as shown in Fig. 1 also show the fluctuations in the production level and thus income level of the general population.

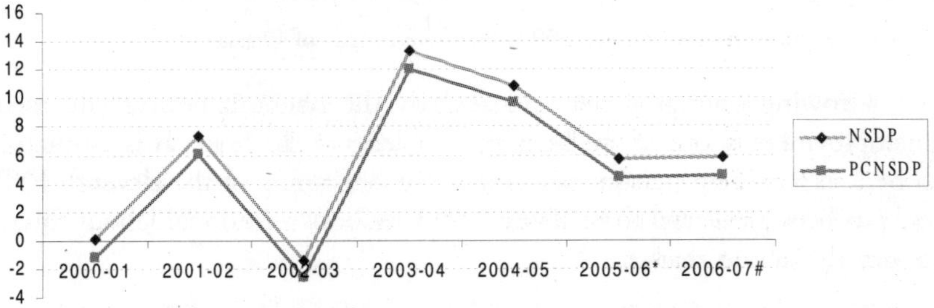

Fig. 1: Annual Growth Percentage in NSDP and PCNSDP of Odisha (1999-2000 prices).

Note: *Indicates quick estimates and # indicates advanced estimates.

(Source: Orissa economic survey, 2007-08, Government of Orissa).

The broad sector-wise NSDP at factor cost of Odisha over the years also reveal the backwardness of the State and the dominance of its rural area population. The percentage of urban population is quite low (15 per cent) (economic survey, GOO, 2007-08). The primary sector (agriculture) dominates in the total share of NSDP over the years.

The primary sector dominates in the total share of NSDP over the years but with fluctuations as shown in the Fig. 2. Such fluctuations in NSDP are due to the fluctuating performance of various sectors.

Agriculture, being the major employment generating sector of the State, fluctuations in its growth, also affects employment level. Besides, with the increase in population and consequent addition to the labour force, supply of labour continues to outstrip demand resulting in increase in levels of unemployment and underemployment. The occupational classification-based on census 2001 shows that, work participation rate among female is generally lower.

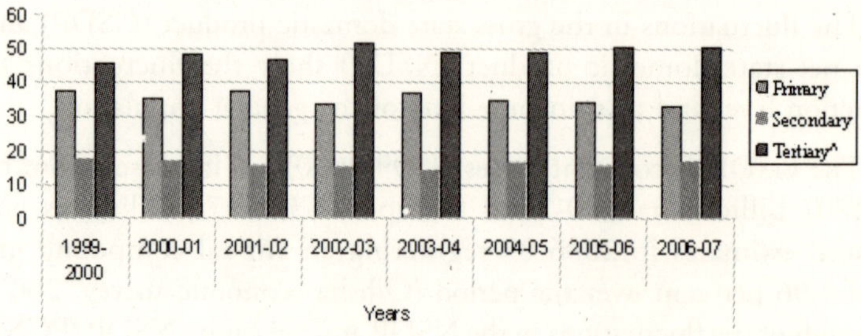

Fig. 2: Broad Sector-wise NSDP of Odisha at factor cost at constant (1999-2000) prices (in percentage).

Note: Indicates that the service sector constitutes a major share of the tertiary sector.

(Source: Orissa economic survey, 2007-08, Government of Orissa).

Growing unemployment particularly the phenomenon of educated unemployment is one of the burning problems of the State. It is estimated to be 1.413 million persons per year at the beginning of the eleventh FYP and has been projected to be about 1.053 millions additional labour forces to join the labour market.

To the tune of 46.8 per cent of the population in Odisha were living below the poverty line (economic survey, GOO, 2007-08) that declined a little and became 46.6 per cent (according to uniform recall period method) or 39.9 per cent (according to multiple recall period method) that is highest among the States compared to all India average of 27.5 and 21.8 respectively, as per the economic survey, GOI, 2010-11. And the percentage of urban population is quite low (15 per cent) (as per economic survey, GOO, 2007-08). The poverty level is higher among the ST's compared to SC's or general castes. The percentage of ST is 22.13 per cent of the total population. The SC and other caste percentage is 17 per cent and 61.34 per cent respectively of the total population (economic survey, GOO, 2007-08). Odisha besides being the poorest State in the country has large concentration of ST's who are basically poor and downtrodden among the masses in the State. As per national human development report, 2001 it occupies the eleventh rank in HDI that is far away from other upper rank holders of the country. Besides, overall literacy rate in Odisha is only 63.08 per cent. While male literacy rate is 75.35 per cent and the female literacy is only 50.51 per cent (population census report, 2001). The disparity in literacy rates between rural and urban Odisha is 59.84 per cent and 80.84 per cent, respectively.

The share of university or higher education and technical education is 12.22 per cent and 1.19 per cent respectively during 2000-01 which is inadequate to meet the growing demands for higher education. A technically educated person is given higher respect and prestige compared to the others in Odisha.There is stronger competition among the students to qualify in the engineering entrance examination and get a seat in one of the reputed institutes (either government or private) of the State. The average per student expenditure in technical or professional T/P courses in urban Odisha is higher than the developed States in terms of human resources such as Kerala and Tamil Nadu. Even, urban girls from middle or high income families have a larger demand for technical or professional courses. Owing to the emerging need of the State for rapid high-tech agro-industrial development by exploiting the diverse natural resources, it has become imperative to generate a stock of highly technically skilled manpower. This in turn has necessitated bringing about sustainable improvement in the overall quality and growth of technical education.

Relative Enrollments and Access to Higher Education in Odisha

The variations in enrollments in education in Odisha compared to the two other highly enrolled States such as Tamil Nadu (with large number of technical or professionalinstitutions and large number of private institutions) and Kerala (with enriched human resources due to higher access to education) the States with higher demand for private and professional institutions are considered for a comparative analysis. The secondary data related to gender, native place, social category, economic status (determined by monthly per capita consumption expenditure on education) and different levels of education, etc., are extracted (and estimated) from the national sample survey (NSS) reports and census report for such analysis.

Gender, Region and Enrollment Level

Looking at the diversified profile of the State in terms of human development indicators, the enrollment level in the State is also quite awkward when compared to few other States and an all-India figure. The actual variations are shown in Table 1.

The enrollment in higher education by the rural area students of Odisha is lower compared to highly enrolled States such as Tamil Nadu and Kerala. Even, the enrollment percentage of Odisha in higher education is lower than an all India average. Girls are more deprived compared to the boys in terms of higher education. But, the urban area students' participation in higher education is quite larger than the higher enrollment States such as Tamil Nadu and Kerala and also the all India average enrollment in higher education. Though, the difference between boys and girls' higher education enrollment in urban areas is visible, the girls' enrollment in higher education

Table 1: Attendance/non-attendance and Enrollment in Higher Secondary (HS) and Higher Education (HE) in Odisha Compared to Others (in percentage)

State	*Level of education*	*Rural*		*Rural persons*	*Urban*		*Urban persons*	*Total persons*
		Male	*Female*		*Male*	*Female*		
ODISHA	HS							
	Attending	4.32	3.23	3.82	6.5	10.25	7.9	2.1
	Not-attending	0.03	0.09	0.5	0.5	1.23	0.75	0.1
	HE							
	Attending	4.12	2.07	3.19	19	14.31	17.13	2.5
	Not-attending	0.03	0.69	0.42	1.36	1.06	1.31	0.18
TAMIL NADU	HS							
	Attending	8.94	9.45	9.09	10.4	10.44	10.42	9.75
	Not-attending	0.03	0.1	0.03	0.1	0.34	0.14	0.18
	HE							
	Attending	8.58	4.82	6.81	12.59	13.86	13.22	9.56
	Not-attending	0.17	0.1	0.03	0.54	0.15	0.31	0.18
KERALA	HS							
	Attending	9.53	11.09	10.27	10.47	9.33	9.81	10.19
	Not-attending	0.01	0.51	0.32	0.16	0.84	0.5	0.32
	HE							
	Attending	12.61	14.9	13.7	11.82	19.01	15.73	14.14
	Not-attending	0.61	1.55	0.97	0.33	0.84	0.67	0.98
ALL-INDIA	HS							
	Attending	6.29	4.91	5.63	9.71	9.6	9.74	6.67
	Not-attending	0.34	0.24	0.37	0.35	0.37	0.31	0.31
	HE							
	Attending	4.89	3.48	4.32	13.12	13.18	13.23	6.54
	Not-attending	0.2	0.2	0.18	0.53	0.75	0.49	0.31

Note: Not-attending implies those who are enrolled but not attending the specific education concerned and HE implies higher education; HS implies higher secondary level of education.

(*Source:* Researcher's own estimations from NSS report, 64th round (2007-08), GOI).

in Kerala State is the largest. The urban area girls in Odisha have also a larger participation in higher secondary (HS) education compared to the boys. The educated parents of urban areas have greater concern for girls' education and among all the students there is the possibility of more percentage of general category girl students whose parents prefer higher studies for their wards. Overall, it is the urban area students in Odisha, who have a wider access to higher education. The larger share of urban students' access to higher education may be due to the fact that there is a growing participation of students of high age groups (as studied by Sinha and Srivastava, 2008) and/or due to the inclination of the urban students towards higher education to get social respect and prestige and to get better prospects for employment (particularly in technical or professional areas). Besides, the growing numbers of private institutes (in technical or professional courses) increases the higher education enrollments.

The resource crunch of the government favours the private players for providing of higher education. Such institutes establish their campus inside the populated regions of the State where there are proper infrastructure facilities and more demand for higher education. Thus, there is greater imbalance in the distribution of institutes. All those students from underprivileged families are unable to compete for such institutes due to the high fees charged by such institutes. Though both public and private sector banks are very active in the State in disbursing educational loan, many students fail to meet all the requirements of the banks (Panigrahi, 2010). The major hurdle lies on the post effect of education loan. The future uncertainty of income or the fear of getting a job due to technological obsolescence or else; prohibit many from poor families from availing of educational loan. These students are eliminated from higher studies due to lack of funds. Even, many students remain unexposed to urban atmosphere where they can get current information. Their access to education remains confined only to primary or secondary education. Such conditions further widen the gap between the privileged and underprivileged.

Economic Status and Enrollment Level

The Table 2 below shows enrollment in terms of economic status.

The 40 per cent of low quintile class of population enrollment in subsequent level of education goes on declining and the enrollment in higher education increases with the increase in the income level. Odisha is backward in terms of enrollment with a lowest of 40 per cent of population in almost all the levels of education compared to other States except the primary level of education. It could be due to the recent universalisation of Elementary

Table 2: Enrollment Status (in per cent) for each Quintile Class of Monthly Per Capita Consumption Expenditure (MPCE in per cent) in Odisha and Few Other States#

Quintile Class	*Level of Education**	*Odisha*		*Tamil Nadu*		*Kerala*		*All India*	
		Rural	*Urban*	*Rural*	*Urban*	*Rural*	*Urban*	*Rural*	*Urban*
00-20	Primary	64.03	57.25	46.78	46.37	40.65	35.55	61.46	51.5
	Middle	24.34	21.24	30.53	30.42	30.95	30.91	22.33	24.71
	Secondary	5.92	11.91	13.03	9.59	10.25	14.08	7.41	9.86
	HS	1.31	4.66	5.17	9.59	5.86	4.82	2.37	5.81
	HE	0.87	1.03	1.96	3.02	7.87	5.03	1.18	3.11
20-40	Primary	55.62	46.7	44.95	43.89	33.02	28.51	56.31	44.67
	Middle	23.35	22.75	30.66	25.95	24.3	25.5	23.81	23.8
	Secondary	11.46	18.36	14.66	14.5	15.59	21.6	9.56	12.43
	HS	1.91	7.18	5.33	7.82	9.71	6.18	3.54	6.85
	HE	1.27	1.99	3.04	7.82	9.71	12.21	1.72	6.55
40-60	Primary	51.37	43.48	45.16	35.49	26.34	24.85	52.16	37.09
	Middle	27.41	18.9	27.89	23.72	26.34	27.52	24.32	22.68
	Secondary	11.73	14.49	12.9	18.62	12.76	15.47	11.06	13.2
	HS	3.24	8.4	8.53	11.37	8.29	14.13	5.2	10.13
	HE	1.72	11.76	4.55	9.8	15.73	14.13	2.55	11.06
60-80	Primary	40.96	34.49	37.31	32.22	27.18	38.38	45.81	29.98
	Middle	27.31	18.66	27.02	21.04	26.09	31.92	25.09	20.84
	Secondary	16.17	9.76	14.88	17.82	14.53	19.59	13.61	14.31
	HS	4.41	9.58	11.21	9.11	12.18	16.76	6.76	13.21
	HE	3.36	20.26	8.45	18.58	13.28	29.09	4.17	16.34
80-100	Primary	38	16.87	30.19	21.77	16.53	23.47	33.26	23.37
	Middle	26.42	20.17	19.27	18.91	22.31	27.3	23.03	18.09
	Secondary	15.65	10.42	13.62	12.88	19.28	11.47	16.14	13.85
	HS	8.33	9.1	17.61	14.39	15.11	10.6	10.76	12.24
	HE	8.73	39.53	19.08	28.14	22.16	24.52	12.18	28.5

Notes: # Indicates that the students who are enrolled and attending the specific level of education are considered and * indicates that the non-formal and pre-primary education are excluded from analysis and HE is higher education HS is higher secondary level of education.

(*Source:* Researcher's own estimations from NSS report, 64th round (2007-08), GOI).

Education Programme of the National government. The low income parents (the lowest 40 per cent of quintile class) due to financial, regional, social factors and many cultural factors fail to send their children to the subsequent levels of education, whether it is Higher Secondary (HS) education or Higher Hducation (HE). The enrollment in secondary level of education is a little better by such a group of urban population compared to the rural population. The majority of enrollment in higher education in Odisha is by the upper 20 per cent income group. The urban area students' larger enrollment in higher education in Odisha is also visible compared to other States and all India average. Though, at the Higher Secondary level there is not much difference in enrollments between the upper 20 per cent quintile class of rural and urban students but the difference between the regions regarding enrollment in higher education is quite larger.

It is clear that, few rural area students despite their high income level like their urban counterparts fail to access higher education due to many other obstructions that are cultural, social and regional. Less educated parents due to lack of awareness or due to distance or due to other socio-cultural factors do not send their ward for higher studies. Overall, it is the most privileged section of population who has gained higher access to higher education in Odisha.

Social Status and Enrollment Level

The differentiation in higher education enrollment becomes more acute when various social groups are taken into the purview of analysis of educational enrollments. Before discussing the income level of the social groups and their enrollment in education, it is necessary to get an idea about their representation in the total population. The Table 3 below gives a comparative representation of the scheduled groups of population compared to the general group of population in various States.

The percentage of ST's is 26 per cent of the total population in the rural areas compared to the less than 2 per cent in other States, taken for analysis and 11 per cent in the all India level. The representation of ST's in urban areas is quite less compared to the representation of the other groups of population. Similarly, the SC's population is quite less in urban areas compared to the OBC's or other categories of population. Such higher representation of ST's and SC's in underdeveloped region of Odisha, also provides a view of the backwardness of this scheduled category in the society when they are compared with the other advanced States of the country. This opinion is supported with the following argument when the lowest quintile class of population (in terms of social class) representation is taken for analysis, as given in Table 4.

Table 3: Percentage Distribution of Population by Social Groups in Odisha and Few other States (Region-wise), by 2004-05

State	*Rural*					*Urban*				
	Social Group					*Social Group*				
	ST	*SC*	*OBC*	*Others*	*All*	*ST*	*SC*	*OBC*	*Others*	*All*
Odisha	25.64	17.58	39.4	17.33	100	9	13.69	30.53	46.78	100
Tamil Nadu	0.54	27.06	70.54	1.86	100	0.64	14.52	74.74	10.09	100
Kerala	1.92	11.19	59.39	27.51	100	0.48	8.28	62.88	28.36	100
All India	10.57	20.92	42.75	25.71	100	2.92	15.64	35.6	45.81	100

(*Source:* Researcher's own estimations from NSS report 61st round (2004-05), GOI).

Table 4: Region-wise Percentage of Population having MPCE below the Average

State	*Rural*					*Urban*				
	Social Group					*Social Group*				
	ST	*SC*	*OBC*	*Others*	*All*	*ST*	*SC*	*OBC*	*Others*	*All*
Odisha	87	69.4	58.6	41.2	64.7	84.2	87.7	70	50.9	64.8
Tamil Nadu	80.8	83.1	66.4	43.6	70.6	81.9	86	67.5	26.6	66.1
Kerala	93.7	86.1	71.5	58.8	70	47.8	93.4	73.9	49.1	68.4
All India	79.6	77.4	64.1	53.3	65.7	74.3	84	75.4	54.5	67.1

(*Source:* Researcher's own estimations from NSS report 61st round (2004-05), GOI).

The percentage of ST's population in Odisha below the average income level in rural areas is greater than Tamil Nadu and all India average. Though SC's from rural areas are a little better off than their counterparts, the urban area ST's and SC's are economically more deprived than their counterparts. The economic status of these underprivileged sections of population also affects their enrollments in higher education.

As studied by Sinha and Srivastava (2008) the enrollment status of the deprived group of population such as SC's and ST's in Odisha has experienced a marginal improvement when compared to the other groups of population. But, in terms of the types of education, the disparity is still continuing to be larger. Both in Tamil Nadu and Kerala the SC's population enrollment in higher education shows an improvement. But, the disparity in enrollment is substantial due to higher enrollment of the other groups of population in higher education.

The participation of SC's in higher education is highest for Tamil Nadu in the year 2001 compared to the other States taken for the analysis. Both Tamil Nadu and Kerala are far ahead of Odisha in terms of equality index. The reason behind this is, the lesser enrollment of the non-scheduled category of population in these advanced States where it is found that after the completion of schooling they choose business within or outside their family enterprise that give way to SC population to access higher education (Sinha and Srivastava, 2008). But, in case of Odisha the enrollment of non-scheduled population in higher education is higher than the scheduled population. Thus access to higher education is less for SC in Odisha though there is an improvement in enrollment over the decade.

While in terms of participation in technical education the ST are ahead of SC in Odisha (and also compared to the two other States) but in terms of equality index in technical education both are the same and poorly represent in technical or professional courses. The dominance of the non-scheduled population in technical or professional courses is quite visible. The reservation of ST's seats in government technical or professional institutes have increased their participation in such institutes but the representation may not be the same in private technical or professional institutes if both government and private technical or professional institutes are studied separately for such an analysis.

Concluding Remarks

The access to higher education is a complex issue associated with a variety of arguments and discussions among the masses, the policy makers and the academia. It is a daunting challenge for the government to tackle the access problem of education. The problem is inherent and deep-rooted in the historical, socio-economic status of the person or group concerned in the society.

In the Indian context, and particularly in case of Odisha, the underprivileged sections of the society are the SC's, ST's, OBC's, and women. Since such categories and sections of population are historically downtrodden, the initiatives taken by the government for their betterment reduces their deprivation but the effect is very slow.

The various policies and programmes undertaken by the government have increased the overall enrollment of these underprivileged sections of population in higher education but when they are compared with the non-scheduled population, the overall achievement seems to be meagre. The positive discrimination policies of the government since the period of independence has increased reservations in educational institutions and occupations for the improvement and for the access to higher education by such groups of population thereby improving their social status by making them mobile in the social strata and increasing the financial resources for them. Once they enter the reputed and recognised universities or institutions they gradually thought to increase their chances of selection in the job market. But, the competition between the reserved category and general category of population is so stringent that the general category of students improves their potential by more credentials. This is true in case of Technical and Professional courses like Engineering, IT, etc. The OBC reservations very recently have increased their enrollments but the poor representation of such reserved categories in urban areas make them incapable of making use of the reservation facilities provided by the government due to their ignorance. The most of the benefits of the reserved categories of population is appropriated by the affluent sections of population of that category.

Women students in general lag behind their male counterparts in enrollments in higher education due to reasons like, low family income, number of dependants in the family, marriage and dowry problem, etc. argued in literature.

Thus, the overall, access to higher education in Odisha is a privilege of the urban area non-scheduled category of population and the dominance is quite acute in case of Technical and professional education and they basically belong to the upper and middle income group of population.

References

- Alexander, K. (1982). Concepts of Equity. In W.W. McMahon and T.G.

Geske (Eds.), *Financing Education Overcoming Inefficiency and Inequity,* Urbana: University of Illinois Press.

- Atkinson, A.B. (1975). *The Economics of Inequality,* New York: Oxford University Press.
- Barr, N. (1993). Alternative Funding Resources for Higher Education. *The Economics Journal,* 103: 718-728.
- Béteille, A. (2002). *Equality and Universality: Essays in Social and Political Theory.* New Delhi: Oxford University Press.
- Béteille, A. (2010). *Universities at the Crossroads.* New Delhi: Oxford University Press.
- Census of India (2001). *National Population Census Report 2001.* New Delhi: GOI.
- Chanana, K. (1993). Accessing Higher Education: The Dilemma of Schooling Women, Minorities, Scheduled Castes and Scheduled Tribes in Contemporary India. *Higher Education,* 26: 69-92.
- Chanana, K. (2000). Treading the Hallowed Halls: Women in Higher Education in India. *Economic and Political Weekly,* 18: 1012-1022.
- Chitnis, S. (1988). Educating the Weaker Sections of Society. In A. Singh and P. Altbech, (Eds.), *Higher Education in India: The social context.* New Delhi: Konark Publishers.
- Chowdhury, K.C. (1998). Dalits in Higher Education: Cooption or Domination. *Journal of Higher Education,* 21: 437-451.
- Geske, T.G. (1982). Educational Finance: Research Findings and Policy Implications. In W.W. McMahon and T.G. Geske (Eds.), *Financing Education, Overcoming Inefficiency and Inequity.* Urbana: University of Illinois Press.
- Government of Orissa (2004). *Human Development Report.* Bhubaneswar: Government of Orissa.
- Government of Orissa (2007-08). *Orissa Economic Survey.* Directorate of Economics and Statistics, Planning and Co-ordination Department. Bhubaneswar: Government of Orissa.
- Halsey, A.H. (1993). Trends in Access and Equity in Higher Education: Britain in International Perspective. *Oxford Review of Education,* 19(2): 129-140.
- Hannum, E. and Buchman, C. (2005). Global Educational Expansion and Socio-economic Development: An Assessment of Findings from Social Sciences. *World Development,* 33(3): 333-354.
- Heynemann, S. and Loxley, W. (1983). Effect of Primary Schooling Quality on Academic Achievement. *American Journal of Sociology,* 88 (6): 1162-1194.

- Mare, R. (1981). Change and Stability in Educational stratification. *American Sociological Review*, 46: 72-87.
- Marginson, S. (2007). The Public/Private Divide in Higher Education: A Global Revision. *Higher Education,* 53(3): 307-333.
- McMahon, W.T. (1982). Efficiency and Equity Criteria for Educational Budgeting and Finance. In W.T. McMahon and T.G. Geske (Eds.), *Financing Education: Overcoming Inefficiency and Inequity*. USA: University of Illinois Press.
- Moore, G.A. (1978). Equity Effects of Higher Education Finance and Tuition Grants in New York State. *The Journal of Human Resources*, XIII(4): 483-501.
- NSS Report (2006). *Employment and Unemployment Situations among Social Groups in India: 2004-05*. No.516 (61st Round), NSSO. New Delhi: GOI.
- NSS Report (64th Round). *Education in India, 2007-08: Participation and Expenditure*, No.532. NSSO. New Delhi: GOI.
- NUEPA (2005). *Report of the CABE Committee on Financing of Higher and Technical Education*. June, New Delhi: NUEPA.
- NUEPA (2008). *Background paper on 11th Five Year Plan in Higher Education Strategies for Effective Implementation*. New Delhi: NUEPA.
- Panigrahi, J. (2010). Determinants of Educational Loan by Commercial banks in India: evidence and implications based on a sample survey, *Journal of Educational Planning and Administration*, XXIV(4), October.
- Patwardhan, V. and Palshikar, V. (1992). Reserved Seats in Medical Education: A Case Study. *Journal of Education and Social Change,* 5: 1-11.
- Psacharopoulos, G. (1989). The Return to Education. *Comparative Education*, 17(3): 321-341.
- Raftery, A.E. and Hout, M. (1993). Maximally Maintained Inequality: Expansion, Reform and Opportunity in Irish Education, 1921-75. *Sociology of Education*, 66: 41-62.
- Rao, S.S. (2002). Equality in Higher Education: Impact of Affirmative Action Policies in India. In E.F. Beckham, (Ed.), *Global Collaborations: The Role of Higher Education in Diverse Democracies*. Washington DC: AACU.
- Rao, S.S. (2001). *Equality in Higher Education: Impact of Affirmative Action Policies in India*, Unpublished Draft Paper, New Delhi: Jawaharlal Nehru University.
- Roemer, J.E. (2001). Equality of Opportunity. In Arrow, K., Samuel, B., and Durlauf, S. (Eds.), *Meritocracy and Economic Inequality*. New York: Oxford University Press.
- Secada, W.G. (1989). Educational Equity versus Equality of Education: An

Alternative Conception. In Secada, W.G. (Ed.), *Equity in Education*. London: Falmer Press.

- Sen, A. (1992). *Inequality Reexamined.* New Delhi: Open University Press.
- Sinha, S. and Srivastava, R.S. (2008). Inclusiveness and Access of Social groups to Higher Education. In *Higher Education in India: Issues Related to Expansion, Inclusiveness, Quality and Finance.* New Delhi: UGC.
- Tresch, R. (1995). *Public Finance: A Normative Theory.* USA: Academic Press.
- Tyler, W. (1977). *The Sociology of Educational Inequality.* London: Sage Publications.
- Walters, P.B. (2000). The Limits of Growth: School Expansion and School Reform in Historical Perspective. In M. Hallinan (Ed.), *Handbook of the Sociology of Education*. New York: Kulwer Academic Press.
- Weisskopf, T.E. (2004). *Affirmative Action in the United States and India: A Comparative Perspective*. London: Routledge.

2 Quality Gap in Higher Education: A Study of Three Generation Groups of Under Graduate Learners in Dombivli

Amit A. Joshi

Abstract

The higher education sector in India seems to expand quantitatively with around 570 universities including central, state, deemed and the private one's imparting education to first, second and third generation learners but this expansion seems to have failed to address the issue of quality in higher education leading to the creation of a quality gap between these three groups. On one hand, we have IITs and IIMs generating world class engineers and managers and on the other hand, we have an educational system where students are deprived of the conditions that develop interpersonal and cognitive skills. The bridging of this quality gap remains the toughest challenges before the *Rashtriya Uchatar Shikshan Abhiyaan*. The rationale for undertaking this study was to trace and study the factors that largely determine the quality gap. The objectives to undertake this study was to identify the determinants of quality gap and to examine the significant differences in relation to skill gap among three groups. For this purpose the undergraduate learners have been arranged into three groups namely the first generation learners, second generation learners and third generation learners. The paper discusses some factors like language problem (speaking in English), knowledge of Mathematics and Statistics, inquisitiveness, independent decision-making, easy accessibility to online resources and extra-curricular activity participation that should fit the quality framework from the students' perspective. The methodology included for the use of purposive sampling where a sample of 20 students selected from each group. The primary data was collected through scheduling where the responses were personally administered. The data was presented in a tabulated form. Kruskal-Wallis statistic test (a non-parametric test) was used to test the null hypothesis. The hypothesis under study was that there is no significant difference in the responses of the three groups with reference to the quality factors. The significant difference between two independent groups was also tested using

Wilcoxon-Mann-Whitney statistic test. The outcome of the study was that the quality factors largely determine the quality gap and it was observed that there was a significant difference in the responses of the different groups and it was accepted as under. Kruskal-Wallis statistic test and moreover the Wilcoxon-Mann-Whitney U statistic test was used to test the difference in the combination of two groups within the three groups, it was observed that the responses were statistically significant. The conclusion of the study is that there is a need to address the issues of quality factors for all colleges and universities to sustain in the global environment.

Introduction

The Education sector in India has expanded in terms of quantity but in terms of quality it has a long way to go. In this era of knowledge economy a wide disparity has been observed in terms of qualitative values among various sections of learners. On one hand, we have IIT's and IIM's generating world class engineers and managers but on the other hand our education system is fighting hard to find the solution to the problem of social exclusions, skill or quality gap among various first generation, second generation and third generation of learners. The quantitative expansion of education is mainly concerned with the acquisition of knowledge and it considers merely the external assessment of the student as the performance indicator. Interpersonal and cognitive skills largely determine the qualitative aspects of the education. The ignorance of these skills among certain group of students results into creation of quality gap which increases after every semester and year. External assessment or public examination fails to assess the cognitive skills as well the quality gap. The quality gap problem becomes grave indeed due to some discouraging feedbacks about the teaching and learning approach in Indian universities by the bright and financially empowered students, who are mainly the third or second generation learners. Most of such learners are hunting for other options like foreign universities for seeking better quality of education. It is quiet possible that the future learners from the higher stratum of the society may aspire for other universities. Given the report on the world university ranking, not a single Indian university can be listed in first 200 top universities of the world. The teachers and the mentors of higher education are the stake holders of the knowledge economy. Therefore, bridging up the quality gap is equal responsibility of a teacher. The bridging of this quality gap remains the toughest challenges before the *Rashtriya Uchatar Shiksha Abhiyaan.*

Review of Literature

The gap model analysis of service quality in the Indian higher education has been studied by Rajsekar (et.al. 2009) where the providers and customers gap is highlighted. Henard (2008) reviewed 29 higher education institutions across 20 OECD and non-OECD countries that focused on the reasons for and effectiveness of quality teaching initiatives. UNICEF (2000) examined the researches related to the political, economic and cultural dimensions of education.

Rationale for the Study

The problems that quality gap might create are indeed grave and therefore the results generated will tend to be half-baked. The rationale for taking up this study to consider the three group of learners independently namely the learners of the first generation (FGL), second generation (SGL) and third generation (TGL). It is imperative to study the factors that undermine and determine the quality issues in higher education. There are various intellectual and behavioural factors that need to be studied in depth to trace the reasons for the quality gap in education.

Objectives of the Study

The following were the objectives of the study:

(1) To identify the determinants of quality gap.

(2) To examine the significant differences in relation to skill gap among first generation, second generation and third generation learners of higher education.

Area of Study

The study focuses on the quality facets of higher education and the area of the study is restricted to the higher education learners of all the three groups from Dombivli city. Moreover, the scope of the study is restricted to the higher education in non-technical stream of Arts and Commerce.

Factors Determining the Quality Framework of Higher Education

The term quality encompasses the holistic development of the learner. The exogenous factors on which the quality framework depends are availability of efficient and dynamic teaching staff, proper assessment mechanism, well-developed infrastructure and pedagogy etc. However, there are some factors that are intrinsic factors like language problem (speaking in English), knowledge of Mathematics and Statistics, inquisitiveness, independent decision-making, easy accessibility to online resources and extra-curricular activity participation that largely determine the quality facet.

Methodology

The methodology involved was the use of purposive sampling whereby a group of 20 students from each group of generations i.e., first generation, second generation and third generation were taken for the study. The first generation learners were identified as those who are the first in their family pursuing higher education. The second generation learners are those whose parents are educated (at least higher secondary). The third generation learners indicate that not only their parents but also grand parents have passed atleast matriculation. The data about the each group of students was collected in the form of group administered questionnaire. It was an ordinal type data and therefore Likert type scalē (four point endorsement scales) were used to quote the responses. The scope of the responses were determined by the level of agreement and there was no scope to provide undecided or neutral responses therefore four point scales representing strong agreement, agreement, disagreement and strong disagreement were taken into account and the scores for the levels were as given below:

Strong Agreement	Agreement	Disagreement	Strong Disagreement
(4)	(3)	(2)	(1)

Since the groups to be tested were more than two independent groups it was tested using Kruskal Wallis test that belongs to the family of non-parametric statistics. Moreover for testing the significant difference in the responses between two groups out of three Mann-Whitney U statistical test was used.

Data Analysis and Intrepretation

(I) Descriptive Analysis

In the descriptive analysis the data was collected through an administered questionnaire. The information related to the quality indicators such as language proficiency, mathematical and statistical know-how, independent decision-making, comfort level to participate in the extra-curricular academic activities, frequent access to internet and self-confidence was extracted from the respondents.

Q. 1. Language problem is the basic hurdle for learning and understanding concepts.

Q. 2. I find it tough to cope up with mathematical concepts.

Q. 3. I find it difficult to take decisions about professional carrier independently.

Q. 4. It feels uncomfortable to actively participate in the extra-curricular academic activities.

Q. 5. There is no frequent access to internet.

Q. 6. I lack self-conviction.

Responses with respect to the quality indicators (in Percentage)

FGL: First generation learners. SGL: Second generation learners. TGL: Third generation learners:

SA: Strongly Agree. A: Agree. D: Disagree. SD: Strongly Disagree.

Learners	*FGL (Group I)*				*SGL (Group II)*				*TGL (Group III)*			
	SA	*A*	*D*	*SD*	*SA*	*A*	*D*	*SD*	*SA*	*A*	*D*	*SD*
Q.1.	45%	45%	—	0%		35%	60%	5%	—	—	45%	55%
Q.2.	15%	65%	10%	10%	5%	35%	55%	5%	—	—	50%	50%
Q.3.	75%	25%	—	—	—	25%	75%	—	—	5%	60%	35%
Q.4.	75%	20%	—	5%	5%	35%	50%	10%	—	—	45%	55%
Q.5.	10%	55%	35%	—	—	30%	50%	20%	—	—	35%	65%
Q.6.	50%	45%	—	5%	—	40%	40%	20%	—	10%	50%	40%

It can be seen from the descriptive analysis that the first generation of learners strongly reveal their agreement with the problems they face in the process of learning. The second generations of learners also have shown their agreement in certain areas where they face difficulty but by and large they are better off as compared to first generation of learner as they disagree to certain questions. The third generation learners with few exceptions are better off as they strongly disagree or with the problems which the first generation learners are more prone to.

(II) Inferential Analysis

The data obtained was an ordinal data and therefore a non-parametric test was used to check the significant differences among three groups. On the basis of three different groups namely the FGL, SGL and TGL the inferential analysis involved the use of Kruskal Wallis test statistics for checking the significant differences in the responses among three groups of learners.

The Kruskal Wallis Test statistic is given by,

H=12/ N (N+1) (Σ (Ti) ^2/ (Ni)) – 3(N + 1)

Since the K samples include more than five observation, the test statistic H is a very close approximation of chi-square distribution with (k -1) degrees of freedom where it denotes the number of groups. To check the significant differences in the responses among a combination of two different groups among the three groups was taken. The null hypothesis that there is no significant difference between the responses of any two groups among the three groups was tested using Wilcoxon Mann-Whitney test.

The test statistic is given by,

U=N1N2 + N2 (N2 + 1)/2 – ΣRi

Results and findings

(A) Kruskal Wallis Test for testing significant difference between three groups

Hypothesis		*Critical Value*	*Remarks*
Under Ho: Responses from 3 groups do not differ significantly	Approximation to Chi-square as N is greater than 5 **Hcal = 44.1032**	At 5 per cent level of significance with (k-1) degrees of freedom i.e. 2 dfs, the critical value is 5.991	There is significant differences in the responses of the three groups

(B) Wilcoxon Mann-Whitney U Test for testing significant difference between two groups

Test-stastic	*Groups*	*Critical Value*	*Remarks*
Under Ho: Responses from 2 groups do not differ significantly	I and II	At 5 per cent level of significance, z = 4.661 and p-value = 0, U value =27 and Critical U value is 127	Significant differences in the responses of group I and II
Under Ho: Responses from 2 groups do not differ significantly	II and III	At 5 per cent level of significance, z = 4.57 and p-value=0, U value=30.5 and critical U value = 127	Significant differences in the responses of group II and III
Under Ho: Responses from 2 groups do not differ significantly	I and III	At 5 per cent level of significance, z=5.27 and p-value=0, U value =4.5 Critical value of U= 127	Highly significant difference exist between the responses of Group I and III

The outcome of the inferential analysis is that the three groups differ significantly in terms of the responses. This implies that there is a quality gap among the three groups. It is obvious from the analysis that Group I and Group III are highly significant in their responses indicating that the quality gap between these two groups is critical.

Some Possible Solutions

After analysing the factors that determine quality education for the three groups of learners, the results showed that there exist significant differences between the responses among the three groups as well as between the three groups. It is obvious the quality gap as studied under the mentioned factors is wide between three groups. The teachers and the mentors of higher education are the stake holders of the knowledge economy and they can play a pivotal role to minimise the quality gap. The investigator strongly feels that only research promotion activites in education among the teachers is not going to solve the problem of the quality gap but application of the research is equally important. There needs a co-ordination between the institutions from the remote villages and the institutions from the cities where the big and well-settled institution can help in guiding the small institutions to solve their problems. The study reveals that there is lack of self-conviction and confidence among the first generation learners. Regular workshops on motivation and developing soft skills at least once in two months can help to minimise the gap among the learners.

Conclusion

It can be concluded that there is an aurgent need to address the issues of quality factors for all colleges and universities to sustain in the global environment as well as to ensure inclusiveness and equity in education. Especially the first generation learners need special attention, mentoring and counselling. Their value, attitude and approach towards education need to be strengthen in order to develop a qualitative balance and reduce the quality gaps.

References and Citations

- Bhandarkar, P. and Wilkinson, T. (2009), Methodology and techniques of Social Research, *The scaling techniques,* (pp. 237-238), Mumbai: Himalaya Publishing House.
- Bhattacharya, D. (2003), Appendix (p. 296), Research Methodology, New Delhi, Excel Books.
- Henard, F. (2010). Learning our lessons: The review of quality teaching in higher education retrieved from http://www.oecd.org/edu/imhe/44058352.pdf
- Jina, H. and Rath, B. (2013). Performance of first year degree students in the internal test assessment in relation to their anxiety and attitude towards internal assessment. In N.Dey (Ed.) *Educational research* (p. 361). New Delhi: APH Publishing Corporation.
- Madan, P., Paliwal, V. and Bharadwaj, R. (2010), Research Methodology, *Testing of Hypothesis-II (Non-Parametric or Distribution Test),* (pp. 283-290) New Delhi, Global Vision Publishing House.

- Rajsekar, M., Muninarayanappa, M. and Reddy, S. (2009). The gap model analysis of service quality in Indian higher education. *E-Journal of Asia Pacific Journal of Social Sciences* (pp. 214-229) Retrieved from http://www.socialsciences-ejournal.org/2.11%20Rajasekar.pdf
- UNICEF (2000), *Defining quality in education*, Document No. (UNICEF/PD/ED/02), New York, Colby. J and Witt, M (p. 3) retrieved from http://www.unicef.org/education/files/QualityEducation.PDF
- Why private universities are set to be the future of quality education in India (2013, June 9).
- *Economic Times*, retrieved from http://articles.economictimes.indiatimes.com/2013-06-09/news/39834862_1_quality-education-manipal-global-education-indian-education.

3 Gender Disparities in Higher Education Enrollment in India—An Overview

Latha M.T.
Dr. Shivanand Nari

Abstract

This paper reviews gender disparities in higher education enrollment in India. Higher education is an important indicator of socio-economic development of a nation. India has experienced rapid growth, expansion, advancement and changes in the number of institutions and the level of education, both in the numbers and the quality of education. However, owing to a number of constraints and socio-economic factors, the benefits of expansion of educational facilities have not reached fully to all, especially women notwithstanding communities and states. There are wide **gender** disparities in terms of access to higher education. In this background this paper examines the trend in women enrollment for higher education in India from the period 2001-2010 and region-wise gender disparities in women enrollment in higher education. Using Exponential Growth model, the Compound Average Growth Rate shows that enrollment ratio of women has increased by 89 per cent compare to men enrollment 82 per cent. The paradox of enrollment is widened by the fact that in regions and region-wise gender disparity is highest in India it is reported that East and North East regions are least in women enrollment. North region has been placed in the middle and the West region has been placed the second highest in enrollment and South region has placed first highest in women enrollment in higher education that is proved through using One Way Anova and post Hoc test. The marginalisation of educated women in research continues priority area within higher education.

Introduction

Higher education is an important indicator of socio-economic development of a Nation. It is regarded as means and ends of development. India has experienced rapid growth, expansion, advancement and changes in the number of institutions and the levels of education, both in the numbers and the quality of education. It also includes the magnitude of research works in all the disciplines. India has the largest educational system in the world; this largeness is mainly due to the large population and their requirements. India ranks second in the world in terms of enrollment of students in higher education institutions. There are 12,600 colleges, 70 lakh students, three lakh teachers occupying 16 central universities, 39 deemed universities, 221 universities, of which 156 are state universities, and 10,555 colleges (2012, UGC). This has provided all sections of the society great access to higher education. However, owing to a number of constraints and socio-economic factors, the benefits of expansion of educational facilities have not reached fully to all, especially women notwithstanding communities and states. There are wide **gender** disparities in terms of access to higher education. Access is generally lower for females as compared to the males the Gross Enrollment Ratio (GER) is 12.42 per cent for males and 9.11 per cent for females. The females belonging to the lower castes and minority groups suffer acutely in accessing higher education than others. Education is paramount for promoting equality between women and men. As we move towards the next century the debate on social and human development has also begun to highlight the instrumentality of education, especially of female literacy and primary education. Education at the primary level is the focus of debate for those concerned with social and human development; higher education is highlighted for social and occupational mobility, for best formation and for intellectual and personal development. (Karuna Chanana). While there are varied theoretical frameworks to explain gender inequality within education, there is general agreement that gender inequality is deep-rooted and universal. Hence, there is need for micro level study pertaining to status of higher education among women.

Educational Policy and Women in Higher Education

The Indian Constitution provides for equality to all Indian citizens irrespective of caste, religion and sex. Further, the deprived groups, namely, the scheduled castes and scheduled tribes are provided supports such as reservation in the state-run educational institutions for purposes of admission and for jobs in the employing organisations. Moreover, religious and linguistic minorities are permitted to establish educational institutions. Thus, education has been perceived as an important instrument for the advancement of the deprived and the minorities, on the one hand, while equality was guaranteed to everyone including Women.

The issue of women entering higher education came firmly on the global political agenda in 1998. The document Higher Education and Women: Issues and Perspectives (UNESCO 1998) prepared for the 1998 World Conference on Higher Education specifically focused on the issues related to women. In India, it was the Kothari Commission, which more than three decades earlier in 1964-66, had emphasised explicitly on equal educational opportunities for women and had also suggested effective steps to achieve it. As pointed out by Chanana, the first two Five Year Plans acknowledged the problems related to women's education and tried to link education with employment. It was after the publication of the Report of the Committee on the Education of Women in 1959 that led to a more focused attention later, which got sharpened with the Report of the Committee on the Status of Women in 1974 and women's education was placed within the broader framework of developmental issues. The National Policy of Education (1986), broadening the vision further underscored the role of education in empowering women that would overcome inequalities and disparities (Chanana 2005).

Subsequent Five Year Plans and various committees including the National Perspective Plan (1988-2000) have stressed the need for greater participation of women in higher education. These efforts have resulted in increase in women accessing higher education from 25.7 lakhs in 1993-94 to 42.6 lakhs in 1999-2000 to 54.06 lakhs in 2004-05. The corresponding figures for men are 51 lakhs, 69 lakhs and 81 lakhs. In absolute terms women continue to lag behind men, but because of accelerated growth rate in women's enrollment, the gap between men and women is narrowing. For example, the growth rate of women students in higher education between 1993-04 to 2004-05 has been 7.72 per cent as compared to 4.73 per cent for men. The census-adjusted figures for two rounds, i.e., 1993-94 and 1999-2000 (the corresponding census years 1991 and 2001), although slightly higher show similar trend, *i.e.,* 8.77 per cent for women and 5.22 per cent for men respectively. Significantly, the growth in enrollment in higher education is much higher for rural women as compared to their urban counterparts – thirteen per cent as compared to five per cent respectively – more than twice as faster for the rural women. The corresponding figures for men are about five per cent (rural) and three per cent (urban) respectively. Although the higher growth rate in case of rural women is partly because of the low base, it cannot be denied that increasingly more rural women are entering the domain of higher education. Currently (2004-05), 40 per cent of the total enrollment in higher education as compared to less than 10 per cent at the eve of independence consist of women (UGC 2005).

There has been phenomenal growth in enrollment of women students in higher education in the country. The share of women's enrollment which was 11.3 per cent of the total enrollment in 1950-51 has increased to 38.6 per cent in 2008-2009. Gross Enrollment Ratio (GER) of women has increased by 4.6 percentage point during 2001-2002 to 2008-2009.

Barriers to Access Higher Education

There are several factors that reduce access and corrective orientations of women in higher education. Factors that inhibit female access to higher education are quantitative, such as non-availability of colleges and inadequate delivery that is unsuitable infrastructure and absence of basic physical facilities. Other factors are qualitative and are rooted in the socio-cultural context (Karuna Chanana) such as inadequate of rest rooms, common rooms, hostels, non-availability of scholarships/fellowships and disciplines of their choice, absence of women teachers, or separate schools and colleges for women; absence of counselling for discipline and career options; etc.

The socio-cultural factors may be divided into two sets viz., those at the macro level and at the micro level. The macro level dimensions relate to caste, tribe, class and regional variations. The micro level factors may be further sub-divided into institutional and societal factors.

Institutional factors that originate from gendered structures. Some of the notable social dimensions of institutional arrangements are: gender stereotyping in course content and subject choices, discriminatory attitudes of teachers and administrators, absence of role models for career options and academic leadership etc. Even in a single sex institution, the faculty may reinforce traditional social roles or not encourage women students to follow the non-traditional role models. Sometimes, the rules and procedures may be too restrictive so as to suffocate the development of young women. Such restrictive practices in the hostel may lead to the dropping out of women students.

Social factors are the push and pull factors that originate from cultural practices, behaviour patterns and social role expectations and the association of women with the private domain of household continues to affect access to higher education. Some of the notable and well-known barriers are: lack of economic resources in the family; the choice between dowry and educational expenses, education being perceived as consumption and being irrelevant for production. As per the socialisation norms, parents may not use the earnings of their daughters. Therefore, either they do not want them to take up jobs or when they do, it is viewed as a short-term goal. This is because the traditional role expectations are such that the future parents-in-law and the husband would decide future career options of the young women.

Thus, even if daughters start working, the reluctance to use daughter's income is quite common except among the very poor. Thus, for a large majority, higher education is not linked to careers. These social role expectations and self expectations affect the aspirations of a large number of women raises their marital prospects of getting a qualified and well-placed husband. Even, if they take up jobs after higher education, dowry demand does not seem to reduce corresponding to her monthly income or salary.

Steps taken to Improve Higher Education Among Women

University Grants Commission (UGC) has taken a number of steps for greater access to women in higher education like Indira Gandhi Scholarship for Single Girl Child for pursuing Higher Technical Education. Construction of Womens Hostels, Development of Women's studies in Universities and colleges, Schemes of capacity building of Women's Manager in Higher Education, Post Doctoral fellowships and also women Junior Research Fellowship candidates can get six months maternity leaves with payments (UGC). All India Council of Technical Education (AICTE) has a scheme to encourage tuitions fee waiver for girl's students by incentivising the technical institutions and relaxation in norms for establishment of technical institutions exclusively for women.

Review of Literature

Sharmistha and Grabowsk (2004) Examine Education has a positive relationship with economic development the casual linkage between educations at all levels and economic growth in India. Levels are primary, secondary and tertiary hence female education at all three levels has potential for generating economic growth (Palanithurai, 2004; GOI, 1966). This argument is more valid in the context of developing countries (Devi, 1994 (a) The economic growth model of development was questioned by the UNDP in its first human development report of 1990, which reiterate that people, not things, are the wealth of nations. In that direction human development is the process of building the capabilities to enable people to lead productive lives (UNDP, 1990). Education is the stepping stone and precondition for building capabilities (Devi, 1994 b). As human development reports reveal most of the South Asian countries are having low human development and India is one such country (UNDP, 2010). Within India all the states are not having same level of human development and there occurs a wide range of disparities in human development of India based on gender, region and other factors (GOI, 2002). Theoretically, and empirically it has been found that males are more literate than females; forward regions are having higher literacy than backward regions and high income states having higher literacy rate than other states (Rampal, 2000; Premakumara, 2006; Kaul, 2001; Caseen, 2002).

Research Gap

From the review of earlier studies, it is evident that empirical studies relating to impact of gender inequality in education on economic growth; but there is no evident in the results of empirical studies relating to research on growth rate of gender-wise enrollment at higher education in India and gender-wise disparity in enrollment at higher education in India. With this backdrop this paper fills this gap by analysing growth rate of gender-wise enrollment at higher education in India and also analysing gender-wise disparities in enrollment at higher education among regions.

Objectives of the Paper

Following are the objectives of the paper.

1. To analyse the growth rate of gender-wise enrollment of higher education in India.
2. To examine the region-wise gender disparities in enrollment of higher education among regions.

Hypotheses of the Paper

1. There is a significant increase in growth rate of gender-wise enrollment in India.
2. There is a significant gender-wise disparity in enrollment of higher education in Indian regions.

Methodology of the Paper

This paper is based on secondary data obtained from Ministry of Human Development Resource and UGC Annual Reports from the period 2001 to 2010. The first hypothesis being tested using Exponential Growth Model in Excel sheet to find out Compound Growth Average Rate (Compound Annual Growth Rate—CAGR' the year-over-year growth rate of enrollments over a specified period of time). The compound annual growth rate is calculated by taking the *n*th root of the total percentage growth rate, where is the number of years in the period being considered. This can be written as follows:

$$\text{CAGR} = \left(\frac{\text{Ending Value}}{\text{Beginning Value}}\right)^{\left(\frac{1}{\#\text{ of years}}\right)} - 1$$

And second hypothesis is being tested one-way analysis of variance (ANOVA) is used to determine whether there are any significant differences between the means of two or more independent (unrelated) groups that is men and women enrollments in higher education. It is important to realise that the one-way ANOVA is a *collection* test statistic and cannot tell which specific region were significantly different from each other regions in gender-wise enrollment in higher education; for this, we using a post-hoc test, in post-hoc test we used Tukey LSD test in one way Anova. Indian states are classified into 5 regions such as North (region 1), North East (region 2), East (region 3), South (region 4) and West (region 5).

Results and Discussions

(a) Growth Rate of Higher Education Enrollment in India

This section provides men and women enrollments' in higher education from the period of 2001-2010 and decadal growth rate of enrollment in higher education. The first objective was proved in this section Compound Average Growth Rate is increased in women enrollment than total growth rate. The numbers are noticeable. And men enrollments are decreased when compared to women enrollment. Growth rate of total student enrollments are analysed by using the following Table 1.

Table 1. Men and Women Students Enrollments in India

Years	*Men*	*Women*	*Total*
2002	5273305	3551468	8824773
2003	6117826	3869028	9986854
2004	7135909	4641665	11777574
2005	6123821	3630508	9754329
2006	8886376	5707533	14593909
2007	6910634	4701871	11612505
2008	7526519	5028729	12555248
2009	8153049	5488759	13641808
2010	9926195	7048688	16974883
CAGR	0.082274657	0.089463	0.0852078

(*Source:* Ministry of Human Resource Development).

Table 1 explains that growth rate of student's enrollment in higher education in India from the period of 2002 to 2010. Compound Growth Average Rate of women's enrollments is highest (0.089463 or 89 per cent) when compare to Average growth rate of all over India total enrollment

Table 2. Enrollment of Men and Women Anova

		Sum of squares	*df*	*Mean Square*	*F*	*Sig*
	Between groups	20014903031541.200	4	5003725757885.300	26.658	.000
	Within Groups	7508128414388.000	40	187703210359.700		
Enrollment of Men	Total	27523031445929.200	44			
Enrollment of Women	Between groups	10510003916732.900	4	2627500979183.240	26.977	.000
	Within Groups	3895912172744.220	40	97397804318.606		
	Total	14405916089477.200	44			

(0.0852078 or 85 per cent) and men's enrollments in higher education. (0.82274 or 82 per cent).

Table 2 shows that Anova test results of enrollment disparity among men and women, here test result that, growth rate of enrollment of men and women has significant difference in enrollment in India last column of the table shows the significance value.000, it clearly shows that there is a significant difference between men and women enrollment in higher education if we considered the F value that's also shows the same result of significance, here calculated F value is greater than the table value (26.658>2.61) at the degree of freedom (3, 31). Null hypotheses is rejected, there is a statistically significant difference (.000) between groups and within groups of enrollment of men in India. And also for women enrollment, calculated F value is greater than the table value (26.977>2.61) at the degree of freedom (3, 31). Null Hypotheses is rejected, there is a statistically significant difference (.000) between groups and within groups of enrollment of women. All over India the growth rate of gender-wise enrollments are increased but there is statistically significant difference between men enrollment and women enrollment growth rate.

(b) Analysis of Region-wise Gender Disparity in Higher Education Enrollment

This section provides the data on enrollment of women, men and across the regions viz., North, North-East, East, South and West. According to the latest statistics the enrollment of women in 2001-2002 was **324158** out of total enrollment of **1076996** in higher education remaining are mens enrollment which **752838** (UGC 2003-04). The number of women has increased from 324158 in 2002 to 7048688 in 2011 out of total enrollment **16974886.** The rises in numbers are noticeable but the region-wise gender disparity in higher education enrollment is high in all regions compared to men except south region where women enrollment is high and in the East region the women enrollments is the lowest compared to all regions of India.

The following Table 3 explains that using a one-way Anova post hoc test was conducted to compare the women enrollment in higher education between the regions.

Here, North region is compared to all other regions, which show that there is statistically significant difference in North-East (.000) and East (.003) regions in women enrollment of higher education. But there is no statistically significant difference in South (.121) and West regions (.114); in these two regions significant value is greater than the 0.05 level. Hence, the women enrollment in higher education is far above the ground in North region when compared to North-East and East regions but compared to South and West regions there is no significant difference in women enrollment.

Then, North-East region when compared with all four regions weighs against to all other regions there is a statically significant difference between North, East, South and West regions. Statistically significant value is less than 0.05 level, in all regions which clearly shows that there is statistically significant difference in women enrollment, consequently in the North-East region's women enrollment in higher education is least when compare to all four regions.

Here, compared to East region to all other regions there is a statistically significant difference between North, North-East, South and West regions, which clears from the statistically significant value, which is less than 0.05 levels. Results shows that in East region's enrollment of women in higher education is difference when compare to all four regions.

Then, South region is compare to all other regions there is no significant difference between North (.121) and West regions (.978) in women enrollment of higher education, it is provide evidence from the significant value is greater than 0.05, but North-East and East regions are significant difference at the .000, which shows that, there is statistically significant difference in these two regions. Hence, women enrollment in higher education is high in South.

And finally, the West region is compared to all other four regions over again the North-East and East regions are significantly difference from other two regions. Which is prove that significant value is less than the 0.05 in North-East and East regions and the significant value is greater than the 0.05 in North (.114) and South regions (.978). It clearly shows the disparity in enrollment of higher education between regions.

Conclusion

The empirical evidence and the results of the present study clearly show that the overall trend of enrollment in higher education is increasing during the reference period of the study; it is evident that the gender-wise disparity in higher education in terms of enrollment is more in India. The disparity is also widespread among different regions of the country. Especially in North-East and East regions are the lowest in women enrollment in higher education. South and West regions are the highest in women enrollment in higher education and North region is between the North-East, East regions and South, West regions in women enrollment in higher education.

Post-Hoc Tests

Table 3. Multiple Comparisons (Between Regions)
Dependent Variable: Enrollment of Women LSD

(I) Region	(J) Region	Mean Difference (I-J)	Std. Error	Sig.	95 per cent Confidence Interval Lower Bound	95 per cent Confidence Interval Upper Bound
1. North	2	1023079.778*	147118.852	.000	725741.49	1320418.07
	3	467015.667*	147118.852	.003	169677.38	764353.96
	4	-233315.778	147118.852	.121	-530654.07	64022.51
	5	-237416.222	147118.852	.114	-534754.51	59922.07
2. North-East	1	-1023079.778*	147118.852	.000	-1320418.07	-725741.49
	3	-556064.111*	147118.852	.001	-853402.40	-258725.82
	4	-1256395.556*	147118.852	.000	-1553733.85	-959057.27
	5	-1260496.000*	147118.852	.000	-1557834.29	-963157.71
3. East	1	-467015.667*	147118.852	.003	-764353.96	-169677.38
	2	556064.111*	147118.852	.001	258725.82	853402.40
	4	-700331.444*	147118.852	.000	-997669.73	-402993.15
	5	-704431.889*	147118.852	.000	-1001770.18	-407093.60
4. South	1	233315.778	147118.852	.121	-64022.51	530654.07
	2	1256395.556*	147118.852	.000	959057.27	1553733.85
	3	700331.444*	147118.852	.000	402993.15	997669.73
	5	-4100.444	147118.852	.978	-301438.73	293237.85
5. West	1	237416.222	147118.852	.114	-59922.07	534754.51
	2	1260496.000*	147118.852	.000	963157.71	1557834.29
	3	704431.889*	147118.852	.000	407093.60	1001770.18
	4	4100.444	147118.852	.978	-293237.85	301438.73

* The mean difference is significant at the 0.05 level.
1=North, 2=North-East, 3=East, 4=South, 5=West.

Notes

- Himachal Pradesh, Haryana Jammu and Kashmir, Punjab, Uttar Pradesh, Uttaranchal, Chandigarh and Delhi.
- Arunachal Pradesh, Assam, Manipur, Meghalaya, Mizoram, Nagaland, Sikkim and Tripura.
- Bihar, Chhattisgarh, Jharkhand, Orissa, Andaman and Nicobar and West Bengal.
- Andhra Pradesh, Karnataka, Kerala, Tamil Nadu, Pondicherry and Lakshadweep.
- Goa, Gujarat, Madhya Pradesh, Rajasthan, Dadar and Nagar Haveli and Daman and Diu.

References

- Damodar, N. Gujarati., and Sangeetha. (2007). *Basic Econometrics* (pp. 304-313). New Delhi: Tata McGraw-Hill Publishing.
- Devi, Nirmala.T. (1994 a), *Socio Economic Profile of SAARC Countries* (p. 33). New Delhi: South Asian Publishers.
- Devi, Nirmala.T. (1994 b). *Socio Economic Profile of SAARC Countries* (pp. 154-56). New Delhi: South Asian Publishers.
- GOI, (1966). *Education Commission 1966.* India: Department of Education.
- GOI, (2002). *National Human Development Report 2001.* New Delhi: Ministry of Human Development.
- GOI, (2004-2012) *Ministry of Human Resources and Development Reports* New Delhi: Ministry of Human Development.
- Karuna Chanana, (2000) "*Treading the Hallowed Hans Women in Higher Education*", Economic and Political Weekly, Vol. 35, No. 12 pp.1012-1022.
- Karuna Chanana (1993) "*Accessing Higher Education: the Dilemma of Schooling Women.*
- *Minorities SC, ST and Contemporary India*", Higher Education Vol. 26, No. 1, 1993, pp. 69-92.
- Premakumara, Riyaz Ahmad (2010) *"Regional Disparities, Inclusive Growth and Educational Development in Karnataka".*
- UGC, (2002-2012) *University Grants Commission Reports,* New Delhi.
- Zakir Husain (2010) *"Gender Disparities in Completing School Education in India Analysing Regional Variations"* Draft dated 24/11/2010: V 2.1, Population Research Centre, Institute of Economic Growth Delhi University Enclave, North Campus, Delhi 110007, India.

4 An Overview of Financing of Higher Education in India

Manjunatha G.
Dr. M. Mahesha

Abstract

Higher education is critical to India's aspirations of emerging as a major player in the global knowledge economy. Knowledge is the driving force in the changing globalised economy and society. The global competitiveness of Indian industry and also its employment generation potential is clearly dependent on availability of quality and quantity of specialised human resources. Better the resources better are the opportunities. This is realised with higher education. It is a national resource and therefore without quality higher education is a curse for a nation. Higher Education is both a social and private are valuable. Funding large population seeking higher education is a herculean task. This paper attempts to analyse the present pattern of financing of higher education in India and to discuss the desirability and feasibility of various alternative methods of funding the same. Exponential Growth model is used to analyse trends in financing. The results conclude that there is significant decline in public expenditure. It is suggested for alternative avenues of financing higher education in the form of private expenditure, tuition fees, aid and scholarships, education loans, graduate taxes and corporate contribution.

Key words: Higher Education, Gross Enrollment Ratio (GER), Rate of Returns, Expenditure, GDP.

Introduction

Education is an essential component for development of a human being. It ensures knowledge, skills of an earning livelihood or trade and makes one eligible for employment. It is also linked with a person's social status. The importance of education is quite clear. Education is the knowledge of putting one's potentials to maximum use. This importance of education is basically for two reasons. Firstly, the training of a human mind is not complete without education. Education makes man a right thinker and decision-taker. Secondly, only through the attainment of education, man is enabled to receive information from the external world; to acquaint himself with past history and receive all necessary information regarding the present so as to improve the present and strive for a better tomorrow. Higher education has social and private implications benefiting both society and individual in non-quantifiable way. Moreover as a policy, higher education institutions play an important role in setting the academic standards for primary and secondary education. But absence of adequate capital retains all positive externalities of higher education. Therefore, financing is an important issue.

The cost for higher education is to be essentially borne by the government or taxpayers (as grants), parents or their substitutes (as tuition fees), students and/or individuals (by availing loans or doing part-time work) and donors (individuals or institutional). The debate, therefore, is essentially whether the higher education should be paid for by the general taxpayer or its beneficiaries, i.e., the students or their parents. Financing of higher education by the government is justified on the ground that education, being a public good or at least a quasi-public good produces many positive externalities. Therefore, government should finance higher education. Finally, the production process in higher education is believed to be subject to economies of scale or decreasing returns to scale. Hence, it is considered more efficient for the government to provide higher education (Tilak, 2005). However, several arguments against public subsidisation of higher education have been put forth (Tilak 2005). The reason is that social rates of returns of higher education are found to be lower than private returns.

There is continuous progress in higher education, especially in Gross Enrolment Ratio (GER), in number of higher education degree holders, number of institutions offering courses in degree programmes—bachelors and masters, diplomas and PhD degrees world-wide, however, these rates are insignificant when compared with their corresponding requirements and targets. This requires huge investment in education sector. Federal governments and state governments have been allocating huge amounts and funding education in their budgets every year. However, fiscal consolidations and critical macro-economic crises have reduced state's contribution to education sector in recent years. Moreover, with the New Economic Policy, economies opened their higher education sectors to open market investments through active participation of private sector, partially or fully. This is in response to fill the investment gap. Nonetheless, improving primary and secondary education sector, higher education would not receive any prominence. Therefore, the present study is undertaken with the twin objectives—to study the present scenario of financing higher education in India and to discuss about the feasibility and desirability of alternative sources of financing so as to maintain standards of higher education in India.

Secondary data is used for verifying set objectives. This data is collected from UGC Reports, RBI Reports, NSSO, Ministry of HRD, Govt. of India and OECD. Exponential Growth model (Regression) is used to explain the trends in financing higher education in India.

Higher Education at Global Level

Since the time of concept of 'welfare state' has been conceived, education has become the domain of state's responsibility. Further with the political and economic changes in twentieth century such as independent movements in Asia and Africa, world wars, cold war between capitalist nations headed by United States and Britain, and socialist nations headed by former USSR led to improvements in education of its people so as to make them aware of their movements and contribute to their respective nations in turn. In addition to this, states recognised that education has positive social and private returns. Governments through successful planning set targets for increasing Gross Enrolment Ratios in primary and secondary education, and higher education. This required huge financial capital. However, financing education sector requires huge investments and budget allocations. Developed countries could reach higher levels in lesser time than developing countries given their economic position. Asian and African countries strived hard to increase enrollments but still remained at lower levels due to constraints set by resource mobilisation. This is clearly evident in Table 1. The GER of Tertiary education (Higher Education) of European and OECD countries is comparatively better than African and Asian countries. The gratifying thing is that they too have increased their GERs from initial GERs. Data of expenditure per student as a percentage of per capita GDP is provided in Table 1. Funding of higher education is based on certain models that respective countries follow. United States, Sweden, UK, Finland have better GERs. These models provide them approximate expenditure that state has to be made, allocate available funds between sectors and institutions, capital expenditure, subsidising education, scholarships, tuition fees, hostelling and accommodation and student loans.

"There ain't no such thing as a free lunch" (Friedman, Milton). Therefore, while investing in education returns are also expected, if not profit at least break-even costs. These come in terms of private returns and social returns. Returns on education is calculated by either using the

Table 1. Gross Enrollment Ratios and Public Expenditure per Student as a Percentage of GDP Per capita

Gross Enrollment Ratios of Tertiary Education				*Public Expenditure per pupil per cent of GDP per capita*		
Country	2008	2009	2010	2008	2009	2010
Argentina	69	71	75	16.5	19.4	18.4
Australia	72	76	80	19.9	20.5	-
Belgium	64	67	71	36.6	37.4	35.6
China	22	24	26	-	-	-
Finland	95	92	94	32.5	38.9	38.5
France	54	55	57	37.1	40	-
India	15	16	18	-	74.7	69.7
Malaysia	37	40	42	-	60	47.3
Norway	73	74	74	45.9	49.1	44.7
Pakistan	5	7	8	-	-	—
United Kingdom	57	59	60	22.1	20.5	-
United States	85	89	95	21.2	19.6	21.7

(*Source:* The World Bank).

"full-discounting" or "elaborate" method or "Mincerian Earnings function Method".

Full Discounting Method involves calculating the internal rate of return based on individual age-earnings profiles that vary over time (t), i.e.,

$$\sum_{t=m+1}^{n} \frac{(W_u - W_s)_t}{(1+r)^t} = \sum (W_s - C_u)(1+r)^t$$

where, (*r*) is the discount rate that equates the benefits from the extra education (proxied by earnings differentials in the economy), to the sum of opportunity costs (foregone earnings of the student while studying), and the direct resource costs of schooling at a given point in time. Thus, $(W_u - W_s)_t$ is the difference in earnings between two levels of education. W_u is the annual earnings of a more educated person. The "Mincerian" earnings function, method starts by fitting a regression to the data in the form,

$$1n\ W_i = \alpha + \beta_p D_p + \beta_s D_s + \beta_u D_u + \gamma_1 EX_i + \gamma_2 X_i^2 + \varepsilon_i$$

where, *EX* stands for years of labour market experience, defined as Age–School starting age, and *D* is a 0-1 dummy variable corresponding to the sub-scripted level of schooling (Mincer 1974). The private rate of return to higher education can then be calculated from the earnings function by the following formula, $r_u = \dfrac{\beta_u - \beta_s}{S_u - S_s}$.

The discounting of actual net age-earnings profiles is the most appropriate method of estimating the returns to education because it takes into account the most important part of the early earnings history of the individual. However, this method requires comprehensive data. Social and private rates of returns are computed by Blondal in 2002. Private rate of returns and Social rate of returns are highest in is highest in UK, US and France and lowest in Italy, Japan and Canada. This is due to benefits accrue to individuals undoubtedly accrue to Society. It is in response to more expenditure and higher GERs in higher education in these countries.

3. Models of Funding in Europe

Models have been the basis of funding of higher education in European Countries. The funding of higher education is a matter of ongoing concern in terms of expansion and diversification, fiscal pressure, market participation, demand for greater accountability and greater demand for efficiency, equity and quality (Peter Maassen, 2000).

The massification of higher education over the last two to three decades has resulted in substantial increase in the level of public funds directed to higher education institutions. In particular during the 1980s and early 1990s, governments have looked for ways to make higher education more efficient in order to put an end to the continuous growth of the higher education budget. In many countries this has led to a growing interest of higher education institutions in non-public sources of income. In other countries the foundation of the funding mechanism changed from input based to output oriented. As a consequence of these developments, and also encouraged by the growing Europeanisation and globalisation of higher education, much interest has emerged in looking abroad for new perspectives on the organisation and funding of higher education and for understanding how other (European) countries have dealt with their budgetary problems concerning higher education. Few important European higher education models are provided here.

(1) **Denmark:** Denmark has around 110 higher education institutions, ranging from comprehensive universities to smaller professional schools. Traditionally, Danish higher education was regulated strongly by the state. The state guarantees funding through the Ministry of Education (MoE) and the Ministry of Research and Information Technology (MoRIT). MoE has the overall responsibility for educational matters, whereas MoRIT has the political responsibility for research, universities, information technology and telecommunications. In 1980 a *formula based budgeting* system was introduced with separate funding of teaching and research. Funding of

teaching was based on "active students" and student/teacher ratios. As a supplement to the basic research funding, a substantial portion of public funds for research is allocated through the *Research Councils*. The universities decide on all matters relating to the use of current and capital resources when lump sum taximeter teaching grant is allocated to them.

(2) **France:** French higher education is much diversified as regards the way it is organised, the type of institutions, and the admission requirements, which vary according to the nature of the institution and the purpose of the courses offered. The French higher education system can be divided into three sectors or types of institutions: universities, state institutions (or public schools for higher education), and private institutions (or private schools for higher education). The public higher education institutions are primarily funded by the government. The private institutions derive their resources mainly from tuition fees and industry. The national French budget for higher education, including recurrent resources, investments and personnel salaries for all types of public higher education institutions, is annually adopted by the Parliament on government proposal.

In budget, funds for research are also allocated. The major part of these research funds were administered by the national 'research organisations'. Funds from both sources are administered separately. Integrating (the administration of) these funds has been contemplated by the ministry. Further, Companies have to pay a specific education tax (*Taxe d'Appretissage*). Firms are allowed to pay it directly to the higher education institution of their choice otherwise it will be levied and redistributed by the Chambers of Commerce. Higher education institutions can compete for funds from these revenues, however, in practice mainly private higher education institutions in the field of business-economics and engineering benefit from it. Research and teaching are funded mainly through separate streams in France. The funding of public institutions is based on contracts negotiated between the institutions and the Ministry of Education. This so-called contract-policy aims at providing institutions with a long-term framework. The institutional contract comprises priorities for the institutions, e.g., the strengthening of the educational programmes aimed at reducing dropout rates. Government also takes care of appointing and recruiting staff for the public institutions. In the same way, buildings are mainly funded and built by the ministry. They are owned by the state and allocated to the universities. They have adopted SANREMO (*système analythique de réparation des moyens*) model in 1993. Since then, funding formula was simplified. According the SANREMO model, the funds are allocated to the institutions on the basis of the number of students and standard costs per student. In this model, the Ministry of Education calculates the product of the costs per student and the number of students in each study programmes per university and thus allocates funds.

(3) Germany: In Germany, an aggregate of sixteen potentially different policies, given that the sixteen states (*Länder*) is responsible for higher education. German higher education is a binary system consisting of universities (*Wissenschaftliche Hochschulen*) and *Fachhochschulen.*

German higher education is publicly funded, and institutions have to follow the budgeting and accounting laws of German public administration. The federal (Bund) and Lander governments fund higher education. The budget is an integrated budget for education and research. Financial investments in new buildings, equipment for new buildings, and equipment above a certain threshold level (150,000 DM) are financed jointly by the *Länder* and the federal Minister of Education. Further, Students are provided study aid, cheap housing and meals.

(4) United Kingdom: The higher education system in the United Kingdom (i.e., England, Wales, Scotland, and Northern Ireland) has a unified structure. After the abolition of the binary line in 1992, all polytechnics, central institutions (Scotland) and a few colleges of higher education obtained university status. The rise in higher education enrolments is a prominent feature of the UK system. It has strongly been supported (even 'commanded') by the government.

The funds for teaching, research and related activities are largely formula-based. The formulae take account of the size and activities of individual institutions and the quality of their research. In distributing funds for teaching and research, the HEFCE aims to maintain diversity and increase opportunities, encourage efficiency in the use of public funding, maintain and enhance quality, and provide stability in the funding from year to year. The formula for teaching funds is price- (or efficiency-) oriented, the formula for research is quality-oriented, and the 'formula' for tuition fees is volume-oriented. Institutions receive teaching funds in the form of an HEFCE grant and student fees. The grant is allocated to institutions by using a so-called 'core-plus-margin' approach. In this approach the core is the part of an institution's grant for teaching that is to a large extent based on the budget allocated in the previous year, thus providing financial stability. However for medical sciences, it employs other approaches to finance.

Higher Education in India

India is a developing economy, where its large population has starved of education. Providing education to all is a herculean task for state. Since from the first five year plan, targets were set to increase in GERs in both primary and higher education sectors. Periodic assessments were also made to assess set objectives and targets. Punnayya committee (1993) has also recommended increasing GER in higher education. However, GER of higher education is not satisfactory. This is evident in Fig. 1. Planning commission has set a target of 22 per cent in twelfth Five year plan. Initially, State has taken the whole responsibility of funding higher education, as private sector didn't consider it as lucrative investment.

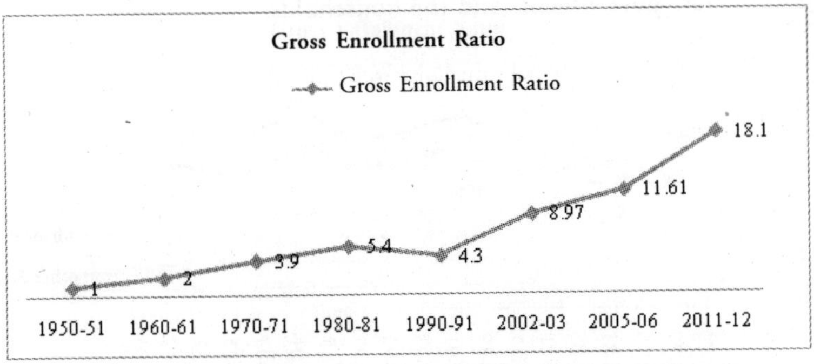

Fig. 1: Gross Enrollment Ratios in Higher Education in India.

(*Source:* UGC Reports).

Exponential Growth model has been used to test the significance in the change of Government spending on higher education in India. The results are presented in the Table 2. It reveals that there are significant changes in funding of higher education by Education department and other departments. Obtained ß (beta) values explain the changes in expenditure given change in time period.

Table 2. Results of Expenditure made on Education by Education Department and other Departments as per cent of GDP

Variables	*β (beta) Co-efficient*	
	1971-72 to 1989-90	*1990-91 to 2008-09*
Expenditure by Education Dept as per cent of GDP	0.76 (0.000)	0.85 (0.000)
Expenditure by other Depts as per cent of GDP	0.085 (0.000)	0.100 (0.000)
Total Expenditure on Education as per cent of GDP	0.179 (0.000)	0.198 (0.000)

From 1971-72 to 1989-90, expenditure by education department and other departments on higher education has increased significantly. Similarly, from1990-91 to 2008-09, changes in expenditure made by other departments is more significant, although both of them are significant. The trend coherently explains increasing trend of public expenditure. However, the difference between two periods is meagre. Fig. 2 explains the increasing trend of financing in India. There has been increasing trend till 1990 and declined thereafter as impact of New Economic policy. However, it increased in 2000-01 as social inclusive policies took prominence in eleventh five year plan. Higher education in India is primarily funded by the government–central or state governments and the households.

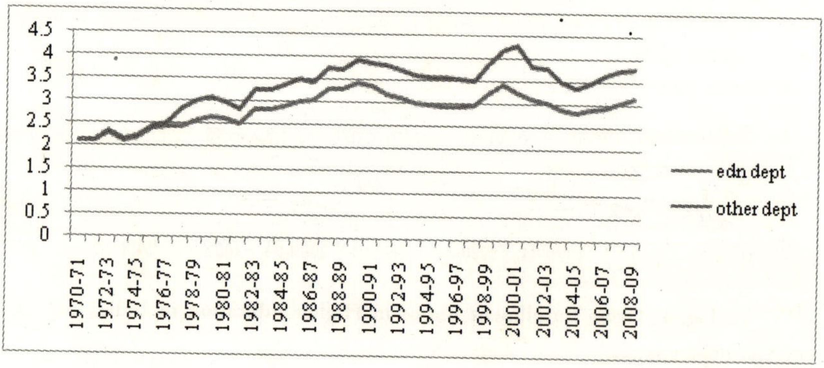

Fig. 2: Expenditure on Higher Education by Education Department and other Departments.

As part of globalisation, the economic reform packages were introduced in India in the beginning of 1991. These reform packages imposed a heavy compression on the public budgets on education sector, more specifically so on higher education. Following the introduction of structural adjustment policies, that include macro-economic stabilisation and adjustment, a fiscal squeeze is experienced in all social sector investments in many developing countries, including in India. This has trickled down to public expenditure on education in general, and higher education in particular.

The process of globalisation is technology-driven and knowledge-driven. Therefore, the very success of economic reform policies critically depends upon the competence of human capital. Human capital competence and efficiency with higher education as it provides one with specialisation. Moreover, it is to be realised that higher education institutions play an important role in setting the academic standard for primary and secondary education. In this regard, Tenth plan documents that, "Since budget resources are limited and such resources as are available, need to be allocated to expanding primary education, it is important to recognise that the universities must make greater efforts to supplement resources from the government". Further, "it is to be realised that while primary education is fundamental to the nation, higher education determines its economic and technological progress in the globalised era, which are the necessary and sufficient conditions for growth and development respectively. Even for very low enrollment ratios in higher education in India, it is increasingly realised that public budgets cannot adequately fund higher education, particularly when sectors of mass education are starved of even bare needs. Hence, the resources from higher education are being diverted to the development of primary education. But it is stressed that while it is mandatory that the nation achieves universal elementary education and total literacy, it cannot at the same time afford to relegate to a neglected position to achieve global standards in higher education (UGC, 1993).

Education, being a subject of concurrent list and acknowledging the spill-over benefits, central government should finance higher education. Nevertheless, it is declining. At the same time states have increased their budget allocations for higher education (Table 3). However, in proportion to India's GDP, they are smaller.

University Grants Commission (UGC) is the apex body for higher education in India.

It is also the main funding agency of the central government. Bulk of the expenditure on higher education is on revenue account and the capital expenditure is a negligible proportion of the total educational expenditure. Fund allocation is done on deficit basis. UGC provides competitive grants to the eligible universities and colleges under various schemes to promote equity, relevance, excellence and research.

The funds for higher education in India come mainly from three different sources, viz., government, fee income from students and other sources of income from philanthrophic works, industry, sale of publications, etc. the demand for higher education has been growing rapidly with comparatively faster growth in enrolment in higher educational institutions, although they are less. It is being increasingly realised that public budgets cannot adequately fund higher education, particularly when sectors of mass education are starved of even bare needs. As a consequence, several policy directions on new ways of diversifying resources, resulting from a variety of pressures and opportunities are continually emerging with several alternatives, including student fees, student loans and privatisation. Maharashtra,

Table 3. Expenditure on Education–As Ratio to Aggregate Expenditure

State	*2000-01*	*2001-02*	*2002-03*	*2003-04*	*2004-05*	*2005-06*	*2006-07*	*2007-08*	*2008-09*	*2009-10*	*2010-11*
(1)	*(2)*	*(3)*	*(4)*	*(5)*	*(6)*	*(7)*	*(8)*	*(9)*	*(10)*	*(11)*	*(12)*
I. Non-special Category											
Andhra Pradesh	13.3	12.5	11.7	11.6	9.8	11.1	10.8	9.0	9.0	10.0	12.5
Bihar	23.7	20.7	18.4	18.9	15.8	19.6	19.7	17.6	18.5	18.1	16.3
Chhattisgarh	13.1	12.4	11.0	10.8	12.3	13.4	12.9	13.5	14.4	15.6	18.6
Goa	11.9	10.5	12.0	12.1	13.9	12.3	13.7	12.3	13.3	14.1	15.4
Gujarat	13.6	12.7	13.5	11.2	11.5	12.6	12.7	13.4	11.7	13.8	15.9
Haryana	14.6	13.8	13.7	10.2	11.6	13.4	11.9	12.9	15.0	16.3	17.3
Jharkhand	–	16.2	19.0	14.2	14.9	15.8	15.2	15.1	18.6	15.4	15.8
Karnataka	17.7	16.0	14.8	12.9	12.7	14.0	13.1	14.4	16.1	14.0	15.6
Kerala	20.0	19.0	17.6	15.7	16.2	16.6	17.1	15.9	16.7	16.8	17.0
Madhya Pradesh	16.3	12.5	12.2	9.9	8.8	10.2	12.4	11.1	12.8	13.0	14.2
Maharashtra	22.3	22.1	18.9	15.5	14.0	15.7	16.4	17.2	17.0	19.1	20.8
Odisha	15.9	14.6	14.3	12.2	12.6	14.7	12.8	14.3	16.9	18.2	18.3
Punjab	13.2	11.7	12.1	10.2	10.1	11.3	8.9	10.3	11.3	12.2	11.7
Rajasthan	18.8	18.2	15.5	14.1	13.8	17.2	15.6	14.6	17.9	19.0	19.1
Tamil Nadu	18.0	17.3	13.8	12.6	11.2	13.6	12.2	12.7	13.1	15.2	15.2
Uttar Pradesh	16.8	16.0	14.6	9.1	12.5	15.2	14.7	14.1	13.2	13.8	16.1
West Bengal	17.1	16.2	15.9	11.8	14.9	13.7	15.2	15.2	13.1	17.7	19.7

(Contd...)

(Contd...)

(1)	(2)	(3)	(4)	(5)	(6)	(7)	(8)	(9)	(10)	(11)	(12)
II. Special Category											
Arunachal Pradesh	6.4	13.3	12.1	9.1	10.7	9.9	10.7	10.8	11.4	12.2	10.8
Assam	25.5	21.9	22.4	22.3	17.0	20.8	20.4	20.1	18.8	16.4	22.0
Himachal Pradesh	17.0	16.2	14.5	12.4	13.5	14.1	14.1	15.4	16.2	16.3	17.9
Jammu & Kashmir	11.1	11.6	10.9	11.1	9.7	9.3	10.0	9.2	10.0	11.3	12.6
Manipur	20.2	13.7	13.3	13.1	15.3	15.4	11.9	14.2	12.0	11.9	10.7
Meghalaya	16.6	17.9	15.3	15.2	15.0	15.5	14.1	15.5	12.8	14.8	16.1
Mizoram	16.2	16.0	14.5	12.0	13.8	13.4	13.8	13.2	14.1	14.9	14.9
Nagaland	13.8	11.0	11.0	10.8	11.0	11.6	12.3	11.4	11.2	11.3	13.4
Sikkim	14.2	8.0	7.6	11.8	8.8	10.4	10.5	9.2	10.6	12.4	17.3
Tripura	19.3	18.6	19.2	18.3	20.0	15.3	15.9	15.1	14.4	16.2	17.2
Uttarakhand	21.5	21.1	20.0	17.6	18.4	17.2	18.1	17.6	18.2	22.6	23.5
All States	17.4	16.2	15.1	12.6	12.7	14.2	14.0	13.8	14.3	15.3	16.6
All States (% to GDP)	2.8	2.6	2.5	2.3	2.3	2.2	2.2	2.2	2.3	2.4	2.5

Source: Budget Documents of the State Governments and State Finance Accounts.

West Bengal, Rajasthan and Tamil Nadu have spending around 20 per cent of their budget expenditure over the years on higher education. However, in some states, it is declining especially in Tamil Nadu, Karnataka, Kerala and Maharashtra. It is appreciable that backward states, Assam and Uttarkhand are increasing their budget allocations for higher education progressively.

Alternative Sources of Financing Higher Education in India

As deficit financing of higher education neither promotes cost-effectiveness nor internal resource generation, the *Punnayya Committee* (1992-93) pointed out that the existing mechanism of funding for higher education perpetuates inefficiency and suggested that the grant-in-aid system should be suitably modified to reward quality, efficiency and innovativeness. The committee recommended the replacement of the existing practice of negotiated block grants based on historical allocations by policy driven funding based on unit cost method. Apart from changing the funding mechanism, the committee also advocated cost recovery by suitably revising, rationalising and enhancing tuition fees. Despite specific recommendations of these committees, the funding of higher education institutions in India continues to have a historical or political basis.

The amount of funding that a higher education institution receives is based largely on what they received the year before or how powerful their friends are in the government or funding agency. As Hauptman (2006) points out, this approach tends to be more input driven and is largely based on staff costs and institutional infrastructure needs. Whereas in many countries there is a shift to policy-driven funding by introducing policy variables into funding process (as in UK) or performance–based funding that recognise outputs rather than just inputs (as in US). Funding process followed in India continues to on the basis of historical allocation. In keeping view with reducing state expenditure and enhancing efficiency of higher education, available optional avenues of funding are private funding, increasing tuition fees, graduate taxes, scholarship and financial aid to economic poor of backward social classes, Education loans, Private investment and compulsory legally abiding donation of medium and large firms to education.

Private funding confers responsibility of affordable parents to educate their children on their own funds. Tuition fees should be in view with ensuring efficiency and equity. Graduate taxes are those payments charged on alumni students whose income is above specified levels, because of large subsidised education they receive at nation's premier institutions. This should not be a burden for them but liability on their part. Education loans should be made available to unaffordable students with or without collateral security easing the process. Although private sector has started investing through their own higher education institutions, should not look always for profits, as most of them are commercialised today, but ensure efficiency, equity and standards. This requires them to invest in enhancing faculty, skill development; infrastructure and research and development. Private investors should also invest in public institutions along with providing campus placements. In addition to these, as in France firms, companies and corporations both national and foreign should contribute their due share to higher education through ASSOCHAM, NASSCOM or such organisations which can disburse collected funds based on requirements or achievements of institutions and universities.

Conclusion

Higher education is of utmost importance for a nation as it creates competitive and efficient human resource. Given the Indian context and resource base in the global scenario, there is a need for creating clear incentives for enhancing institutional efficiencies and improving productivity so as to compete with global standards. Recent Quacquarelli Symonds (QS) list on World University Rankings published by Times Higher Education gives a dismal picture. None of Indian Universities were on top 200. What we are producing are degrees which have not kept abreast of changes. Unprecedented growth in higher education is happening without any commensurate improvement in quality. The quality of higher education has much left to be desired. Therefore, higher education needs radical improvements in infrastructure, productive faculty, administration and management. On the other hand, fiscal difficulties and market fluctuations have reduced state's ability to invest furthermore, as providing universal school education itself requires huge resources. Given these constraints, it is binding to mobilise resources from alternative avenues such as private sector and households while ensuring equity of weaker sections and efficiency of education sector. Government should envisage on changes in Indian higher education through private investment, and public-private participation so as to bring dynamics into it making them on par with global premier institutions, in quality and quantity.

References

- Anindita Chakrabarthi and Rama Joglekar (2006), "Determinants of Higher education – An empirical analysis using state level data", *Economic and Political Weekly,* Vol. 41, No. 15 (April 15-21, 2006).

- B.G. Tilak, Jandhyala and N.V. Varghese (1991), "Financing Higher Education in India", http://www.jstor.org/stable/3447129.
- Chakrabarthy, K.C., (2011), "Indian Education System—Issues and Challenges", *RBI Monthly Bulletin.*
- Geetha Rani, P., (2002), "Economic Reforms and Financing Higher Education in India", http://www.ibbc.lt/economicreformshighereducation.pdf.
- "Higher Education in India—Issues related to Inclusiveness, quality and finance" UGC Report, 2008.
- Massen, Peter (2000), "Models of financing higher education in Europe", Center for Higher Education Policy Studies (CHEPS), University of Twente, Netherlands.
- Tilak, J.B.G., (1995): 'Costs and Financing of Education in India: A Review of Issues', Problems and Prospects, UNDP Research Project, Centre for Development Studies, Thiruvananthapuram, Kerala.
- Pawan Agarwal, June 2006, "Higher education in India—The need for change", Working Paper (ICRIER).
- Peter Dietsch (2006) "Financing higher education: the case for a graduate tax", http://www.creum.umontreal.ca/IMG/pdf/ATELIERS_VOL1N1_06_88_ 102.pdf.
- Prakash, Ved (2007), "Trends in Growth and Financing of Higher education in India", *Economic and Political Weekly* , Vol. 42, No. 31 (Aug. 4-10).
- Shatrugna, M., (1994), "Financing Higher Education—Justice Punnayya committee report", *Economic and Political Weekly*, Vol. 29, No. 32.
- Report of Analysis of Budget Expenditure on Education 2008-09 to 2010-11, MHRD, Govt. of India, Planning and Monitoring Unit, New Delhi, 2012.

5 Challenges in Higher Education: Interpreting Quality in the Context of Expansion in Indian Higher Education

Chetan B. Singai
Reetika Syal
Manisha M.

Abstract

Education in India has undergone substantial expansion and has increased its institutional capacity since independence, with higher education having major share in it. At present the higher education sector constitutes of 16.9 million students in 634 universities as compared to 0.2 million students and up to 20 universities in 1950-51 (UGC, 2012). The country now claims to be the third largest system in the world after China and USA in terms of enrollment and largest in the world in terms of number of higher education institutions.

However, with such an expansion there are myriad of challenges encountering the higher education sector. Challenges witnessed in terms of governing the complex structure of the higher education system; conceptualising quality; ensuring 'universal access' and enhancing funding (UGC, 2011). Among these, the concept and practice of quality in higher education has gained relevance in policy discourses in the last six decades (along with equity and expansion). Quality has myriad of interpretations: it could mean excellence, innovation and efficiency. In addition to this, quality in recent times (given the complex typology of institutions/universities) has further adapted itself to various different forms. Such diversity in its application and meaning therein, calls for critical examination in terms of what constitutes quality and what it does not. Such an investigation is necessary for policy-makers, administrators and scholars in the field of higher education and its governance.

Given this context, the paper aims to analyse the historical engagement with quality in higher education through critical discourse analysis of policies, programmes and institutional mechanisms. To highlight the diversity in interpreting diversity in practice of quality in higher education institutions, the paper aims to examine two case studies – a state university and a private university in order to examine what constitutes quality in these institutions? In what ways quality varies (if any) among these institutions? What are the implications of such convergence and/or divergence for the larger eco-system of higher education in India?

Introduction

In the recent past higher education in India has undergone substantial expansion and has increased its institutional capacity several fold. At present the higher education sector consists of 16.9 million students (GER 18.8 per cent) in 634 universities as compared to 0.2 million students and up to 20 universities in 1950-51 (UGC, 2012). The country now claims to be the third largest system in the world after China and USA in terms of enrollment and the largest in the world in terms of number of higher education institutions (UGC, 2011). (See: Table 1)

Table 1. Number of Higher Education Institutions as per Respective Typology

Type of Institution	*Number*	*Proportion (in per cent)*
Central Universities	43	07
State Universities	297	47
Private Universities	100#	16
Deemed Universities	129	20
Institutes of National Importance plus and *Other University Level Institutions	65	10

(*Source:* University Grants Commission (2012). Higher Education in India at a Glance.VIBA Press Pvt. Ltd., New Delhi).

In the last three years the number of private universities has increased rapidly: In the year 2008-09 – (21 universities); 2009-10 (60 universities) and 2010-11 – (94 universities) (FICCI, 2011).

*Other Institutes include Indian Institutes of Science Education and Research (IISERs) (5), National Institute of Fashion Technology (NIFT), Rajiv Gandhi Institute of Petroleum Technology (RGIPT) and Jawaharlal Nehru Institute of Post-Graduate Medical Education and Research (JIPMER).

After independence, there was a great concern among policy-makers for reshaping and restructuring of the higher education system. Such a concern was reflected in setting up of various committees/commissions to suggest reforms or changes in the then existing system/structure of higher education and its institutions. Commissions/committees like the Radhakrishnan Commission (1948); Kothari Commission (1965); Gajendragadkar Committee (1970); National Knowledge Commission report on higher education (2006) and Yashpal Sharma Commission on higher education (2009) and so on, that emphasised on the need for reforms in higher education governance.

While these official endeavours pressed on reforms, the massive expansion that the higher education sector has witnessed hitherto has been the major cause for concern. Moreover, the expansion is not just in numbers/ size but it has led to a complex typology of higher education institutions– Central, State, Deemed, Private, Polytechnic and Open universities. Today we have private and deemed universities that have been added to the existing typology of higher education institutions: polytechnic institutions, state and central universities, hence forming a complex 'hexagon' from then existing 'quadragon' (Central, State, Polytechnic, Open universities) structure of higher education system in the country.

With such transitions, renewed/new relationship(s) between the state and the higher education and its institutions, finance, autonomy, accountability, quality and equity were some the key considerations in reforming the higher education system and its institutions. However, as the agenda for reforms evolved, higher education system in the country underwent a series of crisis at two levels: at the level of policy, and at the level of institutions (Tilak, 2013).

Given this context, the paper aims to analyse the concept of quality in higher education within the reforms framework (particularly given the growth of privatisation in higher education) through critical discourse analysis of policies, programmes and institutional mechanisms. To highlight the diversity in conceptual interpretations of quality in higher education institutions, the paper aims to examine two case studies of – a state university and a private university–in order to examine what constitutes quality in these institutions? In what ways quality varies (if any) among these institutions? What are the implications of such convergence and/or divergence for the larger eco-system of higher education in India?

Quality in Higher Education: A Conundrum

'Quality' is a much-debated term. Those who are relativists in their orientation believe that 'quality' is subjective and may vary on a case-to-case basis; others believe quality may be objectified and has specific attributes that can be indentified. The word quality comes from the Latin word *quails* meaning 'what kind of'. It is a multi-dimensional and many-layered concept. It has a variety of meanings and connotations associated to it. It is widely debated, frequently objectified and measured, yet elusive in its acceptance. It is therefore not surprising that, it has been referred to as a 'slippery concept' (Pfeffer and Coote, 1991). To illustrate the slippery and elusive nature of quality and the confusion associated with it many scholars (Nigvekar, 1996; Warren et al., 1994; Mishra, 2002) have referred to most often cited quote of Pirsig (1974):

> Quality…you know what it is, yet you don't know what it is. But that's self-contradictory. But some things are better than others, that is, they have more quality. But when you try to stay what the quality is, apart from the things that have it, it all goes *poof!* There's nothing to talk about it. But if you can't say what Quality is, how do you know what it is, or how do you know that it even exists? If no one knows what it is, then for all practical purposes, it doesn't exist at all. But for all practical purposes it really *does* exist… So around and round you go, spinning mental wheels and nowhere finding any place to get traction. What the hell is Quality? What is it? (p. 171, cited in Nigvekar, 1996)

The above-mentioned perception implies quality means different things to different people (and for kind of people i.e., academicians, policy-makers and other stakeholders within the higher education sector). With such ambiguous background, it is important to explore the relevance and challenges in conceptualising quality-its meaning and transitions within the framework of higher education and its reforms.

Conceptualising 'Quality' in Higher Education

The British Standard Institution (BSI) defines quality as "the totality of features and characteristics of a product or service that bear on its ability to satisfy stated or implied needs" (BSI, 1991). Green and Harvey (1993) identified five different approaches to conceptualising quality:

- In terms of *exceptional* (exceeding high standards and passing a required standard);
- In terms of *consistency* exhibited through "zero defects" and "getting right the first time", making quality a culture);
- As *fitness for purpose* (meaning the product or service meets the stated purpose, customer specifications and satisfaction);

- As *value for money* (through efficiency and effectiveness) and
- As *transformative* (in terms of qualitative change).

These different notions of quality have led Reeves and Bednar (2011) to conclude "...The search for a universal definition of quality and a statement of law like relationship has been unsuccessful". However, the concept of quality could be conceptualised as revolving around few central ideas: Quality as absolute, Quality as relative, Quality as a process, and Quality as culture.

When we consider **quality as absolute**, it is given and considered as the higher possible standard. For instance the China Wall could be considered as work of high standard and quality. In other words, there is high brand value, status and positional advantage. Education institutions like OX-BRIDGE set some sought of high standards. Quality as relative suggests that the quality of a product or service can be described in relative terms. According to Mukhopadhyay (2005) the adherence to "product specification is actually the minimum conditions for quality, but not the sufficient condition". The sufficient condition is customer or user satisfaction and beyond" (p. 19). Subsequently, quality as a process, suggests that in order to achieve quality of a product or service it must undergo certain processes and conform to the procedural requirements. Thus, quality is the outcome of systems and procedures laid down for the purpose. Finally, quality as culture–recognises the importance of organisational view of quality as a process of transformation, where each entity is concerned and acknowledges the importance of quality. In this context it is apt to quote (Barrnet, 2010):

> ...a high evaluation accorded to an educative process, where it has been demonstrated that, though the process, the students' education development has been enhanced...not only have they achieved the particular objectives set for the course but, in doing so, they have also fulfilled the general education aims of autonomy of the ability to participate in reasoned discourse, of critical self-evaluation, and of coming to a proper awareness of the ultimate contingency of all thought and action (p. 61).

With private sector operating in this sector, the notion of management or industries has gradually taken root. Quality in industries could be defined as adhering to the stated or implied performance requirements of the customer, but with interpretations as varied as the individuals; it is rather difficult to define the Quality in (higher) educational institutions. Although, the Quality management concepts in business and in education remain same, there are certain limitations in adopting the corporate methods of Quality management because educational institutes cannot be considered as industry and the products are not their students, but it is the education imparted to the students. Students, their parents, and their future employers are the customers of this product (education). In Quality management, the customer is defined as the next person in line. In an educational institute, students directly receive the teaching services and hence are the customers of the teacher, whereas the faculty and the Institute's administrators are the suppliers of the services. Even the supplier-customer oncept of Quality management cannot be applied in education because the customers do not understand what is to be acquired, or what is of good Quality.

From the above-mentioned literature, one could realise that the concept of quality is amorphous and contextual, thus creating a conundrum as such. It ranges from meaning 'standard' to 'excellence'. Both are deeply rooted in their respective values operationalised in individual, institutional, and as national practice. "Standards can be defined in terms of minimum 'threshold' by which performance is judged" (Ashcroft and Foreman-Peck, 2012, p. 21). In this context, quality is assessment in terms of a set of norm-referenced standards (such as NAAC criteria) that are built around what is expected at the minimum and beyond. And other end of continuum is the consideration of quality as 'excellence' (recalling Green and Harvey's reference to 'Exception, mentioned-above). Excellence is a performance stage of exclusiveness that is distinctive from many others and stand out as demonstration of 'zero defect' and highest level of satisfaction of/from the relevant stakeholders. To sum-up, in higher education, our objective is to achieve the 'standard' and move towards 'excellence'.

Governmental Responses to Ensuring Quality

With recent explosion in the Indian higher education sector, it is important we should worry about quality. As teachers, directors, stakeholders, head of departments, planners and policy-makers in higher education, we should worry about this conundrum. Policy-makers and university administrators have strived hard to implement various quality indicators at the systemic as well as at the institution level.

In the recent past, the government set up the National Accreditation and Assessment Council (NAAC in 1994) as a response to policy recommendations suggested in the National Policy on Education (NPE), 1986. The NPE was to address the issue of 'deterioration in quality of higher education'. NAAC as an autonomous body began to assess institutions of higher education in the country based on following criteria's: Curricular aspects, Teaching-learning and evaluation, Research, Consultancy and extension, Infrastructure and learning resources, Student support and progression, Governance and leadership and Innovative practices as the basis for its assessment procedures. This was a significant move from the government. Because quality assurance in higher education would mean little if not monitored constantly. It is interesting to note two critical points: firstly, with NAAC accreditations universities were mandated to evolve their vision, mission and objectives. These are considered to be important parameters for assessment. Secondly, the university website or the university hand books, open with the remark that the university has been accredited by NAAC with following grades. Grades have become an important tool benchmark or an evidence for quality education among these institutions. However, the accreditation process is voluntary as of now, with the National Accreditation and Regulatory Authority (NARA) bill tabled in the parliament (as on 2013), it will be made mandatory.

Further, the UGC in the compendium of flagship programme (titled Quest for excellence specific to public universities) introduced schemes like 'University with potential for excellence', operation faculty-recharge, special assistance programme and laid down stringent accountability measures through Academic Performance Index (API). To substantiate the above, University Grants Commission (UGC) Chairman Professor Ved Prakash said universities should not confine themselves to transmission and certification of knowledge. "A majority of the centres of higher learning in the country have failed in capacity building exercise. There is a crisis in the country in this regard... Unless an institute evolves itself into a centre of excellence, it does not deserve to be called a centre of higher learning" (April, 2012).

Planning Commission in the twelfth five year plan has provided detailed plans for expanding the higher education echoing the eleventh plan recommendations. However, in this plan the focus on expansion is accompanied by providing quality education. The twelfth plan states, that a strong leadership backed by bold vision, clear strategy, creativity competition, critical thinking, quality consciousness, innovative governance and a 'process driven approach; improves the pursuit of quality in higher education institutions in particular and higher education sector in general.

Subsequent to NAAC, UGC and the Five year plan (11th and 12th) intervention at macro level, institutions at the micro level have adopted various strategies to enhance quality or acclaim the brand of excellence. For instance, University of Jammu was the first university to be certified with International Standards Organisation (ISO) 9001:2000.

Private Sector and Higher Education in India

In the last two decades or so, the government made attempts to 'consolidate' higher education–public expenditure on higher education declined, with rise in GER. The government had to respond to this crisis, privatisation was considered as one of the potential way solution. Secondly, there was often a complaint of decline in the quality of education offered among existing public institutions. Here decline in quality was perceived (by scholars) a product of lack of autonomy and consequent innovation in all aspects of higher education including development of curriculum, recruitment, retention and training of faculty, development of infrastructure Decline in quality was also associated with slow expansion of established institutions. The deterioration of quality is most glaring in the state universities (Jayaram, 2006). A private university envisaged as one of the ameliorative/an alternative to this condition by the policy-makers.

With the eleventh five year plan providing major thrust on expansion, the private sector has evolved as a major player. The private sector now accounts for 64 per cent of the total number of institutions and 59 per cent of the enrollment in the country as compared to 43 per cent and 33 per cent respectively about a decade ago (FICCI, 2012).

Analysing/Describing Pointers from the Case Studies

In order to comparatively examine the concept of quality across typologies of universities, two cases have been included. Gulbarga University established in 1980 (Gulbarga) has been taken to represent state universities and Alliance University established in 2010 (Bangalore) has been taken to represent private universities. Both institutions are situated in Karnataka and their comparison is carried out to indicate the differences between the typologies of university they represent and not necessarily the institutions *per se*. The comparison between the state and private university is carried out on the basis of their vision and mission statements and the courses/disciplines that they offer to show differences in the organisation of universities. Below Tables 2 and 3 provide insights into the vision and mission of the two universities (state and private). Further, the type of courses and department profile has also been illustrated in Tables 4 and 5 respectively.

From the above-mentioned tables we can see significant differences in the vision and mission of the two universities. The state university envisions higher education in a 'traditional' notion and aims to achieve quality by empowering the stakeholders with knowledge and in turn achieving socio-economic transformation. The mission statements of the state university also bring out a process-oriented approach, which aims at achieving excellence

Table 2. Vision Statements of State (Gulbarga) and Private (Alliance) Universities in Karnataka

State University	*Private University*
1. Excellence in higher education.	World-class University by 2025. Nurture talent and catalytically transform the lives of millions through excellence in teaching, research, service and community development.
2. Empowerment through knowledge.	To uphold a commitment to shaping lives through scholarly teaching and learning.
3. Inclusive growth for socio-economic transformation and sustainable development.	Contribute to an equitable and holistic transformation of society at large.

Source: Collated by Centre for Research in Social Studies and Education, Jain University (May-June 2013).

Table 3. Mission Statements of State (Gulbarga) and Private (Alliance) Universities in Karnataka

State University	*Private University*
1. To equip students with relevant knowledge, competence, and creativity to face global challenges.	Pursue excellence in teaching, learning and scholarship.
2. To achieve innovations in teaching-learning, research and extension activities to realise national goals.	Prepare students for leadership through enlightened learning partnerships with faculty mentors and the community.
3. To facilitate optimum use of human and natural resources for sustainable development.	Support faculty and other scholars in pursuing world-class research: clinical, theoretical, empirical, experiential and foster creative endeavour.
4. To promote participation of all the stakeholders in the development of the University and the region.	Develop mastery of disciplines and professions and instill confidence among its key constituents in their application for a future of meaningful pursuits and productive work in the service of humanity.
5. To empower students through inclusive growth.	Channelise faculty and student talent for professionally-related service to the university, the community and society at large.
6. To adopt and promote the knowledge output for human development.	Promote and preserve academic freedom, diversity, equality, harmony and justice.
7. To create awareness of human rights, value system, culture, heritage and environment.	

Source: Collated by Centre for Research in Social Studies and Education, Jain University (May-June 2013).

in higher education and in turn benefiting the society, value system and culture. In the case of a private university, the idea of quality is more 'output-oriented' i.e., the main focus here is on providing a kind of education that is professionally-oriented, has international application and can make the students 'world-class' citizens.

Table 4. Types of Departments/Courses Offered by the State University

Departments	*Courses*	*Faculty*
Science and Technology	62	82
Arts	24	19
Social Science	21	28
Law	4	3
Education	8	14
Commerce and Management	6	7

Source: Collated by Centre for Research in Social Studies and Education, Jain University (May-June 2013).

Table 5. Types of Departments/Courses Offered by Private University

Schools	*Courses*	*Faculty*
Engineering and Design	2	33
Management	1	36
School of Business (Commerce and Management)	5	82

Source: Collated by Centre for Research in Social Studies and Education, Jain University (May-June 2013).

Tables 4 and 5 show data for the types of courses offered by the two universities and course-wise distribution of faculty members. For the purpose of this paper, disciplines offering courses with post graduation and above degrees have been included in the tables. As is clear from the data, the state university offers a whole range of courses including social sciences, arts and languages, and the technical disciplines of science and technology, management etc. However, the private university only focuses on the technical courses of engineering and management. This reiterates the point made earlier that the private universities are more 'output-oriented' in their approach. Employability and salability, of the students as well as the institution are the driving force behind the courses offered by these institutions. With a skill based/technical curriculum, the focus is on revenue generation; both for the students (courses with employability) and the institution. Though the focus of the private university is on becoming a world-class university, the path adopted is not knowledge and research oriented but productivity and marketability oriented. Again, the emphasis is on creating a 'world class institution' and not on 'producing world class citizens by empowering them with world class values' which will in turn make the institution as world class university of great repute.

Conclusion

Rapid expansion of higher education in the country has been at the cost of its quality. Given series on macro and micro initiatives (at least in the last couple of decades) it is significant to deconstruct what constitutes quality education. Quality varies widely across institutions. For instance, the case studies illustrate significant differences in conceptualising quality in higher education between a state and private university in the state of Karnataka. State university emphasises on faculty and students competitiveness, and adhere to 'traditional' notion of quality with aim process-oriented parameters. In the case of a private university, the idea of quality is more 'output-oriented i.e., the main focus here is on employability, skill and competence based curriculum, focus on revenue generation and focusing on the international outlook–envision to be a world-class universities.

Despite the general deterioration of quality, some institutions like the IITs, IIMs, a few university departments have maintained standards-'absolute quality', thus creating island of excellence, in the sea of higher education in the country. To sum up, the need for worry in enhancing quality one could refer to various research and policy papers stating that the standards of higher education in the country did not compare favourably with the average standards in the educationally advanced countries.

The hope lies in the existing and forthcoming (improvised) agencies on one hand, and institutions themselves on the other, contribute in ensuring quality in higher education. One of the key challenges in such mechanisms is coming to consensus on what constitutes quality and what it does not.

References

- Barnett, R. (2010). *Improving Higher Education: Total Quality Care,* Bukingham: SRHE & OU.
- BIS (1988). *BIS Quality system vocabulary. ISI 14000 quality system: Guidelines for selection and use of standards on quality system,* New Delhi: BIS.
- Harvey, L and Green, D. (1993). Defining 'quality'. *Assesment and Evaluation in Higher Education.* 18 (1), pp. 9-34.
- Mishra, S. (2002). Guest Editorial: Does technology advancement mean better Education? *Media and Technology for Human Resource Development, 14 (1 and 2), v-viii.*

- Mukhopadhyay, M. (2005). *Total Quality Management in Education,* 2nd Ed., New Delhi: Sage Publishers.
- Nigvekar, A.S. (1996). Quality assurance in higher education: An Indian dilemma, *Journal of Higher Education,* 19 (3), pp. 353-364.
- Peffer, N. and Coote, A. (1991). *Is Quality Good for you? A critical review of quality assurance in the welfare services,* London: Institute of Public Policy Research.
- Pirsig, R.M. (1974). Zen and the art of motorcycle maintenance, New York: Vintage.
- Reeves, C.A. and Bedner, D.A. (2011). Defining quality: Alternatives and implications, *Academy of Management Review,* 19 (3), pp. 419-445.
- Tilak, J.B.G. (2013). *Higher Education in India: In Search of Equality, Quality and Quantity.* New Delhi: Orient Blackswan.

6 Higher Education in Law and Marginalised Sections: Issues and Concerns

Dr. Vishwanath M.

'Higher education should be treated as one of the 'high priority development expenditures' in the state. Without appropriate funding, the state cannot be expected to survive in a knowledge society and a competitive world economy. Hence, it should not be subjected to reduction as a subsidy, but treated as its investment for development'.

Introduction

The report of the Task Force on Higher Education, Government of Karnataka, 2004 clearly identifies and asserts the need of the role of state governments in Higher Education (HE), as it wants a strong state with men of knowledge and who can compete at the highest level, to achieve these results the state need to invest more in higher education which would benefit all sections of society and fulfill the constitutional mandate. Higher education once being only the domain of few influential groups (social and economic) in the society, where hardly few from the Marginalised Section (MS) were able to reach the level of higher education and it was a distinct dream of reaching the portals of Professional courses. Today things have improved as the state machineries have provided opportunities to the deprived groups through many ways which includes reservation, scholarship, separate institutions (especially for women) and the like. With all these measures the question still that hovers around us is whether the marginalised section of society has been benefited as expected? Or there are still some serious issues and concerns that need to be addressed.

The paper is set out into two parts. Part one assesses the importance and constrains of higher education in India with particular reference to the marginalised sections which include Scheduled Caste (SC), Scheduled Tribe (ST) and Religious Minorities and the second part of the paper discusses the issues and concerns in higher education in law in connection with the above stated marginalised sections.

PART-I

Providing access to higher education to its young masses, and ensuring quality and equality in higher education have been a great challenge to all developing and under developed countries and India is not an exception to this challenge. Since 1947, the Central and State governments have been trying to promote higher education to its people ensuring quality and equality and it has been quite successful in ensuring its base goal of reaching higher education to all and especially to those sections of society who have been deprived of education and in particular higher education, the section mainly consists of SCs, STs, the other Backward Classes (OBC), religious minority groups and the inhabitants of educationally backward areas. The Constitution mandates that the state shall provide equal opportunity to every citizen of the country in education, employment and economic interests and more particular of the need to protect the interests of weaker sections through fundamental rights and directive principles of state policy.

Higher Education must necessarily be connected with quality and equity, the National Policy on Education, 1986 has emphasised the need to remove the disparities that has continued in the system even after independence and has pointed out the need to equalise the educational opportunities to the deprived classes. Reservations are provided in educational institutions and admission criteria are relaxed for students from most of these categories. In addition, financial support is provided by governments in the form of scholarship and grants. It appears that the thrust of the educational policy has been on growth with equity though there may be shortfalls in actual implementation.

During the second half of the twentieth century, higher education acquired an egalitarian character with the process of 'massification' being especially intense in the developing countries and particularly in India. The 'logic' of 'massification' is inevitable and includes greater social mobility for a growing segment of the population, new patterns of funding higher education, increasingly diversified higher education systems in most countries, generally an overall lowering of academic standards, and other tendencies. Worldwide, there has been a near seven-fold expansion in the number of students, from 13 million in 1960 to 85 million in 2000. In India the expansion has been even more spectacular. In the last sixty-odd years since independence the number of universities has grown from 20 to 448 (end of 2012). The growth in the number of university-level institutions from independence to the end of 2012 is detailed in Table 1.

Table 1. Categories of University Level Institutions

University-Level Institutions	*Year*									
	1947	*1957*	*1967*	*1977*	*1987*	*1997*	*1999*	*2000*	*2005*	*2012*
Central Universities	3	4	4	7	9	15	17	17	20	42
States Universities	17	35	65	98	134	164	182	183	217	243
Deemed Universities	-	-	7	9	22	39	43	46	106	130
Institutions of National Importance	-	2	9	9	10	11	12	12	13	33
Total of University-Level Institutions	**20**	**41**	**85**	**123**	**175**	**229**	**254**	**258**	**356**	**448**

Source: Association of Indian Universities (2000) Universities Handbook, AIU, New Delhi.

The Central Universities in 1947 were just three and it took 30 years for Central Universities to double their strength from three to seven in 1977, later it doubled its number in 20 years and by the end by 2005 their strength was 20 and by the end of 2012 it increased to 42, which is a phenomenal rise within a span of seven years and is a good sign of development of higher education. The number of state universities almost doubled every ten years in the period 1947-67. Later on the growth in their numbers has been gradual but slow in the subsequent years. By the end of year 2005 there were 217 State Universities and by 2012, there were 243 State Universities. It can be also noted that the number of deemed universities have also multiplied from 2000 to 2012. The number of private universities especially after 2000 has been really an interesting story of how higher education is adding in big industrialist, business houses and other investors to its kitty and the apprehensions expressed many educationist and experts on the number of free private universities needs a relook as to its utility and purpose.

The main question is whether the additions of universities as added any benefits to the MS? It would be really a tough question to answer as Table 2 shows us the comparative analysis of literacy rate among the general population and the MS.

Table 2. Literacy Rate of General Population, SC and ST Population, 1961–2010

Year	*General*			*Scheduled Caste*			*Scheduled Tribe*		
	Male	*Female*	*Total*	*Male*	*Female*	*Total*	*Male*	*Female*	*Total*
1961	34.44	12.95	24.02	16.96	3.29	10.27	13.83	3.16	8.53
1971	39.45	18.70	29.45	22.36	6.44	14.67	17.63	4.85	11.30
1981	46.89	24.82	36.23	31.12	10.93	21.38	24.52	8.04	16.35
1991	64.1	39.3	52.2	49.91	23.76	37.41	40.65	18.19	29.60
2001	75.3	53.7	64.8	66.64	41.90	54.69	59.17	34.76	47.10
2010	NA	NA	NA	73.0	52.1	62.8	70.7	52.1	61.6

Source: Census of India 2001; Selected Educational Statistics 2004–05, Ministry of Human Resource Development Government of India; GOI, NSSO, Primary Data (2009-10).

The literacy rate of SCs has increased considerably, from 10.3 per cent in 1961 to 54.7 per cent in 2001, till recently the gap between literacy rates of the general and SC population had not reduced. In the area of higher education, also, there is a gap between the SCs and the general population. The gross enrollment ratio for the country as a whole in 2000 was about 10 per cent. For the SCs, however, it was significantly lower at 6.4 per cent. Between 1961 and 2001, the literacy rate of STs increased 5.32 times, while that of total population increased 2.69 times. However, the gap between the literacy rates of STs and of the general population continued during the three decades between 1971 and 2001 almost at the same level of 17.70 per cent and above, but with marginal variations.The facts presented above are very conclusive as it clearly shows that the MS are far behind compared with the general sections in the field of education.

Table 3. Literacy Rate among all Religious Communities in 2001

Communities	*Male*	*Female*	*Total*
All religious communities	75.38	53.7	64.8
Muslims	67.6	50.1	59.1
Christians	84.4	76.2	80.3
Sikhs	75.2	63.1	69.4
Buddhists	83.1	61.7	72.7

(*Source:* The First Report on Religion data 'Census of India 2001', pp. XXI, XIII).

Table 3 shows that literacy rates among Muslims, both men and women, have been the lowest among all the religious minorities.

Table 4. Enrollment of General and SC/ST Students in General Higher Education

Year	*General*	*SC/ST*	*Total*	*Male/ Female Ratio*
1947 (not bifurcated)	-	-	45654*	-
1957	570885 (86.24%)	91090 (13.76%)	661975	6.27:1
1987	2950610 (92.79%)	229115 (7.21%)	3179725	12.88:1
1996	4372820 (87.75%)	610509 (12.25%)	4983329	7.16:1
1998	6530098 (89.32%)	780522 (10.67%)	7310620	8.36:1

Source: Government of India (1953) Progress of Education in India (1947-1951), Quinquennial Review, Ministry of Education, New Delhi; Government of India, Education in India (1957-58), Ministry of Education, (1967-68) Ministry of Education and Social Welfare, and (1977-78) Ministry of Education and Culture, New Delhi; Government of India, Selected Educational Statistics 1986-87 and 1995-96, New Delhi: Ministry of Human Resource Development (Planning, Monitoring and Statistics Division), New Delhi.

If we consider the demographic pattern, the percentage of students belonging to the scheduled caste and scheduled tribe categories should be about 23 per cent of the total strength, but these categories have remained very much underrepresented in higher education throughout the last five

Table 5. SC/ST Representation in Central Government Services in 1994, 1999, and 2004 (as on 1.1.2004)

Group	*1994*			*1999*			*2004*		
	Total	*SCs/STs*	*% of Total*	*Total*	*SCs/STs*	*% of Total*	*Total*	*SCs/STs*	*& of Total*
(A)	59016	6046/1727	10.25/2.92	93520	10558/3172	11.29/3.39	80011	9744/3311	12.2/4.1
(B)	103198	12442/2902	12.06/2.81	104963	13306/3512	12.68/2.35	135409	19602/6,274	14.5/4.6
(C)	2381613	374758/128228	15.73/5.38	2396426	378115/145482	15.78/6.07	2040970	344865/136630	16.9/6.7
(D)	1023285	209423/62945	20.47/6.15	949353	189761/66487	19.99/7.00	802116	147212/53776	18.4/6.7
Total	3567112	602670/195802	16.9/5.49	3544262	591740/218653	16.7/6.17	3058506	521423/199991	17.05/6.54

Source: Annual Report, Ministry of Personnel, Public Grievances and Pensions, Government of India, New Delhi 1985-1986, 1989-1990, and 2004-2005).

decades. In fact, the percentage of students of the reserved category in general higher education has not increased up to the mark. It suggests that the benefits of reservation have not percolated to the poor amongst SC/ST and it is important to analyse the reasons and identify the barriers. The total enrollment of learners in 1957 about 13.76 comprised of SC/ST learners however this proportion drastically dropped in 1987 and was recorded to be 7.21 per cent. As per National Sample Survey by 2003 the enrollment ratio for SC/ST was 4.0 and 5.9 respectively. Till date it hovers around 10-13 per cent. Tables 2, 3 and 4 are closely connected because if the primary and secondary education improves, then the changes of representation of MS would improve in higher education both quantitatively and qualitatively.

Education not only makes a man sensible and cultured but it should also normally provide him the skills to earn his livelihood. Table 5 clearly shows that our education system has not provided enough scope to convert knowledge into earning either commercially or intellectually. Table 5 shows a marginal improvement in the percentage of overall SC representation in the Group A, B and C categories of Central Government services from 1994 to 2004, while there was a substantial decline in the Group D category shows a marked improvement in the representation of STs in various categories of services during 1994 and 2004, though they are yet not adequately represented in any of the four categories. The situation is especially unsatisfactory with respect to the A and B categories.

Table 6. Percentage of OBC Representation in Central Government Services (as on 1.1.2004)

Group	*Total*	*OBCs*	*Percentage of total*
(A)	80011	3090	3.9
(B)	135409	3123	2.3
(C)	2040970	106309	5.2
(D)	802116	26158	3.3
Total	3058506	138680	4.53

**(Source:* Annual Report, Do P&T, GoI, 2006–07).

Table 6 indicates that even the OBC section despite 27 per cent posts being reserved from 1993, that the overall representation of OBCs in government service is abysmally low, just 4.53 per cent. Only 3.9 per cent, 2.3 per cent and 5.2 per cent, respectively of Group A, B, and C posts are occupied by OBC persons. Tables 5 and 6 are clear indicators as to the underrepresentation of the MS in government jobs which forces us to relook in to our education system especially higher education, as it is mandatory to have higher education to obtain group A and B posts. The extracts from

Karnatak Human Development Report 2005 gives us much clear picture as do education and jobs:

'At the tertiary level, more SC students enroll in degree classes in government colleges than in aided colleges. In 2003-04, SC students constituted 15.7 per cent and 8.8 per cent of all students enrolled in government and aided colleges respectively. State-run colleges provide access to higher education to precisely those social groups who have been excluded from higher education by social and cultural biases. Aided colleges far outnumber government colleges but their performance in the enrolment of SC students needs to improve. Performance-wise, in 2003-04, out of 17,163 students who enrolled, only 5,475 (31 per cent) completed their courses of study and graduated, as against the 43,007 (49.44 per cent) who graduated out of 86,961 enrolled general students. The attrition rate is very high for all social groups, which is a commentary on the quality of instruction and lack of infrastructure in government colleges, which is further attenuated by the low-income status of the majority of its users. In technical education, SC enrollment in the year 2002-03 was 6.8 per cent in degree courses and a low 0.8 per cent in diploma courses. This is a matter of concern because high-end jobs in the state tend to cluster in technology-driven sectors, and SCs are, therefore, under-represented here'.

The core area of concerns in higher education is the maintenance of quality and strict implementation of the reservation system especially in professional courses. The University Grants Commission (UGC) in 1998 has given guidelines for the establishment of Social Protection Office (SPO) for SCs, STs, OBCs, the People with Disability (PWD) and Minorities in Universities and Deemed to be Universities, the purpose is to help them to implement the reservation policy with regard to the admission of students and the recruitment of teaching and non-teaching staff at various levels. Its function is also to help the SC/ST/OBC/PWD/Minority categories to integrate with the mainstream of the university community and to remove any difficulties, which they may be experiencing. The initiations by UGC seem to be not so successful and it is high time that we boost more economic and social measures to improve the strength of MS. With the universal acceptance of the fact that higher education is a crucial factor in national development, it is necessary to ensure easier and greater access to its young people and especially to those belonging to MS. Inclusive growth demands that all social groups have equal access to the services provided by the State and equal opportunity for upward economic and social mobility. It is also necessary to ensure that there is no discrimination against any section of our society. A broadening and deepening of the higher education base is crucial for social, economic and human development. As the report of the World Bank UNESCO Task Force points out, broadening access as an on-going process that requires continuous efforts and a crucial aspect is helping disadvantaged groups to overcome the endemic problems that exclude them from the system. A major responsibility should be the creation of an environment that discourages discrimination and promotes equality.

PART-II

Law is one of the most faithful mirrors reflecting the fundamental social, economic and political values, at a particular period. The legal profession, including the Bench and the Bar, has played and are playing the most significant role in shaping and operating the legal system and its effects in securing justice in a society. Thus, it becomes pertinent to explore the said core values, or rather a Social Justice Mission in the educational system, which prepares them to play such a fundamental role in society.

The basic concern for the legal system in the early period of free India was to fulfill the objectives set out in the Constitution. Law and justice can no longer remain distant neighbors. To achieve the constitutional goal of access to justice, legal system should ensure moderate court fee, availability of affordable, competent and socially relevant lawyers. Further, Courts with humanistic approach are necessary to narrow the distance between law and justice. In this scenario the legal profession which is the custodian of providing justice is expected to play a dynamic role. Law Schools being recruit grounds for legal profession there is a need to inject a new spirit into the content of legal education to make lawyers and legal professionals socially relevant and professionally competent.

Today, with 740 institutions offering legal education and 40,000 law students graduating every year[6] and 10,20,000 lawyers registered, India has the second largest number of lawyers in the world, second only to the United States. With this staggering number, it is to be expected that Law Schools would play a pivotal role in promoting and providing justice, particularly through legal aid. Unfortunately, there is a general feeling that legal education in India is not "meaningful" and "relevant." The way legal education has been structured in India appears to suggest that it is intended to provide students only with some knowledge of statutes.

In its 1958 report, the Law Commission of India painted a black picture of the standards of legal education:

> "The portals of our law teaching institutions manned by part-time teachers open even wider and are accessible to any graduate of mediocre ability and indifferent merits...there is hardly a pretence at teaching...

this character is followed by law examinations... which the students manage to pass by cramming short summaries published by enterprising publishers... the result, a plethora of LL.B., half-baked lawyers, who do not know even the elements of law and who are let loose upon society as drones and parasites in different parts of the country."

These remarks were made by the Commission when there were only 43 law institutes training 20,159 students. Today about 740 Law Schools with an enrolment of over 2,50,000 are in no better position than in 1958, barring few exceptions. Law Schools became factories, of producing ill-trained law graduates unsuitable to both the profession and society. As discussed in part-I of the paper it is important to not only provides assess and equity in higher education but also quality. The Law Colleges, if they desire to be relevant in the present scenario of legal education, need to realise their role in a socio-economic welfare milieu. They need to take up multiple roles to act as effective instruments participating in the socio legal changes that are happening in the nation. The change brought by globalization and privatization, demands, and rather commands new skills from a lawyer.

Further most of the efforts made for improving legal education till today are concentrated only towards meeting the needs of the Bar and the Bench. But the present scenario requires legal personnel not only for Bar and Bench but for various other fields such as law makers, civil services, academics, corporate, trade and industry, arbitrators, negotiators, social organisations and non-governmental organisations. The change of role of the lawyer from litigator to justice provider requires new array of social skills. The present goal of legal education required to change from meeting the needs of Bar and Bench to maximising social justice and access to justice. Furthermore, the legal profession influences the society more than any other profession. Therefore, to make legal profession meaningful, concentrating only on knowledge input and skills input would not be adequate. Due to its distinct character and capacity, the legal profession requires the third and a very essential component, i.e., socially relevant or community oriented legal profession. There is a considerable consensus among the legal professional all over the world that all these three inputs can be harmonised in Law Colleges.

Table 7 shows the enrollment of students into law colleges in 1998, 2004 and 2012; there is significant improvement from 1998 to 2004 in the strength of law students but it has reduced in 2012 from 22209 to 14910. It appears that from the year 2005 to 2000 courses like B.B.A and B.B.M have taken some share out of law student's enrolment. As discussed in the early part of part-II it legal studies is a very important and vital aspect in the

Table 7. Enrollment of Students in Law Colleges (State of Karnataka) 1998 and 2004*

University	*1998*			*2004*		
	Male	*Female*	*Total*	*Male*	*Female*	*Total*
Mysore	1631	719	2348	2481	1109	3530
Bangalore	4708	2204	6912	6179	2619	8798
Mangalore	176	127	303	248	190	438
Karnatak	3576	767	4343	3412	871	4283
Gulbarga	735	298	1033	1072	261	1333
Shivamoga (Kuvempu)	1809	448	1985	2257	1438	5133
Total	**12699**	**4559**	**17258**	**14830**	**5729**	**22209**

Enrollment of Students in Law Colleges (State of Karnataka) 2012-13*

Karnataka State Law University (Affiliated Colleges) 5-year course and 3-year course and LL.M	General	SC	ST	OBC and others	
Total	2516/ 5596/36 8148	723/ 1494/8 2225	216/ 269/9 494	1568/ 2432/44 4044	**14910**

* *Source:* Status of Scheduled Castes in Karnataka, Karnatak Human Development Report. 2005 (Planning and Statistics Department Government of Karnataka, 2006), p. 392.

* *Source:* Karnatak State Law University, Hubli Admission Statistics Report (2012-13).

education system. Law graduation opens a very large avenue than any other subject, as knowledge of law is mandatory in all most all job requirements. The profession of Lawyers and Judges are respected in society with high esteem and it is a great concern that MS have not been able to mark their footsteps in legal field. Table 7 clearly highlights the low strength of MS in legal studies.

Lawyers are considered to be the social engineers' in society, who are expected to bring in social change for the betterment of the society. This change should benefit all sections of society and it is self explanatory that until MS are involved in these decisions-making system (judges, parliamentarians and legislators) as a decisions-making persons it would be tough to change the system that has been loaded in favour of dominant sections of the society. Legal education remains as one of the major tools in bringing in the desired results that would practically enforce the constitution mandate.

Conclusion

India has one of the largest higher education systems in the world, with 25.9 million students enrolled in more than 45,000 degree and diploma institutions in the country. It has witnessed particularly high growth in the last decade, with enrollment of students increasing at a CAGR of 10.8 per cent and institutions at a CAGR of 9 per cent. India achieved a Gross Enrollment Ratio (GER) of 17.9 per cent, up from 12.3 per cent at the beginning of the Plan period. India's GER of 16 per cent was much below the world average of 27 per cent, as well as that of other emerging countries such as China (26 per cent) and Brazil (36 per cent) in 2010. Differences across communities have been quite evident-14.8 per cent for OBCs, 11.6 per cent for SCs, 7.7 per cent for STs and 9.6 per cent for Muslims. The issues and concerns in higher education is the threat that have emerged from private universities that have mushroomed throughout the country which has created imbalance among the haves and have-nots; it is high time that the governments upgrade their universities and compete (as it is inevitable, as private universities would flourish more and invest more money due to globalisation) with private universities, and provide best quality, access and equity to all sections of society and in particular to the Marginalised Sections.

References

- Report of the Task Force on Higher Education, Government of Karnataka, 2004.
- Constitution of India Article—15, 16 and 46 in particular.
- Philip G. Altbach, Liz Reisberg and Laura E. Rumbley Trends in Global Higher Education: Tracking an Academic Revolution A Report Prepared for the UNESCO 2009 World Conference on Higher Education, (Paris: United Nations Educational, Scientific and Cultural Organisation, 2009), p. (iii).
- United Nations Educational, Scientific and Cultural Organisation, 2001.
- 11th Five Year Plan Report Chapter 6, Social Justice Scheduled Castes, Scheduled Tribes, Other Backward Classes, Minorities, and Other Vulnerable Groups.
- Status of Scheduled Castes in Karnataka, Karnatak Human Development Report 2005 (Planning and Statistics Department Government of Karnataka, 2006), p. 222.
- World Bank and UNESCO (Washington D.C: The World Bank, 2000).

- Sharma, S.S., Legal Aid to the Poor: The Law and Indian Legal System, (Deep and Deep Publications, New Delhi, 1993), p. 1.
- M.R.K. Prasad 'Legal Education in India: Role of Clinical Legal Education in Developing, Institutionalising and Implementing a Social Justice Mission for Law Schools' P.h.D., Thesis Submitted to Goa University (2010), p. 80.
- Chairman BCI, available at http://www.barcouncilofIndia.org/bar-council/chairman.php.
- N.L. Mitra, *Legal Education in India*, Conference of International Legal Educators, Florence, Italy (2000) available at http://www.aals.org/2000international/english/India.htm.
- Chairman BCI, available at http://www.barcouncilofIndia.org/bar-council/chairman.php.
- Dr. Justice A.S. Anand, Legal Education in India – Past, Present and Future, 3 SCC Jour. (1998).
- I.P. Massey, *Quest For 'Relevance' in Legal Education*, 2 SCC (JOUR) 17 (1971).
- *See*: The Law Commission of India, Report on Reform of Judicial Administration (1958).
- Using global definition of GER (pp. 18-22 age cohorts), India's GER was 20.2 per cent in 2011–12 Source: Ministry of Education of People's Republic of China, Twelfth Five Year Plan: Chapter on higher education, UNESCO: Global Education Digest 2011. National Center for Education Statistics USA.
- Higher Education in India: Twelfth Five Year Plan (2012-2017) and beyond.

7 *Rastriya Uchchatar Shiksha Abhiyan* for the Empowerment of Marginalised Sections: An Analysis

Dr. B.P. Mahesh Chandra Guru
Dr. N. Sanjeevaraja
D. Srinivasa

Abstract

Education has been rightly viewed as an effective instrument of individual and collective development. India has one of the largest higher education systems in the world. Knowledge production, knowledge inculcation, personality development, enhancement of employability and development of national economy are the essential aspects of higher education in India which has grown over a period of time both statistically and professionally. *Rastriya Uchchatar Shiksha Abhiyan* (RUSA) is a centrally sponsored scheme which covers 316 states public universities and 13,024 colleges in India. The implementation of the scheme will be spread over twelfth and thirteenth five year plan period and the funding to states will be on the basis of critical appraisal of their plans and activities. A sum of Rs 5,00,00,000 has been earmarked for the implementation of this programme across the country. This scheme intends to improve the quality of higher education, enhance Gross Enrolment Ratio, facilitate inclusive higher education and achieve empowerment of marginalised sections of Indian society. The RUSA warrants state governments to set up State Council for higher education and supporting agencies to assess and monitor the quality of higher education in states and union territories concerned. The governments are called upon to improve the quality of higher education and provide employment opportunities to large number of educated and unemployed youth belonging to socially and economically marginalised sections of India society.

Introduction

The RUSA lays emphasis on the adequate availability of quality faculty in all higher educational institutions and ensure capacity building at all levels of employment. The yardstick for deciding the quantum of funds for the states and institution comprise the norms that reflect the performance in key areas such as access, equity and excellence. The states are required to step up their academic and administrative reforms and fast track their implementation in order to achieve the goals of RUSA. Besides this, higher education councils should perform multiple roles such as strategy, planning, monitoring, evaluation and fund management at the state level. It is necessary to appoint full time faculty, develop institutional infrastructural facilities, upgrade educational technologies, adopt standardised teaching methods, develop communication skills, promote entrepreneurship, increase accreditation facilities and enrich the human resources in the field of higher education. The absence of vision and missionary zeal among the various stakeholders is a major drawback of this programme. New approaches to performance related funding, incentivising well-performing institutions, scientific planning and coordinated efforts for effective implementation of RUSA are absolutely required in the present times. The community of scholars has a social responsibility of scientifically evaluating the objectives of the programme, thrust areas of this programme, awareness building exercises, network development, various stakeholders, professional strategies, status of the programme, drawbacks of the programme and future course of action for the successful implementation of the programme. The paper intends to evaluate the utility of RUSA from the points of view of inclusive educational development and economic empowerment of marginalised sections with special reference to India.

Preamble

India has achieved considerable progress in the field of higher education in the post-independence era. The present approach to higher education is governed by the National Policy on Higher Education of 1986 and Programme of Action of 1992. These two land mark reports practically laid down the basis framework for the national policy on higher education in India. The need for transformation of higher education is seldom questioned since the ultimate goal of higher education in India is to increase productivity, achieve social and national integration and accelerate the process of modernisation and spiritual values. The champions of social justice have advocated the cause of inclusive higher education and empowerment of marginalised sections of Indian society who have contributed significantly for the development of nation as prime producers of national wealth. The *Rastriya Uchchatar Shiksha Abhiyan* (RUSA) aims to improve quality in higher education and enhance Gross Enrollment Ratio in higher education. The scheme also intends to improve provide the benefit of access to higher education in the age group of 18-23 years on the basis of an innovative approach towards funding higher education in state universities and colleges. The RUSA also lays emphasis on adequate availability of quality faculty in all higher educational institutions and ensure capacity building at all levels of employment with special reference to the marginalised sections of Indian society. The paper primarily deals with the role of RUSA in the empowerment of educationally excluded and economically deprived sections of India.

Inclusive Higher Educational Development of Marginalised Sections

Higher education in India has been diversified since early 1950s after the establishment of University Grants Commission in 1953. Several committees also examined the status, problems and prospects of higher education in India and emphasised the need for greater access, quality, relevance and inclusiveness with respect to higher education management in the country. India has also witnessed dramatic increase in the educational institutions, number of programmes, number of teachers and number of beneficiaries over a period of time. In the present times, there are central universities, state universities, deemed universities, and institutes of national importance established through central legislation, and institutions established through state legislation.

The Twelfth Plan has emphasised the need for making higher education relevant in the age of globalisation and removing the inequities in access to education amongst the various socially and economically marginalised groups. Greater emphasis has been laid on the diversification of higher education, improvement of quality of teaching, enhancement of employability and promotion of social and national integration. The most significant paradigm shift proposed by the Planning Commission (2012:15) is in the arena of funding of state higher education system. Strategic funding of this sector has been strongly proposed in order to make a marked difference in the overall resource endowment for the state higher education sector.

Scholars have noted that higher education is a social good which contributes significantly for national development. Education is also viewed as the great hope that can level inequities and differences in a pluralistic society like India. There are certain policies which have addressed the issue of equity for the marginalised sections of society. But, there is no comprehensive, integrated approach towards addressing the issue of equity even though gender, religion, region, class, caste and other factors constitute the critical determinants of inclusive higher education development of marginalised sections in India.

The goals of 'social-effectiveness' is in conflict with the market doctrine of 'efficiency' in the age of globalisation which has witnessed the increasing privatisation of higher education in India and other countries. Jyothi (2009:05) examined the linkage between entrepreneurship and higher education in India and called upon the authorities to promote entrepreneurship among the youth representing marginalised sections through higher education. The existing system of higher education is not good enough to meet the developmental needs of the marginalised sections of society since India is not ready for privatisation of higher education.

Thorat (2006:19) analysed certain issues related to access, inclusiveness and quality with special reference to higher education in India. The scholar noted certain inter-group disparities of multiple natures such as rural and urban, inter-state, inter-caste, inter-religion, male-female, occupation group and poor-non poor groups. He observes: "There are significant disparities in enrollment ratio between rural and urban area. There is considerable inter-state variation in the level of higher education. There are significant disparities across social groups. The Gross Enrollment Ratio (GER) is much lower for ST, SC and OBC as compared with other. The SC/ST/OBC persons belonging to Hindu religion lack far behind the higher caste Hindu population in terms of access to higher education. The Scheduled Castes from all religion suffered from a lower access to higher education as compared with their high caste counterpart. The GER for the poor was 2.4 per cent as against 12.91 per cent for non-poor. Among the occupation group, the enrollment is particularly low for the marginalised sections as compared with the privileged sections of Indian society". There is much yet to be achieved from the point of view of inclusive higher education management despite certain gains. A well-articulated national policy framework geared towards greater inclusion of marginalised sections in the management of higher education is imperative to achieve sustainable development.

Studies have revealed that although the numbers of marginalised students in higher educational institutions have steadily increased, a large percentage of them are either unemployed or underemployed, not finding work of their choice or in their specialised filed. There is a U-shaped rather than linear relationship between higher education and employment, with participation in work dipping with increasing education up to a certain limit, but also increasing beyond that limit. In fact, even definitions of what constitutes a 'marginalised section' are unclear, and that the effects of class, gender, caste and marginalisation are variously experienced in different regions of the country. The policies have failed to come up with a unified framework that can coherently conceptualise or address these issues adequately. The marginalised sections of Indian society still face tremendous disadvantage, discrimination and deprivation, particularly in Indian higher education.

Desai, and Kulkarni (2008:03) have also examined the effects of 'positive discrimination policies' that have long operated in India. They have noted that whilst *Dalits, Adivasis* and others have had improved outcomes in primary schooling, the effects of positive discrimination have not filtered into higher education. The marginalised sections of Indian society show little gain in educational attainment due to absence of social activism and governmental patronage.

Deshpande (2009:04) argues that 'merit' and 'need' are very complex and often interwoven with other factors. His chief argument is that various logics such as power sharing, deprivation and discrimination are erroneously conflated in discussions around concessions and provisions and this in turn leads to policies that sometimes contradict each other and are often confused and ineffective. Weisskopf (2004:22) examined the impact of reservation on admissions to higher education in India and noted that reservation has benefited the various disadvantaged groups, even if not adequately. Practically, there is no evidence to support the popular argument that the creamy-layer of the marginalised sections benefit to the detriment of the group as a whole.

The Twelfth Plan cautions against single-minded and narrow strategies for improving access and equity, as they tend to do so at the expense of distributive educational justice and quality of higher education in India. The state is responsible for redressing multiple and graded inequalities in higher education and enhancing the presence of marginalised sections of Indian society in the centres of excellence, taking care of their post-admission needs and redesigning curricula to take into account their specific requirements. The plan document states: "The challenge of excellence is not just about placing a few institutions and individuals at par with global norms for excellence, it is also about expanding the pool of institutions, scholars and students who continuously strive to improve quality to achieve global excellence. Thus, an interconnected strategy for higher education development is needed to address issues of access, equity and excellence in a coordinated manner.

RUSA for the Empowerment of Marginalised Sections

The *Rashtriya Uchchatar Shiksha Abhiyan* (RUSA) is a new centrally sponsored scheme for higher education which will spread over two plan periods (XIIth and XIIIth) and will focus on state higher educational institutions. There are 316 states public universities and 13,024 colleges that can be covered under RUSA. The funding will be provided in the (Center: State) ratio of 90:10 for North-Eastern States and J&K, 75:25 for Other Special Category States (Sikkim, Himachal Pradesh and Uttarakhand) and 65:35 for Other States and UTs. The private government-aided institutions are also eligible to receive funds subject to fulfilling the conditions laid down by the Government of India.

The Twelfth Plan Document justifies the need for RUSA thus: "Given the pitiable condition, wide reach of the state university system and limitations of the UGC, there is a strong need for a strategic intervention for the improvement of access, equity and quality in Indian higher education, that focuses on state universities and state institutions through a special centrally, sponsored scheme in a mission mode".

The CABE document (2005:01) states: "RUSA is proposed to be an umbrella scheme that would subsume existing schemes and the central funding would flow from MHRD through state councils of higher education to institutions. States would be funded on the basis of plans of higher education prepared by them. All funding under RUSA would be norm-based and future grants would be dependant on the outcome. Certain academic, administrative and governance reforms will be a precondition for receiving funding under RUSA, said the CABE document.

The RUSA has a new approach towards funding higher education in state universities based on key principles of performance-based funding, incentivising well performing institutions and decision making through clearly defined norms, which will establish and rely upon a management information system to gather the essential information from institutions. RUSA will aim to provide greater autonomy to universities as well as colleges and have a sharper focus on equity-based development, and improvement in teaching-learning quality and research. The states are required to step up academic and administrative reforms and fast track their implementation in order to achieve the goals of RUSA. These include the creation of a State Higher Education Council, creation of accreditation agencies, preparation of the state perspective plans, commitment of certain stipulated share of funds towards RUSA, academic, sectoral and institutional governance reforms, filling faculty positions etc. The State Higher Education Council will undertake this process of planning, execution and evaluation, in addition to other monitoring and capacity building functions.

The objectives of RUSA would be to achieve the target of GER of 30 per cent, which the central Government has set for itself, by the year 2020.

The government aims to improve the quality of state universities and colleges and enhance existing capacities of the institutions to become dynamic, demand-driven, quality conscious, efficient and forward looking, responsive to rapid economic and technological developments occurring at the local, state, national and international levels. The salient objectives of the scheme are as follows:

- Improve the overall quality of existing state institutions by ensuring that all institutions conform to prescribed norms and standards and adopt accreditation as a mandatory quality assurance framework.
- Usher transformative reforms in the state higher education system by creating a facilitating institutional structure for planning and monitoring at state level, promoting autonomy in state universities and improving governance in institutions.
- Ensure academic and examination reforms in the higher educational institutions.
- Enable conversion of some of the universities into institutions of excellence at par with the best in the world.
- Create opportunities for states to undertake reforms in the affiliating system in order to ensure that the reforms and resource requirements of affiliated colleges are adequately met.
- Ensure adequate availability of quality faculty in all higher educational institutions and ensure capacity building at all levels of employment.
- Create an enabling atmosphere in the higher educational institutions to devote themselves to research and innovations.
- Expand the institutional base by creating additional capacity in existing institutions and establishing new institutions, to achieve enrolment targets.
- Correct regional imbalances in access to higher education by facilitating access to high quality institutions in urban and semi urban areas, creating opportunities for students from rural areas to get access to better quality institutions and setting up institutions in un served and under-served areas.
- Improve equity in higher education by providing adequate opportunities of higher education to socially deprived communities;

promote inclusion of women, minorities, SC/STs and differently abled persons.

The RUSA intends to provide financial assistance to the states and institutions on the basis of certain healthy norms of higher educational management such as access, equity and excellence. The need for strategic funding of State institutions must ensure that the issues of quality and access are addressed in an equitable manner to facilitate the inclusive growth and development of marginalised sections of Indian society. The broad components of RUSA, therefore, would be creation of new universities, new engineering colleges and new degree colleges by the State Governments. Reforms in the areas of governance of universities, academic and examination reforms and affiliation system of State universities would be another important component of the scheme.

The primary components of RUSA include - creation of new university and colleges, converting existing colleges/cluster of colleges into universities, expansion of courses and disciplines (with special focus on inter and cross disciplinary learning), one model college in each district of the country by creation/upgradation, research and innovation grants/funds one university to be made research university, creation of state higher education councils, creation of accreditation agencies, infrastructure up gradation of existing institutions with special focus on quality and equity (e.g. girls hostels, toilets, libraries and laboratories), expansion of quality distance learning programmes and improvements in usage of ICT for leveraging learning efforts, establishing management information system, faculty support–recruitment and capacity building, administrative/governance reforms, academic and examination reforms, affiliation reforms (target being less than 100 colleges for each university) and leadership development of educational administrators.

The guiding principles of RUSA include-performance based outlays and outcome based reimbursements, incentivising and disincentivising, apolitical decision-making, disclosure-based governance, autonomy for higher educational institutions, equity-based development, quality and research focus. The success of RUSA primarily depends upon the adoption of healthy practices and professional norms by the institutions concerned. The states are expected to fulfill the priority requirements and also honour the commitments made towards certain conditions which must be fulfilled during the course of the RUSA implementation. The implementing agency in the state is required to prepare a plan of action. This should indicate the physical targets and budgetary estimates in accordance with the approved pattern of assistance under the RUSA which follows a Bottom Up approach for planning and budgeting.

Future Course of Action

The RUSA is indeed a well-designed tool to improve the quality of higher education on the basis of critical appraisal of the performance of the higher educational institutions concerned. The continuity of the scheme depends on the performance outcome-based on the well-established parameters referred to above. The scheme primarily provides educational and employment opportunities to large number of persons who constitute the 'marginalised community' in India. The policy-makers, academicians and other stakeholders should deliberate on this scheme and prepare grounds for effective implementation of the scheme for the benefit of the marginalised sections. In the age of globalisation, higher education should be perceived as a long-term social investment for the inclusive, integrated and sustainable development of people who matter most from the point of view of national development.

The globalisation has also necessitated the inculcation of competitive spirit in all spheres of human life including higher education. It is necessary to enhance the employability of youth who are the backbone of national development. Greater autonomy to institutions, recruitment of faculty, improvement in teaching–learning quality, scientific curriculum development, systematic research, monitoring and evaluation, brain storming sessions, media intervention, judicial monitoring, social activism and other measures would go a long way in actualising the goals of RUSA and facilitating the educational and economic empowerment of the marginalised sections of Indian society.

Conclusion

The Government of India aims at an 'optimum' solution to create a centrally sponsored scheme which is an alternate way of facilitating systematic management of higher education in the country. The scholars have also hoped that the reforms initiated under RUSA will build a self-sustaining momentum with a view to push for greater accountability and autonomy of state institutions and impress upon them the need to improve the quality of education. The yardstick for deciding the quantum of funds for the states and institution comprise the norms that reflect the performance in key result areas–access, equity and excellence. The states are required to strictly adhere to the norms of RUSA and achieve the goals of inclusive educational development and economic empowerment of the marginalised sections of Indian society.

References

- CABE Committee (2005) Report on Higher Education Funding, New Delhi.
- Desai, S. and V. Kulkarni (2008) Changin Educational Inequalities in India in the Context of Affirmative Action, *Demography,* 45 (2): pp. 245-270.
- Deshpande, S. (2009) Inclusion versus excellence: caste and the framing of fair access in Indian higher education, *South African Review of Sociology,* 40 (1): pp. 127-147.
- Jyothi, P. (2009) Revisiting Linkages between Entrepreneurship and Higher Education, *Advances in Management,* 2 (10): pp. 39-43.
- Planning Commission of India (2012) Five Year Plan, New Delhi.
- Planning Commission of India (2012) XIIth Five Year Plan, New Delhi.
- Thorat, Sukhadeo (2006) Higher Education in India: Emerging Issues Related to Access, Inclusiveness and Quality, Nehru Memorial Lecture, University of Mumbai, November 24, Mumbai.
- Weisskopf, T.E. (2004) Impact of Reservation on Admissions to Higher Education in India, *Economic and Political Weekly,* 39 (39): pp. 4339-4349.

8 Trends Across Higher Education in Karnataka: An Approach Towards Inclusive Growth

Mohammed Ashfaq Ahamed
Dr. P.M. Honakeri

Abstract

The study analyses the trend across higher educational institutions in Karnataka and the trends in higher education enrollment with regard to gender, SCs and STs in Karnataka. The important findings of the study reveal that the total higher educational institutions in the state have increased from 1681 in 2001-02 to that of 2379 in 2011-12, with an average annual growth rate of 4.29 per cent. On an average, during the period of 2000-01 to 2009-10, the percentage share of male and female enrollment stood at 58.5 per cent and 41.5 per cent with a differential gap of around 17 per cent. Among SCs it stood at 11.35 per cent and across STs, it remained at 3.18 per cent. The GER across males during the period 2006-2009 stood highest than the State's GER in higher education in Karnataka. The GER among SCs in the year 2009-10 has stood at 18.40 per cent, slightly higher than the State's GER with an increase of 6.37 per cent over the period 2006-07. The GER among STs in the year 2009-10 has stood at 14.90 per cent, with an increase of 6.15 per cent over the period 2006-07. The current GER in the state is around 18 per cent. The State Government has evolved a long term integrated policy on higher education in the year 2012 in order to improve the GER in the state. An inclusive database would be much helpful in undertaking ground level research in the areas of higher education and would be beneficial in driving the higher education to the path of inclusive growth.

Introduction

Higher education is of prime importance and should be given high accord for building a knowledge-based society. It is also a powerful tool for achieving inclusive growth as higher education helps in increasing access to highly skilled and high paid jobs. The higher education in India is based on two landmark reports called the University Education Commission (Radhakrishnan Commission) Report in 1948-49 and The Education Commission (Kothari Commission) Report in 1964-66. The National Policy on Education which was amended in 1992 had stated that "Higher Education provides people with an opportunity to reflect on the critical social, economic, cultural, moral and spiritual issues facing humanity and contributes to national development through dissemination of specialised knowledge and skills. Higher Education is therefore a crucial factor for survival."

Karnataka Jnana Ayoga (KJA) has been set-up in the state for increasing the knowledge base of the society. It desires to promote faster, sustainable and more inclusive growth as mentioned in the Twelfth Plan Approach Paper of Government of India. The Karnataka State Government further has constituted a Task Force on Higher Education in 2002, which reiterated the need for a State level planning and co-ordination of Higher Education including University Education through an independent autonomous body for Higher Education in order to bring out better excellence, inclusiveness and accessibility in the Higher Education Sector.

Review of Literature and Research Gap

The following section provides brief literature review on the study. Prakash (2007) examined the trends in the expansion of higher education and also analysed variations in participation across states, gender and social groups. The study came to the conclusion that Quantitative expansion and Qualitative improvement of higher education should command highest priority in the policy discourse. Premakumara and Riyaz (2010) made an effort to analyse regional disparities in primary and secondary education of Karnataka as a backdrop to the policy of inclusive growth. The study concludes that though the enrollment in these areas has increased due to various government programmes, but still high dropout rate prevails. Gupta et.al., (2012), presented the development scenario of the higher education in India by identifying the key challenges that is being faced by the country. It also presented the key initiatives by the Government and recommendations to meet the key challenges.

Based upon the perusal of the literature review, it is found that studies' having their approach towards inclusive growth needs to be undertaken. Further with regard to Karnataka state, there are scanty research studies dealing with higher education and inclusive growth. Therefore, the following study intends to provide an inclusive approach in analysing the trends across higher education in Karnataka.

Need for the Study

The recent five year plan i.e., 11th and 12th have aimed at the objective of fostering inclusive growth in the country. Mr Jeffrey, Chairman and CEO of Manpower Planning, USA argues that "The best way to achieve Inclusive Growth is through developing people's education and skills." Professor Janadhya Tilak has also stressed the importance of education in the context of inclusive growth. Further in the present context, there is no denying the fact that, disparities continue to exist not only between states, but as well as within the districts of the states and the disparities varies among regions, gender and social groups. It has become necessary to study inclusive growth in education sector at rural-urban levels, across male and female segments and across social groups.

Objective of the Study

The study intends to analyse the trend across higher educational institutions in Karnataka and the trends in higher education enrollment with regard to gender, SCs and STs in Karnataka. It also aims to identify policies and programmes implemented by the Government with special focus on inclusive growth.

Methodology of the Study

This study is based on secondary data collected from the Reports of Ministry of Human Resource Development such as Selected Educational Statistics and Statistics on Higher and Technical Education in India. Apart from that, data is also collected from "Statistical Abstract of Karnataka" and "Karnataka at a Glance" of respective years. The study uses statistical and analytical methods such as Averages, Percentages, Annual growth rates, Average Annual Growth Rates and Gender Parity Indices.

Conceptual Framework

Inclusive growth is largely defined as a broad-based growth covering not only the major areas of the state but should also cover villages and smaller towns. It should benefit the widest number of people with special consideration to the marginalised or disadvantageous sections of the society. It should ensure increase in the involvement of people from all the sections of the population into the growth process. Further it demands that all social groups should have equal access to the services provided by the State and equal opportunities for upward economic and social mobility. The four A's framework developed by the former UN Special Rapporteur on Right to Education by name Katarina Tomasevski is used in the study and has been linked with the chief attributes of inclusive growth. It is depicted in the below chart.

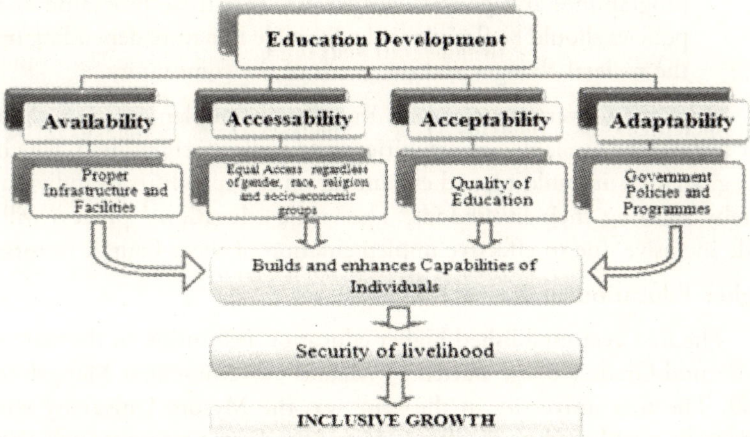

Source: Author's Conceptualisation.

The education development relies on four factors in the context of inclusive growth. They are as follows:-

(a) **Availability:** Government should provide proper infrastructure and facilities in the country so that the individual can utilise the opportunities provided. This in turn will develop their capabilities.

(b) **Accessibility:** After the government provides the means to utilise the opportunities, it should also ensure equal access to these opportunities regardless of the gender, race, religion and socio-economic status they belong. Efforts should be made to ensure the inclusion of marginalised groups and there should be no denial of services to any of the student. This in turn will help them to utilise the available opportunities and helps in building up their capabilities. This also helps them in securing their livelihoods by gaining employment ventures.

(c) **Acceptability:** The next important factor in this arena is acceptability. It speaks out that the quality of education that is imparted should be free from any kind of discrimination, relevant and culturally appropriate. The teaching methods should not confine to any ideologies, should be objective and unbiased.

This helps in developing the skills of the individuals, through which they can secure their livelihoods.

(d) **Adaptability:** This factor focuses on the various government programmes and policies and stresses that these programmes and policies should be flexible and adjustable in nature depending upon the societal changes and the needs of the community.

Once the Government ensures the effective implementation of these four factors, the available opportunities will be effectively utilised, which in turn guarantees in building and enhancing up of capabilities of individuals, thereby securing their livelihoods. The entire educational process will be made inclusive due to effective implementation of these Four A factors.

Higher Education in Karnataka

The first ever established higher education institution in the state was the Second Grade College started by Madras Government at Mangalore in 1869. The first university in the state was the Mysore University which came to be established in the year 1916 and the first engineering college was started in Bangalore in the year 1917. By 1956, 28 general colleges and 14 professional colleges were established in the state. The Department of Collegiate Education came to be established in the year 1960 and is striving hard to make higher education affordable and accessible to all. It looks after the administration of government and private aided colleges in the state. The Department of Technical Education in the state came to being in 1959 and it is playing a vital role in looking after the technical education in the state.

Table 1 presents the overall trend in the growth of higher educational institutions in Karnataka during the period 2001-02 to that of 2011-12. In the year 2001, there were around 16 universities/deemed universities in Karnataka. It has shown a considerable improvement over the period. Now in the year 2011, the total number of universities and deemed universities in the state stands around 40. On an average, there is 9.86 per cent of increase in the number of universities/deemed universities over the period 2001-02 to 2011-12 in Karnataka. With regard to total number of higher education colleges in the state, we have general degree colleges and professional colleges. The general degree colleges include arts, science and commerce colleges, where as the professional colleges include engineering colleges, technical colleges, architecture colleges, medical colleges, polytechnics, teacher training colleges and others.

Chart 1 depicts the trend across general degree and professional colleges in the state. The total no. of general degree colleges in 2001 were around

Table 1. Growth of Higher Educational Institutions in Karnataka

	Total Higher Educational Institutions	*AGR**	*Total Universities/ Deemed Universities*	*AGR**	*Total General Degree Colleges*	*AGR**	*Total Professional Colleges*	*AGR**
2001-02	1681	-	16	-	916	-	747	-
2002-03	1696	0.89	19	18.75	923	0.76	753	0.80
2003-04	1710	0.83	19	0.00	930	0.76	760	0.93
2004-05	1706	-0.23	22	15.79	930	0.00	753	-0.92
2005-06	1904	11.61	23	4.55	930	0.00	950	26.16
2006-07	1457	-23.48	24	4.35	462	-50.32	970	2.11
2007-08	1828	25.46	26	8.33	638	38.10	1163	19.90
2008-09	1961	7.28	30	15.38	647	1.41	1283	10.32
2009-10	2021	3.06	37	23.33	652	0.77	1331	3.74
2010-11	2054	1.63	40	8.11	657	0.77	1396	4.88
2011-12	2379	15.82	40	0.00	669	1.83	1709	22.42
Average AGR*	**4.29**		**9.86**		**-0.59**		**9.03**	

Note: *refers to Annual Growth Rate.

Source: (1) Selected Education Statistics and Statistics on Higher and Technical Education of respective years.
(2) Statistical Abstract and Karnataka at a Glance of respective years, Government of Karnataka.

916, higher than the number of professional colleges in that year. Later in the year 2005-06, the number of professional colleges increased to such an extent that it somewhat levelled the number of general degree colleges. After 2005-06, there was a drastic trend in the number of general degree colleges and professional colleges. The number of professional colleges increased drastically from 930 in 2005-06 to that of 1709 in the year 2011-12. There had been a positive increase over the period 2001 to 2011. The average annual growth rate during this period stood at 9.03 per cent. On the other hand, the number of general degree colleges decreased considerably. It decreased from 950 in 2005-06 to that of 669 in the year 2011-12. There had been a negative increase in the number of general degree colleges in Karnataka over the period 2001 to 2011. On an average, the growth rate stood negative at 0.59 per cent. The total higher educational institutions in the state have increased from 1681 in the year 2001-02 to that of 2379 in 2011-12, with an average annual growth rate of 4.29 per cent.

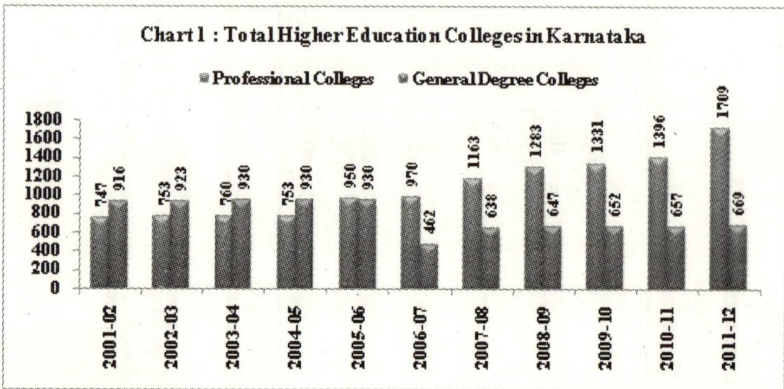

Source: Selected Education Statistics and Statistics on Higher and Technical Education of respective years.

Higher Education Enrollment by Gender

Table 2 provides the enrollment in higher education by gender in Karnataka. The total enrollment across higher educational institutions in Karnataka during the year 2000-01 stood at 552290. The male enrollment constituted around 60.4 per cent and the remaining 39.6 per cent were female enrollment, indicating a gap of around 20.7 per cent. In this respect, the Gender Parity Index remained at 0.66 during this year and there was a gender gap of more than one lakh. In the year 2004-05, the Gender Parity Index improved by 0.14 points and the gender gap in enrollment reduced by around 34,621. The percentage share of male and female enrollment in this year stood at 55.7 per cent and 44.3 per cent respectively, indicating a gap of around 11.3 per cent. However in later years, the Gender Parity

Index saw a slight decline and it picked up after 2007-08. Even the percentage gap in the share of male and female enrollment to the total enrollment decreased slightly after 2007-08. In the year 2009-10, the percentage share of male and female enrollment was 56.6 per cent and 43.4 per cent with a gap of around 13.3 per cent. The Gender Parity Index stood at 0.77. Therefore on an average, during the period of 2000-01 to 2009-10, the percentage share of male and female enrollment stood at 58.5 per cent and 41.5 per cent with a differential gap of around 17 per cent.

Table 2. Higher Education Enrollment in Karnataka by Gender

Years	*Total Enroll-ment*	*Male Enrollment*		*Female Enrollment*		*Gender Party Index*	*Gender Gap*
		Number	*Percen-tage to Total*	*Number*	*Percen-tage to Total*		
2000-01	552290	333374	60.4	218916	39.6	0.66	114458
2001-02	537027	322755	60.1	214272	39.9	0.66	108483
2002-03	544355	328556	60.4	215799	39.6	0.66	112757
2003-04	639190	376128	58.8	263062	41.2	0.70	113066
2004-05	706241	393039	55.7	313202	44.3	0.80	79837
2005-06	951786	565485	59.4	386301	40.6	0.68	179184
2006-07	1061456	634160	59.7	427296	40.3	0.67	206864
2007-08	873528	502554	57.5	370974	42.5	0.74	131580
2008-09	1421886	801714	56.4	620172	43.6	0.77	181542
2009-10	1260038	713536	56.6	546502	43.4	0.77	167034
Average	**854780**	**497130**	**58.5**	**357650**	**41.5**	**0.72**	

(*Source:* Selected Education Statistics and Statistics on Higher and Technical Education of respective years).

Higher Education Enrollment by SCs and STs

Table 3 provides the enrollment across higher education by Scheduled Castes and Scheduled Tribes in Karnataka. In the year 2000-01, the percentage share of SC enrollment to the total enrolment remained at 11.52 per cent. It decreased by 3.43 per cent in the year 2003-04, but in later years it saw a slightly increasing trend. By the year 2009-10, it stood at 15.65 per cent. On an average, the percentage share of SC enrollment across the period 2000-01 to 2009-10, stood at 11.35 per cent.

With regard to enrollment of Scheduled Tribes across higher education in Karnataka, the percentage share in the year 2000-01 remained at just 3.35 per cent. In the later years, there was a decline in percentage share. In the year 2007-08, it declined by 0.40 per cent but however in the year

2009-10 it increased by 2.11 per cent. The percentage share of ST enrollment in this year stood at 5.01 per cent. On an average, the percentage share of ST enrollment across the period 2000-01 to 2009-10 stood at 3.18 per cent.

Table 3. Higher Education Enrollment in Karnataka by SCs and STs

		SC Enrollment		*ST Enrollment*	
Years	*Total Enrollment*	*Number*	*Percentage to total*	*Number*	*Percentage to total*
2000-01	552290	63612	11.52	18514	3.35
2001-02	537027	68410	12.74	19272	3.59
2002-03	544355	48109	8.84	12874	2.37
2003-04	639190	51678	8.08	17664	2.76
2004-05	706241	76716	10.86	16443	2.33
2005-06	951786	99775	10.48	22122	2.32
2006-07	1061456	126448	11.91	36329	3.42
2007-08	873528	102466	11.73	25361	2.90
2008-09	1421886	165494	11.64	53218	3.74
2009-10	1260038	197252	15.65	63122	5.01
Average	**854780**	**99996**	**11.35**	**28492**	**3.18**

(*Source:* Selected Education Statistics and Statistics on Higher and Technical Education of respective years).

Gross Enrollment Ratio (GER) Across Higher Education in Karnataka

Table 4 provides the trend in Gross Enrollment Ratio (GER) across Higher Education in Karnataka. It remained at 15.47 per cent in the year 2006-07. It however increased to 20.70 per cent in 2008-09 but again in the year 2009-10, it decreased by 2.60 per cent. It's around 18.10 per cent. With regard to gender, the GER across males saw an increase from 17.78 per cent in 2006-07 to that of 19.80 per cent in 2009-10. The GER in higher education across males during the period 2006-2009 stood highest than the State's GER in higher education in Karnataka. The GER across females have increased from 12.96 per cent in 2006-07 to that of 16.30 per cent in 2009-10. The gender gap in GER across higher education has reduced from 4.82 per cent to that of 3.50 per cent during the period 2006-07 to 2009-10. The Gender Parity Index in GPR has also shown a considerable improvement. In the year 2009-10, it stood at 0.82, increased by 0.09 per cent over the period 2006-07.

The GER across higher education among SCs in Karnataka has fairly increased from 12.03 per cent in 2006-07 to that of 18.40 per cent in the year 2009-10. During this year, the GER of SCs in higher education has remained slightly higher than the State's GER in higher education. On the other hand, the GER among STs in the year 2009-10 has stood at 14.90 per cent, with an increase of 6.15 per cent over the period 2006-07. The SC-ST gap between the GER in higher education in Karnataka in the year 2009-10 stood at 3.50 per cent.

Table 4. Gross Enrollment Ratio across Higher Education in Karnataka

	2006-07	*2007-08*	*2008-09*	*2009-10*
Total	15.47	12.90	20.70	18.10
Male	17.78	14.30	22.60	19.80
Female	12.96	11.40	18.80	16.30
SC	12.03	9.80	15.60	18.40
ST	8.75	6.20	12.70	14.90
GPI	**0.73**	**0.80**	**0.83**	**0.82**
Gender Gap	**4.82**	**2.90**	**3.80**	**3.50**
SC-ST Gap	**3.28**	**3.60**	**2.90**	**3.50**

(*Source:* Statistics on Higher and Technical Education of respective years).

Government's Policies and Programmes

University Grants Commission (UGC) was established in the year 1956 by the Union Government with the aim of co-ordinating, determining and maintaining standards of higher education in the country. It is striving hard to make higher education accessible to all and also for the inclusive development of higher education. In order to increase the female enrollment in higher education, UGC has been providing financial support for construction of hostels for women and other related infrastructural facilities in colleges of higher education. It is also implementing "Indira Gandhi Scholarship" for single girl child to pursue higher and technical education across the country. These initiatives by UGC have helped in improving the Gender Parity Index across the higher education in the state.

Further several schemes of UGC have also been implemented in the country in order to support the higher education of Scheduled Castes and Scheduled Tribes. These include Remedial Coaching at UG and PG level, coaching classes for preparation of National Eligibility Test (NET), establishment of centers of social exclusion and inclusive policy in universities etc. Every universities of the country have been requested by UGC to set up an "Equal Opportunities Cell" in order to ensure equity and inclusion in higher education. Further Rajiv Gandhi National Fellowship has been implemented by UGC in the country for SCs and STs to pursue their higher education.

Apart from the policies of the Central Government, the State Government itself has evolved a long term integrated policy on higher education in the year 2012 with the assistance of Karnataka Knowledge Commission (KKC) and Karnataka State Higher Education Council (KSHEC) aiming to increase the GER by increasing access of education to all.

Important Findings of the Study

- The total higher educational institutions in the state have increased from 1681 in the year 2001-02 to that of 2379 in 2011-12, with an average annual growth rate of 4.29 per cent.
- On an average, during the period of 2000-01 to 2009-10, the percentage share of male and female enrollment stood at 58.5 per cent and 41.5 per cent with a differential gap of around 17 per cent. The Gender Parity Index stood at 0.72 per cent.
- On an average, the percentage share of SC enrollment across the period 2000-01 to 2009-10, stood at 11.35 per cent and across STs, it remained at 3.18 per cent.
- The GER in higher education across males during the period 2006-2009 stood highest than the State's GER in higher education in Karnataka.
- The GER across higher education among SCs in Karnataka has fairly increased from 12.03 per cent in 2006-07 to that of 18.40 per cent in the year 2009-10.
- The GER among SCs in the year 2009-10 has stood at 18.40 per cent, slightly higher than the State's GER with an increase of 6.37 per cent over the period 2006-07.
- The GER among STs in the year 2009-10 has stood at 14.90 per cent, with an increase of 6.15 per cent over the period 2006-07.

Recommendations and Conclusion

In the light of the above findings, the following recommendations deserve a mention. The Twelfth Five Year Plan of Government of India has set out the target of bringing the GER in higher education to 21 per cent by the plan end and to 30 per cent by the year 2020. The current GER in the state is around 18 per cent. Efforts needs to be undertaken by the Government in order to increase the GER as per the targets specified. The quantitative expansion of the higher educational institutions needs to be undertaken in the state at a faster pace. No doubt, the government has made many initiatives in order to improve the female enrollment across higher education, but despite of this, the female enrollment is bit lower than the male enrollment. Further The Gender Parity Index (GPI) with respect to higher education enrollment in the state is around 0.72 per cent. In this regard, Government should take concrete steps to ensure increase in female enrollment so that the GPI is brought closer to one. The households and families should be made aware of the importance of attaining higher education among females, and subsequently avenues for pursuing higher education of females should be initiated.

The scope for professional education in the state is gaining much prominence since 2005-06 which is evident from that fact that that the number of professional colleges has increased drastically since 2005-06 in the state. Further a proper and an inclusive database for higher education is the need of the hour. The study found some limitations in the database on higher education in the country as the enrollment data for OBCs and minorities were not included in the database. An inclusive database would be much helpful in undertaking ground level research in the areas of higher education and would be beneficial in driving the higher education to the path of inclusive Growth.

References

- Prakash (2007), "Trends in Growth and Financing of Higher Education in India", Economic and Political Weekly, Vol. XLII No. 31, New Delhi.
- Premakumara and Riyaz (2010), "Regional Disparities, Inclusive Growth and Educational Development in Karnataka", Trends in Information and Management, Vol. 6 No. 2, Jammu and Kashmir.
- GOI (2011), "Report of the Working Group on Higher Education for the XII Five Year Plan", Ministry of Human Resource Development, New Delhi.
- Gupta et.al., (2012), "Higher Education in India: Structure, Statistics and Challenges", Journal of Education and Practice, Vol. 3, No. 2.
- GOI (2006 to 2009), "Statistics on Higher and Technical Education in India", Ministry of Human Resource Development, New Delhi.
- GOK (2008 to 2011), "Karnataka at a Glance", Directorate of Economics and Statistics, Government of Karnataka, Bangalore.
- GOK (2010 and 2011), "Statistical Abstract of Karnataka", Directorate of Economics and Statistics, Government of Karnataka, Bangalore.

9 Higher Educational Status of 'Dalit Women' in Karnataka

Dr. Nagaraj. M. Muggur

Abstract

In the present days women's capabilities have not materialised into an equal participation between men and women in terms of access to education, resources and employment opportunities. Historically, the caste system left the lowest castes (*Dalits*) at the bottom of the social, political and economic set up in India. Especially, *Dalit* women are placed at the absolute bottom of the social hierarchy as they face systemic and structural discrimination threefold: as *Dalits,* as poor and as women. And even today the *Dalit* women are forced into the labour market because of the need to sustain themselves and their families. At the same time only occupations that are available and traditionally allocated to them are those which no one else would prefer to do. Better paid and dignified occupations continue to be out of reach for them through a systematic denial of rights to education, training, land and other livelihood resources. Apart from constitutional legal measures and number of policy initiatives have been initiated various governance levels to improve the socio-economic conditions in the last six decades, even though the condition of *dalits* and *dalit* women has not improved much and they do not only remain at the bottom of the social hierarchy, but also face multiple challenges in accessing their rights. Taking into account of this backdrop, the present paper is an attempt made to know the higher educational performance of *dalit* women in the state and over period of time efforts of government programmes towards improving higher educational status of *dalit* women. These are all aspects were discussed under the availability of secondary level information related to Karnataka state.

Introduction

Historically *Dalits* are the most marginalised groups in all walks of life in India. Especially, the caste system has left the lowest castes (*Dalits*) at the bottom of the social, political and economic set up in country.

Moreover, in the present days women's improved capabilities have generally very less as comparing to men in terms of access to education, resources and employment opportunities. Particularly *dalits*, the women of *dalits* are placed at the absolute bottom of the social hierarchy as they face systemic and structural discrimination in threefold: as *Dalits*, as poor and as women. Even today the dalit women are forced into the labour market because of the need to sustain themselves and their families. At the same time only occupations that are available and traditionally allocated to them are those which no one else would prefer to do. Better paid and dignified occupations continue to be out of reach for them through a systematic denial of rights to education, training, land and other livelihood resources. When one considers *dalits* as a homogeneous community and assess their higher educational attainment during post independence period, the event that is to be mentioned is the historic reservation policy and the subsequent changes among the *dalits*. But apart from constitutional legal measures and number of policy initiatives have been initiated various governance levels to improve the socio-economic conditions in the last six decades, even though the condition of *dalits* and· *dalits* women has not improved much and they do not only remain at the bottom of the social hierarchy, but also face multiple challenges in accessing their rights. Taking to account of in this backdrop, the present paper an attempts made to know the higher educational performance of *dalits* women in the state and over period of time efforts of government programmes towards improving higher educational status for dalits women. These are all aspects were discussed under the availability of secondary level information related to Karnataka state.

Dalits Population in India and Karnataka

The majority of caste or caste population is also more important to acquiring of major position in the social caste system as in an independent country like India. In the Indian democracy system the development of any caste is almost depending upon majority of population component as it shows various manifestation of upper as well as lower position of *dalits* through various indexes. Herewith, we have examined the decade wise population of altars social groups in both Karnataka as well as the country as per the census of India from 1901 to 2011. The Table 1 has been provides the information about population changes in across census periods. The share of the SC population in the total population, which was 13.22 per cent in 1961, declined to 13.14 in 1971, then increased to 15.07 per cent in 1981 and to 16.38 per cent in 1991, and thereafter, fell to 16.21 per cent in 2001 and tremendously increased in 2011 as 21.44 per cent. It is comparing to country level statistics the scheduled caste population share is almost similar trend to total population.

Table 1. Percentage Share of SCs/STs and Others to Total Population in Karnataka and India

Decades	*Karnataka*			*India*		
	SC	*ST*	*Others*	*SC*	*ST*	*Others*
1961	13.22	0.48	86.31	14.7	6.8	78.5
1971	13.14	0.79	86.07	14.6	6.9	78.5
1981	15.07	4.91	80.02	15.3	7.6	77.1
1991	16.38	4.26	79.36	16.4	8	75.6
2001	16.21	6.55	77.24	16.2	8.2	75.6
2011	21.44	8.00	70.56	21.87	10.9	67.3

(*Sources:* GOK (2006) p. 212, GOI (2009) p. 30 and GOI (2011) pp. 10, 34-35).

In the other hand, the share of the ST population in the total population, which was 0.48 per cent in 1961, and it has increased decade to decades as in 1971, 1981 and slightly decreased in 1991 and increased 2001 to 2011 is 0.79, 4.91, 4.26, 6.55 and 8.00 as respective decades in the state. But the percentage of scheduled tribe share comparing to country level population is much higher than that of the state from 1961 to 2011.

Literacy Rate

Since Independence the Central and State governments have been given more importance to improvement of educational status of *Dalits* as well as *Dalits* women. The various official reports and studies were pointed out that the rate of growth of literacy among *dalits* has increased; however, the gap in literacy as well as higher education between *dalits* and non-*dalits* communities remains the same. Equally, the gap in educational status between SC males and females remains the same. Census data provide more insight into literacy rate and literacy gap among and across social groups.

The growth in the literacy rate of both male and female SCs and STs between 1981 and 2011 has been present in the table 2. It is evident from the above table the literacy rate of *dalits* as well as other than *dalits* was tremendously increased from 1981 to 2011 in the state. The gender gap in literacy rate among the SCs and STs has difference in some extent from 1981 to 2011. But the gender gap in literacy rate is a reality among SC, ST and general categories, it is more pronounced among STs followed by SCs. Especially, in women literacy concern *dalits* women were improved in the level of literacy as in 1981 to 2011 is 15.5 to 46.7 and 10 to 40.6 increased SCs and STs women respectively in the respective decades in the state.

Table 2. Literacy Rate among SCs and General Population in Karnataka

Years	*SC*			*ST*			*General*		
	Male	*Female*	*Total*	*Male*	*Female*	*Total*	*Male*	*Female*	*Total*
1981	39.4	15.5	27.6	29.9	10.0	20.1	58.7	33.2	46.2
1991	49.7	25.9	38.1	40.6	18.2	29.6	67.3	44.3	56.0
2001	63.8	41.7	52.9	59.2	32.8	47.1	76.1	56.9	66.6
2011	65.3	46.7	56.1	65.4	40.6	40.6	82.9	68.1	75.6

(*Sources:* GOK (2006) pp. 220, 237 and GOI (2011) pp. 10, 34-35).

But comparing to *dalits* women the general caste women's are top in the position as 33.2 to 68.1 per cent in the respective decades. It shows that the *dalits* women are still in the bottom all male including *dalits* as well as general and general women position as literacy level in the state.

District-wise Literacy Rate

According to Karnataka Human Development Report the district-wise *dalits* female both (SCs and STs) literacy rate has been present in the Fig. 1. It is reveals that the SCs female in Udupi, Bangalore Urban and Dakshina Kannada are constituted highest literacy rate 62.8, 62 and 58.4 per cent respectively and other than these district were recorded less percentages.

In the other hand the ST female highest literacy constituted in Dakshina Kannada, Bangalore Rural and Udupi districts is 65.7, 64.8, and 62.8 per

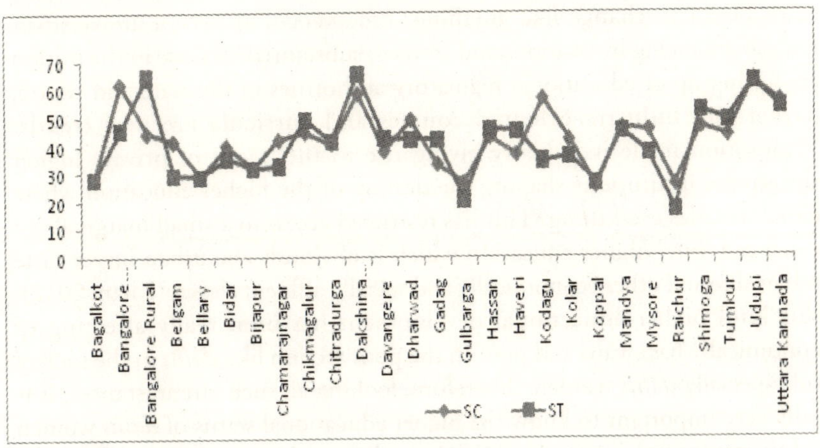

Fig. 1. Female Literacy Rates among the SCs and STs in Karnataka by Districts 2001

(*Sources:* GOK (2006) p. 335).

cent respectively. The lowest literacy rate has been recorded SCs and STs Raichur, Gulburga and Koppal districts. Other than this district were recorded in between of highest and lowest in the state.

Women Participation in Higher Education

According to the Universal Declaration on Human Rights (1948) Education is recognised as a fundamental human right, along with other necessities, such as food, shelter and water. Human development is predicated upon universal access to education, with its implications for equity and social justice and education empowers people to make informed choices about their lives and their rights as citizens in a democracy. And also gender justice gets a boost when women have access to education, which, by enhancing women's knowledge and employment capacity, increases their sense of autonomy and self worth as well as health status improves as their education levels rise. This predicted that education is one of the minimum need for human development and it is also very important to women in the male dominate society like India.

After independence, there was tremendous increase were found in number of higher educational institutions in the country. Teachers and students thereafter also witnessed big increase. The National Higher Education policy adopted in 1986 has emphasised on three basic elements, Access, equal access (or equity), Quality and Excellence. But the process of development in this sector was exclusionary for the sections like Scheduled Tribes, Scheduled Castes continues today. After 1991, the higher education sector began to change like anything. Emergences of private universities, new self-financing institutions and courses, substantial increase in the tuition fee, setting up of educational regulatory authorities in the state and centre, market and industry-oriented courses and curricula are new trends. Privatisation made it industry giving rise to the boom of private higher educational institutions shaping the destiny of the higher education where market decides everything. This has restricted access to a small marginalised which can 'buy' higher education which is obviously the urban upper caste Indian elite and other economically and socially affluent classes (Khan. 2012). This kind higher educational development has been really affecting to economically backward and poor in the poor section like *dalits* in the society and especially *dalits* women. Therefore, looking all such circumstances, it is really very important to know the higher educational status of *dalits* women and their participation in the state. According to 2004 sample survey, made by the Directorate of Economics and Statistics, Karnataka, it has been clear in the table (see Table 3).

Table 3. *Dalits* Profile of the Educational Levels in Karnataka (percentage to population)

Level of Education	*SC*			*ST*		
	Male	*Female*	*Total*	*Male*	*Female*	*Total*
Not literate	43.69	**54.73**	49.08	48.19	**55.30**	51.61
Literate without formal education	2.12	**1.42**	1.78	1.68	**0.72**	1.22
Literate below primary	16.89	**16.88**	16.89	17.01	**18.43**	17.69
Primary	12.33	**11.27**	11.81	10.70	**11.68**	11.17
Higher primary	10.81	**8.71**	9.78	10.53	**7.32**	8.99
High School	8.45	**5.40**	6.96	7.29	**5.27**	6.32
PUC	3.45	**1.10**	2.30	2.36	**0.66**	1.54
Diploma	0.35	**0.13**	0.25	0.34	**0.12**	0.23
Graduate	1.47	**0.22**	0.86	1.40	**0.18**	0.81
Post-graduate	0.21	**0.04**	0.13	0.15	**0.02**	0.09
Technical graduate	0.12	**0.02**	0.07	0.06	**0.00**	0.03
Technical Post-graduate	0.04	**0.01**	0.03	0.05	**0.00**	0.03
Handicrafts (skills)	0.05	**0.07**	0.07	0.23	**0.30**	0.27

(*Source:* GOK (2006) pp. 222, 239.)
Sample Survey, Directorate of Economics and Statistics, Karnataka, 2004A).

It is evident from the Table 3 that the *dalits* (SCs/STs) percentages of level of education gender-wise as per the Karnataka Human development Report 2006 among the Scheduled Caste and Scheduled Tribes women are more illiterate as compare to men as well as less in percentages of education level in the state. More are less high proportion of *dalits* women educational level is below primary followed by primary and higher primary in the state. SCs women are over 5.4 per cent reach high school and 1.1 per cent PUC, 0.13 per cent Diploma, 0.22 per cent graduates, just 0.04 per cent was reaching PG studies and 0.02, 0.01, 0.07 per cent were Technical graduate, Technical Post-graduate, Handicrafts (skills) respectively.

In the other hand, the STs women are similar to SCs in case of illiterate position and also similar in case of high proportion of educational levels below primary followed by primary and higher primary. There are only 5.27 per cent of female were reach high school education and PUC 0.66 per cent, Diploma 0.12 per cent only 0.18 per cent were having graduate level education just 0.02 per cent ST women were post-graduates and 0.30 per cent having Handicrafts (skills). None of the STs female were performed as Technical graduate and Technical Post-graduate in the state. It shows that male are dominate in the educational level as comparing to female *dalit* population and SCs female were dominate in the overall education levels as comparing to STs female. Overall looking to education level of *dalits* in Karnataka as comparing to elementary level education the higher education level is very low in the state.

Student Strength in Degree Collages

According to Report of Taskforce on Higher Education government of Karnataka 2004 *dalits* female strength in degree collages is present in the Fig. 2. It is evident from the figure that there are more percentages of *dalit* female's strength that has dominated in government aided degree collages, whereas less in per cent both scheduled caste as well as scheduled tribes female in government degree collages during the years of 2002-03 to 2004-05 in the state. It is because of most of the government aided degree collages were located in rural areas, due to this reason the both SCs/STs *dalit* female were depending on government aided collages in the state.

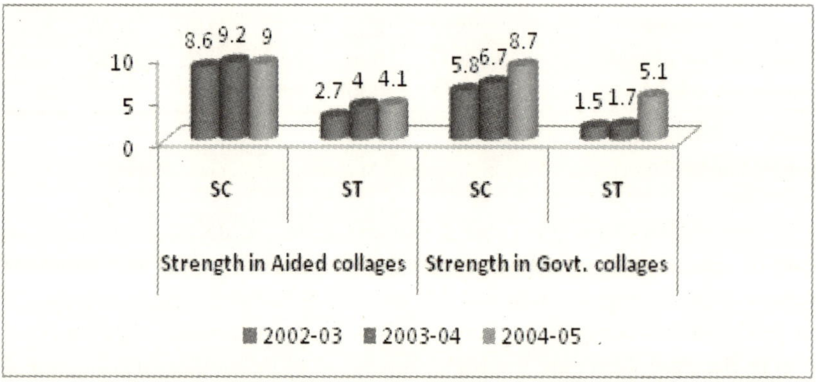

Fig. 2: *Dalits* Female Strength in Degree Government and Aided Collages in Karnataka ('000')2002-03 to 2004-05.

(*Sources:* GOK (2004) 'Report of the Taskforce on Higher Education').

In the other hand, the percentages of ST female as comparing to SCs is very less both government aided as well as the government collages in the state. Looking both strength of government and aided degree collages the *dalits* female participation strength has been increased during the years of 2002-03 to 2004-05 in the state.

Level of Higher Educational Status of *Dalit* Women

According to Status of Education in India National Report 2009, selected educational statistics report 2006-07 and Statistics of Higher Education and Technical Education 2009-10 report of Ministry of Human

Resources Development Bureau of Planning, the *dalits* women educational status of Karnataka has been clear in the table (see Table 4).

Table 4. *Dalits* Female Educational Status in Karnataka 2006-07 to 2009-10

Educational Levels	*SC*		*ST*	
	2006-07	*2009-10*	*2006-07*	*2009-10*
PhD /M.Phil	161	84	9	14
Post Graduate Courses	1282	1953	134	462
Under graduate Courses	29227	48863	9101	13465
Post School Diploma	15884	11714	1845	3533
Post Graduate Diploma	334	249	92	13
Grand Total	**46888**	**62863**	**11181**	**17487**

(*Sources:* GoI (2011) pp.12-18 and Selected Educational Statistics 2006-07, pp. 9-21).

It is evident from the table both SCs and STs female are participating all type of educational levels in the state. Whereas in case of proportion of women educational status is comparing to SCs female to STs females are less in number in the respected years in the state. The SCs female number of participation has increased in all levels of higher educational from 2006-07 to 2009-10 and it is also similar results in the STs number of female participation.

Government Higher Educational Programmes for *Dalits* Women

Dalits women significantly more per cent of the population are illiterate and below the poverty line, the significance of elementary education and higher education becomes even more important for socio-economic disparities have prevented the poor and marginalised, weaker sections of the society from pursuing education, because of the need to earn livelihood and due to lack of affordability. Therefore, after independence, the improvement of *dalits*, the founders of the Constitution of India provided for the reservation of seats in educational institutions for *dalit* students and the Constitutional provision also provided the framework for the proactive policies and Government programmes to provide financial assistance, hostels and learning resources for encouragement of dalits students.

Moreover, the Government of Karnataka has taken the necessary steps and efforts to be made providing reservations in Universities, Government colleges, private aided colleges and private unaided colleges rural as well as urban *taluk* head-quarters. The Department of Social Welfare, Government of Karnataka has made provisions for running hostels for *dalits* women students. In the same time Government of Karnataka to encourage *dalits* students to have access to higher education, apart from exclusively ensuring scholarships and free ships for the students (State and Government of India).

Apart from these steps, the universities have undertaken reservation in Ph.D. and M.Phil, admission, research scholarships for SC-ST students. Cash prizes to rank holders and toppers among the SC/ST students in the University examinations. Orientation programmes for SC/ST students about the opportunities in higher education and employment. Co-curricular activities for personality development (GOK. 2004). SC/ST book bank in colleges and universities. Appointment of teachers as student's welfare officers in colleges and universities. Extra board and lodging fund for students, apart from Government scholarships. Establishment of Dr. Ambedkar Hostels with the Department of Social Welfare. Establishment of Dr. Ambedkar Chairs and study centre's to undertake research and awareness programmes on social justice, empowerment and policies and programmes.

During the eleventh plan of UGC has been implemented some schemes for dalit higher educational encouragement which is Establishment of Equal Opportunity Cells (EOC) creation of SC-ST Cells in the universities, SC/ST amelioration fund to the University, Post-Doctoral Fellowships, Rajiv Gandhi National Fellowships, Post-Graduate Scholarships for professional courses students. Remedial Coaching schemes, Coaching classes for competitive examinations at universities, Construction of Womens Hostels for Colleges. This schemes and government programmes are significantly making efforts to creating further encouragement to *dalits* women for improvement of higher educational status in the state as well as in the country.

Financing of Higher Education

As far as central government is concerned, the share of higher education in its total expenditure on education was well over 40 per cent between 1960-61 and 1985-86, but it has been below 20 per cent after 2000-01. The share of higher education in the states' spending on higher education has, however, fluctuated between 9 and 12 per cent, reaching an average of 12.2 per cent during 1982-1992. The share of higher education in total education expenditure of both Central and State governments rise to 14.2 per cent during 1981-82 to 1991-92, but fell to 12.7 per cent during 1992-93 to 2003-04 (GOI. 2008). Thus, by all accounts, the relative priority given to higher education declined after 1992-93.

Expenditure on Higher Education in Karnataka

According to Economic survey of Karnataka 2012-13 the plan and non-plan expenditure on higher education in Karnataka has been presented in the Fig. 3. It is evident from the figure that plan expenditure lesser than that of non-plan expenditure during the years 2008-09 to 2012-13 in the state. The plan expenditure on education in the year of 2008-09 is 11008.81 lakhs were increased up to 2010-11 is 36110.78 lakhs and comedown in the year 2011-12 is 33678 lakhs and once again increased during the year of 2012-13 in the state.

(Rs. in Lakh)

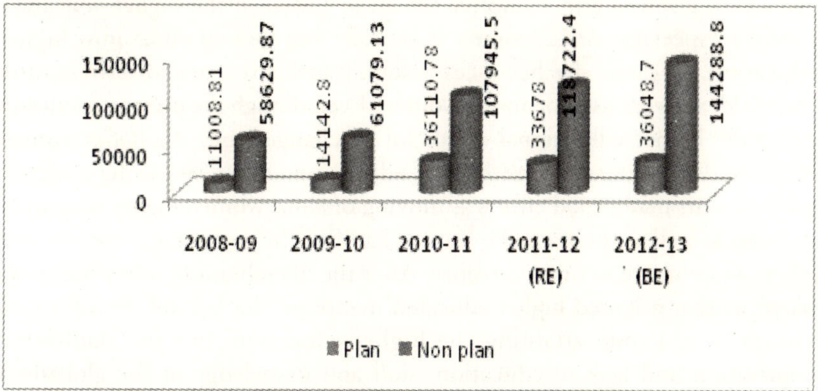

Fig. 3: Plan and Non-plan Expenditure on Higher Education in Karnataka

(*Sources:* GOK (2013) 'Economic Survey of Karnataka 2012-13' p. A-104).

Note: RE: Revised Estimate. BE: Budget Estimate.

In the other hand, the non-plan expenditure were tremendously increased 58629.87 to 144288.8 lakhs from 2008-09 to 2012-13 respectively in the state.

Expenditure for *Dalits* Women Higher Educational Encouragement

The Government of Karnataka has launched a number of schemes for the welfare of SC /ST students. The expenditure for the purpose of welfare was Rs 115.00 lakhs in first five year plan; the same was 28500 lakhs during 9th plan period. (It is projected to be Rs 60218.27 lakhs during 10th plan). The Department of Social Welfare, Government of Karnataka, is the agency for the implementation of welfare schemes. During 2003-04, the Department has taken up 34 state level and 31 district level programmes (plan). The Department also has 29 Special (non-plan) programmes during 2003-04. It had extended post metric scholarships to 93,583 students and merit scholarships to 2,888 students. There are 281 SC/ST hostels, accommodating 20,630 students. Apart from these hostels, it also sanctioned aid to 87 private hostels. And also the state government significant increase in the number of

Government colleges in rural areas, an increase in the enrollment of SC/ST students, especially women, in these Government colleges (GOK. 2004). This government financial support further improved *dalits* as well as *dalit* women educational status over a period of time in the state.

Conclusion

In the social hierarchy the lowest castes (*Dalits*) has at the bottom of the social, political and economic set up in India. In the higher education concern especially *dalits* women it is really big task to enter into higher education. Because she has faces systemic and structural discrimination threefold: as *dalits*, as poor and as women. Even though the present condition especially higher educational sector lot of changed and the *dalits* women have made progress in the higher education. After the independence governments made good efforts as moving of *dalits* women higher education in India as well as the state like Karnataka. But the percentages are very less when we compare to other category. After the liberalisation policy industry-based market-oriented higher educated manpower far behind the advanced groups in not only attaining the higher education, but the traditional deprivation and lack of education, skill and knowledge in the globalised context which make them for poor daiits women from higher education. Even though, government policies of reservations in education have played a remarkable role for *dalit* women, due to lack of identification of the really beneficiary who are poor in the community and lack of awareness? Therefore, government should be strict to maintain the proper implementation of reservation facilities for higher educational attainment of *dalits* poor women and train them modern higher education skills in free cost and create the awareness of higher educational government benefits. Than only progress will expect in the level of higher education with the help of protective policies like avoiding discrimination, otherwise this results will repeat same in the state as well as in the country.

References

- GOI (2008) '*Higher Education in India Issues related to Expansion, Inclusiveness, Quality and Finance*' MHRD, University Grant Commission, New Delhi. p. 17.
- GOI (2009) '*Status of Education in India National Report*' National University of Educational planning and administration for the department of MHRD, Government of India, New Delhi. p. 30.
- GOI (2011) '*Statistics of Higher and Technical Education 2007-08*'. MHRD Bureau of planning monitoring and statistics, New Delhi. p. B-8.
- GOI (2011) '*Statistics of Higher Education and Technical Education*

2009-10, Ministry of Human Resources Development Bureau of Planning, Monitoring and Statistics, Government of India, New Delhi,2011. pp. 12-18.

- GOI (2011) *"Provisional Population Total"* Census of India, Paper 2, Vol. 1 of 2011, Karnataka series 30. pp. 10, 34-35.
- GOK (2004) *'Report of the Task force on Higher Education'* Government of Karnataka Bangalore September 2004.
- GOK (2006): '*Karnataka Human Development Report 2005*' Published by Planning and Statistics Department, Government of Karnataka, pp. 212, 220, 222, 237, 239 and 335.
- GOK (2013) *'Economic Survey of Karnataka 2012-13'* Planning Programme Monitoring and Statistics Department, February 2013, Govt. of Karnataka, Appendix: 10.4, p. A-104.
- Khan Ajmal (2012) '*Higher Education and Social Mobility among Muslims and Dalits in India: A Comparative Perspective in the Globalised Times*' Islam and Muslim Societies, a Social Science Journal, Vol. 5, No. 2-2012. pp. 46-47.

10 New Policy Framework for Regulation of Higher Education in India: A Critical Evaluation of the Higher Education and Research Bill, 2011

Dr. V. Sudesh

Abstract

India started with a very low literacy rate of about 12 per cent in 1947 which has increased to 74 per cent today. Higher education rate in India, however, was placed much lower at 13.82 per cent according to 2001 census which increased to 14.48 per cent in 2003. According to World Bank, India's Education system is the third largest in the world. There are five hundred and fifty-four university level institutions and over thirty-two thousand colleges, both publicly and privately funded. There were about 13.6 Million Students pursuing higher education in 2009 according to UGC. Currently, there are many professional bodies like University Grants Commission, the All India Council for Technical Education and the National Council for Teacher Education, etc. which regulate the system of higher education in India.

Keeping in view of numerous concerns that have arisen with regard to the regulatory structure in various fields of knowledge in institutions of higher learning and the recommendation of various committees, the Ministry of Human Resource Development has proposed the Higher Education and Research Bill, 2011 (hereinafter the Bill).

The Bill calls for overall changes in the regulatory framework by providing for replacement of the University Grants Commission, the All India Council for Technical Education and the National Council for Teacher Education with the all encompassing NCHER which will have overall control over higher education and research. The specialised bodies, in the opinion of the framers, have led to fragmentation of knowledge with different regulatory agencies taking different views on matters of standards and promotion of higher education.

The proposal to introduce the Bill has generated a lot of controversy both in academic and political circles. The scholars/thinkers are divided over idea of establishment of an umbrella body as against the specialised bodies which may result in unmanageable complexities and concentration of power. Various other issues ranging from legislative competence of the Union legislature to challenges of co-ordination among different supplementary bodies and delay in the process of recognition, affiliation and management of academic standards etc. are seen as serious concerns. Owing to too many controversies the Bill has not seen the light of the day till date though originally introduced in 2011. In view of these developments, it is proposed in this paper to examine the different perspectives, address various issues and explore the possibility of agreements on key aspects and evolve consensus to clear the roadblocks in bringing necessary changes to the existing regulatory framework.

Introduction

The present higher education system is a legacy inherited by the Indian state from the British administrators. It is well-known that the Britisher's implanted the higher education system to serve their colonial needs. Some of the earliest Universities in India like the Universities of Bombay, Calcutta and Madras, all founded in 1857 were all exotic institutions established purely as examining bodies. In fact Lord Curzon made a very critical statement about the Indian university by observing that *"Here the university has no corporate existence in the same sense of the term (i.e., as in Oxford or Cambridge); and it is not a collection of bulidlings, it is scarcely even a site. It is a body that controls courses of study and sets examination papers to the pupils of affiliated colleges. They are not part of it. They are frequently not in the same city, sometimes not in the same province*".

However, post independence, with an independent constitution, the emphasis was on setting many state universities to cater to the higher education needs of the growing and vibrant young Indians. The turning point in our policy on higher education may said to be the process of globalisation of Indian economy initiated by the Government of India since the year 1990.

Globalisation meant that the state patronage for higher education has been slowly withdrawing. In order to introduce reforms in higher education in the wake of globalisation and to bring about uniformity in different sectors of education, the Ministry of Human Resource Development (MHRD) has introduced in the Rajya Sabha the Higher Education and Research Bill 2011 (THER). THER is the outcome of the recommendation of the Yashpal

Committee and National Knowledge Commission. Since its introduction the THER bill has been receiving criticism and has been subject of opposition from students, academia and several states.

Regulation of Higher Education Institutions: Current State

At present, higher education in India is regulated by University Grants Commission (UGC) and a plethora of distinct segregated bodies like All India Council of Technical Education (AICTE), Medical Council of India (MCI) and National Council of Teacher Education (NCTE), The Bar Council of Indi (BCI) etc.

UGC set up under UGC Act 1956 is responsible for co-ordination, determination, and maintenance of standards and release of grants to universities and research organisations.

AICTE has been established under the AICTE Act, 1987. The council is authorised to take all steps that are considered appropriate for ensuring coordinated and integrated development of technical education and for maintenance of standards.

MCI was set up by the Indian Medical Council Act, 1956, amended in 1993. The council is empowered to prescribe minimum standards for medical education required for granting recognised medical qualifications by universities or medical institutions in India. The Council is also responsible to give its recommendations to the Central Government for establishing new medical colleges, opening of new or higher courses of study and increase in admission capacity in any courses of study or training.

NCTE is a statutory body set up under the National Council for Teacher Education Act, 1993 to facilitate planned and coordinated development of the teacher education system in the country, and for regulation and proper maintenance of norms and standards in the teacher education system. The Council is empowered to grant recognition of institutions offering courses or training in teacher education.

The BCI (Bar Council of India) of India rules may prescribe for a class or category of person entitled to be enrolled as advocate. The BCI can also specify the conditions subject to which an advocate must have the right to practice and the circumstances under which a person must be deemed to practice as an advocate in a court.

These regulatory bodies prepare coordinated programs for development of higher education in each state. Thus, they seek to consolidate the efforts and investments of institutions of higher education with the state.

(i) Drawbacks

During the recent past there has been a rapid growth of privately funded institutions with the result that their governance has become an area of major concern. There are a number of private educational institutions which have mushroomed to cater to the demands of highly competitive knowledge economy. The management of these institutions has been influenced by the members of trust or society consisting of family members and their relatives. Since these institutions are wholly privately funded, there is an element of profit-making in the collection of admission fee, payment of salary to teachers and administrative staff. Some of this privately funded institution seeks political patronage which further interference in the fair administration of the institution. The attitude of the regulatory bodies with respect to grant of affiliation, recognition of course, enhancement of seats etc., have lead to fragmentation of knowledge and lack of co-ordination. Certain incidents relating to the conduct these regulatory bodies have established the fact that vested interests are controlling the higher education in an **archaic** fashion. The National Knowledge Commission has in its report underlined the over-regulation but under-governed nature of regulatory regime at present in India.

Compartmentalisation and fragmentation of knowledge systems, absence of innovation in learning methods, disconnect with society and too much emphasis of multiplicity of harmful entrance and qualifying tests are some of the concerns expressed even by the Yashpal Committee, which ultimately resulted the recommendation of setting up of National Commission for Higher Education and Research.

National Commission for Higher Education and Research (NCHER): A New Umbrella Body

It is proposed under the THER Bill 2011, that the NCHER as a statutory body will take over the powers and duties of the existing regulatory bodies. The proposed commission is to be assisted by a General Council, a Collegium, and a Board for Research, Promotion and Innovation. The constitution, powers and functions of the commission are clearly defined in the Bill itself. The members of the NCHER shall be appointed by the President of India on the recommendation of the Selection Committee consisting of the Prime Minister of India, the Speaker of the Lok Sabha, the leader of the opposition in Lok Sabha, the Minister in-charge of higher education and the minister in charge of medical education.

Objectives of NCHER

The primary objective of NCHER is to evolve norms and standards for various aspects of higher education including assessment and accreditation. This will be done by abolishing several of the regulating bodies dealing with academic norms for higher education. The NCHER in evolving new policies, procedures, norms and standards has to consult all States, Union Territories and other statutory regulating bodies.

Further the objectives of NCHER are:

- Providing for a comprehensive and integrated growth of higher education and research keeping in view of the global standards of educational and research practices.
- Bringing about greater co-ordination and integration in the planning and development of higher education including research.
- Facilitating determination, co-ordination, maintenance and continued enhancement of standards of higher education and research including university education, vocational, technical, professional and medical education and other than agricultural education.
- Renovating and rejuvenating higher education

Major Concerns over the Proposed Regulatory Body

(i) Compartmentalisation and Fragmentation of Knowledge

The idea of proposing a single regulatory body is to prevent compartmentalisation and fragmentation of knowledge existing in the present system of governance of higher education. However, as one reads the provisions of the Bill, it may be stated that the entire scheme of the Bill is so devised that present autonomy enjoyed by the various bodies including the state governments is being taken away to cater to the needs of the market economy. The all powerful NCHER may henceforth determine the education policy under mining the powers of even the parliament. The overriding provisions of the Bill will provide a single window system for entry of private investment in higher education thereby making *education* as a business venture.

The prevalent corruption in the existing system is proposed to be tackled by establishing an eight member commission whose objective is 'renovation and rejuvenation' of higher education. Concerns are raised on the absolute powers to be enjoyed by the regulatory body and the 'best brains' comprising the commission. Historical evidence suggests that absolutism will lead to corruption and given the caste and religious combination of the Indian society, there is no doubt that over period of time the NCHER will also face the same criticism as the present are facing.

(ii) Autonomy

Further provisions of the Bill make it clear that no university or institution can start conferring or awarding a degree unless it has been 'declared' to do so by the commission. In this regard the powers of the state legislatures to start new universities will be seriously eroded. Due to the centralisation of all aspects of higher education, there is a concern that there will be a serious interference to the powers and independence of the State legislature on the subject of education. The Commission will become an over dependent body on all aspects of higher education. The existing autonomy is bound to be lost. The Bill proposes to undermine the existing autonomy of the institutions by making it subservient to the needs of competitive global environment. The all powerful NCHER will discharge all functions and responsibilities hitherto being done by the academia and academic councils of the universities, thus eroding the autonomy of universities. Under the Bill, based on the report prepared by NCHER once in five years, the state government will be forced to implement the agenda set by the commission. The powers of the state governments have also been limited as they can appoint vice chancellors of their universities only when they satisfy the standards set by the commission.

(iii) Commercialisation

The Bill proposes to establish the higher education financial services corporation. The corporation will notify its memorandum and articles of association. It will disburse grants to higher education institutions in accordance with the regulations yet to be made. Thus corporate culture in funding of institutions of higher education is being developed. The provisions of the Bill in this regard are based on the assumption the economic capacity of the State is limited, resulting in resource crunch for education. If the Bill becomes the law, the constitutional principles of equality and social justice will be eroded by private agencies, who then will treat education as tradable commodity. The new principle under the Bill will be that education is an instrument for producing human resources for corporate needs and the market forces will determine the character of knowledge.

Conclusions

Nearly more than six decades after independence, the education system is on the door step of a major overhauling by the provision of the THER Bill 2011. Along with four other Bills, Indian higher education system is set witness path-breaking changes. The proposals are meant to provide a strong foundation to overcome the present aberrations and elevate the credibility of Indian higher educational qualifications among the community of nations.

However, for the proposed changes to be effective there is a need to address the concerns by seeking public approval. A nationwide debate involving all the stake holders in the academia needs to be organised. Anything done in haste with regard to the implementation of the Bill will have serious and irreversible consequence for public education in our country. In fact, the THER Bill 2011 addresses the critical issues raised by Lord Curzon in his observations (*supra*).

References

- The Higher Education and Research Bill, 2011.
- Dr. Vijender Sharma, "Towards Complete Control over Higher Education" available at vijendersharma.wordpress.com/(http:p.cpim.org/2012/0722_pd07222012_8.html) published in People's Democracy, Vol. XXXVI, No. 29, July 22, 2012.
- Quoted by Anandakrishna, Chairman, Board of Governors, IIT. Kanpur, at the foundation Day Lecture, NCTE, New Delhi. 17th Aug. 2010.
- The Foreign Educational Institutions Bill-2010, the Educational Tribunals Bill- 2010, the national Accreditation Bills-2010, the Prohibition of unfair practices Bill- 2010.

11 Issues in Quality Higher Education in India

Dr. Shriprasad H.

Abstract

India's higher education system is the world's third largest in terms of students, next to China and the United States. Unlike China, however, India has the advantage of English being the primary language of higher education and research. India educates approximately 11 per cent of its youth in higher education at present. In 2011, there are 227 government-recognised Universities in India. Out of them, 20 are central universities, 109 are deemed universities and 11 are Open Universities and rest are state universities. Most of these universities in India have affiliating colleges where undergraduate courses are being taught. There are many basic problems facing higher education in India today. These include inadequate infrastructure and facilities, large vacancies in faculty positions and poor faculty thereof, low student enrollment rate, outdated teaching methods, declining research standards, unmotivated students, overcrowded classrooms and widespread geographic, income, gender, and ethnic imbalances. Apart from concerns relating to deteriorating standards, there is reported exploitation of students by many private providers. Ensuring equitable access to quality higher education for students coming from poor families is a major challenge. Students from poor background are put to further disadvantage since they are not academically prepared to crack highly competitive entrance examinations that have bias towards urban elite and rich students having access to private tuitions and coaching. Education in basic sciences and subjects that are not market friendly has suffered. Research in higher education institutions is at its lowest ebb. There is an inadequate and diminishing financial support for higher education from the government and from society. Many colleges established in rural areas are non-viable, are under-enrolled and have extremely poor infrastructure and facilities with just a few teachers. There is an absence of a well-informed reform agenda for higher education in the country. A few efforts made now and then are not rooted in the new global realties based on competition and increased mobility of students and workforce teachers and their knowledge is very insufficient. Most of the teachers are making money with tuitions.

Industry and Academia connection, Innovative practices are necessary to ensure curriculum and skills in line with requirements. There is also a need to relate the fee structure to the student's capacity to pay for the cost. So that, students at lower economic levels can be given highly subsidised and fully subsidised education. Student-centred education and employment of dynamic methods of education will require from teachers new attitudes and new skills. Methods of teaching through lectures will have to subordinate to the methods personal consultation between teachers and pupils, and dynamic sessions of seminars and workshops. Partnership-PPP is most essential to bring in quality in the higher education system. Need-based Job-oriented Courses, Action Plan for Improving Quality-Stipends to Research Fellows are necessary to enhance the quality education.

Introduction

A nation advances in proportion to education and intelligence spread among the masses. Out of many factors of the development of a nation education occupies a prominent place. The Indian higher education system has witnessed a significant expansion in recent years, both in terms of number of institutions as well as the student enrollment. India has more than 400 universities and over 20,000 colleges of which almost half were set up in last decade. Student enrollment has crossed 12.9 million in 2007-08. The private sector has enthusiastically participated in the growth of the higher education system with about 63 per cent of the total higher education institutions being private unaided institutions. Though these are clearly positive trends, the Indian higher education system continues to demonstrate many structural shortcomings which in turn create challenges in meeting future expectations. Despite having more higher education institutions than any other country in the world, hardly having any feature of the leading institution of the world. At about 12 per cent of our GER is almost half of that of China, being much lower than the national average. Current key issues of higher education can be noted down as under.

1. Excellence

Lack of research activity and shortage of high quality faculty are the plaguing factor in higher education. While enrollment in higher education has grown six times in the last thirty years faculty strengthen has grown only by four times. State universities have 40 per cent and Central universities have 35 per cent of faculty shortage respectively. The student teacher ratio has stood at 26; it is just 15 in the developed countries. Academics in China authored five times more research papers than India in 2011. Besides the relative impact of citation for India is half of that of world average.

As of March 2010 only 32.3 per cent (159) of the total number of Indian Universities and 13.1 per cent (4094) of the colleges in the country had been accredited by the National Assessment and Accreditation Council (NAAC). As of March 2010, NAAC had rated 62 per cent of the universities and 90 per cent of the colleges as average (B) or below average (C) on specified quality parameters.

Industry reports and surveys indicate that the students qualifying from higher education institutes lacks the high quality skills required, which leads to employability issues. According to industry reports only 25 per cent of technical graduates and 10 per cent to 15 per cent of other graduates are considered employable by the IT/TIES industries. According to a survey conducted among 800 MBA students across different cities in India only 23 per cent were considered employable.

2. Equity

Equity is a major concern in higher education in India. There is wide disparity in terms of rural-urban, gender and communities. Access to higher education for all minority social groups is much below the national average. There is considerable gender disparity unfavouring the females. In 2007-08 the Gross Attendance Rate in urban areas was almost three times that in rural areas.

Gross Enrollment Ratio in Education is 15 per cent by 2011-12 (significantly less than the world average of 26 per cent). In addition there is wide disparity in enrollment figures across states, between urban and rural areas. GERs in rural India have increased from 3.95 per cent in 1983-84 to 7.51 per cent in 2004-05, while urban India GERs have increased from 17.68 per cent to 23.79 per cent. Though GER in rural India has increased, the gap between GERs in rural and urban areas has only widened. (FICCI Education Summit, 2009)

3. Poor Foundation

For quality output in higher education there is need for strong foundation in the elementary education. In most of the cases students who enter the higher education found to be lacking basic English, Mathematics and Logics. Without having strong base in these set of knowledge one cannot build a quality higher status of knowledge. Teachers at elementary and higher elementary shall be given handsome salary to attract good teachers in this sector. But in reality there is drastic difference in the pay structure between primary teachers and the rest. However, the work load, responsibility of primary teachers appears to be quiet more.

4. Poor Faculty Position

Large vacant faculty positions and poorly qualified faculty also dilute the quality of research done at higher education. A large section of the faculty in colleges and universities has not completed their PhDs. A survey conducted by UGC shows that a quarter of the faculty in Indian higher education institutions spends less than five hours per week on research. In fact just five per cent of the faculty spends more than 20 hours per week on research.

5. Selection of Faculty for Teaching

Teaching of a person no only depends on his knowledge, but also how he delivers his lecture in the class rooms. As per the UGC norms SLET/NET is the minimum eligibility criteria for the selection of a lecturer at the entry level. Indeed it is only a partial approach in deciding the quality of a teacher. It decides his/her knowledge on the subject not how they delivers his knowledge to the students who are the real beneficiaries. It is noted in most of the colleges/universities teachers are unable to deliver the knowledge in a good language. The communication skill/accent is of low quality. Merely offering a good salary may not attract quality teachers. The selection procedures should concentrate on the communication skill and how loves the profession.

6. Poor Quality Research Papers

In terms of research papers India lags behind in terms of both number and quality. India published about 180,000 research papers from 1994-2004, one fifteenth of the number of research papers published by the USA. Number of times a research paper is cited at is indicative of its quality. India's research papers were cited at an average of 3.2 times, indicating poor quality. India's rank was 119th out of 149 countries in terms of number of citations.

Patent filing in India is limited to a few institutes and is significantly lesser than that of leading international players. Though the number of patent filing is by Indian Institutes is increasing, the pace is slower than that of other Asian countries.

The number of doctoral students has kept pace with and the overall quality of doctoral studies in many institutes is questionable. The number of students pursuing PhD in ratio to the total student population in higher education has been declining. Less than one per cent of the total students enrolled in higher education are pursuing PhD.

A variety of problems are leading to the questionable quality of PhDs:

- There is no uniformity in quality control for the award of PhD has led to wide variations in time of award of the degree. At some universities PhDs are awarded within 18 months while to others it takes almost 3-5 years to complete.
- There is lack of quality guides for research. While those guiding doctoral research have little or no idea on the subject. This has further let to the deterioration of the quality of PhDs.
- Lack of clear-cut definition of PhD, especially so in social science research.
- Difficult to manage research due to heavy teaching schedule in degree colleges, there is no specific time has allotted for research purpose as such.

7. Status of Syllabus

The syllabi of many universities reveal the extent of academic backwardness. They spell out subjects which are neither job-oriented nor life oriented. When students enter the world they are surprised that there is hardly any job for the course they have studies. For a common man spending amount for education raises the question of return for it. Teachers in fact themselves wonder what is the application of the subjects that they teach.

8. Outlay for Education

Despite 2012-13 being the first year of Twelfth Five Year Plan, there seems to be hardly any focus on prioritising for education by the Union Government. The current total government spending (both state and Central) on education accounts for about 3.7 per cent of GDP (2009-10). While India's public expenditure on higher education as a percentage of GDP is comparable to other countries, it is extremely low when assessed on a per student basis. (Making the Indian higher education system future ready 2009)

The R&D expenditure spent on higher education in India is very low. In 2005-06 research at higher education accounted for a mere 4 per cent of the total national R&D expenditure.

9. Island of Excellence

There exists a complete disconnect between the higher education system and government funded research and development laboratory system, which is referred to as the 'two box disease. The research institutions funded by the government sector are established as 'island of excellence'. The staffs of this organisation have no obligation to teach at universities. The facilities and the infrastructure of these institutes are not shared with the higher education system. As such there is no cross pollination of ideas and practices between the research laboratories set up by the Indian government and the Indian higher education system. In comparison R&D centers internationally are co-located with major universities. The research staff engaged by these centers is actively involved in teaching post-graduate as well as under graduate students. Besides there is a lack enablers for Industry-Academic collaboration (FICC Higher education Summit 2009).

10. Regulatory Road Blocks

India's higher education system faces significant regulatory roadblocks. There are limited modes of entries and restriction for foreign players. Some of the government's faculty development initiatives and research/student funding programmes are only applicable for public institutions. Besides there are many conflict regulations for distance education. Also, there are multiplicity of regulators with overlapping roles. (GOI 2012 a).

Key Recommendations

- Encourage the private sector investment in education through development of innovative PPP models.
- Encouraging such environment that generate alternate sources of revenue by Higher Education Institutions.
- Strengthening higher education through a strong foundation of elementary education.
- Under each discipline developing such syllabus which is relevant, practical/market-oriented. Complete elimination of outdated, irrelevant.
- Need to strengthen NET/SLET exams by adding more lectureship oriented components.
- Creating an enabling environment in terms of lesser teaching hours for researchers both in colleges and universities, providing better budget and infrastructure.
- Increase the number and quality of doctoral students through regulating the eligibility for guideship, through the launch of

innovative programmes, provision of attractive fellowships and enhanced industry collaborations.

- Simplifying the regulatory framework by creating single independent body for regulating higher education system.

References

- GOI (2012 a) *'Higher Education in India: Twelfth Five Year Plan (2012-2017) and beyond'* FICCI Higher Education Summit 2012, Planning Commission Government of India.
- GOI (2012 b) ASHE Annual Status of Higher Education in States and UTs 2012 Planning Commission, Government of India.
- Higher Education Summit (2009) Making Indian Higher education system future ready 2009 FICCI *Higher Education Summit.*
- Mishra (2012) '*Higher Education: New Challenges and Emerging Roles'* Odisha Review, July 2012.

12 Economic Empowerment of Women and Inclusive Development Through Restructuring of Higher Education

Mr. Jnaneshwar Pai Maroor
Dr. Ashalatha K.
Dr. B. Vamana Baliga

Abstract

Education is a basic requirement and a fundamental right for the citizens of a free nation. It is also of increasing strategic importance in the new environment of knowledge and information technology-based globalised economy. Education plays a catalytic role in a country's socio-economic development and is one of the principal means available for a deeper and harmonious form of human development reducing poverty, ignorance and exclusion. Higher Education, which is a training ground for a professional, research-based, career-oriented future, must be respected as a potential instrument for bringing about social transformation and ensuring the success of democracy. Education must be provided to all categories of citizens by breaking down constraints and barriers. Once, students have completed primary and secondary education, attention must focus on increasing participation of men and women equally in the field of Higher Education.

The Indian National Policy of Education recognises this when it states 'wider women's access to vocational, technical and professional education at all levels, breaking gender stereotypes, will ensure better financial stability for women and lead to national development'. **Gender discrimination** has been a major obstacle in granting equal opportunity for women in Higher Education. It has been identified as a crucial category and deserves attention in the education-equality paradigm. Today, women's education has become an issue of debate within which it is now necessary to shift the focus from women's intellectual development to women's autonomy in decision-making, freedom of expression and control over resources. This research paper tries to explore answers to the following questions: (a) Will Higher Education institutions and their leaders respond to the required changes? (b) What measures are to be devised to exploit women's potential and promote their subsequent empowerment?

Introduction

Education is a basic requirement and a fundamental right for the citizens of a free nation. It is also of increasing strategic importance in the new environment of knowledge and information technology based globalised economy. Education plays a catalytic role in a country's socio-economic development and is one of the principal means available for a deeper and harmonious form of human development reducing poverty, ignorance and exclusion. Higher Education, which is a training ground for a professional, research-based, career-oriented future, must be respected as a potential instrument for bringing about social transformation and ensuring the success of democracy. Education must be provided to all categories of citizens by breaking down constraints and barriers. Once students have completed primary and secondary education, attention must focus on increasing participation of men and women equally in the field of Higher Education. The Indian National Policy of Education recognises this when it states 'Wider women's access to vocational, technical and professional education at all levels, breaking gender stereotypes, will ensure better financial stability for women and lead to national development'.

Women's Empowerment

Gender discrimination has been a major obstacle in granting equal opportunity for women in Higher Education. It has been identified as a crucial category and deserves attention in the education-equality paradigm. Today, women's education has become an issue of debate within which it is now necessary to shift the focus from women's intellectual development to women's autonomy in decision-making, freedom of expression and control over resources. Empowerment is the manifestation of a redistribution of power that challenges patriarchal ideology, transforming the institutions that reinforce or perpetuate gender discrimination. The parameters of empowerment have been identified as:

- Developing ability for critical thinking;
- Fostering decision-making and action through collective processes;
- Ensuring equal participation in developmental processes;
- Enhancing self-esteem and self confidence in women.

The time has arrived to realise the relevance, in a rapidly developing country like India, of education for leadership-building, especially for women—something which can be achieved only through higher education.

Concerns and Directions of Higher Education

Education is an end in itself as well as a means of realising other desirable ends. In our world of unpredictable social and technological changes, education has taken on a particular significance as a means of understanding and coping with such complexities. The knowledge explosion, supported by tools of information and communication technologies, is a driving force of the Indian economy, facilitating a better quality of life. Thus, Indian Higher Education needs to reorient itself to become more vibrant, competitive, meaningful and purposive. In the emerging global environment, women are required to develop a more skilled approach to cope with the rapid multiple changing environments. If Higher Education is to thrive within contemporary realities, then there needs to be a shift from exclusive reliance on a masculine-orientated curriculum to a more developed market-oriented content that is comprehensively suited to the entire population. Higher Education is a means to achieve vertical mobility which can counteract the deep divisions that exist in society.

Integration of Women in Development

Since access to education allows each person the opportunity to gain an understanding of self as well as of society and its resources, equal educational opportunities should be available to both men and women. Equality and social access became major goals of Higher Education in post-independence India. In 1948-49, the University Education Commission commented that colleges should be established that would serve both men and women simultaneously for Higher Education but, nonetheless, gender inequalities in access to Higher Education have continued through decades. The target of Higher Education is to provide women's access to vocational, technical, professional education and emergent technologies. Identification of skills and occupations suitable for women should be based on the employment potential of women.

Over the years, these four challenges have been faced by Higher Education:

1. To introduce more disciplines and diversity;
2. To satisfy the social demands for new options;
3. To remove gender barriers and role stereotyping;

4. To enable enrollment of women for purposes of productivity and of empowerment.

The questions that we need to explore are (a) Will Higher Education institutions and their leaders respond to the required changes? (b) What measures are to be devised to exploit women's potential and promote their subsequent empowerment?

Women in Higher Education

The first of the following tables reflects the gender status of literacy at high school completion. The remaining two provide gender disaggregated data on participation in Higher Education.

Table 1. Male-Female Literacy Rates in India—as Percentage of Population

Year	*Male*	*Female*	*Percentage*
1981	45.95	21.97	34.45
1991	53.45	28.46	41.42
2001	64.13	39.29	52.21
2011	75.85	51.16	65.38
2011 (Rural)	71.40	46.70	59.40
2011 (Urban)	86.70	73.20	80.30

(*Source:* Ministry of Human Resources. (2005-12). 3rd, 4th and 5th Educational Survey Government of India).

Table 2. Enrollments in Higher Education as Percentage of Total

Year	*Women*	*Men*
2006-07	32	68.9
2007-08	32.7	78.1
2008-09	33.2	66.8
2009-10	33.8	66.2
2010-11	34.1	65.9
2011-12	34.1	65.9

(*Source*: Ministry of Human Resources. (2005-12). 3rd, 4th and 5th Educational Survey Government of India).

Table 3. Enrollments of Women in University—by Faculty

Discipline	*Total Enrollment*	*Women Enrolled*	*Percengage of women to Total Enrollment*
Arts	1,591,012	687,069	43.2
Engg./Technology	181,604	11,263	6.2
Law	228,979	20,024	8.7
Commerce	848,804	173,957	20.5
Science	777,740	253,427	32.6
Medicine	142,125	45,054	31.7
Education	90,803	47,557	52.4

(*Source*: Ministry of Human Resources. (2005-12). 3rd, 4th and 5th Educational Survey Government of India).

Complicating an understanding of these data are widespread disparities in enrollment by regions, caste and tribe, nonetheless there is evidence that:

1. The percentage of women students in the Faculties of Law, Engineering and Technology is markedly low as compared to male enrolments.
2. Compared with nearly 22 per cent of female students overall, only a little over 14 per cent are enrolled in the Commerce Stream.
3. Fifty-four per cent of women are concentrated in Arts and Humanities, as against 40 per cent of males.

The Redefined View of Higher Education

Traditional concepts acknowledge Higher Education as an instrument of personal development, by expanding an individual's intellectual horizons, interests and potential for empowerment and a better quality of life. It has also been taken to be a vehicle of social engineering that conforms people to social values. Theodore Schultz and Mary Backer emphasised the role of Higher Education in the transformation of human beings to human capital. With the unveiling of economic reform policies, the role of Higher Education is being reinterpreted and redefined. Market-promoting policies are posing a challenge to Higher Education, and are being considered as both a driving force of economic development and the focal point of learning in a society. Higher Education has assumed responsibility for transmitting accumulated knowledge both cultural and scientific. The effect of innovation and technological progress will increasingly demand competencies and pose challenges requiring more dynamism in the course content. Higher Education needs to be reoriented to increase women's access to traditionally male dominated courses and equip them to take up entrepreneurial management and leadership roles and responsibilities.

The three specific needs related to women and Higher Education are:

- Recognition of women as an essential human resource base of each country;
- A strong commitment to equip women with the necessary range of managerial skills empowering them in their decision making role;
- Institution of a feminine leadership model-suited to the needs of social development across all sectors.

Role of Universities: Empowering Agents of Higher Education

To be effective agents of empowerment through Higher Education, universities need to give attention to:

- *Mass motivation and mobilisation*: Dissemination of information through newsletters and other social agencies;
- *Literacy Promotion*: Preparation of training packages and development of learning materials;
- *Techno-pedagogic inputs*: Preparation of data based information and transference of matter into technological display;
- *Network Culture*: Monitor activities related to women's studies and women's movements and recommend better implementation;
- *Women and Research*: The University Grants Commission has agreed to provide part-time research associate ships to 100 girls every year;
- *Special access for women*: Women students from scheduled caste and tribes in India will be eligible for Government schemes of scholarship, coaching assistance and remedial classes.

Globalisation and Challenges of the Century

Globalisation has effected changes in educational systems owing to the introduction and exercise of technological and communication developments. Twenty-first century India is facing a number of challenges in the field of education. Adjustment to social demands for new options in Higher Education and for removal of gender barriers is creating pressures on educational leaders. Higher Education is finding it difficult to meet the challenges of a knowledge explosion, uneven growth and inequities in policies. As a consequence, there is a fall in standards, posing a serious threat to India's national development. Strategies to provide management training and research work for women are the areas which Higher Education needs to address to promote women's advancement and empowerment. Evidence of a paradigm shift from pure industrialisation to information-based society is present. From a gender perspective, the questions that arise are:

(a) Does the curriculum content promote research and gender equality?

(b) Does the learning environment foster assertiveness and empowerment in girls?

(c) How will the education system foster sensitisation of members towards girls' Higher Education and empowerment?

(d) Will limited participation in humanities and social sciences help women and society?

(e) Will Higher Education help women's transition from emancipation to empowerment?

Diversity and Dynamism in the Higher Education Curriculum

A restructured curriculum envisaging skill-based, gender-sensitised schemes and guidance services facilitating employment is the responsibility of Higher Education.

To keep abreast of social conditions, social surveys need to check:

(a) The reasons responsible for the poor utilisation and participation in the technological advance by women? and

(b) What measures need to be implemented for women to make use of technological improvements?

The lack of educational and training facilities for studying science and the type of employment available for women holds them back. Thus, one of the thrust areas of Higher Education is to include technology studies to help women's development in research and employment. Academic policy designing must include the enrollment of more women to ensure 'Productivity Ethics'–to increase women's productivity is imperative. Mass communication is therefore becoming increasingly significant as a University course. In India, a technological course for women is prevalent whereby financial assistance is provided to initiate engineering and technology for a period of five years along with training women faculty managers and administrators. To invite participation of women in science and research, fellowships and projects are being given to women to seek affiliation in the local laboratories close to their residences. The funding of courses on science, vocational and professional degrees are made mandatory in women's colleges.

Technical Education and Human Resource Development

Being the apex of the educational pyramid, Higher Education takes responsibility for providing people with an ability to reflect on the critical, social, economic and cultural issues of a nation. Today, technical education is a significant component of Human Resource Development within which women must be included. Preparation of women as part of human capital, having a great potential for adding value to products and services, is being improved by modernisation, promoting institutions-industry interaction, and training women to meet the emerging challenges of science and technology. For this, women are being trained for research, consultancy management and implementation of policies to suit the needs of the industrial society. The UNESCO task-force commented 'without improved human capital, countries will inevitably fall behind and experience intellectual and economic marginalisation and isolation'. In cognisance of this, interdisciplinary and relevant curriculum content with an unbiased open door admission policy for women at par with men is the recent strategy of Higher Education.

Higher Education: Vocational Guidance and Self-employment for Women in India

In India, career guidance and counselling courses in women's colleges are responding to social and market demands with a healthy amalgam of tradition and modernity. With a view to controlling unemployment and increasing women's self-employment, counselling courses, career fairs, exhibitions and seminars are organised to disseminate information, cultivate the required skills and enable women to be productively employed to serve society with dignity. Women are developing self-confidence, self-esteem and a sense of financial security by way of skill cultivation to be entrepreneurs.

A recent shift to provide more options better suited to women is visible in Indian Higher Education. Courses such as Computer Science, Electronics, Information Technology, Home Science, Law and Governance, Molecular Medicine are significant inclusions in the curriculum. Courses in Fashion Designing, Clinical Nutrients and Dietetics, Nursing and Business Administration are also present. Personality development and spoken English classes, commercial and secretarial practice, Media careers, Public Relations, Advertising, Garment Technology, Hotel and Catering studies are offered as certified courses.

Unconventional course inclusions that exploit the creative potentialities of a candidate like event management, puppetry workshops, television script writing, and aviation law are now available to women students. The Indian

Business School, in liaison with Goldman Sachs of USA, has introduced a specialised MBA management degree for women. These new courses aim to provide women students with hands on training building competency to access jobs against competition. In addition to these, the Life Insurance Corporation of India conducts a three-month crash course to train those women who need financial assistance for healthy survival.

Strategies of Empowerment: Higher Education and the Indian Perspective

The Indian National Policy on Education (NPE) is a landmark in the approach to women's education when it proclaims: 'The Education System will play a positive interventionist role in the empowerment of women. It will foster the development of new values through redesigned curricula, textbooks, training and orientation of teachers, decision-makers and administrators'. The programme implementation explains women's empowerment through collective reflection and decision-making. For this Higher Education needs to take responsibility for:

- Cultivation of positive self-image and self-confidence;
- Developing capacity for critical thinking;
- Achieving group cohesion and fostering decision-making and action;
- Providing women's centers in Agricultural and Home Science Colleges;
- Providing Continuing Education and Correspondence Centers for organising vocational and literary skills;
- Revamping the Industrial Training Institutes in terms of diversification of trades and courses, keeping in view of the job potential, facilities for vocational counselling, imparting information about credit, banking, entrepreunal development and access to women's technical education;
- Providing Women's Studies Research centers to identify issues and areas and organise seminars and workshops to discuss and analyse women-related issues and disseminate information and encourage interaction with students and the general public through the media;
- Providing classes on legal literacy, programmes for women's socio–economic development delivered via media, adult education and information and training support;
- A more relevant and responsive curriculum catering to the cultural and occupational needs of women;

- Meeting the expenses of higher education for the rural, backward sections with incentives like scholarships;
- Meeting the requirement of achieving full integration of women within the democratic and developmental efforts of the country.

Curricular reform should include compulsory exposure to and engagement with different kinds of work in the form of summer jobs or internships, according to the circumstances and needs of the female population. Training must include manual and technical exposure to master operational techniques. Evaluation must project an analytical study to check the extent to which women have become capable of applying themselves and being problem solvers.

Gender-fair Education

The main challenge to women's Higher Education is to provide gender-fair education to all citizens. Gender-fair education involves an aggressive move away from emphasis on separate and complementary spheres for men and women and on gender-stereotyped careers to expanded options and outcomes. The attainment of equality, rights, and empowerment should not be accidental or simply an offshoot of a good education but rather an explicit, over-reaching goal in a healthy social environment.

Some major instruments of gender-fair education are:

- Affirmative action and quota systems, aggressive recruitment of female faculty and administrators, reform programmes to remove bias from curricula and teaching materials, gender sensitivity training for teachers and counsellors, a review of policies and procedures for possible gender bias, and active recruitment of women into non-traditional fields of study;
- Identification and projection of role models among faculty, administrators, and alumnae; systematic inclusion of women among speakers and resource persons;
- Gender studies programmes that are platforms for awareness generation in addition to offering courses that involve research, design and conduct training programmes and establish links with women's non-governmental organisations and activists for women's empowerment;
- The challenge of gender-fair women's Higher Education should be the transformation of women's lives as well as the transformation of society itself.

Impact of Higher Education in India: The Road to Comprehensive Development

The focused goal of Indian Higher Education is to acquire, generate, supplement and transmit knowledge that builds up leadership qualities. It has already to some extent empowered women to compete better, perform with precision and efficiency and achieve excellence in multi-tasking. Empowered women challenge men in their workplace and are visible in all forms of powerful corporate positions. Politically and economically women are now in a more commanding situation than fifty years ago. Indian women have made their presence felt in industry, technology, literature, art, banking, insurance and pharmaceutical centers. Educated women are also there in international business and administrative roles. Women's instinctive approach, which encompasses humane concerns, finds its reflection in their ability to combine justice with compassion, concern with rationality. Our vision of a better India free from multiple maladies can only be achieved when educated empowered women take up the mantle of responsibility and commit themselves to restructuring and advancing the development of India.

Conclusion

Higher Education of women plays a crucial role in releasing their energy and creativity and enabling them to meet the complex challenges of the present world. In acknowledging them as potential human resources, investment must be made in developing their capacity in terms of education, skill development, and technology transfers through technical training. Special emphasis needs to be given to Research and Development of appropriate scaled-down occupations in engaging women in large proportions. Illiteracy and cultural barriers need to be removed without any further delay. For women to make personal strides forward, a synergy of effort, concentration, planning and cohesive functioning at the Higher Education level will create possibilities of a different future. By extending women's visibility and their self-sustaining ability, Higher Education must train them to become leaders with decision-making capacities to achieve the best for themselves and the country.

References

- Korres, George M. (2010). *Women's Participation and Innovation – Activities in a Knowledge based Economy*. Delhi: The Women Press.
- Ministry of Human Resources. (2005-12). The 3rd, 4th and 5th Educational Survey Government of India.
- Gupta, Mukta. (2003). *Women and Educational Development*. Mumbai: Swarup and Son Publishers.

13 A Study on Personal Effectiveness of SC and ST Students in a Higher Education Institute

Dr. K.K. Murugan
Mr. C. Radha Krishnan

Introduction

The social stigma and the traditional society system made boundary to the SCs and STs. They cannot involve themselves in many welfare schemes of employment and they are still caught in the traditional whirlpool of occupations. The majority of rural SCs remain landless agricultural labourers and their children do not reach out the higher education. In case of STs there are no such social stigma like untouchables and slavery but they suffered under poverty and backwardness. The common character feature among SC and ST is educational reach out and employability even with their personality is much adequate to any civilised and developed people in the modern society. The lowest of the castes was the *shudras*, the servants and farmhands from the native tribes and conquered societies. They did not own their own land, but were forced to work for others. Beneath all castes was the group known as the "Untouchables"—delegated the worst jobs, like cleaning up the gutters, collecting garbage, cleaning up human waste, and burying the dead.

The untouchables call themselves *Dalit*, meaning "depressed". Until the late 1980s they were called *Harijan*, meaning "children of God". This title was given to them by Mahatma Gandhi who fought for Indian society to accept untouchables as equals. Legally, the government has banned the caste system, but in-reality it allows discrimination of the lower classes. The untouchables have few rights in society. In various parts of India, they are treated in different ways, but in most regions the attitude towards the untouchables is still harsh and strict. Some Indians have become more flexible in their caste system customs. In general, the urban people in India are less strict about the caste system than the rural. In cities one can see different caste people mingling with each other, while in some rural areas there is still discrimination based on castes. Most of the communities who were low in the caste hierarchy remain low in the social order even today including scheduled castes and tribes.

The present study was focused on Scheduled Caste and Scheduled Tribe students' academic achievement and their personality traits of personal effectiveness. The study was conducted in a higher education institute amongst SC and ST candidates with following objectives.

Objectives

1. Academic achievement of SC and ST students.
2. Comparison of academic excellence between SC and ST students.
3. Personal effectiveness of SC and ST students.

Hypotheses

Based on the above objectives, the following hypotheses formulated and tested.

1. There is no significant difference between SCs and STs with regard to academic achievement.
2. There is no significant difference between male SCs and female SCs in academic achievements.
3. There is no significant difference between SC and ST students with regard to personal effectiveness.

Methodology

With the above objectives, the present study was done by quantitative method and accordingly the student's achievement data of scholastic scores were collected from the academic records of respective college which is located in Mysore city. In addition to this, PE Scale–S (Personal Effectiveness Scale –Students) was administered to the selected students of SC and ST in order to understand their personal effectiveness at the college atmosphere.

Sample of the Study

Table 1. Sample of the Study

Course	*Boys*	*Girls*	*Total*
B.Sc.Ed/B.Sc	18	18	36

Table 2. Category of the Students

Category	*Boys*	*Girls*	*Total*
SC	10	10	36
ST	8	8	

Students of B.Sc.Ed in a higher education institute were chosen in which, thirty-six SC and ST students were included as samples of the study, while twenty candidates belong to Scheduled Caste from southern region of India including ten boys and ten girls. In other hand, eighteen tribal students of same college hail from southern region of India were included. Their age group was between 18 to 20 years.

Tools Used in the Study

PE Scale–S is meant to be used with students as it has been specially adapted for them. The tool was developed by Udai Pareek for Indian population with suitable norms and reliability. It gives the profile in terms of the following personality domains or behavioural patterns.

1. Self-disclosure
2. Openness to feedback
3. Perceptiveness

The tool contains 15 statements, five for each of the three aspects as mentioned above. Each domain consists of eight categories which indicate the personal effectiveness of the individual. Those eight categories are; Effective, Insensitive, Egocentric, Dogmatic, Secretive, Task-obsessed, Lonely, Empathic, and Ineffective

To fulfill and achieve the first and foremost objective of the present study, the academic performance data especially fourth semester marks of all the students who were included in the study was collected. The data as mentioned in the following tables.

Table 3. Performance in English

Category	*Average*	
	Boys	*Girls*
SC	61	62
ST	60	53

Table 4. Performance in Regional Language

Category	*Average*	
	Boys	*Girls*
SC	65	69
ST	62	68

Table 5: Performance in a Core/ Major Subject

Category	*Average*	
	Boys	*Girls*
SC	59	59.2
ST	49	55

Note: First Category refers to SC; Second Category refers to ST.

The high performance was observed in Regional Language comparatively with other subjects in case of all the students while the lowest average was performed in core subject by male students of first category with average of 59 per cent. The overall performance of first category in all three subjects was 62.5 per cent while second category students performed overall of 57.8 per cent which is lower to the first category. According to the second objective of the study, the statistical data reveals that first category students performed better than the counterpart of second category.

The third objective of the study was framed to understand the personality or behavioural pattern of the SC and ST learners at a higher education centre. As a part of Psychological assessment, an instrument called PE-Scale (Personality Effectiveness-Scale) was used and administered to all 36 students who were considered as samples of the study.

Table 6. Personality Domain of First Category Students

Sex	*Personality Pattern*			*Category of Behaviour*
	Self-disclosure	*Openness*	*Perceptiveness*	
Boys	Low	High	High	Secretive
Girls	Low	High	Low	Task-obsessed

Table 7. Personality Domain of Second Category Students

Sex	*Personality Pattern*			*Category of Behaviour*
	Self-disclosure	*Openness*	*Perceptiveness*	
Boys	High	Low	Low	Egocentric
Girls	Low	Low	High	Lonely Empathic

Self-disclosure can be defined as the intentional sharing of personal information about oneself. Disclosure may include sharing both high-risk and low-risk information as well as personal experiences, ideas and attitudes, feelings and values, past facts and life stories, and even future hopes, dreams, ambitions, and goals. In sharing information about yourself, you make choices about what to share and with whom to share it. Here, the data reveals that the first category students both boys and girls were low level in Self-disclosure pattern whereas in the second category of students, boys have showed high level while girls have showed low level.

Openness to experience is one of the domains which are used to describe human personality in the Five Factor Model. Openness involves active imagination, aesthetic sensitivity, attentiveness to inner feelings, preference for variety, and intellectual curiosity. A great deal of psychometric research has demonstrated that these qualities are statistically correlated. Thus, openness can be viewed as a global personality trait consisting of a set of specific traits, habits, and tendencies that cluster together. Here, the study reveals that First category students shown significantly high level while the second category students shown very low level in the openness of behavioural pattern.

Perceptiveness the ability to pick up verbal and non-verbal cues from others indicates perceptiveness. If a person is too conscious of others' feelings he/she may inhibit his interactions. Similarly, a person who is too conscious of his own limitations will tend not to take risks. Effective perceptiveness can be increased by checking others reactions to what is said. A person who does not do this (in other words, if he is not open), may become over concerned about the cues he receives. In this study, boys and girls of both categories have secured high level in perceptiveness while first category of girls and second category of boys have secured low level.

The test scores of **PE Scale-S** revealed that the fist category of male learners has been identified under the domain of **Secretive** personality and female learners have been identified under the domain of **Task-obsessed** personality. Similarly, the second category of male learners has been identified under the domain of **Egocentric** personality while female learners have been identified under the domain of **Lonely Empathic** personality.

Data Analysis

Keeping all the three hypotheses in mind, the statistical analysis such as Mean, Standard deviation, range and inferential techniques such as t-test and Anova for the purpose of comparison between boys' and girls' performance and accordingly the data interpretation was done.

Table 8. Comparison: SC and ST in English

Category	*N*	*Mean*	*SD*	*t-value*
SC	20	61.5	7.8	1.67
ST	16	56.5	8.7	

There is significant difference between first and second category of students in terms of academic performance in the English subject. So, the null hypothesis is rejected.

Table 9. Comparison: Boys and Girls of First Category Students in a Major Subject

Category	*Sex*	*N*	*Mean*	*SD*	*t-value*
SC	Boys	10	59	12.30	-0.044
	Girls	10	59.2	7.03	

There is no significant difference between boys and girls in terms of academic performance in a particular major subject what they achieved. The t-value is found to be -0.044 at 0.05 levels so the null hypothesis is accepted.

Table 10. Personal Effectiveness Among SC and ST Samples

Anova						
Source of Variation	*SS*	*df*	*MS*	*F*	*P-value*	*F crit*
Between Groups	2	2	1	0.07	0.93	4.25
Within Groups	124.25	9	13.8			
Total	126.25	11				

The personal effectiveness among the first and second category students was observed that both groups have no significant difference in the personality domain of self-disclosure, openness to feedback and perceptiveness. The calculated value is lesser than table value at 0.05 levels so the null hypothesis is accepted.

Conclusion

As per as this study is concerned every individual has his/her own potentiality irrespective of caste, tribe, religion, region and other social categories. This particular study on the personal effectiveness of SC and ST students at a higher education centre reveals that they are no way inferior or backward in all personality traits when we compare to upper groups. They are the basic instruments in the society to bring the economic, political, and social changes.

The personal effectiveness determines by various factors including the family background, socio-economic status, level of awareness, motivation, implementation of various government policies etc. If psycho social aspects are to be improved for the better effectiveness in the given task particularly college going students there must be Psychological Counselling services need to be rendered at every higher education centre. In the change of scenario which is taking place among the *'Y'* generation learners, the traditional way of education, occupation and placement need to be counselled to our deprived groups to compete with privileged one. The counselling service should be the objectives of personal, social, educational, vocational, marital, and other related issues. Even though, constitutional provision, reservation policy and other benefits are provided by the central and state governments but still various obstacles play spoilsport, so it has to be re-examined and verified at various levels. For example, opportunities are denied on the name of rigid criteria in various job selections by labelling simply not up to the mark. This is one of the serious concerns at state and union government level, there should not be any prejudice which affects the weaker section enters into mainstream.

References

- Parvathamma C. (1984). Scheduled Castes and Tribes: A Socio-economic Survey, Ashish Publication House, New Delhi.
- Pareek, Udai and Purohit, Surabhi (2011). Training Instrument in HRD and OD, Tata Mcgraw-Hill, New Delhi.
- Omprakash, S. (1989). Development of Weaker Sections: problems, Policies and Issues, Uppal Publishing House, New Delhi.
- Yadav, S.K and Jangira, M.K. (1985). Dynamics of Social Stagnation, Shree Publishing House, New Delhi.
- Vakil, A.K. (1985). Reservation Policy and Scheduled Castes in India, Ashish Publishing House, New Delhi.

14 Deemed Universities: A Partial Remedy to Indian Higher Education Ills—A Case Study of Christ University, Bangalore

Prof. Mallika Krishnaswami

Abstract

The distinct identity of a deemed university offering specialised courses that are otherwise not available in any of the state or private universities has been diluted to such an extent that now it means only professional courses like medical or engineering as they constitute a major portion of the existing deemed universities. Compartmentalisation of universities has not resulted in creating new benchmarks to engineer economic or intellectual growth. Many institutions have made their mark outside the state patronage but they have lost the disciplinary balance in the process. This is against the spirit of Indian knowledge tradition. Though there is an increase in the number of State and Central Universities in the past few years the GER did not show any corresponding increase. The Central Universities with their stringent admission policies and the elite private universities have just become islands of excellence. A multi-stream university takes care of all the civilisational, economic and cultural issues apart from offering sufficient scope for inter-disciplinary and trans-disciplinary studies. In the absence of any meaningful research and development wing in Indian higher education, it became imperative for the concerned private players to enrich and innovate, Indian higher education without making compromises on access, equity and relevance. Broad-based knowledge with a holistic approach was adopted by certain universities including deemed and private universities and Christ University is one among them. This paper attempts to trace the dialectics of higher education by redefining higher education using Christ University as a case study.

Introduction

Higher education in India has had a long innings since the setting up of the three Universities of Bombay, Calcutta and Madras in 1857. Meant to be modelled after the London University, the role of these Universities unfortunately stopped with being purely examining bodies. Little would the British have dreamt that their initiatives in establishing these centres of higher learning, carried on by spirited nationalists like Tagore, Pandit Mohan Malviya, Sir Syed Ahmed Khan and Maharishi Karve would, more than a hundred and fifty years later, remain just initiatives.

There is no authentic data to make any quantitative analysis of Indian Higher Education. The statistics change almost every month making it difficult to form any hypothesis. This is owing to the changes that a 'particular India' is undergoing. Innovations in transport and communication have made the 'growth jump' shortest in terms of 'time' and longest in terms of 'space'. Higher education is no exception to this 'growth jump'. Changes that have happened in the last ten years or less have overtaken the changes that occurred in the previous 50 years. There is a 47 times increase in the number of colleges (33 thousand), 35 times increase in the number of teachers (8 lakhs) and more than 100 times increase in the number of students (1.7 crores) in a span of 60 years (1950-2010). As against 30 universities in 1950, there are 634 universities now. Yet, the gross enrollment ratio has hardly reached significant levels, just about 15 per cent, that too because of the sheer volume of population and the demand for job-oriented courses. Despite phenomenal growth of engineering and management institutions, more than 50 per cent of the students still opt for arts and science courses. More than 75 per cent of the students stop their education at the graduate level.

The Role of the State in Higher Education

Countries across the world are cutting their grant for higher education and India is no exception. When the total allocation for education is around four per cent of the GNP, the share of the higher education is hardly one per cent.

In Karnataka, government grant is extended only to 652 colleges out of 2221 colleges making their contribution to only 29 per cent. Higher education gets only about 12 per cent of the total expenditure allocated for education with about 85 per cent going towards primary and secondary education. (*University Finance: A Study of Karnataka State Universities*, Karnataka Knowledge Commission, 2011).

Committees, Commissions and Beyond

The Radhakrishnan Commission (1948) recommended extensive reforms to resuscitate the ailing higher education system of the country. The biggest incentive for those, who prefers teaching as a career was the announcement of newer and better pay scales. Other facilities were also recommended in order to bring the profession on par with other professions. Merit was made the sole criteria for selection and promotion. Transfer from one grade to another was no longer automatic or on the basis of mere seniority of service.

The Kothari Commission (1966) is remembered for its strong recommendation of linking teaching with research. The Commission was convinced that research would always lead to economic development and it was a means to reach the level of developed countries.

It was the National Policy on Education (1986) which accorded the rightful status to the teachers and codified their role in society. It expected the Government and the communities to create conditions which would help motivate and inspire teachers on constructive and creative lines.

The recommendations of the National Knowledge Commission are termed too idealistic and unrealistic (J. Tilak, 2007), their focus on large scale privatisation of higher education will result only in putting the teachers at the mercy of unscrupulous managements.

The Yashpal Committee (2009) was clear about the role of universities in the national development. 'Since a university is based on the fundamental principle of transcendence and meeting of minds from diverse backgrounds, higher education was increasingly perceived as a means to overcome caste and class hierarchy, patriarchy and other cultural prejudices and also a source of new knowledge and skills, a space for creativity and innovations. Higher education, therefore, was and continues to be considered a national responsibility and the state has to make necessary provisions to realise its potentials'. (Yashpal, 2009)

Higher education in India is split into two broad categories: one for scholarly pursuits and the other for vocational purposes. Among the different kinds of universities are Central Universities, state universities and private universities. While the IITs, NITS and IIMs occupy the pride of place in the educational sector, colleges offering polytechnic and vocational courses can also be counted to contribute towards higher education. Pandit Jawaharlal Nehru's convocation address.

To the University of Allahabad in 1947 sums up the purpose of a University—"*A University stands for humanism, for tolerance, for reason, for the adventure of ideas and for the search of truth. It stands for the onward march of the human race towards even higher objectives. If the universities discharge their duties adequately, then it is well with the nation and the people.*"

In the contemporary world, higher education is constantly evolving. Unlike the traditional role of teaching and serving to advance knowledge, higher education in the modern age is expected to assume new functions. Some of them include seeking and cultivating new knowledge, interpreting old knowledge and beliefs in the light of new discoveries, providing the right kind of leadership, tapping the potential of youth, helping to cultivate the right moral and intellectual values, and striving to promote equality and social justice. But is it really so? The present scenario of higher education indicates otherwise. The unwieldy growth of the system, the lack of resources to sustain the rapid and relentless pace of its growth, the need to keep pace with the advancement of knowledge and technology, and provide relevant knowledge and technology to a developing society besides reservation policies, political pressure and an ineffective state control, and the picture is dismal. Macro level experiments seem to have failed due to lack of planning, lack of innovation and ineffective governance. In a country where accountability is not taken seriously enough, more stringent measures need to be adopted if higher education is to be accorded the status it deserves. This is where the role of private players assumes significance.

Access, equity and quality are the key areas that need to be addressed in higher education. As the first two, access and equity, are very much the concerns of the state, the state has a right to exercise control over the private institutions to have access and to maintain equity albeit only to a certain extent. One of the experiments in economic liberalisation, the Public-Private-Partnership (PPP) has succeeded in many spheres and it has happened in higher education as well. From the state controlled macro-level operations, it has moved to micro-level operations by committed private players with no-profit motif. Christ University, Bangalore is one such private institution which has realised its full potential, making use of the opportunities provided by the state and the public. This paper will focus on the strategy and methodology adopted by Christ University to achieve growth horizontally and vertically through quality measures, giving due representation to access and equity.

Started by an indigenous congregation, the Carmelites of Mary Immaculate (CMI), founded by Blessed Kuriokose Elias Chavara, an educationist and a social reformer of the nineteenth century, Christ College took off as an affiliated college under Bangalore University in July 1969. Granted Autonomy status on 7th October, 2004, it became the first college in South India to be reaccredited with A+ by the National Assessment and Accreditation Council (NAAC) in May 2005, and identified as an Institution with Potential for Excellence in June 2006. On 22nd July, 2008, Christ

College was declared as a Deemed to be University under Section 3 of the UGC Act, 1956, by the Ministry of Human Resources Development of the Union Government of India, a status it enjoys even today despite the litigation surrounding it.

With a few traditional courses in the early years, the change came about in the early nineties with the introduction of industry related and postgraduate courses which brought about the much needed newness to programmes. This was followed by the signing of the first MOUs in the late nineties which paved the way for the internationalisation of programmes. At the beginning of the twenty-first century, sweeping changes transformed the very colour of higher education.

The introduction of vocational as well as industry-oriented courses over the years has witnessed a steady growth. A glance at the statistics of the past thirteen years clearly shows in Fig. 1 that an institution that is committed to its cause can contribute significantly to higher education.

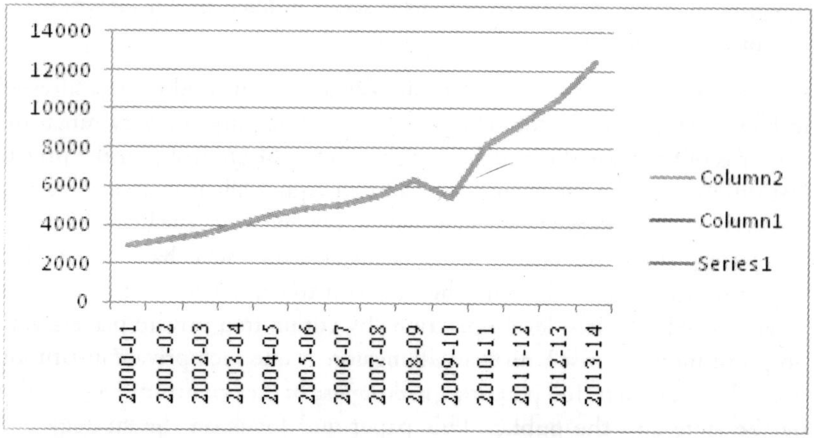

Fig. 1: Showing the Strength of Students over the Past Thirteen Years

Increase in the strength of the students is an indication of the faith reposed in the institution by parents and students alike. A notable point here is the all round growth of disciplines both in terms of teaching and research justifying the role of a university in a developing country. "The new type of university retained the aspirations of the old one to accommodate all the principal branches of study within its scope. When the first universities were set-up in India in the nineteenth century that was the implicit understanding although they themselves did not undertake much research or even teaching in their early phase of existence. New branches of science and scholarship began to emerge throughout the nineteenth century, and

Courses	*2000-01*	*2001-02*	*2002-03*	*2003-04*	*2004-05*	*2005-06*	*2006-07*	*2007-08*	*2008-09*	*2009-10*	*2010-11*	*2011-12*	*2012-13*	*2013-14*
B.Ed							70	57	34	71	72	98	99	98
BBA	60	68	75	57	59	56	82	85	185	282	387	399	416	526
BBM)	179	180	184	241	401	537	614	632	744	633	818	800	804	845
BCom	856	850	878	1023	1166	1257	1198	1271	1399	1216	1714	1983	2337	2577
BHM	148	147	159	215	227	234	229	225	224	127	226	192	195	213
Science	742	847	909	945	934	889	809	837	887	681	697	738	814	1087
Arts	665	802	921	1045	1100	1120	1095	1101	1197	950	1071	1183	1316	1486
LLB							79	163	235	259	478	637	825	1073
PG	314	308	367	449	623	805	940	1174	1454	1149	2453	2795	3076	3561
MPhil											103	101	90	92
PhD										33	24	56	37	
B.Tech										17	83	299	518	749
Int.B.Tech											53	68	112	137
Total	**2964**	**3202**	**3493**	**3975**	**4510**	**4898**	**5116**	**5545**	**6359**	**5478**	**8179**	**9349**	**10639**	**12444**
Int. Prog.														
BS	22	35	05											
ECE		05	10	05										
AMBA			09	28	36	31								
ABBA			09	08										
MATRM				02	02	01								
Total	**22**	**40**	**33**	**43**	**38**	**32**								

(Student statistics as on 16th July, 2013)

(*Source:* Int.Prog- International Programmes - BS-Bachelor of Science, AMBA and ABBA- Assumption University, MATRM- Masters in Tourism Management).

this tendency became accentuated in the twentieth. In the twenty-first century, it has become increasingly difficult for a university to cover every branch of knowledge and yet retain its coherence and unity as an institution unless the conditions are exceptionally favourable". (Béteille, 2009)

One characteristic feature of this growth is the composition of the students and the faculty which has moved from regional to national to international, which has ensured the academic anonymity necessary for a healthy exchange of ideas, generation and dissemination of knowledge devoid of any regional, religious, caste or linguistic bias. Another feature is the spurt in growth after 2009-10 due perhaps to the revival of interest in humanities, social sciences and pure sciences with engineering education becoming stagnant as more than 40 per cent of the seats went unfilled.

From a mere handful of faculty members in the early years, the university has today, a faculty strength of 453, comprising 268 men and 185 women, of whom only 43 belong to the grant in aid category. In addition there are 75 adjunct faculties. 127 of the faculty have PhD and 152, M Phil. From the non-teaching side there is a resource pool of 347 personnel, 198 men and 149 women, with 23 from the grant in aid category.

The curriculum is enriched through various programmes. Orientation towards the holistic education is done through well-structured training, seminars and conferences. Students are exposed to quality research both through internal publications and online knowledge resources. National Talent Promotion Programme, Scholar-in-Residence and Public lectures are other programmes included. ICT integration is introduced in a big way both at the administrative and academic spheres with LMS programmes. A well patronised staff community ensures professionalism and accountability. Timelines are maintained. A liberal mix of students from other parts of the country and the world gives the campus an international look, with many areas in the campus turned into 'knowledge spots'. Industry-academia partnership offers hands on experience to the students and a very healthy 'placement record' boosts the brand image of the university. Effective networking and proper co-ordination among all the University Centres makes the functioning of the University, a smooth affair.

All admissions to undergraduate and postgraduate courses are centralised with standardised admission procedures. The **Office of Admissions** organises and executes the selection process of eligible candidates for the respective programmes before the admissions are processed. Representation is given to the marginalised in accordance with the norms laid down by the government, as well as fee concessions to the needy, depending on the social, economic and family background of the student. In keeping with the vision of the institution, students with special needs are also admitted into various academic programmes, giving them thus, access to educational opportunities. Need-based fee concessions are made available to these students besides an environment conducive to their needs and an alternate pattern of evaluation for the differently abled. Scholarships are also given to the meritorious students and those excelling in co-curricular and extra-curricular programmes. Cross subsidisation of the fees collected from the self-financing, industry oriented courses makes it possible for the unaided faculty to be paid salaries on par with the UGC scales.

In charge of the conduct of mid semester and end semester exams through computer generated question papers, the Office of Examinations also handles the valuation of answer scripts (centralised for ESE), computing of marks, grades and issue of marks cards and degree certificates, all through a digitised process. Based on the credit system which allots three credits for 45 hours, four credits for 60 hours and two credits for practical /dissertation/ projects equivalent to one course, a student can earn 15-20 credits a semester. Every course is generally assessed with a 50 per cent weightage for continuous internal assessment which includes 5 per cent for attendance, and 50 per cent for the end semester examination.

All matters relating to data processing, attendance, computer systems, web page management, web security, reports, transcripts and question paper management are handled efficiently by the Information Processing and Management (IPM).

Operating under the Total Quality Management System (TQMS) which is in charge of ensuring the general organisational culture of the University, the Quality Review and Development Cell (QRDC) reviews the programmes and ensures quality in all spheres of academics while the Centre for Education Beyond Curriculum (CEDBEC) coordinates seminars and conferences at the regional, national and international level, networking to offer the best to the academic fraternity. Understanding the limitations of compartmentalised knowledge which is not adequate to meet the challenges of the world, the Holistic Education Development Cell (HED) makes up for this by designing the curriculum and imparting the necessary personal, interpersonal and societal skills for an all-round development of the students.

With access to five specialised centres spread over two campuses through KOHA, an open source Integrated Library System, the Christ University Library houses more than 2,50,000 books, 600 periodicals, 27 newspapers,

5000 CDs and DVDs. Keeping pace with technology, the libraries subscribe to 15 online databases with campus wide access and have more than 250 computer terminals to facilitate access to the digital world. The library goes beyond its traditional role of just offering books for reference, by organising programmes like Book Club where teachers and students across the university, introduce books and initiate discussions on various topics. The library also organises Book Mark, an event for the exhibition and sale of books by publishers and book sellers. Around 40 publishers including Oxford University Press, Cambridge University Press, Sage Publishers and Central Sahitya Akademi participate in the annual three-day event.

The Research Development Cell (RDC) headed by the Deans and monitored by the respective departments is intended to initiate, promote and facilitate research among faculty members by helping to identify research areas and providing financial assistance to undertake and publish research studies/minor projects. Currently, 12 projects have been completed in 2011-12, 30 on-going in 2012-13 and 24 new projects in 2013-14.

Conceptualised to facilitate a meaningful transition from acquiring knowledge towards an advanced stage of creation and application, in keeping with the transition from a teaching college to a teaching-cum-research University, the **Centre for Research** strives to promote the research culture and motivate scholars to cultivate an aptitude for intercultural and transnational communication in all disciplines. Of the 33 candidates registered for PhD in 2009-10, 16 have been awarded the Doctoral Degree. twenty four candidates registered in Fig. 2 shows in 2010-11, 56 in 2011-12 and 37 in 2012-13.

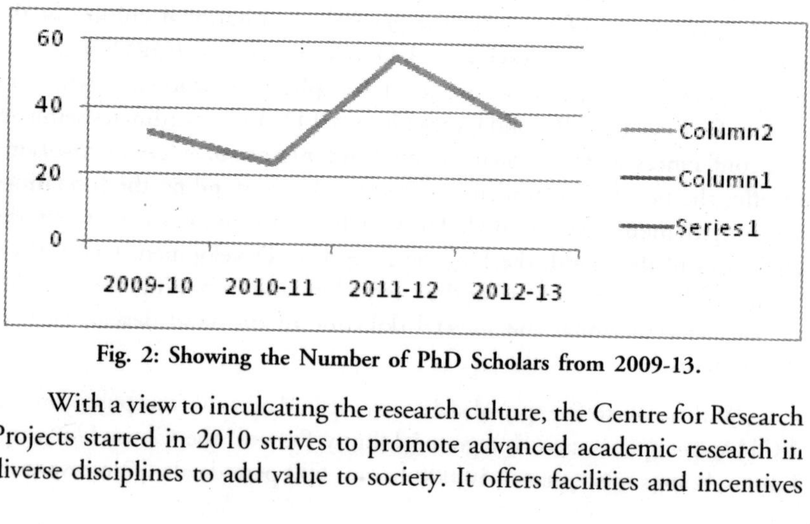

Fig. 2: Showing the Number of PhD Scholars from 2009-13.

With a view to inculcating the research culture, the Centre for Research Projects started in 2010 strives to promote advanced academic research in diverse disciplines to add value to society. It offers facilities and incentives for Major Research Projects, Monographs which involve an in-depth study on a specific subject or concept and Working Papers which give scope for further research. The projects undertaken are contemporary and applied, covering topics of emerging importance and significance in humanities, management, law, and pure sciences. The centre aids faculty members with a financial support of upto Rs 10 lakhs for research expenses and Rs 10,000 per month as research incentive for Major Research Projects (MRP) and upto Rs. 4.5 lakhs for research expenses and Rs. 3,500 per month as research incentive for Monographs. Currently the Centre has 39 on-going MRPs – 19 in 2010-13, 11 in 2011-14 and 12 in 2012-15. It has 16 Monographs – 1 in 2010, 6 in 2011 and 9 in 2012, besides 9 Working papers–1 in 2011 and 8 in 2012 as well as 6 independent projects.

MPhil programmes intended to initiate young scholars into research in various disciplines are coordinated by the respective departments. The overall statistics for the last five years are as shown in Fig. 3:-- 61 in 2009-10, 105 in 2010-11, 102 in 2011-12, 92 in 2012-13 and 95 in 2013-14.

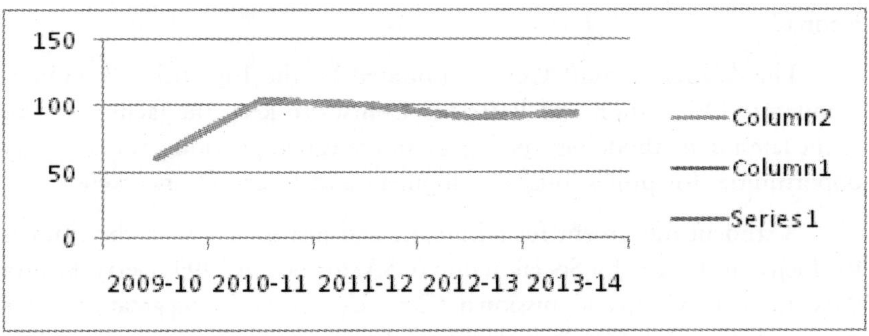

Fig. 3: Showing the Number of MPhil Scholars from 2009-14.

Going beyond traditional academic structures, the Centre for Social Research (CSR) functioning under the Department of Social Work provides more space for social research by conducting fundamental and policy-oriented research studies on social and cultural phenomena of contemporary relevance in interdisciplinary areas, through seminars, workshops and study programmes.

The Centre for Publications started in 2002 has two quarterly journals– Artha-Journal of Social Sciences and Mapana—Journal of Sciences and four biannual journals-Ushus-Journals of Business Management, Tatva—Journal of Philosophy, Atna-Journal of Tourism Studies and CULJ-Christ University Law Journal. Research and newspaper articles are also routed through this centre. Artha-Journal of Social Sciences (ISSN 0975-329X) is a quarterly that publishes articles in all the major branches of human sciences such as Political Science, Sociology, Social Work, Literature, Media, Psychology, Economics and Education. Mapana-Journal of Sciences (ISSN 0975-3303) is published every quarter with articles covering chemical, physical, biological and mathematical sciences. Ushus-Journal of Business Management (ISSN 0975-3311) is a quarterly journal that publishes articles in various Commerce and Management disciplines such as Human Resource, Finance, and Marketing. Atna-Journal of Tourism Studies (ISSN 0975-3281) is a specialised journal on research in tourism. Started in 2008, it is published bi-annually. Tattva-Journal of Philosophy (ISSN 0975-332X) also started in 2008, is a half-yearly journal which publishes research articles in philosophy. Christ University Law Journal (ISSN 2278-4322) is a new journal published since 2012, which gives a platform for the dissemination of scholarship in law and issues related to law. All articles published in the six journals are blind peer reviewed. The Christ University Kannada Sangha, with 227 publications to date, is renowned all over the country for its promotion of Kannada literature and literature of other languages in Kannada.

The Academic Staff College initiated by the Institution, conducts mandatory Orientation and Refresher Courses to keep the faculty abreast of the latest in methodology, pedagogy and research, providing the necessary opportunities for professional development and career advancement.

A student movement for a humane and just society with the child as the focus, the Centre for Social Action (CSA) formed in 1999 operationalises the core values, vision and mission of Christ University, laying great emphasis on social responsibility. It is committed to women empowerment, child development, vocational training for youth, livelihood promotion and water shed development programmes. Through the centre, students are exposed and sensitised to various social issues and involved in development projects undertaken by the Centre. Currently, CSA works with four urban slums, 35 villages in Bangalore Rural, 15 villages in Andhra Pradesh and 24 villages in Maharashtra. The child sponsorship programme undertaken by the students of the University fetches Rs 25 lakhs a year, enough to sponsor 600 children from the slums. To encourage students from rural areas to pursue higher education, 30 students are given full fee concession, free accommodation and a monthly allowance of Rs 1,300. Free lunch prepared by the students of the Hotel Management course caters to about 200 needy students. The Centre is committed to several unique sustainable practices which are not only environment-friendly but create a livelihood option for the underprivileged as well. A paper recycling unit on campus makes it possible to use recycled paper. Products made from recycled paper made by women from the low income group are sold through outlets. Through continuous awareness campaigns, proper segregation of waste generated on campus, is ensured. Food waste which is composted into manure is used for the vegetation on the campus. A water treatment plant treats about three lakh litres of water on a daily basis which is reused to water the gardens. Rain water harvesting is done on Kengeri campus. A Bio-gas plant that treats about 55 kg. of food waste everyday produces methane gas which serves for cooking purposes upto 4 to 5 hours a day.

With the services of eight full time professional counselors, clinical social workers and a medical practitioner, the Centre for Counselling and Health Services helps students cope with anxiety problems and facilitates the development of remedial systems for students whose inadequate motivational factors keep them away from achieving their potential. The objective of the Centre is to provide counselling and basic health services in an accessible and student focused environment, keeping in mind the needs of the student community. The Psycho-educative sessions organised by the Centre are intended to help students deal with issues concerning addictions, managing relationships, reproductive health and personal safety. These issues are also handled through the Peer Education System which comprises student volunteers. Students can also avail the services of a part time medical practitioner in campus.

Part of the Nine Karnataka Battalion, the **National Cadet Corps (NCC)** unit offers training for over 200 cadets under the Army wing for both boys and girls, which include training in drill, arms, map reading, weapons and parades of firing, social service and other adventure sports.

The **Centre for Placements and Career Guidance** focuses on the professional development of the students and trains them to get entry to the career of their choice by helping in career planning through career counselling and programmes on the different skills, corporate etiquette and working effectively in teams.

Recognising that theatre can be a powerful medium in imparting education, the Theatre in Education (TIE) offers a vibrant platform to nurture dramatics through the curriculum by providing assistance to all departments that require it.

The Student Welfare Office (SWO) coordinates all the extra-curricular activities of the University, providing a fair platform for all students to exhibit their talents and skills in literary, art and stage events and is also responsible for selecting the cultural ambassadors of the University.

A 50-member nominated student body with representatives from all the UG and PG programmes, constituted to promote quality in student life within and outside the University, the Student Council, is a support system for the holistic development of the students and acts as the link between the General Administration and the Departments.

Started in 2013, the Centre for Advanced Research and Training (CART) is conceived to be an active network cutting across different disciplines engaging in pure and applied research. The centre offers training in SAP, Basics and Advanced Courses in SPSS besides consultancy services and promotes societal development through knowledge dissemination.

The launching of the digital drive in 2013 is intended to make the faculty at Christ not only comfortable in the use of technology but also to reach out to a generation of 'natives of technology' who are well adjusted to the virtual world. Besides approving all content that go out in the form of print, the Centre for Concept Design (CCD) supports the departments in making high definition innovative audio and video learning resources, helps in developing *e*-learning certificate courses and aids in archieving research projects of the University in the digital format.

A reflection of the past, a representative of the present and a link to the future, Christ University Alumni Association strives to foster a legacy for all future generations of Christites through an environment that invites and presupposes post collegiate involvement and interaction at the local, regional and national level. Besides helping to enhance the growth of the University through its activities and providing a wide range of resources and opportunities, the association has also instituted scholarships for deserving students from all sections of society.

Moving beyond the boundaries, Christ University through the Office of International Affairs co-ordinates with international academic institutions and offers many twinning programs and credit transfers with some of the leading Universities abroad like Liverpool Hope University, Sheffield Hallam University, Swansea University and Birmingham City University, UK; IESEG School of Management, Lille Catholic University and Catholic University of Paris, France; Griffith University, Australia; Western Michigan University, Baldwin Wallace University, Berea, Ohio and Catholic University of America, USA; Norwegian University of Science and Technology, Norway; Duta Wacana Christian University, Indonesia; India Gateway Programme (IGP), University Studies Abroad Consortium (USAC) as well as MOUs with several South Korean Universities besides short International Programs. There are about 450 students from over 50 countries presently on the rolls of the institution.

Deanery of Humanities and Social Sciences

When an imbalance growth of disciplines was noticed across the country the Research and Development wing of the university devised means to attract students for Humanities and Social Sciences. This was made possible through certain innovative programmes. With nine undergraduate programmes, B.A in Theatre Studies being the latest to join the bandwagon, four Honours programs and thirteen postgraduate programs, the Deanery of Humanities and Social Sciences has the student strength of 2083 at the undergraduate level and about 931 at the postgraduate level. True to its commitment to quality, the Deanery plays a multi-faceted role by creating and maintaining a data bank modelled as Resource Centre, monitors the evaluation of students and faculty with the threes C's-constant thirst for knowledge, commitment to life-long learning and courage to embrace change; and aims at good behavioural and operational standards through professionalism and commitment.

The Information and Knowledge Network (IKN) an initiative of the Deanery of Humanities and Social Sciences, is an internal network whose *raison d'être* is the acquisition and dissemination of knowledge. An open forum, it encourages the faculty members to participate in it actively by sharing their thoughts, be it by way of a report of a seminar/conference attended, an interesting reading or discussions revolving around current issues in the relevant domains. Launched in June 2008, the portal has been receiving a good response with the academic year 2012-13 alone accounting for 112 reports. Into its sixth year, IKN promises to continue in the same vein, keeping alive the conversational traffic much required as the Academic Community forges ahead in its attempt to become a model in the field of Higher Education through academic intellectual entrepreneurship.

The purpose of the Scholar-in-Residence (SIR) program stretching from three days to a week with a minimum of seven sessions is to offer the students and faculty an interaction with reputed scholars in interdisciplinary areas, and expose them to the current exploratory fields of knowledge. Dr. N. Jayaram, Professors Girishwar Mishra and Dr. Susie Tharu are some of the scholars who visited the campus under the scheme. Special Guest Lectures (SGL) ranging between two and three days, with about five sessions are meant to serve the same end.

The National Talent Promotion Programme (NTPP) aims at promoting research culture among the young generation and initiating young, inquisitive minds into contemporary issues in the fields of Psychology, Sociology and Economics at the National level. Entries from colleges across the country are received and the shortlisted papers are presented before an audience of over 1000, comprising students and teachers. The papers are adjudicated by a panel of eminent scholars from respective fields. An amount of over Rs one lakhs is spent on each competition.

The monthly Faculty Development Programme (FDP) of the Deanery called Christ University Forum of Humanities and Social Sciences (CUFOHSS) provides an opportunity for all the teachers of humanities and social sciences to meet at least once a month to embark upon a meaningful venture, both in teaching and research domains. The programme is also to make the teachers aware of the existence of certain key concepts from the disciplines other than theirs and to initiate them into possible collaborations both within and outside the department. The forum primarily serves as a catalysing agent in a cordial atmosphere personally and academically. The purpose of the programme is to see the entire deanery of humanities and social sciences as one single unit in the sense that any issue that is discussed has some relevance to an issue in some other discipline and making contact with the person engaged in the study will enrich the study. The sixty minute programme is split into two parts of 30 minutes each, 20 minutes presentation followed by a ten minute discussion. While the first part called Knowledge Sharing, is a collective presentation from any of the departments, of a book, an author or a concept, the second called Research Concerns is an individual research presentation.

Extending the research benefits of CUFOHSS to the student community of the Deanery, the Student Consortium for Academic Negotiations (SCAN) is intended to encourage students to engage in research production and public defense of academic ideas. Coordinated by faculty members and comprising a select enthusiastic and dedicated community of young scholars, it is an initiative of the students, by the students and for the students, to offer a space beyond the classroom for interdisciplinary, transdisciplinary areas and general awareness relating to global concerns.

Conclusion

Adhering to all the regulations of the University Grants Commission, Christ University follows a systemic approach in its day to day administration. Showing transparency in admissions and fee structure, it offers excellent working conditions and an attractive salary package on par with the UGC pay scales. Providing opportunities for continuing education and for undertaking projects, it exposes the faculty to a network of organisations and scholars in the process of organising academic programmes. Faculty development programmes including the monthly faculty seminars go a long way in equipping the faculty and interacting with faculty from other streams. What could otherwise take months, if not years, to achieve in other universities, is possible in weeks at Christ University. Commitment, dedication and a spirit of oneness are the keywords of all its major endeavours.

Economic globalisation has created 'islands of prosperity'. It has also created 'islands of excellence' and Christ University may be one among them. It is a standing example of public-private partnership providing achievable results. Constantly trying to change the well-entrenched mindset of an anti-change national character of Indians, it involves all the major share holders in higher education in a continuing dialogue for a change. This is a small minority but it was always a minority group, a thinking one that is, that changed destinies.

The micro level experiment will succeed only with an effective regulatory system by the authorities. The limitations of this experiment would also include failure to address the major issues involving national interests. These 'islands of excellence' can be merged to form an 'Ivy league' to address quality issues collectively.

References

- Béteille, André. (2009). The Third Foundation Day Lecture of the National University of Educational Planning and Administration (NUEPA) on *Universities in the Twenty-first Century*. Delhi.
- Kaul, Sanat. (2006). *Higher Education in India: Seizing the Opportunity*, ICRIER, New Delhi.
- Yashpal Committee Report. (2009) *The Committee to Advise on Renovation and Rejuvenation of Higher Education,* New Delhi.
- Tilak, Jandhyala B.G. February 24, (2007). *Knowledge Commission and Higher Education,*Economic and Political Weekly.
- Christ University Handbook and Staff Handbook 2013-14.
- Centres of Christ University, Bangalore.

Web Reading:

- http://www.css.ac.in/download/ip_desai_lecture/IPD-10_Suma%20Chitnis.pdf **accessed 5/7/13.**
- http://www.ey.com/Publication/vwLUAssets/Higher_Education_in_India/$File/EY-FICC_Higher_Education_Report_Nov12.pdfaccessed 19/7/13.

15 Gender Equality in Higher Education: A Case Study of Mysore University

Dr. Indira. M.
Prabhavathi P.O.
Basava Raja

Introduction

In recent years, there has been a focussed attention on trying to understand institutions and organisations from a gender perspective. The capacity of institutions to incorporate a gender equality perspective is a fundamental cornerstone of a mainstreaming strategy. The emphasis on mainstreaming gender perspectives in all sectors reflects recognition that the interests and needs of women must be systematically pursued in the formulation and execution of all policies and programmers, if institutions and organisations are to serve women as well as men appropriately, and to fulfill commitments to reducing inequalities between women and men, the gender perspective must become part of the process of formulating, implementing and evaluating policies and programmers.

Despite government policy of positive discrimination, very few women are reaching the levels of higher education. Though there is some improvement in the enrollment of girls in higher education, still there is a gender gap between men and women among the faculty in higher education. The present study makes an attempt to understand the gender gap in the University of Mysore by taking up gender audit. This is a situational analysis to assess the gender bias in the University.

Background of Gender Audit

About 20 years ago, in 1983, the Australian parliament made a precedent setting decision at the initiative of "femocrats" from the labour party, the political party then in power, a resolution was passed to look into how the national budget of Australia was likely to affect the status of women in the country. A year later that resolution was implemented when the national budget was presented to the Australian parliament together with the first women's budget statement. The statement was an extensive report detailing the implications of the proposed budget for Australian women and girls.

The gender audit process was developed by commission on the advancement of women; it was designed to be used by NGO's and private voluntary organisations (PVOS). It means to systematically take stock of and address the status of gender equality in all aspects of their operations and work.

Gender Audit

A gender audit is a self-assessment methodology, which focusses on improving the performance of an organisation with regards to the promotion of gender equality and women's empowerment. It is a skill enhancement tool of self-reflection in people's daily lives and working environment in relation to the promotion of gender equality a gender audit is a participatory process aimed at measuring the level of gender input/incorporation, language, sensitivity and awareness in organisation. It is also learning process through sharing of experiences information, knowledge and best practices. A Gender audit is one aspect of what is referred to as "mainstreaming" analysing main stream Public Policy, including legislation, regulations, allocations, and social projects, from the point of view of their effect on the status of women in a given society, gender audits analyse the income and expenditures of the government from a gender perspective, the basic assumption of gender audits is that public policy impacts differently on men and women. The variance stems form the different roles of women and men in the family and from the lower economic status of women. The purposes of gender audits is:

1. To lead to changes in Public Policy that contributes to an increase in gender equality.
2. Profile the representation and participation of women in the organisation.
3. Identify the developmental dimensions that provide opportunities for advancement of women in an organisation, and
4. Identify the structural barriers that impede their growth.

The process of gender audit is anchored within a framework of gender equity and justice, an audit of the outcome of initiatives taken for promotion of women's development in an organisation and for according visibility, and significance to gender concerns can be a pointer to how women resources are being utilised in that organisation.

The earlier studies have looked at gender issues at the institutional level focussing at macro-level. There are very few studies which made a micro-level study. The present study is an attempt to understand the gender factor in the University of Mysore which is one of the oldest universities of the country. The focus is on the gender differences in admissions, scholarships, PhDs awarded and faculty at different levels.

Objectives

The Important objectives of this paper are:

- To examine women's participation in higher education.
- To analyse the trends in participation of girls in higher education.
- To analyse gender factor in the university of Mysore.

Methodology

This study is based on unpublished data of university of Mysore. Data about the enrollment in PG courses, performance of boys and girls, gender factor among faculty was collected from the various records of the administrative office and individual departments of the University of Mysore.

Secondary data were collected from books, journals, articles, internet and other secondary sources after the collection of the data the available data has been presented in a tabular form.

Area of the Study

The University of Mysore is one of the public universities in India. It was founded by the then Maharaja of Mysore. His highness Sri Krishnaraja Wodeyar IV and his Dewan the renowned engineer states man Sr. M. Visvesvarayya on July 27th 1916, the Maharaja of Mysore become its first chancellor. The university of Mysore became the first university outside the domain of the English administration in India the sixth university in India as a whole and the first ever university in Karnataka at the University of Mysore founding. The entire princely state of Mysore came under its jurisdiction, now this is confined to the Mysore, Mandya, Hassan and Chamarajanagar districts. The university has 43 postgraduate departments that together offer about 55 regular academic programmes to 3,500 students it also runs a number of employment oriented diploma courses and certificate programmes with a student strength of 4,200 at present.

Trends in Enrollment of Girls in Higher Education in India

Due to several measures to encourage the education of girls at different stages there is a considerable increase in the number of girls in higher education.

Percentage share of girls' enrollment to total enrollment at different stages of higher education during 2003-04 to 2008-09 is presented in the Table 1.

Table 1. Percentage Share of Girls' Enrollment to Total at Different Stages of Higher Education during 2003-04 to 2008-09

Stages	*2003-04*	*2004-05*	*2005-06*	*2006-07*	*2007-08*	*2008-09*
Diploma/Certificate	32.70	35.80	33.74	33.80	40.08	40.87
Graduate	37.50	40.90	39.93	40.10	40.41	41.50
Post Graduate	39.50	42.20	42.04	42.04	42.18	40.39
Research	36.10	38.90	37.95	39.04	39.98	40.01

(*Source:* Various issues of UGC Annual Reports, New Delhi).

There has been a substantive increase in the number of separate colleges for women. There were 1902 in 2006-07 as compared to 950 in 1991-92. Despite this the percentage of girls has not increased substantially. For example the percentage of girls in post graduate courses has remained at 40 per cent between 2003-04 and 2008-09. However, there is some marginal increase in the case of girls in research. But there is a considerable increase in the percentage of girls in Diploma/Certificate and Graduation courses. The percentage increased from 32.70 to 40.87. Similarly, the share of girls in graduation increased from 37.50 to 41.50 per cent.

Faculty-wise Distribution of Women Students Enrolled in Higher Education

Traditionally there is a gender segregation of faculties at higher education. More girls were enrolled in arts and commerce subjects and less were observed in science, engineering, and law. However, there is a change in the situation with the development information technology and more girls are entering into engineering subjects. Trends in Faculty-wise distribution of girl students is presented in the table below.

From Table 2 it is clear that more women who are taking up higher education opt for arts and humanities (above 51 per cent) of those in higher education during 1997-98 to 2007-08 to science, commerce and

Table 2. Faculty-wise Distribution of Women Students as a Proportion of Total Women Enrolled in Higher Education in India

Faculty	*97-98*	*98-99*	*99-00*	*00-01*	*01-02*	*02-03*	*03-04*	*05-06*	*06-07*	*07-08*
Arts	54.4	54.4	54.4	54.4	54.3	51.1	51.79	51.13	51.01	51.07
Science	20.1	20.1	19.2	19.2	19	19	19.9	19.94	20.22	20.08
Commerce//Mgt	14.1	14.1	13.6	13.6	13.9	16.7	16.56	16.48	16.43	16.45
Education	3.9	3.9	3.4	3.4	3.2	2.4	1.69	1.81	1.9	1.86
Engg/Tech	1.2	1.2	2.1	2.1	2.3	3.6	3.75	4.17	4.13	4.15
Medicine	-	-	3.3	3.3	3.3	3.9	3.5	3.63	3.63	3.63
Agriculture	-	-	0.6	0.6	0.6	0.4	0.26	0.25	0.25	0.25
Veterinary Science	-	-	0.1	0.1	0.1	0.1	0.09	0.08	0.08	0.08
Law	1.8	1.8	2	2.	2	0.8	1.62	1.68	1.56	1.62
Others	4.5	4.5	1.3	1.3	1.3	1	0.84	0.83	0.79	0.81
Total	100	100	100	100	100	100	100	100	100	100

(*Source:* Various issues of UGC Annual Reports).

management courses are the 2nd and 3rd most popular options (19-21 per cent) and 13-17 per cent) while courses in law, medicine, engineering and technology etc. come a distant least choice (less than 51 per cent), as far as enrollment of women in higher education is concerned. However, there is a distinct change in the trend. There is an increase in percentage of women in engineering courses. While the share of girls in Engineering and Technology was 1.2 per cent during 97-98 it increased to 4.18 per cent by 2007-08.

Table 3. Share of SC and ST among the Girls Enrolled in Higher Education

Year	*PG & Ph D*	*Graduation*	*BE*	*BEd*	*MBBS*	*Total*
(A) Share of Enrollment of SCs (per cent)						
2006-07	8.7	8.7	5.7	8.4	8.6	8.5
2007-08	10.1	9.6	8.7	12.3	9.6	9.7
2008-09	11.4	12	6.7	13.9	13.2	11.3
(B) Share of Enrollment of STs (per cent)						
2006-07	1.8	2.2	1.1	2.3	0.7	2.1
2007-08	2.6	3	3.3	5.3	3.6	3
2008-09	2.7	3.7	3.2	5	4.9	3.6

(*Source:* Gol 2008-09).

Trends in the participation of SCs and STs in different courses during 2004-05 to 2008-09 is presented in table. The share of SC enrollment total enrollment has increased to 11.3 per cent in 2007-08. STs constituted only 2.1. per cent in the total enrollment in higher education in 2004 which went up to 3.6 per cent in 2008 the participation of girls in higher education is relatively low in Rajasthan, Orissa, West Bengal, Madya Pradesh, Uttar Pradesh, Jharkhand, Chattisgarh and Bihar, the tradition although the participation rates of girls, SCs and STs have been increasing the years, social and gender disparities still remain subjects of major concern.

Gender Gap in Enrollment in Mysore University

Gender gap in enrollment to all disciplines from 200-01 to 2008-09 is presented in the table below.

According to the table the percentage of SC boys students enrollment in Mysore University during the year 2000-01 was registered 74.70 per cent and in the year 2003-04 it declined to 66.62 per cent. But now in the year 2008-09 it increased to 69.23 per cent.

During the year 2000-01 the enrollment of SC girls students was 25.30 per cent and it increased to 33.38 per cent in the year 2003-04. Between the

Table 4. Gender Gap in Enrollment in Mysore University

	Scheduled Caste				Schedule Tribe				Others			
Year	*M*	%	*F*	%	*M*	%	*F*	%	*M*	%	*F*	%
2000-01	496	74.70	168	25.30	70	76.09	22	23.91	1308	56.72	998	43.28
2001-02	539	74.04	189	25.96	80	77.67	23	22.33	1188	52.75	1064	47.25
2002-03	485	68.89	219	31.11	65	69.89	28	30.11	1095	47.94	1189	52.06
2003-04	459	66.62	230	33.38	73	71.57	29	28.43	1060	46.47	1221	53.53
2004-05	506	70.97	207	29.03	66	68.75	30	31.25	1198	51.70	1119	48.30
2005-06	444	66.67	222	33.33	63	60.00	42	40.00	1037	44.05	1317	55.95
2006-07	588	67.12	288	32.88	98	62.03	60	37.97	1475	46.37	1706	53.63
2007-08	552	67.48	266	32.52	104	63.80	59	36.20	1201	46.99	1355	53.01
2008-09	495	69.23	220	30.77	117	61.26	74	38.74	1206	46.69	1377	53.31

(*Source :* Various Annual Reports of University of Mysore).

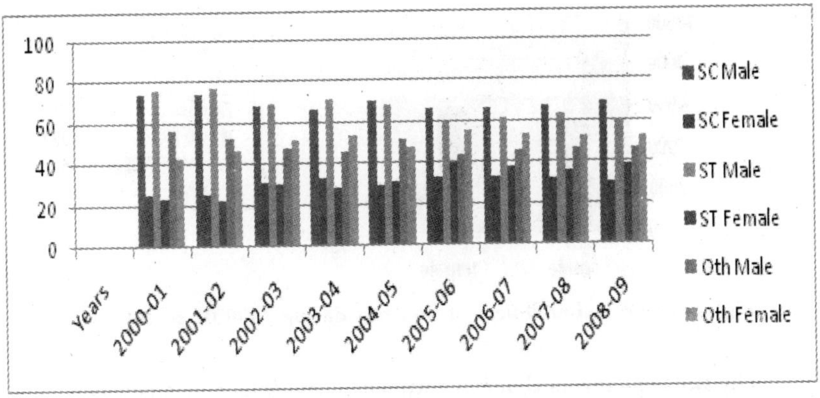

Fig. 1. Trend in Gender Gap in Enrollment in Mysore University.

year 2001-01 to 2007-08 it increased from 25.30 to 30.77. During 2005-06 the share of girls went up to 33.00 per cent.

Coming to ST boys students during the year 2000-01 the boys enrolment was 76.00 per cent. It decreased to 61.26 per cent in the year 2008-09. The enrollment of ST girls during the year 2000-01 it shows that 23.91 per cent and it has been increased to 40.00 per cent during the year 2005-06. Compared to 2005-06 year it is decreased to 38.74 per cent in the year 2008-09. In the case of others male students enrollment in the year 2000-01 was 56.72 per cent and it decreased to 46.69 per cent by 2007-08 and during the year 2000-01 the female enrollment was 43.28 per cent it increased to 55.95 per cent by 2005-06. But in 2008-09 it decreased to 53.31 per cent.

Faculty-wise Enrollment of Students in Mysore University

Faculty-wise student enrollment between 2000-01 and 2008-09 was collected and presented in the table below.

Table 5. Enrollment of Students during 2000-01 to 2008-09

		Boys	*Girls*
1.	Arts	8356	5118
2.	Sciences	4992	5674
3.	Commerce's	2513	2697
4.	Law	207	235

(*Source :* Various Annual Report of University of Mysore).

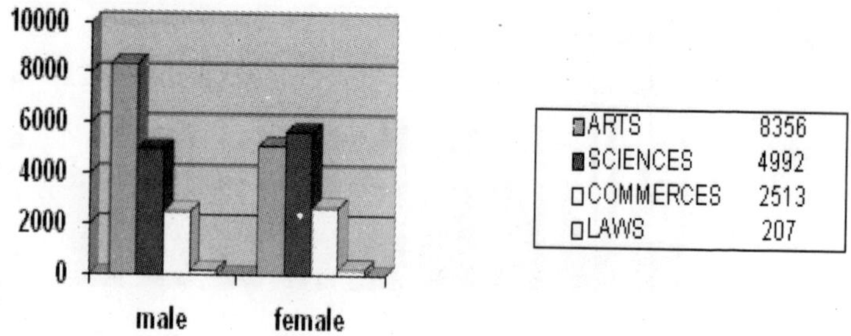

Fig. 2: Trend in Enrollment of Students during 2000-01 to 2008-09.

The findings shows that boys students enrollment in arts was 8, 356, and girls students enrollment was 5118 and coming to sciences department boys enrollment is 4992 in case of girls 5674.

Boys students enrollment in commerce 2513 is female percentage is 2697. Law department boys students enrollment is 207 and girls is 235.

This analysis points to two significant features.

- The proportion of girls students is slightly higher in science commerce and law, and not in arts despite the conventional stereotype of arts discipline being associated with girls.
- The proportion of girls student in law is higher than boys. While there are 207 boys, there are 235 girls during 2000-01 to 2008-09.

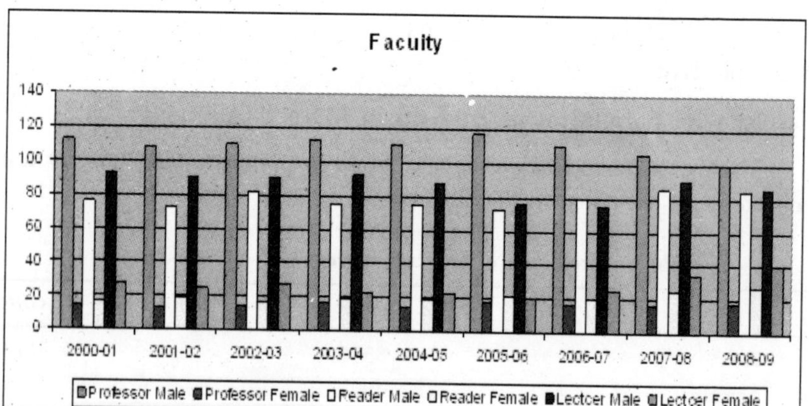

Fig. 3. Trends in Gender Factor in Faculty of University of Mysore.

During the year 2001-01 male professors constitute 88.89 per cent of the total professors in the university of Mysore in all disciplines. In 2001-02 it increased upto 89.26 per cent but it has been decreased to 84.62

Table 6. Gender Factor in Faculty of University of Mysore

Year	*Professors*					*Associate Professors*					*Assistant Professors*				
	M	*%*	*F*	*%*	*Total*	*M*	*%*	*F*	*%*	*Total*	*M*	*%*	*F*	*%*	*Total*
2000-01	112	88.89	14	11.11	126	76	81.72	17	18.28	93	93	76.86	28	23.40	121
2001-02	108	89.26	13	10.74	121	73	79.35	19	20.65	92	90	78.26	25	21.74	115
2002-03	110	88.71	14	11.29	124	82	82.83	17	17.17	99	91	76.47	28	23.53	119
2003-04	112	86.82	17	13.18	129	74	79.57	19	20.43	93	92	80.00	23	20.1	115
2004-05	111	88.80	14	11.20	125	75	79.79	19	20.21	94	88	79.28	23	20.72	111
2005-06	117	86.67	18	13.33	135	73	76.84	22	23.16	95	76	79.17	20	20.83	96
2006-07	110	86.61	17	13.39	127	79	79.80	20	20.20	99	75	74.26	26	25.74	101
2007-08	106	86.18	17	13.82	123	85	77.27	25	22.73	110	91	72.22	35	27.78	126
2008-09	99	84.62	18	15.38	117	84	75.00	28	25.00	112	86	68.25	40	31.75	126

(*Source:* Various Annual Reports of University of Mysore).

per cent during the year 2008-09. The share of female professors was 11.11 per cent during 2000-01 and it increased to 15.38 per cent by 2008-09. The share of female professors is showing an increasing trend in the University of Mysore.

In case of associate professors, the share of female increased from 18.28 during the year 2000-01 to 25.00 per cent by the year 2008-09. 81.72 per cent. Consequently, the share of male associate professors working in University of Mysore decreased to 75.00 per cent during.

The share of male assistant professors was 76.86 per cent the year 2000-01 and it has decreased to 68.25 per cent in 2008-09 year. The share of female Assistant Professors increased from 23.40 in 2000-01 to 31.75 by 2008-09.

Women Faculties in Different Disciplines of University of Mysore

An attempt is made to understand the presence of women faculty in different disciplines in the University of Mysore. The data is presented in table. In the arts faculty the number of associate Professors has not increased over a period of nine years. The number of professors has increased from nine to 12. Another important observation is that there are more professors in arts faculty than in science faculty. The member of Professors in sciences is only four. However, among associate professors there is not much difference in arts and science disciplines. There is not even a single female faculty in law faculty. In the case of commerce up to 2006-07, there is not even a single female associate professors up to the 2007-08. Presently there are two professors, one assistant professor working in the same department.

Gender Factor in the Award of Degrees

Gender-wise trends in the award of Ph.D degree and Post-graduate degrees is analysed for nine years starting from 2000-01 and the data is presented in the table below.

Ph.D Degrees

The data shows that during the year 2000-01 68.96 per cent of the Ph.D awardees were boys and it increased to 82.22 per cent during the year 2001-02. But it reduced to 65.15 per cent. by 2008-09. When we came to the girls, 31.03 per cent of the awardees were girls in the year 2000-01 and it was reduced during the year 2001-02. But by the year 2008-09 it increased to 34.84 per cent indicating that more gender equity is achieved in receiving Ph.D degrees in recent times.

Post-graduate Degrees

In the case of post-graduate degrees there is a consistent increase in the

Table 7. Woman Faculties in Different Disciplines

Year	Arts			Science			Commerce			Law		
	Prof.	Assoc. Prof.	Asst. Prof.	Prof.	Assoc. Prof.	Asst. Prof.	Prof.	Assoc. Prof.	Asst. Prof.	Prof.	Assoc. Prof.	Asst. Prof.
2000-01	9	14	16	4	3	11	1	-	1	-	-	-
2001-02	8	15	14	4	4	10	1	-	1	-	-	-
2002-03	9	14	17	4	3	10	1	-	1	-	-	-
2003-04	12	13	12	4	6	10	1	-	1	-	-	-
2004-05	10	·13	12	3	6	9	1	-	2	-	-	-
2005-06	13	16	10	4	6	8	1	-	2	-	-	-
2006-07	12	12	16	4	8	9	1	-	1	-	-	-
2007-08	12	14	20	4	10	12	1	1	3	-	-	-
2008-09	12	14	25	4	13	13	2	1	2	-	-	-

(*Source:* Various Annual Reports of University of Mysore).

Table 8. Trends in the Number of Students Awarded Degrees and Ph.D by the University of Mysore

	Ph.D					*Post graduation Degrees*				
Year	*Boys*	*%*	*Girls*	*%*	*Total*	*Boys*	*%*	*Girls*	*%*	*Total*
2000-01	60	68.96	27	31.03	87	1360	63.70	775	36.23	2135
2001-02	111	82.22	24	17.77	135	1608	59.91	1076	40.08	2684
2002-03	92	69.69	40	30.30	132	1134	61.34	713	38.60	1847
2003-04	128	74.85	43	25.14	171	1149	58.74	807	41.25	1956
2004-05	107	67.29	52	32.70	159	1023	54.12	865	45.81	1888
2005-06	105	63.63	60	36.36	165	1107	56.12	850	43.43	1957
2006-07	135	72.97	50	27.02	185	963	49.51	982	50.45	1945
2007-08	177	72.83	66	27.16	243	1133	51.61	1062	48.34	2195
2008-09	172	65.15	92	34.84	264	1160	51.62	1087	48.34	2247

(*Source :* Various Annual Reports of University of Mysore).

number of girls. While girls constitute only 36.23 per cent during 2000-01, their share increased to 48.34 by 2008-09. Consequently, the share of boys decreased from 63.70 per cent to 51.62 per cent during the same period.

Gender Differences in the Award of Gold Medals and Cash Prizes

An attempt is made to understand the gender differences in the performance of the students by analysing the trends in the award of gold medals and cash prizes and the data is presented in the table below.

Table 9. Trends in the Number of Students Awarded Gold Medals and Cash Prizes by the University of Mysore

	Gold Medal					*Cash Prizes*				
Year	*Boys*	*%*	*Girls*	*%*	*Total*	*Boys*	*%*	*Girls*	*%*	*Total*
2000-01	40	42.10	55	57.89	95	23	36.50	40	63.45	63
2001-02	62	45.56	74	54.41	136	21	28.00	54	72.00	75
2002-03	53	50.00	53	50.00	106	20	35.71	36	64.23	56
2003-04	32	37.20	54	62.78	86	22	37.23	37	62.71	59
2004-05	35	38.89	55	61.11	90	15	30.61	34	69.34	49
2005-06	36	36.34	63	63.63	99	17	28.81	42	71.12	59
2006-07	47	45.63	56	54.34	103	23	39.65	35	60.34	58
2007-08	38	34.89	71	65.13	109	14	22.56	48	77.41	62
2008-09	42	44.67	52	55.31	94	24	42.10	33	57.89	57

(*Source:* Various Annual Reports of University of Mysore).

Gold Medals

As far as the award of gold medals is concerned, there appears to be no gender gap. While 42.10 per cent of the awardees of gold medals during the year 2000-01 were boys, 57.89 per cent were girls. The marginal difference may be due to some of the medals were exclusively for girl students.

The share of girl students increased to 65.13 per cent in during the year 2007-08. But it has been decreased to 55.31 per cent by 2008-09.

Cash Prizes

In the case of cash prizes girls are our numbering boys. During 2000-01 36.50 per cent of male students received prizes and it is reduced 22.56 per cent during the year 2007-08 and increased to 42.10 per cent in 2008-09. During the year 2000-01 63.45 per cent of girls received the cash prizes. It has been increased to 77.41 per cent in 2007-08 and it decreased to 57.89 in the year 2008-09.

Gender Differences in the Award of Student Scholarships

Faculty-wise analysis of award of scholarships to SC, ST and OBC during the year 2009-10 is presented in the table below.

Table 10. Faculty-wise Students Scholarship (SC, ST and OBC) during 2009-10

Faculty	*Male*	*%*	*Female*	*%*	*Total*	*%*
Arts	3351	74.45	1151	25.56	4502	100
Sciences	869	55.92	685	44.00	1554	100
Law	49	56.32	38	43.67	87	100
MBA	214	72.78	80	27.21	294	100

The data shows that 74.45 per cent male students of arts availed scholarship while 25.56 per cent female students benefitted during the year 2009-10. In science department, 55.92 per cent male students and 44.00 per cent female students availed scholarship. In Law department, 56.32 per cent male students and 43.67 per cent female students availed scholarship. In MBA 72.78 per cent of male students and 27.21 per cent female students were the recipients of these scholarships. There appears to be gender equity in the science and law and it is due to the gender parity in the enrollment in to these faculties.

Gender Differences in Category-wise Award of Scholarships

Table 11. Category-wise Award of Scholarship 2001–02 up to 2009- 10 (Arts)

	Arts	
	Boys	*Girls*
SC	2663	814
ST	412	151
OBC	276	186

(*Source:* Various Annual Reports of University of Mysore).

The table shows that among SC category 2663 boys availed scholarship while 814 girls availed scholarships. In case ST category 412 boy students and 151 girl students availed scholarship. In OBC category 276 boy students and 186 girl students were recipients there scholarships. There appears to be greater gender disparity in the utilisation of student scholarships.

Table 12. Category-wise Award of Scholarships 2001–02 upto 2009-10 (Science)

	Science	
	Male	*Female*
SC	617	526
ST	110	100
OBC	142	59

Source: Various Annual Reports of University of Mysore.

In science Department 617 of SC boy's students and 526 girls students availed scholarships. In ST category, 110 boys students and only 100 girls students are only recipients scholarships. In OBC category, 142 boys students and 59 girls students are availed their scholarships.

Table 13. Category-wise Award of Scholarships 2001–02 upto 2009-10 (Law)

	Law	
	Boys	*Girls*
SC	34	28
ST	10	4
OBC	5	6

(*Source:* Various Annual Reports of University of Mysore).

In law department 34 of SC boys students and 28 of girls students are availed the scholarships and in ST category 10 boys students and four girls students are availed. There scholar's its and in OBC category only five boys students and six girls students are availed the scholarships.

Table 14: Category-wise Award of Scholarships 2001-02 upto 2009-10 (MBA)

	MBA	
	Boys	*Girls*
SC	138	53
ST	29	6
OBC	47	27

(*Source :* Various Annual Reports of University of Mysore).

In MBA Department among SC students 138 boy and 53 girl students are recipients the scholarships. In ST category 47 boy students and 27 girl students availed the scholarships. The data shows that there is a wide gender gap in the case of Management faculty.

Findings

- Enrollment of Girls in technical education in India is not uniform across all the states in India. There is wide differences among the states.
- There is still wide gender gap in enrollment at the university level.
- Gender factors in faculty level shows wide gender differences among the Professors Category and Associate and less in the category of Assistant Professors.
- Girl students availed less scholarship than boys in all the disciplines.

Suggestion

- University should offer more scholarships for the girl students.
- Better hostel facilities should be provided for the girl students.
- Supporting facilities like travel, child care etc., should be provided for female faculty.
- The course in all disciplines should include one paper on gender issues.

Concluding Remarks

The specific purpose of undertaking a gender audit of the university was to profile the representation of women in the organisation and to assess their contribution to the decision-making and academic output of the university. The broader aim is to enable the findings of audit to underscore the necessity of firstly, taking positive measures to enhance the proportion of women at managerial and decision-making levels in higher education institutions and secondly, raising awareness of gender-based values for greater understanding of the socio-cultural barriers to women's empowerment.

The increasing number of women at the entry level positions in recent years documented in this university is the only redeeming feature in the otherwise uniformly low profile of women in the organisation. This is perhaps a sign portending a future wherein there will be greater gender equity and balance at all levels. Alternatively, it can also be an indicator of "feminisation" of higher education with more men opting for careers in the aggressively competitive corporate sector and women settling for the allegedly "famine and docile" occupations of teaching and research.

Regardless of which direction it takes, it is hoped that an exercise of this kind will create an awareness of the urgency to take up gender positive measures in the organisation.

References

- B.G. Sudha, A.S. Ramesh (2010) "Access Equality and Quality Dimensions of Higher Education in India" Edutracks Vol. 9 No. 5 January 2010.
- Chhaya Sukla (2004) "Reforms in Higher Education", Sumit Enterprises, New Delhi, 2004, pp. 94-112.
- D.D. Agarwal (2003) "History and Development of Higher Education in India" Sarup and Sons, New Delhi 2003, pp. 68-81.
- Harsh Gandhar (2005) "Gender Disparity in Higher Education in Independent India" University News, Vol. No. 43, No. 42, October 17, 2005.
- Jahdhyala B.G. Tilak (2007) "Women Education and Development", Gyan Publishing House, New Delhi 2007, pp. 72-98.
- Jandhyala B.G. Tailak (2010) "Nets Weighter Vision for Policy for Education" Economic and Political Weekly, Vol. XLV No. 13, March 27. 2010.
- Lalit Gupta, L.C. Parwani (2001) Quality Assessment and Governance Audit in Higher Education, University News, Vol. No. 39, No. 51, December 17, 2001.
- Neeraj Kaushal (2009) "Full Literary for Women" Supreme Saviour, Vol. No. 64./6 June, 2009.
- Outsiders within (2001) "Identity and Difference in Higher Education", Asgate Publishing Limited Gower House, Croft Road do shot Hampshire GULL 3HR England, 2001, pp. 44-66.
- R.C. Batia (2003) "Gender Auditing, Vikas Publishing House Pvt. Ltd., 2003, pp. 100-110.
- S.Gurumurthy 1979 "Higher Education in India" Newer Publications Madras 1979 pp. 140-148.

- Samer Prahlad Narkhede (2001) "Challenges of Higher Education in India" Sarup and Sons, New Delhi 2001, pp. 109-136.
- V.K. Rao (1999) "Trends in Education" Rajat Publication, New Delhi 1999, pp. 296-312.
- Ved Prakash (2007) Trends in Growth and Financing of Higher Education in India" Economic and Political Weekly, Vol. No. 36 August 4, 2007.
- Vighuti Patel 2008 "Gender Mainster Caming in Social Protection" Economic Political Weekly Vol. No. 16, April 18, 2009.

16 Higher Education and the Marginalised: The Kerala Scenario

Dr. Santhosh Areekkuzhiyil

Abstract

Kerala is known for higher literacy rate, higher enrollment rate of students in school education and higher education. Level of higher education is an important factor which contributes to the empowerment of the individuals and the different strata of the society. Lack of higher education became one of the major reasons for the continued backwardness of the marginalised strata of any society. There are much studies anlysing the status of the marginalised in school education in Kerala. But with respect to higher education, studies are very scanty and even adequate data are not available. In this context, the present study focusses on the status of higher education of the marginalised sections in the state of Kerala.

The objectives of the study are to analyse the status of marginalised sections in higher education in Kerala. The study uses secondary data. The study indicates that the status of higher education of the marginalised in Kerala is not as much as planned and expected. The findings of the study helps to understate the backwardness of the marginalised sections in higher education and its impacts.

The Context

The level of education, especially the higher education is an important element contributing to the development of any society. The 18 to 23 age segment forms the core of future manpower. Hence, the quality and pattern of higher education is of pertinent significance in the qualitative development and progress of any society. Higher education is of vital importance for the society, as it is a powerful tool to build knowledge-based society of the 21st Century. The University Grants Commission (UGC) has chalked out several plans to increase Gross Enrollment Ratio (GER) of students in higher education from the present level to 30 per cent during the 12th Five Year

Plan (2012-17). However Indian higher education is confronted with formidable challenges and must undertake fundamental changes and renewal to create qualitative and competitive force. Hence, Government of India needs to give emphasis on expansion, inclusion, and excellence as the pillars of higher education.

Objectives of the Study

Quality education is vital for overall development of a country. For the last few decades Indian education system focussed to achieve quality education. The objective of the study is to analyse the status of marginalised sections in higher education in Kerala.

Data and Methodology

The present study is based on secondary data published by various government and non-governmental agencies.

The National Scenario

Since independence, higher education has always been identified as a critical component of India's growth story. This ongoing emphasis has resulted in India having one of the largest higher education systems in the world. Growth in numbers, however, has not been accompanied by an improvement in the delivery of higher education. The Indian Higher Education system continues to be bogged down by the challenges of inadequate access, poor quality and inequity. The Gross Enrollment Ratio (GER) in India has grown slowly and now it is estimated to be at 17.9 per cent, which means we need to travel a lot to achieve our dream of universal higher education. India's Gross Enrollment Ratio (GER) in higher education has been presented in the Table 1 and Fig. 1. It shows that the India's Gross Enrollment Ratio (GER) in higher education is not satisfactory when comparing with some developed and developing countries like US, UK, China etc.

Table 1. Gross Enrollment Ratios of Countries

Countries	*Gross Enrollment Ratio*
United States of America	89
United Kingdom	59
China	28
India	17.9
Brazil	3
World Average	27

(*Source:* Ministry of Higher Education, Govt. of India).

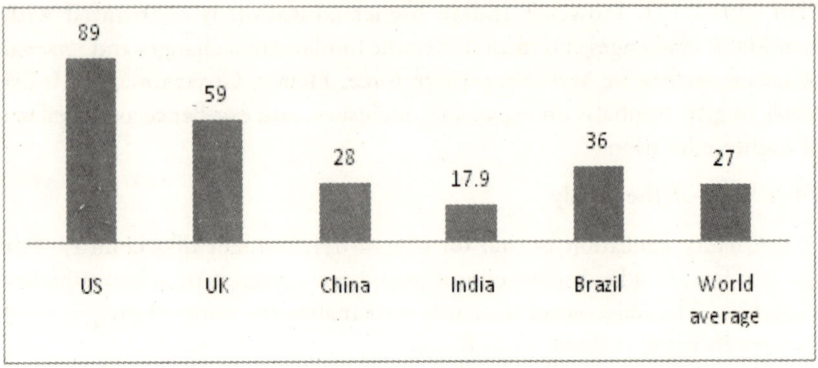

Fig. 1. Gross Enrollment Ratios of Countries.

The data shows that the developed countries, United States of America and United Kingdom have very high GER like 89 and 59 respectively. However, the India's gross enrollment ratio in higher education is 17.9 per cent and it is too low compared the world average of 27 per cent, as well as that of other emerging countries such as China (28 per cent) and Brazil (36 per cent) in 2012.

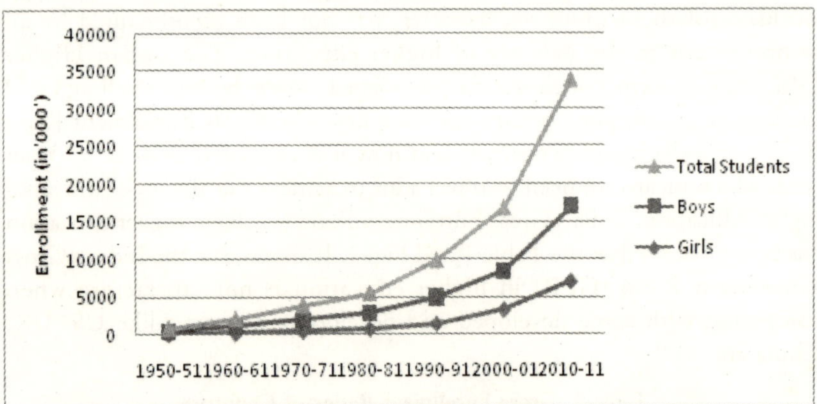

Fig. 2. Growth of Students Enrollment ('000') in Higher Education in India.

Fig. 2 shows the growth of student enrollment in higher education. For the last decades India get slowly improved the rate of enrollment in higher education. But the gap between female enrollment and male enrollment is becoming wider even though the government making new policies and programmes to eradicate the same.

Higher Education Scenario in Kerala

In Kerala the GER in higher education remain at 16-18 per cent and this figure is not uniform throughout the State as there are many areas like Malapuram, Palakkad, Wayanad, Kannur and Idukki districts whose GER is less than 10 per cent (KSHEC, 2012). There are disparities in the pattern of student enrollment in the higher education sector of the state with respect to gender, region, and the nature of course etc. For the proper and balanced development of the society in the coming days of global competition, we need to plan the higher education system in such a way as to ensure the optimum development of the human capital of the state.

Rural Urban Divide in Higher Education

There are rural urban divide in higher education in India. The GER of Higher Education of Rural and Urban population in India is presented in Table 2.

Table 2. GER of Higher Education of Rural and Urban Population in India

Year	*Rural*	*Urban*
1987-88	4.77	19.96
1993-94	4.66	20.17
1999-00	5.58	20.44
2004-05	8.42	16.18
2007-08	11.06	19.33

(*Source:* National Sample Survey).

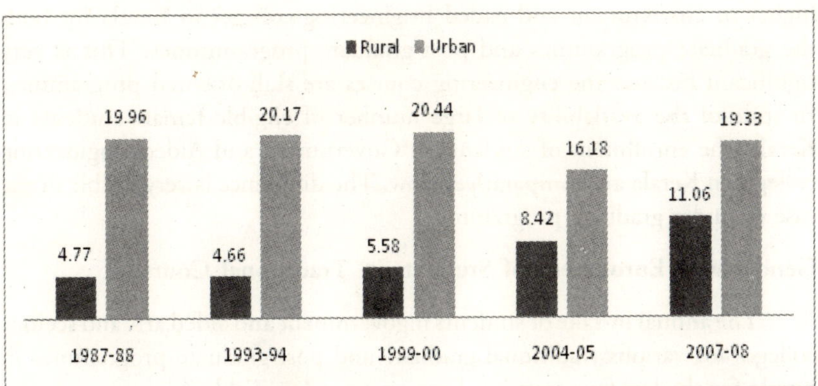

Fig. 3. GER of Rural and Urban Population of Higher Education in India.

Gross Enrollment Ratio of rural and urban areas in higher education are depicted above. In the year 1987-88 GER of rural population in higher education is 4.77, and in the same year urban GER is 19.96. And in the year 2007-08, the GER of rural population is 11.06 and Urban population 19.33. Even now there exists a wide gap between urban enrollment and rural enrollment of students in higher education. Thus, the Indian higher education system suffers from a large rural-urban divide in access.

Gender-wise Enrollment of Students Engineering Education

The annual in-take of students in Government and Aided Engineering colleges for graduate and post-graduate programmes in Kerala for the last few years has been presented in Table 3.

Table 3. Annual In-take of Students in Government and Aided Engineering Colleges in Kerala

Course	*Years*	*Boys*	*Girls*	*Total*
Graduate Programme	2010-11	2896(64.13%)	1620(35.87%)	4516
	2011-12	2740(60.03%)	1824(39.97%)	4564
	2012-13	2927(61.45%)	183638.55%)	4763
Post Graduate Programme	2011-12	501(55.3%)	405 (44.7%)	906
	2012-13	445(54.67%)	369(45.33%)	814

(*Source:* Directorate of Technical Education, Govt. of Kerala).

The Table 3 reveals that the annual enrollment of male students are higher in Government and Aided Engineering colleges in Kerala for both the graduate programmes and post-graduate programmmes. This is very significant because the engineering courses are skill-oriented programmes. In spite of the availability of large number of eligible female students in Kerala, the enrollment of students in Government and Aided Engineering colleges in Kerala are comparatively low. The difference is very visible in the case of under graduate programme.

Gender-wise Enrollment of Students in Traditional Courses

The annual in-take of students ingovernment and aided arts and sceince colleges for various traditional graduate and post-graduate programmes in Kerala for the last few years has been presented in Table 4.

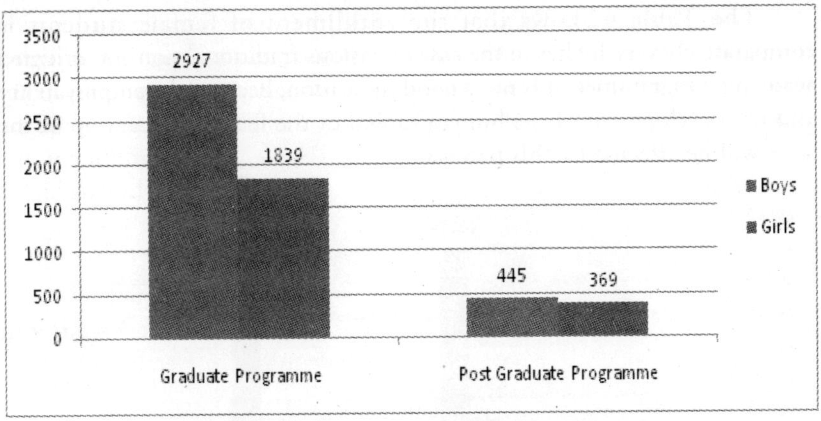

Fig. 4. Annual Gender-wise in-take of Sstudents in Government and Aided Engineering Colleges in Kerala for the year 2011-12.

Table 4. Enrollment of Students in Government and Aided Art and Science Colleges in Kerala

Course	*Years*	*Boys*	*Girls*	*Total*
B.Com	2006-07	3308 (41.86%)	4595 (48.14%)	7903
	2007-08	3352 (39.41%)	5154 (60.59%)	8506
	2008-09	3592 (39.56%)	5487 (60.41%)	9079
	2009-10	3269 (41.24%)	4657 (58.76%)	7926
	2010-11	3379 (39.29%)	5221 (60.71%)	8600
	2011-12	3734 (40.47%)	5492 (59.53%)	9226
M.Com	2008-09	830 (74.44%)	285 (25.56%)	1115
	2009-10	684 (71.47%)	273 (28.53%)	957
	2010-11	222 (22.65%)	758 (77.35%)	980
	2011-12	389 (33.30%)	779 (66.70%)	1168
BA	2009-10	7922 (33.02%)	16072 (66.98%)	23994
	2010-11	7171 (28.96%)	17589 (71.04%)	24760
	2011-12	7726 (29.88%)	18134 (70.12%)	25860
MA	2008-09	577 (18.86%)	2482 (81.14%)	3059
	2009-10	735 (22.85%)	2482 (87.15%)	3217
	2010-11	630 (19.76%)	2558 (80.24%)	3188
	2011-12	503 (15.85%)	2675 (84.15%)	3174
B.Sc	2007-08	6111(22.82%)	15090 (87.18%)	21201
	2008-09	6212 (28.44%)	15627 71.56%)	21839
	2009-10	5932 (27.14%)	15907 (72.86%)	21855
	2010-11	5960 (27.24%)	15918 (72.76%)	21878
	2011-12	6081 (26.3%)	17037 (73.7%)	23118
M. Sc	2008-09	442 (13.61%)	2806 (86.39%)	3248
	2009-10	869 (21.63%)	3149 (78.37%)	4018
	2010-11	656 (19.45%)	2716 (80.55%)	3372
	2011-12	699 (17.39%)	3321 (82.61%)	4020

(*Source:* Directorate of Collegiate Education, Govt. of Kerala).

The Table 4 shows that the enrollment of female students is comparatively very higher in the case of various traditional non-job oriented academic programmes. It is not a good indication, because the employability and the development of the human capital of the female population of the state will be affected by this pattern.

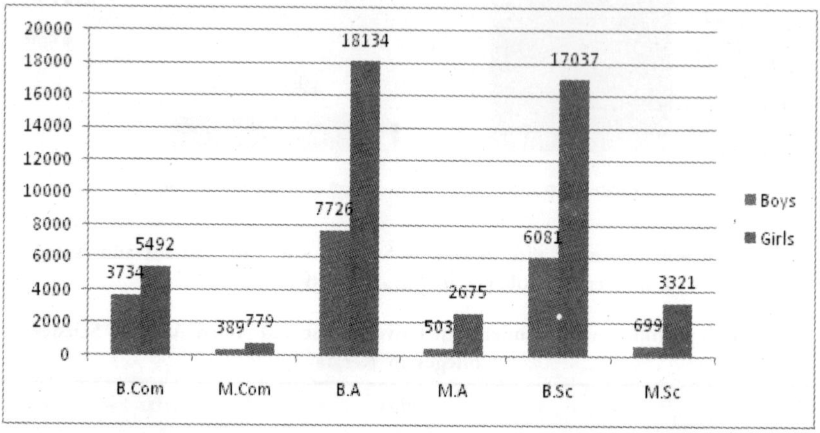

Fig. 5. Annual Gender-wise in-take of Students in Government and Aided Arts and Science Colleges in Kerala for the Year 2011-12.

Unemployment Rate among Educated People in Kerala

The State of Kerala being one of the most awakened and a literate state of the country has been ahead in many respects, particularly in the Human Development Index and Universal Primary education. Kerala is number one in women literacy, enrollment of school and higher education. Although state reported these development index, but the statistics shows that employment rate of women in Kerala is too low compared to many other states in Kerala. On the other hand, it is one of the states which have higher unemployment rate. The unemployment rate in Kerala is presented in Table 5.

Table 5. Unemployment Rate (Per 1000) for Persons of Age 15 Years and Above in Kerala

Year	*1993-04*		*1999-00*		*2011-12*	
Level	*Rural*	*Urban*	*Rural*	*Urban*	*Rural*	*Urban*
Total	94(18)	120(52)	108(19)	125(52)	82(34)	145(50)
Male	72(20)	76(45)	76(21)	69(48)	32(27)	34(29)
Female	158(14)	244(82)	197(15)	264(71)	214(56)	262(69)

(*Source :* Ministry of Labour and Employment, Govt. of India).

Figures in bracket refers to all India figures.

Table 5 shows that unemployment rate in Kerala is increasing. In the year 1994, rural women unemployment rate was 158 and urban women unemployment rate is 244. But now it is increased to 214 for rural and 262 for urban area. This implies that the State could not get the potential contribution of the higher educated segment of women population. It shows that these large segments have not playing their due role in the economic development of the family and the society. According to NSSO (2001), the prevalence of unemployment is more among the educated persons. It is more visible in the Kerala case. The statistics shows that female enrollment in engineering, technical and vocational education is comparatively low. One of the main reasons for this paradox is the lower rate of enrollment in engineering and other professional courses. Majority of the female students in Kerala are enrolling for traditional academic courses.

Social and Financial Divide in Higher Education

In Kerala, enrollment of SC and ST students are very low. The details of scheduled caste and scheduled tribe students studying in government and aided arts and science colleges in Kerala during 2011-12 is presented in Tables 6 and Table 7.

Table 6. Enrollment of SC/ST Students in Government and Aided Arts and Science College in Kerala

	Scheduled Caste			*Scheduled Tribe*		
	Boys	*Girls*	*Total*	*Boys*	*Girls*	*Total*
B.A	3831	7323	11154	532	924	1456
B.Sc	2949	5748	8697	251	390	641
B.Com	1534	2295	3829	320	228	458
M.A	192	588	780	65	97	162
M.Sc	169	512	681	60	74	134
M.Com	77	201	278	28	35	63
Total	8752	16667	25419	1166	1748	2914

(*Source:* Directorate of Collegiate Education, Govt. of Kerala, 2011-12).

Table 7. Ratio of SC/ST Students Enrollment in Arts and Science Colleges in Kerala

Course	*SC*	*ST*
B.A	15.9	1.9
B.Sc	12.8	0.9
B.Com	15.1	1.7
M.A	13.0	2.2
M.Sc	10.8	0.8
M.Com	15.4	1.8

SC students constitute nearly by 14 per cent of total students in 2011-12. Girls' students constitute 65.6 per cent of total SC students in Arts and Science colleges. 2914 Scheduled Tribe students were enrolled for courses in arts and science colleges in 2011-12. The enrollment of ST students in degree and post-graduate courses are 2555 and 359 respectively. Girls constitute 60 per cent of total ST students in Arts and Science colleges. Enrollment of SC and ST students in Arts and Science Colleges in Kerala is comparatively low.

Conclusion

In Kerala, students from the marginalised sections of the society are not getting their due representation in higher education. This is directly and indirectly affecting the marginalised section of the society. This is evidenced from the higher rate of unemployment among the female and the rural youth in Kerala. It is a paradox to see that in spite of the higher rate of enrollment in higher education, there is higher rate of unemployment among females in Kerala. This is due to the nature of higher education programme undergone by the females and the rural students. This indicates the need for more planned reforms in higher education especially for the marginalised sections in Kerala.

References

- Government of Kerala, (Various Issues), *Economic Review*, State Planning Board, Thiruvananthapuram.
- David A. Gabbard. (2000). *Knowledge and Power in the Global Economy: Politics and the Rhetoric of School Reform*. NJ: Lawrence Erlbaum Associates.
- Ministry of Human Resource Development (2011). *All Indian Survey on Higher Education*. New Delhi: MHRD, Govt. of India.

17 The Study of Higher Education for Marginalised Sections in India

Dr. Huchhe Gowda

Abstract

In any nation education is the basic necessity for the socio-economic development of the individuals and the society. In reality, only 20 per cent of the population is higher educated in India. So, Higher education in India is undergoing rapid changes. The challenges ahead are multi-faceted and multi-dimensional. Inclusive development is one of the important goals of the Twelfth Five Year Plan. Since economic resources, mobility, and socio-cultural background are important criteria in determining the accessibility and cost of higher education for a student, disparities are widely visible across geographical regions, genders and socio-economic and socio-religious groups. The GER amongst SCs and STs is much lower than the national average, Muslims also have very low GER. Scheduled Castes and minorities have lower access mostly due to socio-economic factors while tribal areas have lesser number of institutions serving them. Students from these groups are often required to migrate for education, in which case, non-availability of residential facilities and supporting infrastructure in the institutions is a major concern. Gender disparities are an important issue to reckon with. In the age group 18-23 years, females are way behind males. While GER for women and girls is estimated to be 15.8 per cent, it is 22.8 for men. This calls for a more sustained effort in addressing gender disparities spanning the issue of inclusion is another consideration, disparities between various caste groups. Data show the GER among Schedule Castes, Scheduled Tribes and Other Backward Classes are very low. Higher education brings in positive social change. Higher education and quality of life are becoming inter-dependent and go hand in hand. Increasingly, quality of life is being determined by the level of education pursued. Relate to this issue present paper attempts to study the higher education system related to marginalised sections in India, here secondary data were used to analyse this paper.

Introduction

It is widely acknowledged that education has an important role to achieve a greater degree of social justice. The educational institutions are expected to equip children to the best of their ability for securing a meaningful place in society and thus fostering a process of developing an egalitarian society. However, a large number of children are still excluded from the educational system and hence cannot participate meaningfully in the economic, social, political and cultural life of their communities.

The concept of Marginalised Groups is generally used to analyse socio-economic, political, and cultural spheres, where disadvantaged people struggle to gain access to resources and full participation in social life. In other words, marginalised people might be socially, economically, politically and legally ignored, excluded, or neglected, and, therefore vulnerable. Marginality' is demeaning, for economic well-being, for human dignity, as well as for physical security. Marginalisation is generally described as the overt actions or tendencies of human societies, where people who they perceive to be undesirable or without useful function are excluded, i.e., marginalised. The people who are marginalised are outside the existing systems of protection and integration. This limits their opportunities and means for survival.

The present day globalisation has given rise to many dichotomies in the Indian higher education system. Socially backward obviously economically weak will be further marginalised in the market-oriented model. The private and foreign institutions may provide better quality of education, but with high cost, which is not affordable to majority. No doubt, this will be an advantageous to few 'elite' in the society who comes from upper strata, who can meet the financial conditions of such education, at the same time the poor and marginalised minority groups are deprived from this benefit.

In this background, the paper briefly touches the present scenario of Higher Education in the marginalised sections in India and examines the role of the system in democratising the education in India. The paper further assesses the GER (Gross Enrollment Ratio) of the Marginalised groups in terms of empowering the learners in expanding their livelihoods. The study is based on the periodical review reports of the different government agencies, Census and NSSO.

Nature of Marginalised Groups

Marginalisation is, to place in a position of marginal importance, influence, or power marginalised is a multi-dimensional, multi-causal, historical phenomenon. To relegate or confine to a lower or outer limit or edge, as of social standing. There are no general laws to understand and comprehend the complex nature of marginalisation. Marginalisation can be due to class, in relation to specific social, cultural, economic and political conditions, as well as ideological systems, social awareness, and human action.

Marginalised Groups vary in different settings. The religious, ecological system, patriarchy, political economy of a country, and the overall social system have an impact on the marginalisation of specific groups or an individual. Marginalised Groups happen simultaneously at the micro and macro levels.

Marginalised also varies from culture to culture. This can be seen in relation to elderly people living in different countries and cultures. The strong and supportive traditional family system in some cultures often provides better respect and care to elders than the public aided system available in others. Level of awareness among the marginalised groups plays very important role. Organised communities which are aware of their rights, demand more justice than unorganised communities. This also depends upon the support of the political-economic system of the country where they live in. Democratic institutions are favourable for most of the disadvantaged groups.

Marginalised Groups occurs at different levels, i.e., individual, group, community, and global. Discrimination happens across different social institutions, such as family, schools and neighbourhood, at work places, or places of worship. Many communities, a result of colonisation, experience marginalisation such as aboriginals, or women too face discrimination. Globalisation too has increased the gap between rich and poor nations. The influx of capitalism, information technology, company outsourcing, job insecurity, and the widening gap between the rich and the poor, impacts the lives of individuals and groups in many capacities.

Marginalised Sections and Education in India

Indian Constitution recognises socially marginalised communities based on the Caste they belong to. On the basis of caste, Scheduled Castes (SC), Scheduled Tribes (ST). Other Backward Classes (OBC) and the religious minorities, and also women are marginalised in the field of education. According to census of India 2011, the total population of SC account for 16.2 per cent of Indian population, ST account for 8.1 per cent of the total. Though there is no official head count for OBCs the National Surveys suggest that the population of OBCs form 41 per cent of the population.

The differences in the levels of education among the different social groups are examined on the basis of the data shown in Table 1. It presents the area-wise and sex-wise educational levels among the social groups in India during 2009-10.

It is observed from the table that among the rural males, the rate of illiteracy ranges from 35.8 per cent among the ST, 33.1 per cent in the case of SC, 25.3 per cent for the Other Backward Class (OBC) and 17.4 per cent in the case of others. This indicates that the proportion of illiterate population is considerably higher among the ST and SC communities than among the OBC and others. Among the literates, the proportion of those with primary level of education is higher among the ST (26.4 per cent) and SC (27.6 per cent) than among the OBC (25.2 per cent) and others (23.1 per cent), which underlines the fact that among the marginalised section (ST and SC), educational level is mostly centred at the primary level. This is underscored more so by the fact that at higher levels of education, the rate is less among the marginalised section than among the OBC and others.

Moreover, such difference aggravates with the level of education. For instance, at the middle school level, the difference in rate between the marginalised section and others is only 1-2 per cent, which grows to 2-5 per cent at the level of graduation and above.

Among rural females too, there are inter-group variations, in which the marginalised section lose out to the others not only at the higher rungs of education, but even at the primary level of education and needless to say, the rate of illiteracy is higher among the ST (58.3 per cent) and SC (58.1 per cent) than among the OBC (51.4 per cent) and others (36.6 per cent). However, the degree of difference in the rates of education does not go up as in the case of males, but remains constant at around two per cent in favour of the OBC and others. This is not due to higher levels of education among the marginalised section, but because of the low educational levels among the OBC and others. For instance, the proportion of those who have graduation or above level of education among the SC and ST is around one per cent, which is 1.8 per cent among the OBC and 3.5 per cent in the case of others.

Apart from the differences among the social groups within both the rural males and rural females, there are inter-gender and intra-group differences as well. For instance, the rate of illiteracy among the rural ST males is 35.8 per cent, while it is 58.3 per cent in the case of the rural ST females and such differences can be seen across all groups and all levels of

Table 1. Area and Sex-wise Levels of Education among the Social Groups in India, 2009-10

Social Group	Not Literate	Upto Primary	Middle	Secondary	Hr. Sec	Diploma/ Certificate	Graduate and Above	All
	Levels of Education							
Rural Male								
ST	35.8	26.4	18.3	11.1	5.7	0.6	2.2	100.0
SC	33.1	27.6	19.7	10.9	5.4	0.5	2.7	100.0
OBC	25.3	25.2	21.3	15.0	8.0	1.1	4.1	100.0
Others	17.4	23.1	20.9	18.6	11.2	1.3	7.2	100.0
All	**26.0**	**25.3**	**20.5**	14.7	**8.0**	**1.0**	4.5	100.0
Rural Female								
ST	58.3	21.7	10.3	5.7	2.7	0.3	0.9	100.0
SC	58.1	20.2	11.6	6.3	2.6	0.2	1.1	100.0
OBC	51.4	20.8	13.5	8.1	4.0	0.4	1.8	100.0
Others	36.6	25.2	16.3	11.2	6.7	0.5	3.5	100.0
All	**49.8**	**22.0**	**13.5**	**8.2**	**4.2**	**0.4**	**2.0**	100.0
Urban Male								
ST	12.7	17.6	19.3	18.2	14.3	2.6	15.3	100.0
SC	18.4	22.4	20.1	15.9	11.0	1.8	10.3	100.0
OBC	12.0	19.0	19.7	19.7	12.5	3.0	14.0	100.0
Others	6.3	11.3	14.6	20.5	16.0	3.1	28.1	100.0
All	**10.4**	**15.9**	**17.5**	**19.5**	**13.9**	**2.9**	**19.8**	100.0
Urban Female								
ST	31.3	16.7	15.3	14.7	11.1	1.0	9.8	100.0
SC	36.4	20.7	14.5	12.3	8.0	0.8	7.2	100.0
OBC	28.1	18.9	16.4	15.6	10.1	1.5	9.3	100.0
Others	15.2	14.5	14.6	17.3	15.2	1.3	21.9	100.0
All	**23.6**	**17.2**	**15.3**	**15.9**	**12.1**	**1.3**	**14.7**	100.0

Note: Figures in percentage.

(*Source:* Government of India, (2012), "Employment and Unemployment Situation among Social Groups in India", NSS 66th Round, National Sample Survey Organisation, New Delhi, p. 29).

education. Thus, overall, 26 per cent of the rural males are illiterate during 2009-10, which is 49.8 per cent among the rural females; 25.3 per cent of the former are literate upto the primary level, which is 22 per cent in the case of the latter and 4.5 per cent of the males are graduates or educated more, which is only two per cent in the case of the females. Thus, the ST and SC communities are the least educated, which is even much worse among their female folk. The data also indicates the fact that the rate of literacy is lower among the ST and SC males than among the females belonging to the others. Thus, those who are educated upto the higher secondary level among the rural ST males is 5.7 per cent, which is 6.7 per cent among the other females, and it is 2.2 per cent and 3.5 per cent respectively in the case of those who have graduation or above qualification.

Hence, the educational levels of the males among the marginalised sections is worse than that of the females belonging to the others category. Similar differences can be seen within urban males and urban females, wherein the educational levels of the ST and SC population lagging behind that of the OBC and others and similarly, even within the same social group, there are gender differences. The only point of deviation is that the degree of difference in the level of education is greater between the marginalised and others, which is particularly true at the higher rung of education. Even in the urban areas, the males belonging to the marginalised group fails to outshine the females belonging to the others.

Gross Enrollment Ratio's (GER) of Marginalised Sections

Inclusive development is another important goal of the XIIth Plan. Since economic resources, mobility, and socio-cultural background are important criteria in determining the accessibility and cost of higher education for a student, disparities are widely visible across geographical regions, genders and socio-economic and socio-religious groups. The GER amongst SCs and STs is much lower than the national average, Muslims also have a very low GER.

Scheduled castes and minorities have lower access mostly due to socio-economic factors while tribal areas have lesser number of institutions serving them. Students from these groups are often required to migrate for education, in which case, non-availability of residential facilities and supporting infrastructure in the institutions is a major concern. These inferences are drawn from the estimates of NSSO's 61st (2004-05) and 64th (2007-08) round.

Table 2. Gross Enrollment Ratios Across Categories

Sl. No	*Categories*	*GER (Percentage)*	
		2004-05	*2007-08*
1.	SC	8.7	11.5
2.	ST	8.4	7.7
3.	OBC	11.5	14.7
4.	Others	22.5	26.6

(*Sources:* NSSO 2007-08).

Table 3. Gross Enrollment Ratios Across

Sl.No	*Categories*	*GER (Percentage)*	
		Male	*Female*
1.	SC	9.0	13.0
2.	ST	7.5	13.1
3.	Total	12.7	17.1
4.	Others		

(*Sources:* NSSO 2007-08).

Gender disparities are an important issue to reckon with Table 3. In the age group 18-23 years, females are way behind males. While GER for women and girls is estimated to be 15.8 per cent, it is 22.8 for men. This calls for a more sustained effort in addressing gender disparities spanning the issue of inclusion is another consideration, disparities between various caste groups. Figs. (14, 15 and 16) show the GER among Schedule Castes, Scheduled Tribes and Other Backward Classes across States based on the 66th round of NSSO estimates. Interstate variations amongest these groups in the development of Higher Education are glaring in India. Some states have expanded Higher Education Systems fast but some are lagging behind. It is observed that efforts taken in the XIth Plan for improving equal access among social groups has paid dividends. However, much more needs to be done to reduce interstate disparities amongst social groups and improve their GER. Further, GER amongst Caste Groups (SC, ST, OBC and others) point out that more efforts need to be put in improving GER of SC (12.2 per cent) and GER of ST (9.7 per cent) in order to enable them to reach the national average. While, the GER of (SC, ST and OBC) according to the 66th round NSSO estimates (Table 3) are a definite improvement over the earlier NSSO estimates, more needs to be done.

Table 4. GER amongst Caste Groups

Sl.No.	*Category*	*GER*
1.	SC	12.2
2.	ST	9.7
3.	OBC	18.2
4.	Others	27.6

(*Sources:* NSSO 2007-08).

An analysis of the GER amongst caste groups along Rural and Urban areas bring out stark inequities. It is observed that GER for SC (9.6 per cent), ST (7.1 per cent), OBC (15 per cent) in rural areas is quite low compared to their respective GER in urban areas (Figure 19). This major difference calls for greater attention and there is a need to improve education facilities as well as opportunities for these social groups to have access to higher education.

Table 5. GER amongst Caste Groups along Rural and Urban Areas

Sl.No	*Categories*	*GER (Percentage)*	
		Rural	*Urban*
1.	SC	9.6	22.4
2.	ST	7.1	32.2
3.	Total	15.1	28.2
4.	Others	19.2	41.2

(*Sources:* NSSO 2007-08).

The other aspect of equity is women's access to higher education. Many socio-cultural factors contribute to lesser women enrolling for higher education and inadequate infrastructural support at the institutions further reduces their participation. Rajasthan, Odisha, Chhattisgarh, Jharkhand, Assam and Bihar are amongst the lowest in terms of gender parity in higher education, with alarmingly low levels amongst the ST and SC populations. Given the socio-cultural make-up of our society, it has often been felt that opening women's colleges and universities is a useful way of increasing access as the parents are more comfortable in sending female students to such establishments, especially if the students are sent to other states or cities. The proportion of women's colleges is (8.6 per cent) is more than women's universities (1.1 per cent), however, these proportions are still fairly low.

Problems Related to Education for Marginalised Groups

The challenge of poverty associated with disability: With an estimated 1,027 million people, India is the world's second most populated country.

It has 17 per cent of the global population and 20 per cent of the world's out-of-school children. Despite impressive gains in the last few decades India still has more than 260 million people living in poverty. A large number of children with disabilities live in families with income significantly below the poverty level. While disability causes poverty, it is also possible that in a country like India, poverty causes disability. The combination of poverty and disability results in a condition of "simultaneous deprivation. This is a syndrome that sets up barriers to the participation of persons with disabilities in the normal routines and activities of the community, including regular schooling.

The challenge of modifying deeply held attitudes: Attitudes of the non-disabled are proving to be a major barrier in the social integration of persons with disabilities. "The more severe and visible the deformity is, the greater is the fear of contagion, hence the attitudes of aversion and segregation towards the crippled". Such attitudes reinforced by religious institutions may militate against any attempts to include students with disabilities into regular schools. For example, Hindus believe that disability is a consequence of misdeeds performed in the previous life (often referred to as the doctrine of *Karma*). Any attempts to improve the life of a person with a disability may be considered a "defiance of the wills of Allah or as interference with a person's *karma*."

The national educational policy (1986) stressed the need of the liberalisation of education to liberate marginalised sections of the society. The policy recommended for the use of distance education media in a massive way to reach those unreached. A large majority of our people SC/ST's, backward classes. Women and physically disabled remained for reaching out of educational institutions. Distance education provides them with new avenue for getting education. To realise the mission 'education for all' India launched its ODL system in the early 80s.

Suggestions and Recommendations

Mainstreaming is the process, to integrate (a student with special needs) into regular school classes.To incorporate into a prevailing group.The prevailing current of thought, influence, or activity. Representing the prevalent attitudes, values, and practices of a society or group. Efforts have been made to reach education to all. However, there is wastage and stagnation in education. There are economic, social and educational causes that hinder the education of children coming from lower strata of society.

- Incentives to families to send their children regularly to schools till they reach the age of 14.

- Pre-metric scholarships for all children regardless of incomes.
- Constant micro-planning and verification to ensure enrollment, retention and successful completion of courses.
- Remedial measures to better their chances for further education and employment.
- Recruitment of teachers from scheduled castes.
- Provision of hostel facilities.
- Location of school buildings, *balwadis*, and adult education centres to facilitate participation especially in rural areas, hill and desert districts or remote and inaccessible areas.
- Priority given to opening schools in tribal areas with help of tribal welfare schemes.
- Developing curricula and instructional materials in tribal languages with facility to switch to regional language.
- The curricula in the states to depict rich cultural identity of the tribal people.
- Teacher training to tribal youth with assured employment.
- Residential schools including *ashram* schools, *anganwadis*, non formal and adult education centres to open on priority basis.
- Incentive schemes, scholarships for higher education with emphasis on technical, professional and para-professional courses.
- Remedial programmes to help overcome psycho-social impediments.

Conclusion

Higher Education is a very powerful agent of social change. If the higher education system is not streamlined or improved according to the needs of the present day, the primary promise of justice-social, economic and political, equality of status and of opportunity, liberty of thought, faith and worship will ever remain unfulfilled. Higher education should aim at socialisation and democratisation in true sense of the word. The marginalised groups existing in society have historically suffered deprivation in all walks of life in general and in education in particular. Efforts have been made towards economic, social and educational progress of the marginalised people of India. The examination reforms have been suggested right from the time of independence by various committees set-up for the purpose. There is great diversity in the population and the government of India has passed regulations with respect to inclusion of all irrespective of any kind of disability.

There are efforts to provide equal opportunities and inclusion of all in the process of education. Not only are we aware of the vital role that education plays in counteracting disadvantages over which people have little control, but also its important role in shaping their opportunities for education and wider life chances. Protecting the rights of, marginalised and vulnerable persons is probably the most overlooked and disregarded area of human rights law. Marginalised groups are generally marginalised by society, making them easy to ignore. Since they only ever represent a small percentage of the population they lack the critical mass that is often needed to successfully assert human rights claims. Furthermore marginalised themselves are often antagonistic towards each other.

Knowledge is power and therefore has remained one of the most important driving forces of sustaining human existence. For any economy to achieve exponential economic growth, it is essential to gear up skill-based activities through a potential, vibrant and dynamic higher education system. Over the years, trade, investment, mobility of people and the economy have grown significantly and so the need of revamping the higher education system replacing the age-old and non-relevant practices. Looking at the deficiencies in most of the key areas of higher education system of India like accessibility, quality, financing and governance, a strategic paradigm shift in the policy framework and overall functioning is needed to meet growing expectations and societal needs.

References

- Dr. Maheshwari V.K., Education of the Deprived Marginalised Groups Posted on November 23, 2012.
- Government of India, (2012), "Census of India, 2011", Provisional Population Tables, Census of India, New Delhi.
- Government of India, (2012), "Employment and Unemployment Situation among Social Groups in India", NSS 66th Round, National Sample Survey Organisation, New Delhi.
- Government of India, (2010), "Education in India: 2007-08, Participation and Expenditure", NSS 64th Round, National Sample Survey Organisation, New Delhi.
- National Educational Policy (1986), Department of Human Resource Development, Government of India, New Delhi.

18 Foreign Universities and Higher Education: Impact on Affirmative Programmes

Dr. S.V. Girikumar

Abstract

> ***If you are planning for a year, sow rice; if you are planning for a decade plant tree;***
>
> ***If you are planning for a lifetime, educate people.***
>
> **Chinese Proverb**

A well developed and equitable system of higher education that promotes quality learning as a consequence of both teaching and research is central for success in the emerging knowledge economy. It is widely acknowledged that education contributes significantly to economic development. The developed world understood much earlier the fact that individuals with higher education have an edge over their counterparts. They are the ones who always believed that any amount of investment in higher education was justifiable. It is, therefore, imperative for developing countries too, to give due importance to both the quantitative and qualitative expansion of higher education. Indian higher education system is, indeed facing several challenges like access, equity, relevance and quality. Even after significant expansion in the post-independence period, access to higher education in India continues to be poor and more so for the disadvantaged groups resulted from breakdown of state system. It is clear from the history that, at least India like country does not require foreign Universities for giving higher education, the self-sustained abundant resources of knowledge is self-sufficient and also can be spread through the world wide by protecting the affirmative programmes under the constitution of India. There are people aspiring for higher education in the segment of SC/ST/OBC and minorities and the foreign university scheme definitely will not have such reasonable welfare schemes in admission as well in scholarships, and however, the higher education will not be of affordable, thereby it is clear denial of opportunity and representation of unrepresented communities in the higher education and also in higher levels.

Introduction

Education is a process of understanding the nature and oneself in the society, which is growing and expanding by various human inventions. Higher education is refining and grading the human quality to keep environment and surrounding safe for him and for future. "Education for All", education being a basic human right and an instrument of social change. It is the single-most vital element in combating poverty, empowering women, safeguarding children from exploitative and hazardous labour, promoting human rights and democracy and protecting the environment.

Education is not only an instrument of enhancing efficiency but also an effective tool of augmenting and widening democratic participation and upgrading the overall quality of individual and society. India has vast population and to capture the potential demographic dividend, to remove the acute regional, social and gender imbalances, the government is committed to make concerted efforts for improving the quality education as mere quantitative expansion will not deliver the desired results in view of fast changing domestic and global scenario.

The National System of education as envisaged in the National policy is based on a National curricular framework, which envisages a common core along with other flexible and region-Specific components. While the policy stresses widening of opportunities for people and it calls for consolidation of the existing system of higher and technical education. Further, it also emphasises the need for a much higher-level of investment in education of at least six per cent of the national income. The higher education requires a serious attention with reasonable investment in proportionate to social development.

The very basic structure in to the education was realised at the time of independence but there was no demand for education, then it was only to human survival and in the later decades slowly and steadily there was a movement for education. The first policy in its first paragraphs emphasis as "Education has always been accorded an honoured place in India society" The great leaders of the Indian freedom movement realised the fundamental role of education and throughout the Nation's struggle for independence, stressed its unique significance for National development. Gandhi formulated the scheme of basic education, seeking to harmonise intellectual and manual work. This was a great step forward in making education directly relevant to the life of the people. Many other national leaders likewise made important contributions to national education before independence.

There were 20 Universities and 500 colleges at the time of Independence. At present, there are 544 Universities and University level institutions as on 31 December, 2009 of which there are 261 State Universities, 73 Private Universities, 42 Central Universities, 130 Deemed Universities 33 institutions of National importance established under Acts of Parliament, and five institutions established under various State Legislations there is however lots of improvement in the numbers of the Universities imparting higher education from the date of independence in India which records a gradual development in the higher education.

The matter of entry of foreign Universities into India is an economic trade and they do not have any schemes for the welfare of the host countries. It is a fact that the foreign University or foreign education set-up in the Indian Territory is always a foreign rule and does not have the incorporation or intake of the Indianism nor the Constitutional philosophy in itself, further it will diversify the unity of culture and class. It is however the Indian system in the name of Globalisation, Liberalisation and Privatisation and in the anticipation of the development, having the idea of collecting of the foreign Universities entry fee, the Foreign Universities Bill was approved by the Union cabinet in March 2010 and was introduced in the Loka Sabha on May 3rd, 2010, the Bill is unclear whether reservation of seats for OBC and SC/ST students would be an eligibility criterion for the foreign educational institutions to be notified as foreign Education Providers (FEP) which has ignored the affirmative programmes and as well uncared of our own education policy.

Indian Universites *vis-à-vis* Foreign Universities

> *"A University stands for humanism, for tolerance, for reason, for the adventure of ideas and for the search of truth. It stands for the onward march of the human race towards higher objectives. If the universities discharge their duties adequately, then it is well with the nation and the people."*
>
> —Pandit Jawaharlal Nehru

Indian Nalanda University, which flourished from 5th to 12th century, was considered to be the honour of ancient Indian system of Education, as it was one of the best Universities of its time in the sub-continent. Nalanda was one of the first in the world to have residential status of University which had dormitories for students and could have accommodated over ten thousand students and two thousand teachers, the Nalanda University taught and covered every field of learning, it attracted pupils from Korea, Japan,

China, Tibet, Indonesia, Persia and Turkey during the period of Harsha, the then Library was located in a nine storied building where meticulous copies of texts were produced.

Universities are essentially a community of teachers and students where, in some way, all learn from one another or at any rate strive to do so their principal objective is to deepen our understanding of their role in the society and to disseminate this throughout society and to apply it in service of mankind. The ancient Indian universities were of the great potential in its kind and has proven to the world about its value-based education and its contribution to the world. The Indians were and are not less than global competency. Aryabhatta the Indian scientist invented digit *"0"*, trigonometry, algebra and calculus studies were originated in India, so India seems to be the center of education since the ancient days, further in the course of the invasions into India and other countries, the colonial legacy also imposed certain rigid conditions, which has made many developing countries difficult to education system to suit the current socio-economic demands and challenges. The Universities has to strive for the development of humane demands of the society, further the developmental University education should not lead to destructive edge. The Indian Universities have to relook back towards the ancient University system and also have to reserve their willingness to upgrade all the sections of the people at a formula making it affordable.

Foreign University

The very nomenclature of the word "Foreign" denotes the following meaning:

(a) Not native or belonging to a certain country; born in or belonging to another country, nation, sovereignty, or locality; as, a foreign language; foreign fruits.

(b) Held at a distance; excluded; exiled.

(c) Outside; extraneous; separated; alien; as, a foreign country; a foreign government.

(d) Remote; distant; strange; not belonging; not connected; not pertaining or pertinent; not appropriate; not harmonious; not agreeable; not congenial;—with to or from; as, foreign to the purpose; foreign to one's nature is a distinctly, differently, distant one and cannot have the oneness in to the existing system, a system is a mechanism which prepares for the present situation of any state of affairs, further modulated to fit in which could be of the following:

(a) A set of detailed methods, procedures and routines created to carry out a specific activity, perform a duty, or solve a problem

(b) An organised, purposeful structure that consists of interrelated and interdependent elements (components, entities, factors, members, parts etc.) these elements continually influence one another (directly or indirectly) to maintain their activity and the existence of the system, in order to achieve the goal of the system.

All the systems have:

(i) Inputs, outputs and feedback mechanisms.

(ii) Maintain an internal steady-state (called homeostasis) despite a changing external environment.

(iii) Display properties that are different than the whole (called emergent properties) but are not possessed by any of the....

The entry of the foreign Universities in the global economy is the fear and destructive impact, is the loss of National social policies. The developing countries are finding it increasingly difficult to follow independent domestic policies, more inflow of money has aggravated deep-rooted problem of corruption and top colleges of different streams. The entry of foreign universities leads to inequality as its bases the foreign policy and the foreign universities will have greater financial gains at the cost of Indian all types of resources.

Privatisation of Higher Education

The 1990's saw a major turn in the history of contemporary higher education in India. The decade was of turmoil, with an important development being sustained efforts toward privatisation of higher education in India. The financial privatisation of higher education, through reduction in public expenditures and the introduction of cost–recovery measures were accompanied by policy measures toward the "*direct*" privatisation of higher education, the financial necessity has given to forego a social necessity and have created a private sea to pass through the underprivileged section.

Dr. Jayaprakash Narayan, Foundation for democratic reforms in Reforming Higher Education in India has widely canvassed regarding the failure of the state to secure the higher education values in the public sector narrating as follows:

> *It is without serious debate or preparation; the state opened the gates for private provision of higher education. In much of the west, especially in the US, the private providers of higher education are huge philanthropic and charitable endowments which are of a non-profit nature, but unfortunately, in India, in spite of socialist mindset of political class, private for profit higher education institutions were allowed as a matter of routine. In fact, the bulk of education sector in India especially higher education has been privatised on the sly without much of debate! In an insightful paper, the noted political scientist Pratap Bhanu Mehata states: "**This privatisation is not a result of changing ideological commitments of the key actors–the state, the judiciary or India's propertied classes; rather, this privatisation has resulted from the breakdown of the State system. ...***
>
> *Unbridled growth in private provision of education has resulted in the middle classes becoming detached from the public education system as they don't have any stakes in ensuring that they function well. In the absence of demand from vocal middle classes and the consequent lack of political pressure, the state's abdication of education of education sector is accelerated, resulting in vacuum that is filled by a large private for profit sector ....*
>
> *The big difference between the higher education systems of Pakistan and India was that elites in the former usually sent their children abroad even for undergraduate education, and consequently had little stake in the system. The results were disastrous for higher education in Pakistan. Soon India may face a similar problem....*

The deep-rooted thought is not weakened in the higher education, the public system in India will be week if not confident on the public education system and policies.

Impact of Privatisation of Higher Education in India

1. Social protection is defeated.
2. Resulted in social and political chaos.
3. Private monopolies have created irrational competition and profit orientation.
4. Imbalance development of the society.
5. Problems of affordability affecting the educational development.
6. Detaching the public from the public education system etc.

Privatisation of higher education is at the social costs, in a polity such as India's, where structured inequalities have been entrenched, privatisation is sure not to reinforce existing inequalities. The private public partnership model of higher education has not worked well and has ceased to co-opt the ideology of socialistic approach.

The Concept of Higher Education

The change and the reforms are propelled by the vibrant system of higher education in the wake of severe compulsions of economic, social, cultural, political, strategic and global demands. The concept of education only meant learning and imparting of knowledge. The definition of higher education includes a hierarchy of programmes. Many different kinds of University level institutions such as central Universities, Private Universities, IITs, NITs, IIMs, IISERs, occupy the upper end of the higher education spectrum. The various colleges offering general or specialised education, professional education, provide higher education to nearly eighty per cent of students. Then, there are several other post secondary institutions such as community colleges and technical training institutions. In a sense, the polytechnics and vocational institutions, which are not strictly post secondary, are also considered as higher education.

Affirmative Programmes

Affirmative action is a federal agenda initiated in the 1960's that's designed to counteract historic discrimination faced by ethnic minorities, women and other underrepresented groups. To foster diversity and compensate for the ways such groups have historically been excluded, institutions with affirmative action programmes prioritise the inclusion of minority groups in the employment, education and government sectors, among others.

It is even though assuming that accessibility to the higher education is not a major constraint, inclusion of marginalised section of the society like poor, first generation learners, socially and economically backward communities, *Dalits*, tribes etc. may not be ensured, if inclusive measures and affirmative actions are enforced through legislation and persuasion.

There are lots many areas where in the reservation policies are not even cared for the implementation. In a newspaper report "Reservation policy not implemented properly" It is in one of Principal Secretary, Government of Karnataka said that the *dalits* had not been getting the benefits of reservation in many public sector undertaking in the state and further he addressed the gathering stating that reservation policy not implemented properly in PSU's such as the Karnataka State Road Transport Corporation and Karnataka State Power Corporation and termed it as "injustice to *dalits*". There is no reach of the so-called reservation policy and will again defeat the interest in the wake of non-affirmative programmes in the wake of foreign universities to India.

The Affected

The SCs and STs students are distributed equally across India and in the cases of admissions in master's and PhD programmes is tended to be under represented. There is no representation of *dalits* in higher studies due to lack of social and economical supported. The limited evidence indicates that the student enrollment has increased under reservation. In 1981, one estimate put the proportion of graduate students around 3.3 per cent for SCs and 0.8 per cent for STs, which is highly disproportion ate to the actual population share of SC/STs. By the late 1990 the proportion of SC students to the total number of students enrolled rose to 7.8 per cent and fro STs, it rose to 2.7 per cent. This is nevertheless low if we look at the actual share of the SC/ST population to the total population–16 per cent and 8 per cent respectively...In many cases, despite reservation being the norm, it is accepted only in theory and defies implementation of any sorts. It is that the government of India policy itself is being tested in Indian floors for implementation of reservation policy and the rule on foreign Universities will not be implemented for want of strict regulatory system and the implications are negative on Indian secular system. The higher education has to be socialised rather than the privatisation in the entire context.

Education and Human Rights

Education as an economic necessity, integration of economic, social, cultural and political facets of education is facilitated by the indivisibility of human rights. Education not only nurtures the talents but also prepares for responsible citizen and gradually evolves in to the system, leading to strengthen the foundation of the country. Education is a fundamental right of all human rights.

The Right to Education is not a right to mediocre education but, an education which is to be fashioned with the quality of Human right with awareness to the education. The education and human right have a long standing inter and intra-relative development of human life. The Constitution of India was basically framed after an in-depth study into poverty, long years deprivation and inequalities based on caste, creed, sex and religion. The Constitution of India promises to all its citizens justices-

social, economic and political; liberty of thought expression, belief, faith and worship; equality of status and of opportunity; and to promote among all and fraternity assuring the dignity of the individual and the unity of the nation.

It is apart from A-21 as fundamental right and also in A-41 which recognises every citizen's right to work, to education and to public assistance in cases of unemployment, old age, sickness and disablement and in other cases of undeserved want. The social problem presented by the existence of a very large number of citizens. These provisions under the Constitution are made to achieve socio-economic justice in this country. Education shall be for the fullest development of human personality and it is for the strengthening human rights and fundamental freedoms to be enjoyed out of education. It is the children are the assets of the nation and to the world. It is in the Universal Declaration of Human Rights, 1948 in Section 26 has envisaged about the rights of the children in elementary education and the convention recognises education as an important value to be added to the children as a human right and the word of the merit have to be replaced with affirmative merit. Further, the right to development is the integral part of human right and within the ambit of social development; education is one of the essential elements.

The development should not only mean the materialistic development but also humane development which would lead to social justice. Man in the society has moved out of being mere animal existence to the meaning full and dignity to life. Education is not only the requirement but also a prominent indicator of social development and justice. The state governments should realise the social justice into social reality.

The Constitution of India is based on the social justice and stands for all round development of the individual and the state. The UN on Right to development Declaration creates obligations on the states to undertake at National level necessary measures for the realisation of the right to development and shall ensures *inter alia*, equality of opportunity for all in their access to basic resources, education, health services, food, housing, employment and the fair distribution of income.

Concluding Thoughts

The National Universities are better in understanding the social and scientific education and if necessary the National universities be partnership by the Indian industries in the field of science and technology be encouraged and promoted. It is evident that the World class curriculum and attracting good experienced personalities in the area of research and academics exist in our country the services be utilised, and the concept of self-reliance and the Indian future vision are fulfilled. The entry of foreign university is contrary and against to the social justice formula as in the Indian Constitution and ideals of socialistic pattern of society which is not existing in any Bill. The action of the government in inviting the foreign universities is against the interest of reserved class and any amount of precaution trade related agreement will not work with the foreign universities for the lack of jurisdiction and applicability etc. The privatisation is a threat to the public system, the developmental activities should involve all the section of the society only then constitutional values and obligation will be fulfilled else there could be serious lack of social justice....

19 Educational Backwardness Among Muslim Women in India

Kaikashna Begum

Abstract

India is a land of diversity. Among the different religious groups in India, Muslims constitute the largest minority group, i.e., 13.4 per cent of the India's total population. Indian Muslims are facing various socio-economic problems in today's age, among all problems one of the major problem is the educational backwardness of Muslims especially among the Muslim women. In India, Muslims are at a double disadvantage with low-level of education combined with low quality of education. According to Sachar Committee report, the educational status of Muslims in general and Muslim women in particular as according to the data produced in census of 2001 indicates that literacy rate among Muslim is low, i.e., 59.1 per cent and literary rate of Muslim women is 50 per cent. It is very low as compared to male counterparts. The gap between the education of boys and girls in India in the case of Muslims has been a ***yawning chasm***. So, this paper will try to analyse the literacy and educational status of Muslim girls and women in India, the social, cultural and economic factors and forces hindering their educational participation against the backdrop of existing policies, programmes and schemes to promote education of Muslim girls and women. The paper will interpret the existing data on all relevant indicators available from secondary sources, official documents, reports and earlier studies on education of Muslim girls and women. The paper will aim at exploring future directions and strategies for integrating and galvanising Muslim women of all walks of life for an equitable social order.

Introduction

Education has always played a very important role in every society. It makes an individual to internalise the values and norms of the society and simultaneously offers the specific skilled persons to serve different functions in society. It refines sensitivities and perceptions that contribute to national cohesion, a scientific temper and independence of mind and spirit–thus furthering the goals of socialism, secularism and democracy enshrined in our Constitution. **Article 14** of the Constitution confers on men and women equal rights and opportunities in the political, economic and social spheres. **Article 15** prohibits discrimination against any citizen on the grounds of religion, race, caste and sex. **Article 15(3)** makes a special provision enabling the State to make affirmative discrimination in favour of women. **Article 16** provides for equality of opportunities in matters of public appointment for all. Article 21A (The 86th Constitutional Amendment Act, 2002) makes education is now a fundamental right of all children of the age of 6-14 years, the state to provide free and compulsory education to all children of the age of 6-14 years in such a manner as the state by law determines. A new Fundamental Duty Article 51A in Part IV makes it a duty of a parent or a guardian to provide opportunities for education to his child or as case may be ward between the age of 6 and 14 years. Beside these, the Constitution have also made various provisions to safeguard educational rights of religious minorities, such as Article 29 and 30 "Cultural and Educational Rights" of the Indian Constitution.

Though India has one of the most impressive sets of laws for girls and women and yet little is known about them either by women themselves or by men. The Indian socio-legal framework has; therefore, to contend with deeply entrenched customs and traditions, beliefs and practices of a highly patriarchal and feudal past and present that contributes to the continued subordination of women.

In Islam education is the birth right of every Muslim and *Muslimah*. Islam puts considerable emphasis on its followers to acquire knowledge. Islam is perhaps the first religion which has given greater significance to learning. A number of verses from the Holy Quran and the traditions of Prophet Mohammed emphasise the acquiring of knowledge by Muslims whether male or female.

"The pursuit of knowledge is a duty of every Muslim, man and woman", said the Prophet (swa). With this instruction it became a religious duty of Muslims to educate themselves, their families, and their societies. Education and learning became a religious duty; no Muslim could prevent another human being from the pursuit of knowledge. Gender or race, culture or tradition could not become the cause for prohibiting a person from educating one's self. Pursuit of knowledge became a religious law, therefore necessary to attain. With such instruction, the Prophet (swa) not only created an equal right to education, but also opened the door to a better understanding.

"My Lord! Enrich me with knowledge"—(Quran, 20:114)

The rise of Muslims to the zenith of civilisation in a period of four decades was based on Islam's emphasis on learning. This is obvious when one takes a look at the Qur'an and the traditions of Prophet Muhammad(s), which is filled with references to learning, education, observation, and the use of reason.

Every Muslim man's and woman's prayer should be:

"My Lord! Enrich me with knowledge". (Quran, 20:114)

The Holy Prophet *(Sallallaahu Alayhi Wasallam)* said, 'The searching of knowledge is incumbent for every Muslim (male and female).' Every boy or girl, man or woman should pursue his/her education as far as it is possible. In the history of Islam you will find that there were women who were narrators of Hadith, mystics, scholars, writers, poets and teachers, in their own right. They utilised their knowledge within certain precepts of Islam. Hazhrat Aaisha with her intellect and outstanding memory was one of the most important scholars of her time. More than two thousand Hadith are reported by her and she is regarded as one of the best teachers of Hadith. Shaykha Nafisa who was such a great authority on Hadith that Imaam Shaaf'ee sat in her circle. The famous mystic, Rabia-al-Adawiyya (Basria) was also a woman with great wisdom and knowledge. There are numerous other women who are held in the highest respect by the Muslim world in the history of Islam.

Investment in education is the best investment one can make, because it eventually leads to intellectual property. So far as the minorities in India are concerned Muslims are the largest minority in the country, i.e., 13.4 per cent according to the Census report of 2001. But unfortunately majority of this community is educationally and economically most backward. A High Power Panel appointed by the Ministry of Home Affairs and headed by Dr. Gopal Singh identified Muslims and Neo-Buddhists as two educationally backward minorities at the national level and proposed that special efforts have to be made to bring the educationally backward minorities on par with rest of the society. In India, Muslims are at a double disadvantage with low-level of education combined with low quality of education: their deprivation increases manifold as the level of education rises. It has been seen that after the first few years of the primary education afforded to the Muslim girl child, one of two things usually happens. Either the girl is plucked out of formal education by the time she reaches puberty and for all practical purposes lapses into virtual illiteracy, or if she continues in school and does climb up the education ladder, with every rung, the quality of education available to her is so inferior that it equips her for very little. The quality of education in some Urdu-medium schools is low as the calibre of teachers in such schools is so inadequate that the girls who do come out from such institutions–many privately run, others with dubious affiliations from quasi-religious bodies–cannot cope in a competitive environment. Muslims women have not been able to get their due share in total welfare work done by the Government, for economically weaker sections of the society in the country since independence. With respect to Muslim women education it is pity that Muslim has not facilitated women folk to acquire minimum education, or least nominal education. According to the data produced in census of 2001 indicates that literacy rate among Muslim is low i.e., 59.1 per cent and literary rate of Muslim women is 50 per cent, it is very low as compared to male counterparts.

The gap between Muslim male and female education has a ***yawning chasm***. It means that over 50 per cent of Muslim women in India are illiterate today—literacy being officially defined rather generously to include just about anyone who can read and write a sentence or two. The situation in the northern states, especially in rural areas, is said to be particularly dismal. About 85 per cent of rural north Indian Muslim women are unable to read or write. On the other hand, the situation in the south, especially in urban areas, was found to be considerably better, with 88 per cent urban south Indian women said to be literate. The so-called modern society treats women as second class citizens, in the field of education in general and higher and technical education, their share is very low. According to the 1991 Census, there were over 48 million Muslim women in India; in 2001 census the number rose to 62.5 million. In popular perception, these women are typically seen as a monolithic entity undistinguished and indistinguishable in their homogeneity. When compared to women from other faiths in India, the majority of Muslim women are among the most disadvantaged, least literate, most economically impoverished and politically marginalised sections of Indian society. The right to education, especially at the primary level is mandated by the Constitution, yet over six decades after Independence less than 50 per cent of Muslim women in India are literate. Compare this with other women from other minorities: 76 per cent literacy among Christians, 64 per cent among Sikhs, 62 per cent among Buddhists and a whopping 90 per cent among Jain women. On all-India basis, 66 per cent Muslim women are stated to be illiterate. The illiteracy is most widespread in Haryana, Bihar while Kerala has least illiteracy among Muslim women closely followed by Tamil Nadu. Muslim women are found to be more literate than their Hindu counterparts in the states of Madhya Pradesh, Maharashtra, Andhra

Pradesh, Karnataka and Tamil Nadu. Most of the northern states are in urgent need of vigorous and sustained literacy campaigns.

In the study of Zoya Hasan and Ritu Menon (2004) the following figures have been projected in accordance to a survey conducted by them in 2000-01 in 40 districts in 12 states of India, it was found that roughly 60 per cent of Muslim women report themselves to be illiterate while the school enrollment rate for Muslim girls is 40-66 per cent. The proportion of illiterate Muslim women is substantially higher for the rural north than it is for the rest of India where more than 85 per cent women in the rural North report themselves to be illiterate. Less than 17 per cent of Muslim women enrolled in schools completed eight years of schooling and less than 10 per cent completed higher secondary schooling, which is below the national average. The educational status of Muslim girls in north India is particularly abysmal, resulting in substantially lower enrollment rates at the middle school and higher secondary school levels (4.58 and 4.75 per cent respectively as opposed to the national average of 17.86 per cent and 11.42 per cent respectively). The proportion of Muslim women in higher education is only 3.56 per cent, lower even than that of the SCs, which is 4.25 per cent. The overwhelming majority of women reported themselves as not working. The average work participation rate for Muslim women is 14 per cent, which is lower than for Hindus (18 per cent), SCs (37 per cent), and other backward Classes (22 per cent). Few Muslim women are employed in the formal sector. The survey also found that Muslim women had very little awareness of government schemes, and like many of their Hindus sisters, had little power of decision-making in their homes. The authors point out that contrary to prevalent stereotypes about forces of conservatism being the cause for low levels of education among Muslim girls, financial constraints outweigh parental opposition as chief obstacle to girls continuing their studies. In the north zone, financial constraints are much more important for Muslims than they are for Hindus, underlining once again the poverty of Muslim households in this part of the country and this provides the most powerful explanation for the poor levels of women's education in the north as a whole. The south presents a different picture. Girls belonging to lower socio-economic classes have as good a prospect of continuing in school as girls from higher classes. This is because of higher levels of state investment in education, a larger percentage of female teachers, extensive network of roads and good transport facilities that enable easy access to schools. This is a critical determining factor for both girls and female teachers. Even though Kerala is not a prosperous state, it is spending 6.3 per cent of its gross domestic product on education. Uttar Pradesh's ratio is around 3.7 per cent. Over 60 per cent of teachers in Kerala and over 40 per cent primary school teachers in the south zone are women, in contrast to 18 per cent in Uttar Pradesh. Further, road transport is reliable and readily available in Kerala enabling female teachers to travel long distances to teach in rural schools. While regional factors, poverty and the role of the State in providing resources are critical, the impact of violent communal conflict as well as impact of communalisation of education on Muslim girls is significant.

Though different Governments have appointed various committees from time to time to find out the causes of educational backwardness among Muslims in general and Muslim women in particular and various programmes have been initiated but the still goal remains unfulfilled.

Committees and Programmes for Development of Minorities

It was only in late seventies that backwardness of education of Muslim minority started receiving attention and resulted in some action on the part of the State. The Minorities Commission was set-up in 1978. It was a non-statutory body until 1992, when Parliament enacted the National Commission for Minorities Act, and set up the first statutory commission in 1993, called the **National Commission for Minorities (NCM)**. The state governments of Bihar, Karnataka, UP, MP, West Bengal, AP, Tamil Nadu, Maharashtra and Rajasthan have also set-up State Minorities Commissions, and the governments of Assam and Gujarat have set-up Minorities Boards. Still there are many states which do not have Minority Commissions. It was only after Census 2001 which brought out its First Religion Report that statistics on several aspects of population by religion (literacy, educational attainment, sex ratio, work participation) became available in the public domain that has led to public debate and action. A High Power Panel appointed by the Ministry of Home Affairs and headed by Dr. Gopal Singh identified Muslims and Neo-Buddhists as two educationally backward minorities at the national level and proposed that special efforts have to be made to bring the educationally backward minorities on par with rest of the society.

Various Programmes for the uplift of the minorities are as follows:

- The 15-point Programme for Minorities 1983.
- The National Policy on Education (NPE), 1986 and Revised Programme of Action 1992.
- Programme of Action, 1992 (POA): The (POA) 1992, first took note of the existing programmes for the Muslim Minorities and also suggested a large number of short-term, medium-term and long-term measures to promote education of minorities.

- Prime Minister's High-level Committee on Social, Economic and Educational Status of Muslim Community (Sachar Committee) in India 2005.
- New 15-point Programme for the Welfare of Minorities (2006).

Besides these Programmes there were various foundations, council and committees set-up for the educational uplift of Muslim girls and women. Some are mentioned below:

- The **Maulana Azad Education Foundation** (MAEF), set-up in 1989 and fully-funded by MSJE, promotes education among educationally backward minorities. It provides financial assistance for establishment and expansion of schools, residential schools and colleges, provision of laboratory and infrastructure facilities, establishment of computer and vocational centers, construction of hostel buildings, and Maulana Azad National Scholarships for Meritorious Girl Students, as well as Maulana Azad Literacy Awards.
- The **Central Wakf Council**, a statutory body, implements various charity and educational programmes for weaker sections of society.
- The **National Monitoring Committee for Minorities Education** Women are in no way portrayed lesser being than that of man in the Constitution. Various programmes are undertaken by government time to time to ensure equality to women in education. Despite of all such measures the social delineation and dogmatic interpretation have for ages subordinated women to men and emphasised her subservient role. The gap between the education of Muslim men and women is wide. Gender inequality in education is one important aspect of educational disparity.

Literacy Rates of Religious Minorities and other Groups

For the first time, the Census of India provided hard data about the literacy rate among various religious groups in India.

- Giving the picture of all India, the literacy rate for the population age seven years and above for the country as a whole stands as 64.8 per cent.
- Literacy rate among the Jains is the highest at 94.1 per cent followed by Christians 80.3 per cent and Buddhists 72.7 per cent then Sikh 69.4 per cent whereas the lowest literacy rate is among Muslim. The Muslim have returned lower than the national average literacy rate at 59.1 per cent.

Table 1. Literacy Rate among Religious Communities in India Census 2001

Community/ Caste	*Total*			*Rural*			*Urban*		
	Person	*Male*	*Female*	*Person*	*Male*	*Female*	*Person*	*Male*	*Female*
India	64.8	75.3	53.7	58.7	70.7	46.1	79.9	6.3	72.9
Hindu	65.1	76.2	53.2	59.1	71.7	45.7	81.3	7.9	73.9
Muslim	59.1	67.6	50.1	52.7	62.3	42.7	70.1	6.3	63.2
Christian	80.3	84.4	76.2	74.5	79.5	69.7	90.9	3.6	88.3
Sikh	69.4	75.2	63.1	64.2	70.6	57.2	63.6	7.5	79.2
Buddhist	72.7	83.1	61.7	66.9	78.8	54.6	81.6	9.8	72.9
Jain	94.1	97.4	90.6	87.5	94.2	80.3	96.1	8.4	93.6
Others	47.0	60.8	33.2	43.9	58.2	29.5	75.3	3.8	66.5

(*Source:* Based on Census Report, 2001, Government of India).

Gender Gap in the Literacy Rate among Religious Communities

Religion	*Total Population*	*Rural*	*Urban*
All Religion	21.59	24.57	13.41
Hindu	22.95	25.90	14.04
Muslim	17.47	19.67	13.11
Christian	8.18	9.83	5.38
Sikh	12.14	13.49	8.32
Buddhist	21.44	24.25	16.91
Jains	6.82	13.89	4.64
Others	27.61	28.65	17.33

(*Source:* Based on Census Report, 2001, Government of India).

- In 2001, literacy rate of Muslim women was 50.1 per cent compared to 53.7 per cent for all other communities. It is to be noted that the literacy rates are much higher amongst other minorities, Jains lead, followed by Christians, Sikhs and even Buddhist, the lowest literacy rate is among Muslim women.
- Literacy rate is higher among the urban residents in comparison to the rural residents in all the religious communities. The degree of difference, however, varies for different religious groups. Among the minorities, it is the lowest urban literate for the Muslim females (63.2 per cent). Similarly, Muslim males constitute the lowest literate urban population (76.3 per cent) among the minority groups.
- Of course for each of the communities, the overall literacy rate is substantially higher than the female literacy rate, indicating a gender bias existing in all the communities with regard to access to literacy.

> But the Muslims show a relatively low gender disparity in literacy rates, as compared to other religion. The gender disparity in literacy rates among the total Muslim population is about 17.47 percentage points; it is 19.67 percentage points in rural and 13.11 percentage points in urban areas.

If we go through NSSO's 61st Round Prime Minister's high-level Committee, Report, 2006. It has been found literacy rate as Proportion of Muslim Population of age groups 6-13 years in 2004-05 is 74.68, for 14-15 years is 79.5, for 16-17 years is 75.5, for 18-22 years is 70.5 for 23 years and above is 46.1. Here we notice that literacy rate is declining sharply by increase in age of 23 and above among Muslims. And further it is found that the Gender Gap in the Literacy Rate among Muslim is high. Among Muslims it has been found that 3.9 per cent females have acquired Higher Secondary education compare to 5.0 per cent Muslim males. Among rural Muslim female literates, only 1.9 per cent have attained higher secondary level compare to 6.1 per cent for the urban Muslim females. When we look at Muslim literates who are graduates and above, only 2.4 per cent females have attained this level compare to 4.4 per cent males. Here we find that the dropout rate among girls is high. Here also, rural urban divide is sharp. Among rural female only 0.9 per cent are graduates and above compare to 4.3 per cent urban females.

It has been found at the state level the highest literacy rates among Muslims has been recorded in Andaman and Nicobar Islands at 89.8 per cent closely followed by Kerala at 89.4 per cent. Although the national average Muslim literacy rate is low at 59.1 per cent, yet as many as 15 states and union territories recorded more than 70 per cent literacy among Muslims, including the major states of Tamil Nadu, Maharashtra, Chhattisgarh, Gujarat, Odisha, Madhya Pradesh and Karnataka. As many as 16 states and union territories have returned a lower figure than this. Haryana has recorded the lowest literacy rate of 40 per cent cent among Muslim population. This is closely preceded by the states of Bihar, Meghalaya, Jammu and Kashmir, Uttar Pradesh, Nagaland and Assam, all below 50 per cent. With a literacy rate of just 59.13 per cent, the overall literacy rate of Muslims gives them a standing lower than that of 'All Religions'. The Muslim literacy rate is significantly lower than 'all religion' population literacy rate (by 5.71 per cent) percentage point. A similar trend is observed in the case of male and female population of the Muslim community. The literacy rate for Muslim males is lower than 'all religion' literacy rate by 7.7 percentage points, while for females the difference is about 3.58 percentage points.

Educational backwardness among the Muslim population is chronic in the rural areas of northern and north-eastern states, while southern states of India far better. Rapid inclusive growth for all minorities especially the educationally backward minorities in all spheres could be achieved by bringing about equity in access to various forms of educational opportunities taking into account wide disparities that exist in our society across social and religious groups and also regions of India.

There are several social, economic and cultural causes for the backwardness of Muslim Women in the field of education, they are as follows:

The factors and forces hindering the educational participation against the backdrop of existing policies, programmes and schemes to promote education of Muslim girls and women are mentioned below:

1. Economic poverty/financial constraints.
2. Illiteracy among parents.
3. Larger families.
4. Social customs.
5. Early marriages, i.e., girls are withdrawn at early age from primary education to marry them off; therefore dropouts' rate is very high.
6. Assigned task of being domestic/Domestic responsibility of women and additional labour.
7. Procreators of children.
8. Lack of girls school/inadequacy of women's colleges.
9. Poor facilities in Muslim schools.
10. Lack of proper infrastructure as well as number of teaching staff, especially in Urdu medium sections.
11. Lack of visibility of Muslim presence in the service sector, giving rise to a perception of discrimination in jobs in public and private sectors.
12. Negative attitude towards girls education/Hesitation of Parents to send their girl child to school after the attainment of puberty. There is common belief that Muslims parents feel that education is not important for girls as it may instill wrong set of values.
13. Parents hesitate to send their girls to co-educational colleges.
14. Lack of vocational education.

15. The escapist religious leadership and movements.
16. The Indian Muslim socio-cultural ethos partly derived from the imperfect understanding of Islam.

The following remedies could be considered in improving educational standards among Muslim:

The need of hour is a time-bound action on a war-footing to remedy the situation. The following suggestion are made:

1. Government and voluntary sectors should equally take responsibility for extending the necessary physical infrastructural, motivational and academic facilities in higher education to Muslim in general and Muslim women in particular towards making education meaningful to them.
2. An organisation which may be a federation of all Muslim social and educational organisation and institution may be formed at National level with branches at the State, district and Village/Town level.
3. A plan of action which put emphasis on educational development for Muslim women should be prepared at each level for implementation within specific period of time.
4. The Committee at different levels should be monitored the activities at their respective levels and review the progress at end of specified intervals at each level.
5. Adequate funds should be raised to finance various educational projects at different levels.
6. Minority cells at different levels (national, state, village) should be formed and strengthened for effective implementation of the programmes for the uplift of Muslim in general and Muslim women in particular. There must be continuous and meaningful rapport between these Government cells and the Committees formed by Muslims at each level.
7. Minority Commission and Minorities' Development Corporation should be formed or strengthened in every state and center with necessary statutory powers and sufficient financial allocations.
8. The Government should adopt liberal policy in sanctioning grants to educational institutions and industrial units to the minority community.

9. The Government should set special quotas and introduce reservation for the minorities in Government jobs and employment in public and private sectors undertaking with view of bringing backward minorities on a par with the other communities.
10. A demand for protective discrimination in favour of Muslim women into admission in various courses of study, this affirmative action by the state can be an excellent mechanism for equalisation of opportunity in education for them.
11. There is a need of Muslim leadership to get new educational Policy and Programme of action concerning Muslim should be materialised.
12. Reform and a review of syllabus and curricular programmes of institution of traditional religious instructions is one of the urgently needed steps that the community can take to meet the challenge of modernity to Islam as well as making traditional education more relevant.
13. Opening of Muslim girls school and appointing of women teachers, opening of girls hostels, provision for incentives like mid-day meals.
14. Production-cum-training centre for crafts exclusively for girls in district of Muslim concentration.
15. Setting up libraries, reading room in district with Muslim areas.
16. Periodic survey assessing Muslim literacy and educational attainment.
17. Proper implementation of Scholarship scheme.

If the above suggestions are taken into consideration and translated into action with utmost sincerity, it would go a long way towards removing educational backwardness among Muslims. These directions and strategies mentioned above will help in integrating and galvanising Muslim women for an equitable social order. There is a growing hunger for education among Muslim girls and women that can no longer be ignored. Several initiatives have been taken by women themselves when they feel the State or patriarchal society is not giving them their due. The Government of India, as well as the Muslim leadership will be on trial for next few years. The former for its sincerity of purpose, i.e., seriously it means to take affirmative action with regard to Muslims and specially the Muslim women who are educationally backward, the latter to prove that they have no vested interest in keeping Muslims in general and Muslim women's in particular backward. Last but not least, the Holy Quran (Quran, 13:11) says: *"Verily never will God change the condition of a people until they change it themselves"*.

References

- Ahmad, H. (2012), "Empowerment of Muslims through Quality education", in Empowerment of Indian Muslims: Perspectives, Planning and Road Ahead, eds. M.A. Beg and A.R. Kidwai, New Delhi: Concept Publishing Company Pvt. Ltd., p. 1.
- Ansari, I.A. (1988), "Muslim Educational Backwardness: New Educational Policy and Programme", The Muslim Situation in India, New Delhi: Sterling Publishers.
- Azim, S. (1997), "Muslim Women: Emerging Identity", Jaipur: Rawat Publications, p. 11.
- Bhat, P.N. Mari and A. J. Zavier (2004), "Religion in Demographic Transition: The Case of Indian Muslims", in S. Irudaya.
- Bose, S., and Ayesha, J., (eds), Nationalism, Democracy, Development: State and Politics in India, New Delhi, Oxford University Press, 1998.
- Brass, P. (1994), 'The Politics of India since Independence', New Delhi, Cambridge University Press.
- Census Report of India, 2001.
- Engineer, Asghar A. (1995), 'Problems of Muslim Women in India', Orient Longman Ltd., Bombay.
- Engineer, Asghar A. (1992), 'The Rights of Muslim Women in Islam', New Delhi, Sterling Publication, New Delhi.
- Ephroz, Khan N. (2003), 'Women and Law: Muslim Personal Law Prespective', Rawat Publication, Jaipur and New Delhi.
- GOI (2006), "Social, Economic and Educational Status of the Muslim Community of India–A Report", Prime Minister's High Level Committee, Cabinet Secretariat, Government of India (Chairperson–Justice Rajindar Sacchar). New Delhi. p. 85.
- Hasan, Z. and R. Menon, (2004), "Unequal Citizens: A Study of Muslim Women in India", New Delhi: Oxford University Press, p. 71.
- Hussain, S. (2010), "Educational Attainment of Muslim Women in India: Obstacles and interventions", in Minority Education in India: Issuers of Access, Equity and Inclusion, ed. A. Waheed, New Delhi: Serials Publications, p. 53.
- MHRD Annual Report, Department Elementary Education and Literacy; Department of Secondary and Higher Education (2005-06).
- Mondal, S.R. (1997), "Educational Status of Muslims: Problems, Prospects and Priorities", New Delhi: Inter-India Publications, p. 19.

- National Policy on Education 1986, MHRD, Department of Education, New Delhi.
- NSSO 55th and 61st Rounds.
- Ruhela, S.P. (1998), "Religion, Social Class and Educational Opportunity: Case Studies of Eight Muslim Girls", Empowerment of the Indian Muslim Women, New Delhi: MD Publications.
- Saheb, S.A.A. (2003), 'Dudekula Muslims of Andhra Pradesh: An Ethnographic Profile', Economic and Political Weekly, November 15, pp. 4909-10.
- Salamatullah (1994), "Education of Muslims in Secular India". Chandigarh: Centre for Research in Rural and Industrial Development.
- Siddiqui, Z., and Zuberi, A., (eds), Muslim Women: Problems and Prospects, New Delhi, MD Publications, 1993.
- Siddiqui, M.K.A. (2011), 'Muslims in India: Issues and Challenges' (A collection of articles), Kolkata: Abadi Publication, p. 213.
- Siddqui, Mujibul Hasan Siddiqui (1999): Islamic Education: An Objective Approach, A.M.U. Press, Aligarh.
- Talib, P. (2012), "Educational Initiatives to Transform Muslim Community", in Empowerment of Indian Muslims: Perspectives, Planning and Road Ahead, eds. M. A. Beg and A.R. Kidwai, New Delhi: Concept Publishing Company Pvt. Ltd., p. 103.

Notes: Despite of the fact that the provisional data of the Census report of 2011 conducted by the Government of India, New Delhi, has been accredited on 31st March, 2011, however, to avail the religion-wise data, it will take some more years for the data to be made available to the public. Owing to this rationale, the discussion is based on the Census data of 2001, Government of India.

20 Higher Education in India—An Overview

Dr. Siddaraju V.G.

Introduction

Education is universally recognised as an investment in human capital. It is the basic requirement and the most effective instrument of social empowerment and can contribute to socio-economic development by endowing individuals with the means of improving their health, skill, knowledge, and capability for productive work. The knowledge, skill and values acquired through education not only meet the education needs of the society, but they are also permeated with a social content corresponding to the socio-economic and political structure, and consequently social stratification and distribution of power in society.

Higher education is of vital importance for the country, as it is a powerful tool to build knowledge-based society of the 21st century. India possesses a highly developed higher education system, which offers facility of education and training in almost of all aspects of human creative and intellectual endeavours, i.e., arts and humanities, natural, mathematical and social sciences, engineering, medicine, dentistry, agriculture, education, law commerce and management, music and performing arts, national and foreign languages, culture, communications etc. the expansion in institutional capacity in terms of number of universities/colleges and teachers has provided grater access to the students to post higher secondary education.

The expansion in the field of education provided great access to all sections of the society. However, owing to a number of constraints, and socio-economic factors, the benefits of expansion of educational facilities have not fully reach to all the communities specifically among the Scheduled Castes (SC) and Scheduled Tribes (ST). In 2004-05, the GER (Gross Enrollment Rate) was about 10.84 per cent at overall levels, the GER among the SC's (6.30 per cent), the ST's (6.33 per cent), and the OBC (16.60 per cent). Thus, the GER for the SC/STs was three times and that of the OBCs was about two times lower as compared with the others. Between the SC/ST's and the OBC's, however the GER was lower among the former by two per cent points (Sukhadeo Thorat, 2008). Gender discrimination has been a major obstacle in granting equal opportunity for women in Higher Education. It has been identified as a crucial category and deserves attention in the education-equality paradigm.

The Prime Minister, Dr. Manmohan Singh (2005) has optimistically forecast that the 21st Century will be the "knowledge century", by which he refers to the socio-economic transformation that the country is projected to go through in the 21st century as a result of knowledge creation. Mattoo (2009) explicates the notion succinctly: "The whole idea of building a knowledge society is the idea of empowering young men and women through education and ensuring that all our delivery systems are built on the premise of the latest knowledge" (as cited in Bhatia and Dash, 2010, p. 46).

In the next few decades, India is speculated to have the world's largest set of young people. While the correlation between higher education and nation-building is indisputable, the working age population can be an asset only if their potential employability is brought to fruition. Conversely, if the state does not harness the endowment, this demographic group can turn out to be a heavy economic and social millstone.

The Prime Minister, Mr. Singh affirmed the Government's avowal thusly: "the time has come to create a second wave of institution building and of excellence in the field of education, research and capability building so that we are better prepared for the 21st century". With the singular purpose of modelling recommendations and means to tap into this reservoir, the Government founded the National Knowledge Commission (NKC) in 2005. The raison d'être was expressed in the following declaration: "our demographic profile, with 550 million below the age of 25, has the potential to constitute one-fourth of the global work-force by 2020" (as cited in Bhatia and Dash, 2010, p. 47).

The Commission aims to provide a channel to harness the country's vast human capital, more specifically the demographic dividends that accrue from the working age population. The decision to set up the Commission suggests the Government's cognisance of the importance of developing the appropriate paradigm in which to invest in intellectual capital by developing the skill set of the population and encouraging research, innovation and entrepreneurship.

In this context, the present paper is an attempt to analyse the progress of higher education system in India and to analyse the status of women in higher education in India. The preset study is based on secondary data. Secondary data was collected from various reports, i.e., Annual report of MHRD, Economic survey, UGC etc.

Analysis and Discussion

Higher Education in India has evolved in distinct and divergent streams with each stream monitored by an apex body, indirectly controlled by the Ministry of Human Resource Development. Progress of higher education and status of women in higher education in India is presented in the following tables.

Table 1. No. of Universities in India

Year	*No. of Universities*
1970-71	103
1980-81	133
1990-91	190
2000-01	256
2006-07	387
2011-12	659

(*Source:* Various annual reports of MHRD, Government of India).

The above table shows that the No. of universities in India has been increased from 103 to 659 during the period of 1970-71 to 2011-12. The data clearly shows that the number of universities has grown more than six times in the last four decades.

Table 2. No. of Colleges in India

Year	*No. of Colleges*
1970-71	3,604
1980-81	4,722
1990-91	7,346
2000-01	12,806
2006-07	21,170
2011-12	33,023

(*Source:* Various annual reports of MHRD, Government of India).

Table 3. No. of Students Enrollment in Higher Education in India

Year	*No. of Students (Million)*
1970-71	2.0
1980-81	2.8
1990-91	4.9
2000-01	8.4
2006-07	16.6
2011-12	25.9

(*Source:* Various annual reports of MHRD, Government of India).

The Table 3 shows that the No. of students enroll in higher education in India have been increased from 2.0 million to 25.9 million during the period of 1970-71 to 2011-12. It is indicated that the student enrollment in higher education in India has grown 12 times in the last four decades. Further, the India has one of the largest higher education systems in the world, with 25.9 million students enrolled in more than 33,000 degree and diploma institutions in the country.

Table 4. GER in Higher Education in India

Year	*GER in higher education (Percentage)*
1979-80	5.0
1989-90	6.0
1999-2000	10.0
2006-07	12.3
2011-12	17.9

(*Source:* Various annual reports of MHRD, Government of India).

The Table 4 shows that the Gross Enrollment Ratio (GER) in higher education has reached close to 18 per cent in 2011–12. During the Eleventh Plan period (2007–2012). India achieved a Gross Enrollment Ratio of 17.9 per cent, up from 12.3 per cent at the beginning of the Plan period. Various legislative actions were also taken during this period, including the introduction of the Higher Education and Research Bill, the Educational Tribunal Bill and the Foreign Educational Institutions Bill, to enhance transparency and quality in the sector. However, in spite of the significant progress made during the past few years, India's higher education sector is still plagued with several challenges, e.g., its relatively low GER, inequitable access to higher education by community, gender and geography, and lack of high-quality research and education institutions, resulting in sub-optimal outcomes.

The Twelfth Plan recognises these challenges and proposes several initiatives around six focus areas to address them.

- **Expansion**—augmenting capacity in existing institutions.
- **Equity**—creating targetted schemes for backward and minority communities.
- **Excellence**—building excellence through research and innovation, faculty development and internationalisation.
- **Governance**—enhancing institutional autonomy and transparency.
- **Funding**—increasing public and private funding and linking them to outcomes.
- **Implementation and monitoring**—improving co-ordination across ministries and agencies.

The Twelfth Plan emphasises on building "excellence" in India's higher education system. Several institutions are already pursuing this objective, albeit in a less holistic manner. For example: Manipal University, Indian School of Business (ISB), India-UK Advanced Instability Methods (AIM) Network, BITS Pilani etc.

Table 5. Country-wise Students' Enrollment and GER in Higher Education

Year	*Percentage of students enrollment in Higher education*	*GER*
India	25.9	17.9
USA	19.1	95
China	29.3	26

Source: Ministry of Education of People's Republic of China, Twelfth Five Year Plan: Chapter on higher education, UNESCO: Global Education Digest 2011. National Center for Education Statistics, USA .

The Table 5 shows that the Comparison of percentage of students' enrollment and GER in higher education with other countries like USA and China. The data clearly shows that India ranks second in the world in terms of enrollment of students and third rank in GER in higher education during 2011-12.

The Table 6 shows that women enrollment throughout the decade (2001-10) is very normal. In Arts, it is 43 per cent to 46 per cent, in Science, it is 39 per cent to 42 per cent and in Commerce, it is 38 per cent to 44 per cent. The Figs. are showing very steady increase in the general education.

Table 6. Women Enrollment in General Education

Year	Arts			Science			Commerce			Total		
	Total	Women	%	Total	Women	%	Total	Women	%	Total	Women	%
2005-06	4209248	1841682	43.75	1809602	752760	41.60	1612171	636712	39.49	7631021	3231154	42.34
2006-07	4372872	1902249	43.50	1874910	779745	41.59	1613090	610694	37.86	7860872	3292688	41.89
2007-08	5263397	2449813	46.54	2056675	879059	42.74	1916171	743392	38.80	9236243	4072264	44.09
2008-09	5768749	2684371	46.53	2382993	945661	39.68	1888866	863169	45.70	10040608	4493201	44.75
2009-10	7057663	3263293	46.24	2588681	1090368	42.12	2269577	1019934	44.94	11915921	6508383	54.62

(*Source:* Various annual reports of MHRD, Government of India).

Table 7. Women Enrollment in Professional Education

Year	Education			Engineering/Tech., (Including Polytechnics)			Medicine			Law			Total		
	Total	Women	%	Total	Women	%	Total	Women	%	Total	Women	%	Total	Women	%
2004-05	155192	68049	43.85	1085236	252492	23.27	256748	89052	34.68	319671	68596	21.46	1982447	526459	26.56
2005-06	244825	111557	45.57	2358638	593383	25.16	305629	144903	47.41	NA	NA	NA	2909092	849843	29.21
2006-07	271858	122144	44.93	2530362	631270	24.95	319811	150942	47.20	NA	NA	NA	3122031	904356	28.97
2007-08	370660	198723	53.61	1490618	411609	27.61	449333	207843	46.26	293996	69165	23.53	2882318	980066	34.00
2008-09	486186	221494	45.56	1758804	491194	27.93	304391	134761	44.27	215202	58834	27.34	3351011	1107334	33.04
2009-10	545077	274680	50.39	2005563	576851	28.76	354184	168679	47.62	216954	63668	29.35	3790456	1404360	37.05

(*Source:* Various annual reports of MHRD, Government of India).

The Table 7 shows the women enrollment in professional education during 2001 to 2010. It is indicated that there is a dominance of male in all types of education in absolute terms and percentages. Higher number of women is in General Education as compared to Professional education. In Professional education, the male dominance in engineering and Law disciplines are male dominated as compared to education and medicine. Majority of women are pursuing teacher-oriented course around 50 per cent in comparison to other courses in higher education.

From above tables, it is clearly visible that women are more admitted to the general education than professional education. Professional education like Law, Engineering, Medicines and polytechnic courses are more dominated by males where as "Education" is one discipline where all women are joining at large number. We are bringing all these tables to point at a direction that education is one ground where women can develop their situation and gender discrimination at all level can be minimised. The basic reason behind the women enrollment in professional education is declining because of;

- Most of the parents are not interested to join their girl child to the professional course.
- Economic condition of their families is not supportive.
- Parent's awareness is very low.

Summary and Conclusions

The study shows that the past few years, India's higher education sector has witnessed tremendous growth. Today, the country has the largest higher education system in the world in terms of the number of institutions; it is the second largest in terms of enrollment. While India has shown impressive growth in the number of institutes and enrollment in the country, but it still faces challenges on several fronts including low and inequitable access to higher education, shortage of faculty, deficient infrastructure as well as low-quality and inadequate research. Today, a key concern for India is the creation of an employable workforce to harness its demographic dividend to the maximum extent. In the emerging global environment, women are required to develop a more skilled approach to cope with the rapid multiple changing environments. If Higher Education is to thrive within contemporary realities, then there needs to be a shift from exclusive reliance on a masculine-orientated curriculum to a more developed market-oriented content that is comprehensively suited to the entire population. To achieve this, the country needs an education system that can deliver quality in terms of a skilled and industry-ready workforce, without diluting focus on excellent research and innovation.

References

- Bhatia, K. and Dash, M.K. (2010), National Knowledge Commission–A Step towards India's Higher Education Reforms on India's Higher Education. In *International Research Journal of Finance and Economics* (53).
- Sukhadeo Thorat (2008), 'Higher Education in India: Status, Emerging Issues and Approach in the Eleventh Plan'.
- Thorat, S. (2006), "Higher Education in India: Emerging issues related to access, inclusiveness and equity" *Nehru Memorial Lecture, University of Mumbai, Mumbai.*
- United Nations Educational, Scientific and Cultural Organisation (2000), "Women and girls: education, not discrimination" *Paris: UNESCO.*
- Various Annual Reports of MHRD, Government of India.

21 Higher Education and Empowerment of *Dalits*: Ambedkar's Perspective

Dr. H.K. Mariswamy
Dr. C.K. Puttaswamy
Dr. Gopala

Abstract

Higher education is a social good which plays a significant factor in the process of national development. Higher education has grown considerably in India since independence. Access to higher education is uneven and severely inadequate in India. The GATS and WTO agreements have thrown new challenges to higher education in India in the age of globalisation. The new pressures have adversely affected the nation's ability to forge judicious and sound transnational linkages in higher education. The commodification and internationalisation of higher education have created several barriers to the educational empowerment of *Dalits* 0who constitute the most marginalised section of Indian society. Scholars have also noted the complex terrain of Indian higher education and the many problems and challenges that beset it. The studies have emphasised the different logics and justifications that motivate the provisions made in institutions of higher education on the basis of caste, particularly for the *Dalits,* who constitute 30 per cent of the population in India. Various logics such as caste system, capitalism, power structure, power sharing, deprivation and discrimination are erroneously conflated in scholarly discussions around concessions and provisions. These factors have impeded the inclusive higher education of the *Dalits* in the post-independence era. The Gross Enrollment Ratio (GER), Net Enrollment Ratio (NER) and Enrollment of Eligible Ratio (EER) are much lower for *Dalits* as compared with others according to the statistics provided by the official sources.

It is also true that *Dalits* belonging to Hindu religion lack far behind the higher caste Hindu population in terms of access to higher education. *Dalits* have also suffered from a lower access to higher education as compared with their high caste counterpart. The poor non-poor enrollment rate of higher education is the lowest among *Dalits* according to Thorat (2006:08). The scholar has also noted that although the enrolment ratio is generally lower for the female compared to the male, the female belonging to *Dalit* community suffer more in access to higher education than female from other communities due to inbuilt constraints. The various policy provisions in India to encourage more widespread participation in higher education, particularly among *Dalits*, have failed in practice. The elitist curricula in institutions of higher education is a hangover from colonial times and unsuited to the task of enhancing the employability of *Dalits* in modern times. In reality, the effects of positive discrimination have not filtered into higher education in Indian environment due to lack of political will and social activism. Studies have also noted that the so-called 'creamy layer' of *Dalits* do not make disproportionate gains at the cost of their counterparts who are of lower rung economically. The studies on the impact of reservation on *Dalits* in the field of higher education have revealed that reservations in admission, appointment and promotion have partially benefitted *Dalits* in India. There are no adequate empirical evidences to support the popular argument that the creamy layer of the *Dalit* groups benefit to the detriment of the group as a whole. There is an urgent need to expand Indian higher education both in terms of quantity and quality. The most important and urgent reform needed in higher education is to transform it, to endeavour to relate it to the life, needs and demands of *Dalits* and thereby make it the powerful instrument of empowerment of *Dalits* in India.

Educational Background of Ambedkar

Ambedkar was born on April 14, 1891 in a poor family belonging to Mahar community, a Hindu untouchable community in Maharashtra. Ramji Sakphal and Bhimabai were his parents. The boy was named Bhim who became a greatest revolutionary of the 20th century. His father retired from military service when Bhim was hardly two years old. He was put to school at Dapoli when he was five years old. His father moved to Bombay and secured a job in the military quarters at Satara. Bhim lost his mother when he was six years old. His father took lot of interest in the education of children and enabled Bhim to complete his high school education with great difficulty. Bhim was able to continue his education against several humiliations since he was an untouchable. A *Brahmin* teacher in the high school loved him so much that he dropped daily a part of his meal. Bhim drew his surname *Ambavadekar* from his native village Ambavadi. The teacher even changed his surname from Ambavadekar to his own surname Ambedkar in his school records.

Bhim developed in his youth a passion for reading. His father ungrudgingly supplied him with new books by borrowing money from relatives and friends and at times even pawning the ornaments of his married daughters. Bhim was sent to the Elphinstone high school which was one of the leading educational institutions situated in Bombay. Bhim studied hard under the great care, guidance and supervision of his father who had cultivated an ardent desire that his son should become a man of letters and light. Bhim pursued his studies against several odds and obtained a second class in matriculation examination held in 1907. He was compelled to get married at the age of 17 under the existing social tradition and accepted Ramabai as his life partner. He joined Elphinstone College in Bombay and passed the Inter Arts Examination.

Sayajirao Gaekwad, the Maharaja of Baroda provided scholarship to Ambedkar and facilitated higher education. Ambedkar passed B.A. examination in 1912 and was appointed to the post of Lieutenant in the Baroda State Forces in 1913. Ambedkar had cultivated a strong desire to acquire highest qualifications of those years in order to emancipate his people from all oppressive forces and tendencies. Ambedkar signed an agreement in 1914 which stated that he would serve the Baroda State for ten years after the completion of higher studies. He was the first to receive instruction in the land of Lincoln and Booker Washington.

Ambedkar enjoyed the real fragrance of equality, freedom and fraternity in America and engaged in his studies with great diligence, devotion and sincerity. He worked for more than 18 hours a day and obtained M.A. degree in 1915 for his thesis 'Ancient Indian Commerce' at Columbia University. He worked simultaneously on another thesis and obtained Doctor Philosophy for the **Dissertation** in 1916 which was published in the form of a book entitled 'The Evolution of Provincial Finance in British India'.

Ambedkar obtained admission in the Grays Inn Law School and London School of Economics and Political Science. He had to come back to India in 1917 since the period of scholarship was over. Ambedkar was appointed as Military Secretary to the Maharaja of Baroda. He suffered worst kind of humiliation in the office and society for no fault. He had to leave Baroda and serve as Professor of Political Economy in Sydenham College, Bombay in 1918. He was highly respected by the students for his scholarship and devotion to teaching profession. He also organised the Depressed Classes and fought for social justice.

Ambedkar was fortunate enough to receive timely financial assistance from the Maharaja of Kolhapur and left for London in July 1920 to realise his dream of completing higher studies in Law and Economics. He resumed his studies in Economics from September 1920 at the London School of Economics and Political Science and Law at the Grace Inn. He putforth best efforts and was greatly inspired by Benjamin Franklin, who upheld the values namely–industry and frugality. Ambedkar submitted his thesis entitled 'Provincial Decentralisation of Imperial Finance in British India' and earned the Degree in Master of Science in June 1921. In October 1922, he submitted his famous thesis namely–'The Problem of the Rupee' to the University of London in March 1923 which caused a furore in the academic world of London. He returned to India 1923 and resubmitted the thesis which was considered for the award of the Degree of Doctor of Science. Ambedkar emerged as a great scholar with series of efforts and struggles.

Upendra Baxi (1991:02) writes about Ambedkar as an exemplar of scholarship thus: "The student–scholar Ambedkar worked for eighteen hours a day in Columbia University to obtain absolute scholarship. He grew into a bibliophile and purchased about 2,000 books in the city of New York. In London, he toiled there from dawn to dusk till the watchman had to seek him out to leave. He lived on frugal diet so that he can use his savings for buying books. He was a voracious reader, a hardworking student and a polymath. Even as opportunities for university education have grown very substantially, the methods of study and dedication which Ambedkar displayed as a student do not provide any more for the bulk of Scheduled Caste students any model of excellence. He took self-consciously to learning and education as instrumentalities for the eminent leadership of the depressive classes of India".

Educational Perspective of Ambedkar

Ambedkar was a true Buddhist and firmly believed in search for truth and adoption of humanitarian principles in life. The Buddhist principles of *Prajna* (understanding) and *Karuna* (compassion) influenced the educational perspective of Ambedkar. Raghavendra Rao (1991:07) observes: "Inspired as he was by the rational approach of the Buddha in the east and John Dewey in the West he called for inculcation of rational thinking and scientific temper among masses in general and students in particular. He called upon the teachers and students in Elphinston College, Bombay to meet the requirements as well as challenges of the modern world by production as well as application of rational knowledge. He warned that universities should continue to be sacred abodes of learning and not workshops centres which trained an army of clerks".

Ambedkar believed that material negligence and indifference to knowledge were the major reasons behind the backwardness of the Indian people particularly of *Dalits*. His efforts were directed at the removal of social inequities and economic disabilities through opening of avenues of educational advancements and provision of better opportunities for economic progress of *Dalits*. He did not visualise education merely as a means of livelihood but as a powerful weapon to liberate the *Dalits* from ignorance and to strengthen their fight against in justice and inequity in all spheres of life in India. He rightly considered education as a prerequisite for any kind of organisation and movements of the depressed classes. He organised several educational institutions under the banner of 'People's Education Society' to raise the level of consciousness of the serf-like people in India.

Ambedkar had great respect for M.G. Ranade who was a champion of rationalism, evolutionalism and moderatism, particularly, in politics. Ranade had firmly believed that education was the best and surest warranty of social change, for changes primarily have to germinate in the minds of men before they could fruition to its inexorable end. Ambedkar inculcated these ideas and spurned the idea of force as against education as an instrument of social change and economic development in a pluralistic society like India. Ambedkar firmly believed that education could bring not only a new consciousness among untouchables but also impel them toward praxis of self-liberation.

Ambedkar had understood the role of education in a democratic society. He considered acquisition of knowledge to the *sine qua non* for the success of democratic experience. He said that when three-fourths of the population were drenched in ignorance and did not know its rights and responsibilities there could be no hope for self-government. There would be a rule of wealth against poverty, of power against weakness. He further observed: "If we desire to have provincial autonomy, we must ensure two things. One thing is that every access must be given to every grade of modern education to the communities which are educationally backward, in order that they may realise their rights and liabilities of citizenship, and secondly, in order that every access may be given to the communities, it is absolutely necessary, under the present circumstances, that special representation should be provided to them".

Ambedkar had also pointed out that British managed education in India during the pre-independence era in order to create clerks and slaves who remained loyal to them. He had rightly stated that education is the master key which enables the people to gain political power and all other privileges. He appealed to the authorities long ago to consider right to education as a fundamental right and incorporated series of progressive provisions for the educational advancement of Dalits and other oppressed sections of Indian society. He realised that "Education of masses is a matter of great cost". He emphatically observed that education is something which ought to be within the reach of common masses who are the producers of national wealth.

Ambedkar was a great champion of universal primary education. He contended that the Gandhian Scheme would deprive Scheduled Castes people of the curiosity and adventure of learning for they were the poorest of the social studies could be tempted earn a little more than learn, unless until education was sought to be made compulsory. He strongly believed in the educational modernisation of masses under the auspices of the state. In his concept of State socialism he allocated a major role for the State in discharging its duties in respect of education of the unlettered millions of citizens in the country.

Justice V.R. Krishna Iyer endorsed the educational perspective of Ambedkar thus: "Excellence in education is a non-negotiable value, true. Who can deny that, given opportunity, many a flower now wasting its sweetness in the desert air, will not blossom and brighten the garden? And they are the ignored *Harijan/Girijan* talent. On the other hand, demonstrably sub-standard candidates from among moneyed classes are dampened by allowing them to join private colleges, medical, engineering and other institutions by payment of capitation fee although in the competitive market they have no chance, judging by the marks. Our 'meritarian lobby' has not yet shouted against this monetary infection of educational health".

Ambedkar had great faith in the uses of education and its potentialities to alter the values of individuals and prepare them for change. He was greatly inspired by John Dewey's ideas on education and developed a doctrinal belief in the efficacious and transformatory character of education. Dhananjay Keer (1961:03) recalls: "Ambedkar believed that increments in education would enhance the abjuration of traditional values and would also inculcate value preparation for change. Education coupled with law would usher in a great degree of social change, for law was the essence of state".

Higher Education and Empowerment of *Dalits*

Ambedkar was against the privatisation of educational sector since it went against the spirit of social justice in a pluralistic society like India. He strongly advocated nationalisation of education and health sectors since it would empower the marginalised sections of Indian society in letter and spirit. Saroj Khaparde (1991:06) recalls the vision of Ambedkar on inclusive higher education of *Dalits* thus: "It is the duty of a modern university to provide facilities for the highest education to the marginalised sections of society. The oppressed communities should have control in the affairs of modern universities".

Ambedkar wanted to modernise higher education in India since he was inspired by the freedom of choice of learning in American universities. He advocated a reorganisation subjects and courses to provide a wider exposure of knowledge to the pupils. He also pleaded for removal of inequalities of pay scales and status among academics involved either in teaching or research in the universities. He also abhorred the idea of differentiated status for under graduate and post-graduate colleges within the university system. He called upon the students not only to learn, but must be well-versed in the subject concerned. He had also advised the students in schools and colleges to maintain distance from active politics since it would mar their educational progress. He exhorted the students to put a premium on industry and creativity.

In the field of higher education, the actuals fall far less than the formal percentages of reservation. Ambedkar emphasised the role of higher education thus: "I firmly believe in the efficacy of education as a panacea for our social evils. The problem of lower order in this country is not only economic but also cultural. It is not enough to house them, feed them and then to leave them to serve the higher classes as was the ancient ideal of this country. It is even more necessary to remove from them that feeling of inferiority which has shunted their growth and made them slaves of others and to create in them a consciousness of significance of life for themselves and for their country of which they have been cruelly robbed by the current social order of this country. I am convinced that nothing can achieve this except the spread of higher education".

Ambedkar was convinced that mere reservations, liberalising age restrictions and minimum marks could not do. He had suggested that special training and coaching, tuition geared to overcoming handicaps should be a first priority if reservation in higher education is to bear fruit. In scientific and technological fields, preferential treatment should be extended to *Dalits*. He had stated that social revolution, educational revolution and public service revolution should be achieved in order to create a just society in India. He was critical of the educated *Dalits* who betrayed their fraternity for want of power and promotion. Ambedkar (1956:01) lamented: "What is more, when a few members of the SC/ST get a little education, they forsake the lower layers in their own communities and engage themselves in selfish pursuits of promoting their own families. The educated–highly educated class (from *Dalit–Shoshit Samaj*) have betrayed me. I had expected that after acquiring higher education, they will serve the society. But I see here a crowd of clerks who are engaged in feeding their own stomach".

Ambedkar looked upon the university "primarily as a machinery, whereby educational facilities are provided to all those who are intellectually capable of using those facilities to the best advantage, but who cannot avail themselves of those facilities for want of funds or for other handicaps in life. He strongly recommended the nomination of members of marginalise communities on the university bodies which functioned like legislative bodies and were supposed to put forth the needs of the depressed class and to suggest the facilities that were necessary for meeting them".

Conclusion

Ambedkar was one of the great personalities of the world whose life, mission and scholarship have influenced the people across the globe including the marginalised sections. He achieved highest educational progress and emerged as the champion of humanism. He emerged as the chief architect of Indian Constitution by virtue of scholarship and statesmanship. He had frankly admitted that he accepted the chairmanship of the drafting committee mainly to safeguard the interest of marginalised sections of Indian society. He incorporated series of progressive measures in the Constitution of India for the inclusive education progress and integrated development of *Dalits* and other marginalised sections. He strongly advocated that higher education policy framework in India should be geared towards greater inclusion of disadvantaged sections of society since it is imperative to achieve sustainable development. He had called upon the various stakeholders of higher education to reform higher education in India in order to facilitate socio-economic empowerment of *Dalits* and other weaker sections more effectively than certain initiatives such as reservations and regulations. Ambedkar's perspective on inclusive higher education could lead to humanisation of higher education in India with a focus on educational equity, justice and empowerment of *Dalits* and other marginalised sections.

References

- Ambedkar, B.R. (1956) Public Speech Delivered at Ramlila Ground, Agra, March 18.
- Baxi, Upendra (1991) Inaugural Oration at Baba Saheb Ambedkar Centenary Celebration, University of Madras, December 5.
- Keer, Dhananjay (1961) Ambedkar: Life and Mission, Popular Prakashan, Bombay, p. 441.

- Khaparde, Saroj (1991) Dr. Ambedkar's Concern for *Dalit* Education, Paper Presented in the National Seminar on The Life, Mission, Contributions and Relevance of Baba Saheb Dr. B.R. Ambedkar, organised by Ministry of Social Justice and Empowerment, Government of India, New Delhi, April, 15.
- Rao, Raghavendra, J.V. (1991) Dr. Ambedkar and Education, Paper Presented in the National Seminar on The Life, Mission, Contributions and Relevance of Baba Saheb Dr. B.R. Ambedkar, organised by Ministry of Social Justice and Empowerment, Government of India, New Delhi, April, 15.
- Thorat, Sukhadeo (2006) Higher Education in India: Emerging Issues Related to Access, Inclusiveness and Quality, Nehru Memorial Lecture, University of Mumbai, November 24, Mumbai.

22

Quest for Quality Higher Education to the Marginalised —In View of RUSA

Vidhya, V.
Dr. Baiju. K. Nath

Abstract

Indian Education sector is under rapid and progressive changes through the last decade, propelled by the momentum of SSA and now RMSA. Beyond USE, what is next can be UHE (Universal Higher Education) under RUSA. There are special focus groups as target in RMSA, to mainstreaming of the marginalised. It is conceived that the marginalised section is constituted by certain sectors of the society who are segregated on the basis of Religion, Socio-economic status, Physical abilities, Gender and Locality.

The objective of this paper is to analyse the provisions for marginalised sections of the community in the proposed *Rashtriya Uchchatar Sikhsa Abhiyan* (RUSA) and analyse the provisions of the project in terms of adequacy to the needs of students who availed the benefits in *Rashtriya Madhyamik Shiksha Abhiyan* (RMSA); especially those belong to marginalised sections. The method followed for the study was Document Analysis.

RMSA has been given stress to secondary education system. The objective of RMSA is to achieve USE under the tripod; access, equity and quality. Special focus groups of RMSA include girls, scheduled caste and tribal children, children from educationally backward minority community and children with disability. Various strategies were put forward by RMSA to identify the benefit that will accrue to the children from the minority sections of society for the successful completion of secondary education. RMSA is a comprehensive and well-planned programme to cater to the needs of marginalised during their secondary level education. Thereafter, these children are supposed to go for higher education.

According to the RUSA document, there might have a completely new approach towards tending higher education in state universities, distinct from the provisions in RMSA. The document highlighted the key principles of Privatisation for Expansion, Performance-based funding, autonomy of well performing institutions and decision-making through clearly defined norms. A management information system to gather the essential information from institutions is retained in this scheme also. By analysing the draft document it is evident that, the RUSA does not give much emphasis to marginalised sections, though need of their promotion is stated. The dream of mainstreaming of those sections might not be possible with the existing provisions of RUSA.

Introduction

The term "**Marginalisation**" generally describes the overt actions or tendencies of human societies whereby those perceived as being without desirability or function are removed or excluded (i.e., are "marginalised") from the prevalent systems of protection and integration, so limiting their opportunities and means for survival. In India, the problem of marginalisation then, is very real. We see it with women and women's rights—perhaps not as much in Metropolises, but definitely in smaller cities and towns, and villages. Discrimination exists against women at every level, from Female Infanticide to Widow Remarriage, and so on.

Different religious sections also face some marginalisation, as well as people belongs to geographically vulnerable areas, such as hilly and coastal zones.

Marginalisation also referred to as social exclusion is a concept used in many parts of the world to characterise contemporary forms of social disadvantage and relegation to the fringe of society. It is a term used widely in United Kingdom and Europe, and was first utilised in France. It is used across disciplines including education, sociology, psychology, politics and economics. Social exclusion refers to processes in which individuals or entire communities of people are systematically blocked from rights, opportunities and resources that are normally available to members of society and are essential for social integration. The resulting alienation or disenfranchisement is often connected to a person's social class, educational status, relationships in childhood and living standards. Marginalisation also applies to some degree to people with any disability, minorities, people of all sexual orientations and gender identities, to the elderly, and to youth. Anyone who deviates in any perceived way from the norm of a population may become subject to coarse or subtle forms of social exclusion. It is also conceived as, the marginalised section is constituted by certain sectors of the society, who are segregated on the basis of Religion, Socio-economic status, Physical Weakness, Gender and Locality.

Higher Education Sector and Marginalised–Present Status

The National Policy on Higher Education (1986) translated the vision of the Radhakrishnan Commission and Kothari Commission (1966) into an actionable policy by setting five main goals for higher education.

- *Access:* Greater access requires an enhancement of the education institutional capacity of the higher education sector to provide opportunities to all who deserve and desire higher education.
- *Equity:* Equity involves fair access of the poor and the socially disadvantaged groups to higher education.
- *Quality and excellence:* Involve provision of education in accordance with accepted standards so that students receive available knowledge of the highest standards that helps them to enhance their human resource capabilities.
- *Relevance:* Involves promotion of education so as to develop human resources keeping pace with the changing economic, social and cultural development of the country; and
- *Value-based Education:* Involves inculcating basic moral values among youth.

The Programme of Action of 1992 included schemes and programmes that were directed towards the expansion of intake capacity in general, and with respect to the disadvantaged groups such as the poor, SCs, STs, minorities, girls, physically challenged persons, and those in the educationally backward regions, in particular. The Schemes/Programmes were designed to improve quality by strengthening academic and physical structure, in order to promote excellence in those institutions which have exhibited potential for excellence, and to develop curriculum to inculcate right values among the youth.

An analysis of the past Five Year Plan indicates that, there have been continuous efforts to strengthen the base by developing the infrastructure, improving the quality through several programmes and schemes, introducing reforms in content and evaluation and encouraging creation of new knowledge through research. The focus of Fifth five year Plan was on infrastructure development; the Sixth Plan onwards the focus shifted to consolidation and quality improvement. The Seventh Plan laid emphasis on research and academic developments. It was from this plan onwards that the development of centers of excellence and area study programmes got special attention. From the Eighth Plan onwards, the need for differential funding was recognised, it was envisaged that the developing departments would be provided necessary funds to bring up their facilities and activities to an optimum level for their teaching and general research programmes. The Ninth Plan aimed at gearing the system of higher education to meet the challenges arising out of the major social, economic and technological changes. The focus of the tenth Plan was on quality and relevance of higher education, research and development, management in financing and the use of the new information and communication technologies. The Tenth Plan provided the basis for higher education in the 21st century. The Eleventh Plan laid renewed emphasis on higher education and the three targets of broadening access, making higher education inclusive and promoting improvements in quality. In the Eleventh Plan, the share of education in total plan outlay increased from mere 6.7 per cent in the Tenth Plan to 19.4 per cent, of which 30 per cent was earmarked for higher education. This was a nine-fold increase over the Tenth plan. Over the years, considerable progress has been made in higher education in the country.

UNESCO institute for statistics marked that the Gross Enrollment Ratio (hereafter GER) in higher education crossed the threshold 15 per cent to 18.8 per cent still remains below the world average 29 per cent. It is evident that the increase in GER is due to the hike in number of universities and colleges from 30 and 365 to 634 and 33,023 respectively. In other words, low GER reminds the inadequacy of institutions to cater to the need of quality and suitable higher education. The data estimated by TISS, the details of State wide GER in higher education, which tells Goa is in first position with GER of 50.30 per cent and the UT–Lakshadweep with lowest GER 4.80 per cent. Since economic resources, mobility and socio-cultural background are important criteria in determining the accessibility and cost of higher education, disparities are widely visible across geographical regions, gender, and socio-economic and socio-religious groups. The GER among SCs and STs which come under the category of marginalised is much lower than the national average. Ministry of Statistics and Programme implementation, MHRD, Statistics of Higher and Technical education identified the facts that for SCs GER is 8.70 per cent (2004-05) and 11.50 per cent (2007-08), similarly for STs GER is 8.40 per cent (2004-05) and 7.70 (2007-08). Considering the marginalised on the basis of religion the Muslims also have very low GER, 8.50 per cent (2004-05) and 9.5 per cent (2007-08). When compared to the national average scheduled castes and minorities have lower access mostly due to socio-economic factors while tribes have lesser number of institutions serving them. Students from these groups are often required to migrate for education in which case non-availability of residential facilities and supporting infrastructure in the institutions is a major concern. These inferences are drawn from the estimates of NSSO'S 61 st and 64 thround. As far as the marginalised categories are concerned, gender is an important issue to be noticed. By the data obtained from TISS, it is evident that the age group 18-23 years females are very behind males, i.e., 15.8 and 22.8 for females and males respectively. The estimated GER in higher education among SCs, STs and other backward classes across different states showed wide variations. Some states have expanded higher education system fast but some are lagging behind. Further GER amongst caste groups (SC, ST and other) point out that more efforts need to be put in improving GER of SCs (12.2 per cent) and GER of STs (9.7 per cent) in order to enable them to reach national average. Locality also plays major role in the enrollment of students. It is observed that GER for SCs (9.6 per cent), STs (7.1 per cent), and OBC (15 per cent) in rural areas is quite low compared to their respective GER in urban areas. This major differences calls for greater attention and there is a need to improve education facilities as well as opportunities for these social groups to have access to higher education. Religious group disparities are evident that Muslims for various socio-cultural reasons have lagged behind in education including higher education. Muslims with lowest GER 6.70 per cent and Zoroastrians with highest GER 65 per cent are remaining in same India. More than this locality also have influence over the GER of religious groups evidently Muslim OBCs 11.20 per cent, Hindu STs, nine per cent and Hindu SCs 12 per cent. If we consider GER in accordance with the location of residence, urban enrolment is in between 30 and 35 per cent whereas rural is in between 10 and 15 per cent.

All of these indices show the need of reframing facilities available for the marginalised section especially in higher education. Coming to the secondary level of education, RMSA (*Rashtriy Madhyamik Siksha Abhiyan*) is playing key role in bringing up minority as well as marginalised to the main stream.

Rashtriya Madhyamik Siksha Abhiyan–Salient Features

Secondary education is the link between elementary education and higher education. The programme *Rashtriya Madhyamik Siksha Abhiyan* aims at bridging the wide gaps between elementary and higher education. In India, quality of secondary education is more important. The decision to implement RMSA programme was taken in the year 2009, which was launched in 2010. A success of SSA/UEE mission in the improvement of enrollment, retention and completion of elementary education has positive impacts on secondary education. After universalisation of access and improvement of quality education at elementary stage, completion and transition rates have enormously improved resulting thereby more demands in secondary education. In order to cope up with these emerging challenges sincere efforts have to be put for extension and expansion of secondary schools throughout the country. Vision of RMSA is enumerated as:

- To provide a secondary/Senior Secondary School within a reasonable distance of 3-km for every habitation.
- Ensure universal access of secondary education by 2017 (GER of 100 per cent) and universal retention by 2020.
- Providing access to Secondary Education with special reference to economically weaker section of the society, the educationally backward girls, children with special needs and other marginalised categories like SC, ST, OBC and educationally backward minorities.

RMSA has considered marginalised section as a special focus group and has been giving stress for their development. The plan of action to cover special focus groups (namely girls, SC and ST children, children from educationally backward minority community and children with disabilities) is comprised below.

Education for girls is the primary focus of RMSA. Efforts will be made to mainstream gender concerns under RMSA framework. The participation of women in the affairs of the school will be ensured through constitution of school management committee. The distribution of uniforms, scholarships and other educational provisions are taken into account in the gender focus. Every activity will monitor or evaluate on the basis of gender component. Every group will undertake extensive community mobilisation programmes to overcome barriers in girls' education in higher secondary level. The district programme coordinators of high population of SC/ST/Educationally backward minorities and BPL families will be allowed to spent community mobilisation and innovative interventions grant up to Rs 1.00 lakh per annum out of six per cent management and monitoring cost on such activities at school level, habitations, urban settlements, and slums. Taking note of the fact that there is a gross shortage of secondary schools, the dropout of girls is extremely high mainly in northern states. The incentives for girls' education need to be revisited. The measures taken need to be of such nature, force and magnitude that they are able to overcome the obstacles such as poverty, domestic/sibling responsibilities, girl child labour, low preference to girls education, preference to marriage over education etc. Many states have started various incentive schemes like provisions of bicycle, scholarship schemes, cash incentive schemes etc. At the national level to encourage participation of girls National scheme of Incentive to Girls for Secondary Education has been launched in June 2008. According to this scheme, Rs 3000 will be deposited as fixed amount to eligible girls, and they can withdraw it when they reach the age of 18. These are some of the extensive programmes to enhance the GER in secondary and senior secondary levels of education.

When children reach to colleges for their higher education such provisions should be there to hold the whole eligible ones to train to their own taste. And special attention should be given to the marginalised sector to mainstream them. RUSA (*Rashtriya Uchchatar Siksha Abhiyan*) is underway with a plan to eradicate the scarcity of higher education facility. Some key features of RUSA is as follows.

Features of *Rashtriya Uchchatar Siksha Abhiyan*

On the basis of recommendations of the planning commission, the need for reforms in state higher education sector, using central funds in a strategic manner to ensure holistic planning at the state level and enhancement of allocations for the state institutions, a new centrally sponsored scheme is proposed which spread over two plan periods (12th and 13th). The centrally sponsored scheme is called RUSA. The objective would be to achieve the target of GER of 30 per cent by the year 2020. The salient objectives of the scheme are enumerated as follows:

- Improve overall quality of existing state institutions by ensuring that all institutions conform to prescribed norms and standards and adopt accreditation as a mandatory quality assurance framework.
- Bring state higher education system and to establish autonomous institutions for higher education.
- Ensure academic and examination reforms in higher education.
- Enable conversion of some of the universities to Global standard
- Create opportunities for state higher education council to perform well.
- Ensure adequate availability of quality faculty in all higher educational institutions.
- Give stress to research and innovations through higher education.
- Achieve enrolment target in higher education by 2020.

- Correct regional imbalances in providing higher education to all irrespective of their place of living.
- Improve equity in higher education by providing adequate opportunities to socially deprived communities; promote inclusion of women, minorities, SC/ST and differently abled persons.

Project will support state universities and colleges from all states and union territories across the country in policy, academic and management practices. By making a baseline survey, the states can access funding from RUSA to the weakest point to create new system and progress. The state higher education council (SHEC) will be the key in the state level to channelise resources to the deserving institution and SHEC will undertake the process of planning and evaluation, in addition to other monitoring and capacity building function. The project will be implemented through the Ministry of Human Resource Development (MHRD) of the Government of India as "Centrally sponsored scheme" with matching contribution from state governments and UTs. Funding will also be provided for private aided institution, for permitted activities based on certain norms and parameters, in ratio of 50:50. The states would be free to mobilise private sector participation through innovative means, limited to a ceiling of 50 per cent of the state share. The following are the primary components of RUSA that capture the key action and funding areas that must be pursued for the fulfillment of targets:

- Creation of new university and colleges.
- Converting existing colleges or cluster of colleges to universities.
- Expansion of courses and disciplines.
- One Model College in each district by creation/upgradation.
- Research and innovation grants/funds – One university to be made Research University.
- Creation of state higher education council.
- Creation of accreditation agencies.
- Infrastructure upgradation.
- Establishing management information system and ICT for better learning.
- Faculty support – recruitment and capacity building.
- Administrative/governance reforms.

- Academic and examination reforms.
- Affiliation reforms (100 colleges to 1 university, 100:1).
- Leadership development of educational administrators.

Equity interventions are being built into the scheme rather than as stand-alone, low impact interventions. The following components would address the equity issues in a more holistic and integrated manner, thereby making a significant impact on enrollment facilitation of deprived and marginalised sections

- Girls hostels.
- Hostels with 50 per cent reservation to marginalised sections.
- Converting existing buildings to disabled friendly ones.
- Special facilities to disabled.
- Model colleges in each district.
- Special innovative programmes for focus groups and ODL strategies.

RUSA advocates autonomy in establishing universities. The issue of autonomy is crucial to growth and development of higher education. Autonomy has been a subject of discourse in the reports of the commissions and committees set-up from time to time to review the system of education and to initiate the needed reforms and innovations. It is acknowledged that there exist a strong bond between autonomy and accountability. The university autonomy in the present context is not absolute, as it has to function within the regulatory framework. In the autonomous institutions, appointment and promotion of teachers should be based on a nationally determined transparent criterion. The activities of university will subject to scrutiny by a team of experts from the identified area.

It is clear that the expansion of the higher education system in India would not be possible without sufficient levels of private sector funding. With a clear gap in the availability of this private sector funding there is a need to look at partnerships to create progress on this front in the near term. RUSA is seeking private participation (PPP) or contribution in strengthening higher education sector in the form of

- Philanthropic contribution
- Donation from private companies/trusts/NRIs
- Public-private partnership

- Knowledge parks
- Two per cent corporate social responsibility funding
- Rural infrastructure development fund
- Innovative debt instruments.

The corporate sector as key stakeholder in higher education can play a pivotal role in improving our current system. RUSA plan to give direct ownership and management of institutions to stakeholders and accessing help in collaborating with higher education institutions for academic and non-academic support. But it should be ensured that there is no dilution in the quality of education delivered by such institutions. International appropriate accreditation standards may be prescribed by the Government.

RUSA follows a bottom-up approach for planning and budgeting. The process begins at institutional level, which prepares the institutional action plan based on the inputs/discussions with multiple stake holders and sends to SCHE. Also, SCHE considers the requirements of states and initiating necessary action plans with governing bodies. These action plans are the aggregated to form State Higher Education Plan (SHEP). All SHEPs are reviewed and compiled to estimate the next year's fund requirements for programme. This requires setting up of planning teams and committees at various levels, i.e., at underserved and backward districts, regional zones educational institutional level through active participation of multiple stake holders which will help perform both planning and on-going monitoring functions. As the financing of RUSA is concerned, it is based on performance of the institution. The SHEC will create state higher education plans; these would serve as the benchmark against which the performance of the state and particular institutions will be graded. Depending on the level of achievement in various spheres of the plan, funding for the future would be decided. This assessment would clarify state and institutions ability to fulfill the targets it sets for itself; it will also trigger healthy competition among the institutions. These are the outlines regarding the plan of RUSA.

The fact is that apart from the initial part of the document, it does not discuss any particular plan or action to uplift status and standard of marginalised. So far it seen that the schemes SSA as well as RMSA are rising unambiguous plans for upgrading the status of marginalised. It is described under the head "Role of RMSA" in this paper. RMSA entitled RMSA as special focus groups and suggested plans for their development where as in RUSA it is not clearly defined plans to allocate marginalised in higher education sector. Apart from the current concessions which are availed by them, some more has to be put for betterment. Past condition, present status etc. of marginalised are considered in detail in preparing RUSA proposal but the proposal delimited to strategies for financing institutional structuring, privatizing, bringing innovative reforms etc.

Issues to be Resolved under RUSA

There are various issues to be resolved under the proposed reforms in higher education. The major issues may be inclusion of young ladies, PPP in higher education, Inclusion of marginalised in private institution, issue of migrants, etc.

Gender differences persist in educational attainment, employment rates and earnings. In OECD countries, younger women have higher attainment rates than younger men in upper secondary and tertiary education. But, despite a larger proportion of women than men having a tertiary education, women's employment rates and wages are lower than those of similarly qualified men (OECD 2013). Early marriages are another main reason preventing young ladies to continue their education to tertiary level. So, specific schemes should be included to address this issue also.

PPP in Higher Education

Public/Private Partnership means an arrangement between a government/statutory entity/government owned entity on one side and a private sector entity on the other, for the provision of public assets and/or public services, through investments being made and/or management being undertaken by the private sector entity, for a specified period of time, where there is well-defined allocation of risk between the private sector and the public entity and the private entity receives performance linked payments that conform (or are benchmarked) to specified and pre-determined performance standards, measurable by the public entity or its representative. (ministry of finance, India).

In India, both public and private educational institutions operate simultaneously. In fact, India higher education system is intertwined with political, economic, demographic, social and international dimensions. With the result, the higher education system in India differentiates itself in terms of status, governance, ownerships, funding, and administration and control arrangements. There is little suspicion and negative associations regarding private institutions within public education. By and large in India, higher education system has been "over-regulated" and "under governed" making it more complex giving rise to ambiguities. The rational of PPP in the Indian context lies in access, funding and infrastructure. It is important to analyse dynamics between the two and lay policy dimensions in the best interest of the nation without diluting education standards. PPP models in support of higher education extend enough opportunities. In a significant verdict aimed at improving the standard of higher education especially engineering education in the State, a Division Bench of the Kerala High Court directed the State government and the All India Council for Technical Education (AICTE) to take steps to derecognise and close down the colleges which have been continuously performing badly for the last three years. This came as an after-effect of the booming of self-financing or PPP institutions in state. Another issue in professional courses is that, they started functioning by providing admission in a 50:50 ratio, but gradually the proportion changed to 35:65, the fee hike and reduced number of allotment to private institutions, badly affect students belong to marginalised sections. So without making any compromise in quality of education; connecting with PPP will be a hope for developing countries. And the fee structure followed by various institutions is found to be different for same courses; such disparities are the weak points of PPP mode. Since, the self-financing institutions turned out as majority they have influence in decision-making and policy making bodies, which gradually increase social inequalities in the country.

Issue of Migrants

Nowadays, there are a number of people of young age, migrating from other states to Kerala for doing unskilled/semiskilled labors. The wage for them is comparatively less when to the labor done by own people of states; for mass construction works the other state labors are recruited by private agencies and they avail their commission for linking labors with job. Hence, the section so coming migrants are rising as a marginalised group in the state. To lift the whole population including marginalised such a kind of education (primary to higher) required, as the discussion is upon higher education, the suggestion to improve status of the new emerged migrants are to train them in unskilled/semiskilled jobs. Such vocation oriented learning programme will make them masters in their field and hence it will contribute to develop nation. This is not only the issue of Kerala; other states are also facing similar challenges to address the needs of migration.

Conclusion

The proposal of RUSA evokes the need for a comprehensive vision as quality higher education to all in terms of quality in life. By giving suitable and appropriate training, either in academic-oriented or vocation-oriented after completing senior secondary education can place each individual successfully in their own path. Such kind of higher education system is required, i.e., to meet the needs of everyone. Tertiary education may redefined as 'field-based education', in place of institution-based and theoretical education.

Goal of achieving GER by 100 per cent may not lift the status of society; threshold should be given to the needy areas. More than sticking over GER, sustaining good and fruitful education will rewrite the future of the country.

References

- Women tops in higher education but still earn less. 29th June, 2013 Issue No. 278.
- Federation of Indian Chambers of Commerce and Industries, Sector Profile-Education, 2011.
- Consolidated working group report of the Department of Higher Education for XII Five Year Plan, Higher Education, Technical Education and Private Sector Participation Including PPP in Higher Education - Dept. of Higher Education, Ministry of Human Resource Development, 2011.
- University world news.

  http://www.universityworldnews.com/article.php?story=20130628104730556
- European Commission's Green Paper, On Public-Private Partnerships and Community Law on Public Contracts and Concessions, Brussels 30 April, 2004, COM (2004) 327.
- National PPP Policy 2011—Draft for Consultation, Ministry of Finance, Government of India.
- Report of the Task Force on Higher Education, Dept. of Higher Education, Government of Odisha, 2009.
- Executive summary, Leveraging partnerships in India's education sector — The Federation of Indian Chambers of Commerce and Industry (FICCI).
- Introduction to Sociology- e-book:The concept of Marginalisation by Aditya Anupkumar.
- All India Survey on Higher Education, Ministry of Human Resource Development, 2010.
- (Provisional).
- XIIth Five year Plan, Planning Commission of India, New Delhi.
- Working Group for the 11th Plan on Higher Education, Ministry of Human Resource Development.
- Report of the Steering Committee, Secondary Higher and Technical Education for XIth Plan, Planning Commission, April 2009.
- Estimated from unit level data contained in CD of NSS 66th Round of Employment and Unemployment by Bino Paul, Labour Market Research Facility, TISS.
- Selected Education Statistics, MHRD.
- UNESCO Institute for Statistics.
- XIIth Five year Plan, Planning Commission of India, New Delhi, 2012.

23 Status of SCs/STs Women Students in Higher Education: A Case Study

K.R. Bommarayanayaka

Dr. Gopalaraju, R.

Introduction

Education is the most important single factor in achieving rapid economic development and technological progress. Education is considered to be one of the most important means of empowering for SCs and STs students with the knowledge, skills, and self-confidence necessary to participate fully in the development process. Education for SCs and STs has gained a wider role and responsibility all over the nation in the 21st century. One cannot afford to ignore the importance of education for SCs and STs any longer.

Higher Education

Higher education is provided by universities, colleges, and other institutions that award academic degrees. Higher education includes both the under-graduate and the post-graduate levels. Higher education includes most professional education and is strongly vocationally or professionally oriented. It offers a number of qualifications ranging from higher national diplomas and foundation degrees to honours degrees and as further step. Post-graduate programmes such as Master degrees and Doctorates.

Higher education system of India is the third largest in world but as such many have issues like:

- Access to the higher education system is currently restricted to a small portion of society.
- Low public expenditure on higher education as the percentage of GDP comparable to other countries.
- Large rural-urban divides in access, gender inequality, and large differences in GERs in various communities.

India's Gross Enrollment Ratio (GER) in higher education is about 12.6 per cent, in USA-82 per cent, China-23 per cent and Brazil-75 per cent have much higher enrollment rate. Expenditure on higher education is also not satisfactory. The USA expenditure on higher education of GDP is 3.1 per cent, Russia-2.0 per cent, UK-1.3 per cent, Japan-1.1 per cent and China-1.5 per cent and India spends around 1 per cent of GDP on higher education (UGC, KPMG, IMF-world economic outlook data base of April 2011).

Scheduled Caste and Scheduled Tribes

The scheduled caste and scheduled tribes have been specified by 15 presidential orders issued under the provisions of articles 341 and 342 of the Indian Constitutions. The Indian Independence Act 1947, defined the term as "*Scheduled Caste means such castes, races, and tribes or parts or groups which appear Governor-General to correspond to the classes of persons formerly known as depressed classes as the Governor-General may order specify*".

The term Scheduled Tribes is a recent origin which came into being with the birth of the Republican Constitution of India on January 26th, 1950. The term Scheduled Tribes is defined under Article 366(25) as *"Scheduled Tribes means such tribes or Tribal communities or parts of or groups with such Tribes or Tribal communities as are deemed under Article 342 to be Scheduled Tribes for the purpose of the Constitution."*

Objectives of the Studies

1. To know the status of SCs and STs, Women student's enrollment in higher education and also examine the trend of women studying subject offered through various faculties in higher education institutions.
2. To find out the SCs and STs women's students parental socio-economic status and how it is impact on the students carrier.

Study Area

Krishnaraja Nagara is one of the town, and also *taluk* Head nearly 44-km far from its district main city Mysore. Krishnaraja Nagara was founded between 1925s and 1930s as a New town, when a flood by river Kaveri damaged the nearby old town called Yedatore. The town was shifted to a place three miles south and at a higher elevation, now called Krishnaraja Nagara. It was named after Krishnaraja wodeyer, The Maharaja's of Mysore. As of 2001 India census [1], Krishnaraja Nagara had a population of 30.603, males constitute 51 per cent of the population and female 49 per cent. Krishnaraja Nagara has an average literacy rate of 73 per cent. Higher than the national average of 59.5 per cent; male literacy is 78 per cent, and female literacy is 68 per cent. The old name of this college was Municipal First Grade College, which was started on 1971. The college was later taken over by the Government of Karnataka in 1990. And it is now newly called as Government First Grade College.

Higher education in K.R. Nagar is defined as the education attained after the completion of twelve years of schooling. The women students are enrolled in various programmes offered through Department's in higher educational institutions. The total women students' enrollment in higher education during the year 2008-09 was 963 against the total student's enrollment (men and women) of 2388. The position of SCs and STs Women's student enrolled 129 and 61 respectively. The position of women's student's enrolment in the year 2009-10 was 853 against the total student's enrollment of 2296, among the SCs and STs Women's students enrolled 115 and 59. In the year 2010-11 was 812 against the total students enrollment of 2480 and 117 of SCs women's students, only the women's students of STs students is 53 in the year 2008-09. The women's students enrolled in higher education increase, but where as SCs and STs women's students enrolled are very low. In the year 2009-10 and 2010-11, there were some low enrollment in SCs and STs women's student's in higher education, but at the same time the enrollment of women's is also very low, but higher education enrollment of SCs and STs women's students decreases categorically.

SCs/STs Women Students' Enrollment in Various Departments (GFG College, K.R. Nagar)

In the system of higher education there are several areas of disciplines which are offered through department. Therefore, the tables mentioned depict the position of Scheduled Caste and Scheduled Tribes women students' enrollment in various departments.

Table-1 indicates SCs and STs, women student enrollment in department of Arts, Science, B.Com and BBM in the year 2008-2011, the science SCs and STs women student enrollment it is very low, where as SCs and STs women student in Arts department increases, but not up to the mark of higher education, where as B.Com and BBM department student SCs and STs women student enrollment gradually in stagnation position, respectively where as in three years women student enrolled 291(SCs) and

Table 1. SCs, STs Women Student Enrollment

Year	*SCs and STs women students enrollment*					
	2008-2009		*2009-2010*		*2010-2011*	
Department	*SCs*	*STs*	*SCs*	*STs*	*SCs*	*STs*
Arts	104	47	94	45	93	42
Science	13	8	6	5	11	3
B.Com	4	4	9	5	7	3
B.B.M	8	2	6	4	6	5

134 (STs) are enrolled in Arts department. In Science department 30 (SCs) and 16 (STs) students are enrolled. Where as in B.Com and BBM 40 (SCs) and 23(STs) women students enrolled in above mentioned year, it shows that SCs and STs Women student enrollment in department of Science decreases every year, but in department of Arts shows. That there is some normal enrollment among the SCs and STs Women students, at a same time B.Com and BBM department is not satisfactory.

Socio-economic theories regard higher education as playing on integral part in schoolings complicity in the generation of an unequal and hierarchical position of women. Basically, SCs and STs Women student in higher education are found in restricted numbers and in limited subject fields because this is what? Society expects, Even 'needs'. The area of the case study also up holds the unequal and hierarchical, social injustice.

The Economic and Social Gains from Education

If with educational parents contribution to economic development is access to fulfill their desirable goals. Education will enhance SCs and STs women's capacity to contribute to economic progress so in these regard the given table shows that education is also an important part is considered to status of the member of society and also a media to up hold the new generation.

Table 2. SCs/STs Women Students Parental Educational Level

Parental Educational Level	*Arts*		*Science*		*B.Com*		*B.B.M*	
	SCs%	*STs%*	*SCs%*	*STs%*	*SCs%*	*STs%*	*SCs%*	*STs%*
Edu-Nil	17	17	00	67	00	00	00	00
Primary	31	33	57	00	50.50	40	67	00
Middle	4	00	00	00	00	00	00	00
High School	26	25	29	00	16.50	40	00	33
PUC	9	17	00	00	16.50	20	00	67
Degree	13	8	14	33	16.50	00	33	00

The above data indicate that SCs and STs women students parents educational level in Arts department is 18 per cent, where as B.Com students education level is 36 per cent, variably BBM students parents educational qualification is very high 52 per cent, but in science department students parent educational level is more than other department. Educational level of parent is also important factors to decide the student's educational level in future.

The multiplier theory occupies on important place in modern economy, the basic concept of multiplier says that the effect of investment on income, output and employment is manifold than the original investment. The same can distinctly demonstrated in any programme for the rural poor, through the continuous expansion of their economic base. The vices cycle of low income, low savings, low investment, low income, low educational department and also low social status, it can be broken with the injection of higher education in the cycle. Higher education-job opportunity-more income-more savings, more investment-more higher education is the result that sought through higher education it is assured that though who are getting higher education to grab more employment opportunity and an come up through more income-more social status. Experience throughout the globe here proves that higher education can improve the lively hood, as poor and low income people in a significant manner. It helps poor people here get access to higher education, job opportunity, more income, savings and other financial services so that they are co-up with an everyday needs more confidently. The below statistical Table 3, is also the best example of the above theoretical approach.

Table 3. SCs/STs Women Students' Parental Occupational Level

Parental Occupational Level	*Arts*		*Science*		*B.Com*		*B.B.M*	
	SCs%	*STs%*	*SCs%*	*STs%*	*SCs%*	*STs%*	*SCs%*	*STs%*
Agriculture	75	92	72	67	50	60	67	67
Self	4	00	00	00	00	00	00	00
Private	4	00	14	00	00	00	00	00
Government	17	8	14	33	33	20	33	33
Business	00	00	00	00	17	20	00	00

Totally Table 3 indicates that 75 per cent of the SCs and STs Women student's parents' occupation (Arts) totally depend upon agricultural-field. But whereas in B.Com department, 50 per cent SCs and STs student's parent's occupation stands on government sector, in science department 14 per cent of student's parents occupy private sector. About 47 per cent occupy government sector the rest of 49 per cent of SCs and STs students' parents stands on the ground of agricultural-field. In the department of BBM again 40 per cent of SCs and STs Student's parents acquired government job. The rest of 60 per cent concentrate on well-versed agricultural sector, it reflects that even the poor sector part of the society is not in a position to take a stand of their own.

Need for Expansion of SCs and STs Women in Higher Education

There is a is prevailing view that it is necessary to give special attention to SCs and ST women's education at the level of higher education since women are taking advantage of it increasing numbers adequate to the needs of society. Shortages of higher educated SCs and STs, women's available for taking up position of directional and organisational responsibilities in various professions and occupations, however, point to the need for special efforts to expand women's education at the college and university stage. The figures of comparative enrollment of men and women and SCs and STs women students at the higher education's stage reveal that the proportion of SCs and STs women students to the total enrollment in Government First Grade College K.R. Nagar. The below tables indicates that the need and expansion of SCs and STs women's higher education in the *taluk*.

Table 4a. SCs and STs Women's Student's Enrollment: 2008-09

Department	*Total strength*	*Women's students enrollment*	*Total %*	*SCs students enrollment*	*Total %*	*STs students enrollment*	*Total %*
Arts	1642	558	33.98	94	16.84	45	8.06
Science	168	93	55.35	6	6.45	5	5.37
B.Com	187	81	43.31	9	11.11	5	6.17
BBM	299	121	40.46	6	4.95	4	3.30
Total	2296	853	37.15	115	13.48	59	6.91

Table 4b. SCs and STs Women's Student's Enrollment: 2009-10

Department	*Total strength*	*Women's students enrollment*	*Total %*	*SCs students enrollment*	*Total %*	*STs students enrollment*	*Total %*
Arts	1693	629	37.15	104	16.53	47	7.47
Science	266	150	56.39	13	8.66	8	5.33
B.Com	147	63	42.85	4	6.34	4	6.34
BBM	282	121	42.90	8	6.61	2	1.65
Total	2388	963	40.32	129	13.39	61	6.33

Table 4c. SCs and STs Women's Student's Enrollment: 2010-11

Department	*Total strength*	*Women's students enrollment*	*Total %*	*SCs students enrollment*	*Total %*	*STs students enrollment*	*Total %*
Arts	1703	504	29.59	93	18.45	42	8.33
Science	208	92	44.23	11	11.95	3	3.26
B.Com	207	84	40.57	7	8.33	3	3.57
BBM	362	132	36.46	6	4.54	5	3.78
Total	2480	812	32.74	117	14.40	53	6.52

(*Source:* government first.grade.college. K.R. Nagar 2008-2009 to 2010-2011).

The above tables indicate that education is central to the process of sustainable development.

Swami Vivekananda rightly pointed that *"It is only in the homes of educated and pious mothers that great men are born"*.

Findings

The womens fight side by side with men in equal partnership will have to continue to fight against hungry, poverty, ignorance and ill health, the following are some of the main problems of SCs and STs Women's higher education in Govt First Grade College. K.R. Nagar. Here after higher education of SC and ST women their expected expansion in the *taluk* is 85 per cent. However, the SCs and STs women students are not in a position to aim their higher education because of lack of specialisation and at a same time 75 per cent of SCs and STs women students point out the lack of guidance and counselling in the college and 68 per cent SCs and STs women's students suffering from English as a medium of instruction. Sixty per cent of SCs and STs Women's students said that there is a wide gulf between the teachers and the students, and also lack of necessary facilities in the campus, mean while the poor role of the teacher and indiscipline's. Poverty and undeveloped condition, lack of women faculties is also the main problems of students. Last, but not least social evils, group party politics and out- dated conventions is also major facts.

Conclusion

Women higher education in SCs and STs is the key to make women self-reliant and self-confident. SC and STs Women's higher education in particular is expected to holdup the dignity of women as equal partner societal development. It is not only necessary but also expedient to remove the problem and the decline in the standards of teaching methodology, social evils, group party politics, outdated conventions, co-up the wide gulf of students and teachers and try to eradicate local politics and groupism. Possible efforts should be made to improve existing standard of SCs and STs, women's higher education. If we wish to come at par with other well established colleges of cities. It should be our sacred task to work sincerely to raise the standard of SCs and STs women's higher education.

References

- Akadasi Senapathi (2008), Women Participation in Higher Education. Mittal Publication, New Delhi.
- Government First Grade College. K.R. Nagar. Mysore-district, Karnataka.
- Jagannath Patnaik (2001), Women are in Higher Education, Authors Press, New Delhi.
- Rao R.B. (1992), The Position of Women in Higher Education, Chugh Publication, Allahabad, India.
- Shah B.V. and Shah K.B (1998) Education of SCs and STs in India: Rawat Publication, New Delhi.
- Upadhyay H.C. (1991), Reservation for Scheduled Caste and Scheduled Tribe's, Anmol Publication, New Delhi.

24 Impact of National Knowledge Commission on Higher Education with Reference to Gender, Caste and Economic Class

Nagma Sona
Harish D.N.
Chandan D.N.
Suresh Kumar M.B.

Abstract

The National Knowledge Commission (NKC) was founded in 2005 with the main purpose of establishing a knowledge-based society. Despite over 500 universities and 32,000 colleges, the Gross Enrollment Ratio (GER) continues to be low with only 12.4 per hundred of students between 17-23 years accessing higher education which is way far behind the developed countries' average of 45 per cent and even countries like China (22 per cent). The GER for *Dalits*, and other socially and educationally backward minorities, and other socially backward classes is even lower than the national GER. The Centre has set a GER target of 15 per cent by 2015, has planned to increase it to 30 per cent by 2020 and for this, the number of universities and colleges would have to be increased manifold, quality of existing institutions to be enhanced, and existing colleges and universities will have to be expanded. While the IITs have brought about a technological revolution, it is unfortunate that we have not seen such a revolution in other fields of higher education.

However, it is a sorry state of affairs to learn that 50 per cent of the children in government schools between 8-14 years cannot read a simple para, while 65 per cent of them cannot do a simple, two-digit multiplication. Only with improvement in school education, can India become a knowledge-based society.

The Constitution of India offers a framework for aims of education. The socio-cultural aims enshrined in the Constitution assign a transformative role to education. Therefore, in the first parameter the report of 'The

Committee to Advise on Renovation and Rejuvenation of Higher Education' headed by Professor Yash Pal suggested the application of criteria, which derive their value from the categories in terms of which the inequality and social injustice prevailing in Indian society are commonly understood and expressed. *Gender* is the first and foremost category of this kind. The higher education system offers pervasive instances of gender asymmetry. Perhaps no instances are as glaring as the ones we see in our best institutions of technology and management, but the situation is quite grim in several other domains, especially if we extend the scope of our enquiry to cover the composition of the faculty at the highest levels and administrative positions like that of the Vice-Chancellor. *Caste* and *economic class* are two other categories on the basis of which a university's performance can be assessed by asking what steps it has taken to reduce gender, caste and class asymmetries, the modality of such steps, and their outcomes. By definition, a university is a place where India's diversity must find adequate and visible expression.

This paper focusses on NKC, implementation of its suggestions, their ramifications in the context of gender, caste, and economic class based on its knowledge pentagon—access to knowledge, knowledge concepts, and creation of knowledge, knowledge applications, and delivery of services.

Introduction

The term higher education in India includes the entire spectrum of education beyond the twelve years of formal schooling (Jayaram, 2004). Candidates who are successful at the secondary school certificate (SSC) examination have the choice of two tracks of post secondary education. The first track consists of several vocational, technical, and paraprofessional courses leading to variety of certificates and diplomas. These courses vary in duration from one year, in industrial training or teacher training institutes, to three years, in polytechnics. Of these, only the three-year polytechnic courses leading to a diploma is regarded as 'higher education.'

The second track generally described as the 'plus-two' stage, is prerequisite of college level education. Candidates who successfully complete the plus-two stage can take up either a general degree course (such as B.A., B.Com., B.Sc., *et cetera*) of three years' duration or a professional degree course–such as MBBS (5 1/2 years), BDS (4 years), BE (4 years), *et cetera*.

In both type of courses a post-graduate degree (master's degree) would entail two to three years of further education. In all courses, further higher education leading to Master of Philosophy (1-2 years) and Doctor of Philosophy (3-5 years) is possible.

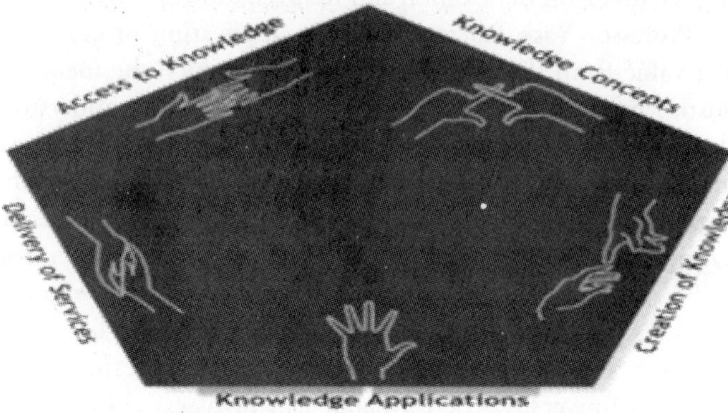

Fig. 1.1. Knowledge Pentagon Suggested by NKC.

Background of the Study

For many decades, 'growth with equity and social justice' has remained on the development agenda of developing countries (Aggarwal, 2001). This was particularly so as the temporal stability of illiteracy and other factors of socio-economic deprivations have resulted in the perpetuation of disparities in social and economic development. Historically, education was used as a potent instrument for exclusion of certain population groups and regions from participation in the development process. Available information suggests that middle-income or lower-income households spend a large proportion of their modest income on sending their children to relatively expensive English medium schools. Such educational opportunities for children are a priority that is almost at par with health care for the family. But there are a very large number of people who simply do not have the resources for such investment. The outcome is exclusion. The researchers believe that inclusion is possible through public provision. The development planners in the latter half of the twentieth century realised that all types of disparities have to be reduced to the minimum in the shortest possible time frame. Therefore, international conventions came out with agreements among governments which prohibit discrimination in access to educational and other social services.

Objective and Scope of the Study

The study would focus on the recommendations of the NKC– submitted in 2006 through 2009– and its implications in the current scenario of higher education in India. An attempt is made to focus on the women, minorities, regional/economic disparities in higher education with exclusive emphasis on the twelfth five year plan's implementations and other initiatives taken by the Central government of late to improve the higher education.

National Knowledge Commission–The Genesis

Knowledge has been recognised as the key driving force in the 21st century and India's ability to emerge as a globally competitive player will substantially depend on its knowledge resources. To foster generational change, a systemic transformation is required that seeks to address the concerns of the entire knowledge spectrum. This massive endeavour involves creating a roadmap for reform of the knowledge sector that focusses on enhancing access to knowledge, fundamentally improving education systems and their delivery, re-shaping the research, development and innovation structures, and harnessing knowledge applications for generating better services. Such a knowledge revolution that seeks to build capacity and generate quality will enable our country to empower its human capital– including the 550 million below the age of 25. Our unique demographic dividend offers a tremendous opportunity as well as a daunting challenge which requires creative strategies for a *new knowledge-oriented paradigm*.

To take its mandate forward the Commission focussed on five key aspects of knowledge (see Fig. 1.1): enhancing access to knowledge, reinvigorating institutions where knowledge concepts are imparted, creating a world-class environment for creation of knowledge, promoting applications of knowledge for sustained and inclusive growth, and using knowledge applications in efficient delivery of public services. Specific focus areas were identified to realise each of these objectives. NKC carried out wide stakeholder consultations, in particular engaging non-government organisations and experts in the form of Working Groups, while formulating recommendations.

National Knowledge Commission had a designated time-frame of three years from 2nd October 2005 to 2nd October 2008, which was extended to 31 March, 2009. In three years NKC has submitted recommendations on 27 focus areas in the form of letters to the Prime Minister. These have been widely disseminated in three compilations: 'Report to the Nation 2006', 'Report to the Nation 2007' as well as 'Towards a Knowledge Society' which is a compilation of the education recommendations. The final Report of NKC contains the full text of all the recommendations submitted by the Commission in the last three years. It also includes follow-up on the recommendations, baseline figures on the key focus areas as well as details of NKC consultations. NKC has also reached out to State Governments for developing knowledge initiatives at the state level.

Organisation

The National Knowledge Commission (NKC) was constituted on 13th June, 2005 as a high-level advisory body to the Prime Minister of India. The vision for NKC was articulated by Dr. Manmohan Singh, Prime Minister of India, in the following words: *"The time has come to create a second wave of institution building, and of excellence in the fields of education, research and capability building."*

NKC consists of eight members, including the Chairman. Mr. Sam Pitroda (Chairman), Dr. Ashok Ganguly, Dr. P. Balaram, Dr. Jayati Ghosh, Dr. Deepak Nayyar, Mr. Nandan Nilekani, Dr. Sujatha Ramdorai, and Dr. Amitabh Mattoo. All Members perform their duties on a part-time basis and do not claim any remuneration. The members are assisted in their duties by a small Technical Support Staff. The Commission is also free to co-opt experts to assist in the management of its tasks.The Planning Commission is the nodal agency for the NKC for planning and budgeting purposes as well as for handling Parliament submissions or responses.

Methodology

The methodology followed by the NKC involves identification of focus areas in the first instance. This selection arises from wide consultation, within and outside the government. After the identification of focus areas, Working Groups of specialists and practitioners are constituted. Working Groups typically consist of five to ten experts, and meet periodically over three to four months in order to prepare a report. Working Group reports are one of the inputs used by the NKC during deliberations to frame its recommendations. In addition, workshops and seminars are held periodically along with informal consultations with concerned experts and stakeholders to get as broad-based a point of view as possible.

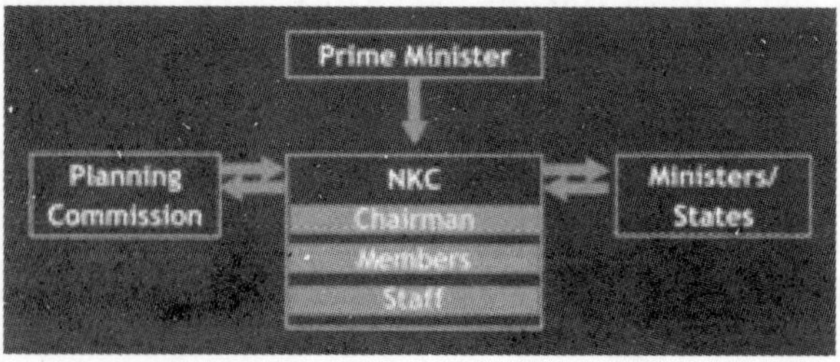

Following this, NKC members discuss the issues raised during consultations and in the Working Group Reports to finalise recommendations. After several rounds of deliberations, a letter is sent to the Prime Minister containing key recommendations. Widespread dissemination of NKC recommendations to State Governments, civil society, and other stakeholders takes place after the recommendations have been received by the Prime Minister and the relevant ministries. The implementation of the recommendations under the aegis of the PM's Office is then initiated, along with coordination and follow-up with various implementing agencies. Key steps include:

- Identification of key focus areas;
- Identification of diverse stakeholders and understanding major issues in the area;
- Constitution of Working Groups and organising of workshops/ seminars, extensive formal and informal consultations with concerned experts and stakeholders;
- Consultation with administrative Ministries and the Planning Commission;
- Discussion in NKC to finalise recommendations in the form of letter to the PM from the Chairman;
- Letter to PM containing key recommendations, first steps, financial implications *et cetera* supported by the relevant explanatory documents by NKC;
- Dissemination of recommendations to State Governments, civil society, and other stakeholders;
- Initiating the implementation of the recommendations under the aegis of the Prime Minister's Office; and
- Coordinating and following-up implementation of proposals.

Impact of National Knowledge Commission

Vocational Training and Skill Development–Inclusive Growth

Launch a National Skill Development Mission with an outlay of 31,200 crore to increase capacity from 2.5 million to 10 million per annum. The National Skill Development Mission would:

Encourage Ministries to expand existing public sector skill development infrastructure and its utilisation by five folds.

Modernise existing public sector infrastructure to get into PPP mode with functional and governance autonomy, establish a credible accreditation system and a guidance framework for all accrediting agencies, encourage agencies to rate institutions on standardised outcomes, and establish a "National Skill Inventory" and a "National Database for Skill Deficiency Mapping" on a national web portal.

Set-up a National Qualifications Framework, which establishes equivalence and provides horizontal mobility between various Vocational, Technical, and Academic streams at more than one career points and a Trainee Placement and Tracking System for effective evaluation and future policy planning.

Enlarge the coverage of skill spectrum to 1000 trades, with relevance to our emerging needs while making a distinction between structural, interventional, and last mile unemployability and correspondingly set-up programmes for 24 months, 12 months, and six months duration. "Finishing Schools" will be encouraged to take care of last mile unemployability.

Create a "National Skill Development Fund" imposing a universal skill development obligation on industry to invest in skill development of SCs/STs/OBCs/Minorities/other candidates from BPL families–as their contribution to affirmative action combined with matching government contribution.

Facilitate repositioning of employment exchanges as out reach points of the Mission for storing and providing information on employment and skill development and to function as career counselling centres.

Enlarge the 50,000 Skill Development Centres programme eventually into a "Virtual Skill Development Resource Network" for web-based learning.

Higher and Technical Education–Social Sector

Expansion, inclusion, and rapid movement in quality by enhancing public spending, encouraging private initiatives and initiating the long overdue major institutional and policy reforms, will form the core of the Eleventh Plan effort.

Improve Quality: Work on a detailed reforms agenda including: Admission, curriculum, and assessment;

Teachers' competence and motivation;

Accreditation and ratings; and

Restructure affiliated colleges and research for policy formulation.

An apex Independent regulatory mechanism accompanied by greater autonomy and internal accountability; establish a high level committee to suggest specific reforms.

Quantitative expansion through establishment of new government and private-funded institutions and increased intake in existing institutions.

Reduce disparities based on gender, caste, region, *et cetera* through differential support.

Establish 30 new Central Universities, 16 in States where they do not exist and 14 as World Class Universities (all India admissions, course credits, regular syllabi revision, incentives for faculty, strong linkage with industry and research institutions, no affiliated colleges, outsource non-teaching functions).

Establish eight new IITs, seven new IIMs, ten new NITs, three IISERs, 20 IIITs, and 2 new SPAs.

Provide flexibility to universities to raise fees accompanied by scholarships, fellowships, and student loans.

Establish a National Science and Engineering Research Board for rejuvenation of research in Universities.

Launch a national Mission in education through ICT coverage in all the universities and colleges; broadband connectivity through National Knowledge Network and requisite nodes within institutions; to be implemented through an Empowered Committee.

Revitalise and reform polytechnics through industry linkage and teacher development, establish 210 community colleges and 700 polytechnics.

Strengthen Open Universities and reform statutory bodies, scale up SAKSHAT as the education portal for 50 crore people.

Implications of NKC Recommendations

The existence, nature and prevalence of the caste system are themselves matters of much debate. The upper classes, insulated from the effects of caste-based discrimination, tend to believe that the caste system is a part of India's antiquated past, an age-old system that no longer has relevance. Invisibility of caste is a fallacy. The caste system is very much a part of modern Indian society and politics. Its interactions with gender, religion, and other variables make it a defining factor in many social and economic processes and its effect on these processes must be considered in any accurate analysis of the Indian polity.

Dalit communities, schedule castes (15 per cent of the population) and schedule tribes (seven per cent) are the largest and most well-known lower caste groups in India today (Census of India, 2001). Historically, discriminated against, studies show that poverty rates among these groups are still markedly higher than those among other groups. However, the position of women within these groups is worth noting. *Dalit* communities have only marginally lower Gross Enrollment Ratios for girls than the national population, and there is only a negligible gap between GERs for boys and girls, unlike other sections of the population where this gap is pronounced. Studies of intra-community and household processes in these communities are also lacking, making it hard to quantify any assessment of their economic and social status.

Given that caste is not just an economic variable, economic development alone will not erase caste-based discrimination. Reservations have been introduced in government jobs, colleges and universities. It is thought that men have gained more from these reservations than women, but the lack of gender-disaggregated datas make such an assertion difficult. There is a high degree of antagonism against the reservation policies amongst the general population, shown by the widespread riots against the 1981 Mandal Commission report, which sought to increase reservation for SC/ST candidates.

India has 30 per cent of the world's total illiterate population and 70 per cent of them are women (Bandyopadhyay and Subrahmanian, 2008). As per 2001 Census, women constitute 48 per cent of the total population, but around 46 per cent of women are still found to be illiterate. Problems of gender disparity and discrimination begin with access to schooling. Female education has long been established to have strong correlations with other dimensions of human and social development.

Despite strong economic and social evidence of the high returns to female education, most communities continue to under-invest in female education relative to male education. Even as the thresholds of schooling completion increase, with significantly narrowing gender gaps in primary education in particular, discrimination against girls in secondary and higher education remains an issue. Economic and social privilege also affect gendered patterns of access, with girls in secondary and higher education predominantly drawn from higher income and social groups, endowed with higher social status.

Even as the low GER is a matter of concern, another serious issue is the inequality in GER across social groups (Higher education in India, 2008).

While the overall GER in higher education is about 10 per cent, the GER for SCs/STs/OBCs is only six-seven per cent, compared to 17 per cent for others. Similarly, the GER is lower for girls (eight per cent) compared to boys (12 per cent). In terms of religious groups, the GER for Muslims are 5.2 per cent compared to 10.4 per cent for Hindus, 11.2 per cent for Sikhs and 18.6 per cent for Christians and other religious groups.

Government reservation policies reserve seats for SC/ST students at schools and colleges. The lack of any gender consideration within these policies ensures that these policies mainly affect the richer and male members of the lower castes (Bhan, 2001). High drop out rates amongst tribal groups, and tribal women in particular, may be due to a number of reasons including the distant location of the nearest school, social-ostracism, familial pressure *et cetera*. Specific attempts, perhaps originating from within the communities themselves, must be made to retain *Dalit* and other lower caste women in school.

General belief is that Muslim women are constrained in their access to education although the lack of data makes this difficult to quantify. Data is needed to better understand this trend and be able to determine the influence of religion itself in the higher levels of illiteracy of Muslim women as compared to regional location, income levels and caste. The use of religious schools, or *madrassas*, by non-elite Muslim families and the use of secular schools by elite Muslims are indicative of a divide in the provision of education along class and gender lines. Provision of single-sex facilities, particularly at a post-primary level, is critical to the advancement of secondary education among Muslim girls.

Education is the fundamental mechanism for social inclusion through the creation of more opportunities. It is therefore essential to ensure that no student is denied the opportunity to participate in higher education due to financial constraints. All the same, NKC proposes National Universities (NUs) that will admit students on an all-India basis by adopting the principle of needs-blind admissions requiring an extensive system of scholarships for needy students. This would make it unlawful for educational institutions to take into account any financial factor while deciding whether or not to admit a student. There must be a well-funded and extensive National Scholarship Scheme targeting economically underprivileged students and students from groups that are historically, socially disadvantaged. Undergraduate degrees in the National Universities, in a three-year programme, should be granted on the basis of completing a requisite number of credits, obtained from different courses. The academic year will therefore be semester-based and students will be internally evaluated at the end of each course. Transfer of credits from one NU to another would also be possible. An appropriate system of appointments and incentives is required to maximise the productivity of faculty in these NUs. Strong linkages would be forged between teaching and research, universities and industry, and universities and research laboratories. The NUs shall be department-based and shall not have any affiliated colleges.

NKC's recommendations require action at three different levels: reforms within existing systems, changes in policies, and amendments in, or the introduction of, new statutes. The suggested changes would also be implemented at three different levels: universities, State governments, and the Central government. India has three global advantages (Natarajan, 2005): (a) communicative competence via ICT systems and the widespread use of English; (b) flexibility in cross-border dealings via local autonomy, which facilitates engagement, and, alongside a rather conservative orthodox university sector; and (c) a technical education sector with 7,74,072 students in 2002 and a high-degree of flexibility in provision. Technical education ranges from higher technological institutions (HTIs), some with autonomy and "deemed-to-be university status", and engineering colleges that grant doctoral degrees, to polytechnic diploma programmes and certificate programmes in industrial training institutes (ITIs). The best vocational education in India is highly innovative. Among the autonomous institutions the research-intensive commercialised IITs have attracted much attention; 40 per cent IITians seek employment overseas.

Conclusion

A major aim of the higher education system must be to ensure that access to education for economically and historically socially underprivileged students is enhanced in a substantially more effective manner. Reservations are essential, but they are only a part, and one form, of affirmative action. Disparities in educational attainments are related to caste and social groups, but are also strongly related to other indicators such as income, gender, region and place of residence. There is need to develop a meaningful and comprehensive framework that would address the multi-dimensionality of differences that still persists. For example, a deprivation index could be used to provide weighted scores to students and the cumulative score could be used to supplement a student's school examination score.

It is important to recognise that there is a quiet crisis in higher education in India which runs deep. The time has come to address this crisis in a systematic and forthright manner. NKC's recommendations constitute an important beginning; the changes suggested would make a real difference.

Of course, the process of reform and change is continuous. There is more to be done, and NKC will continue to think about its next steps, but it emphasises the urgency of the situation, because India's future depends on it. It is important to act here and now.

References

- Aggarwal, Y. (2001), Disparities in Educational Development. New Delhi: NIEPA (DISE). p. 22.
- Bandyopadhyay, M., and Subrahmanian, R. (2008). Gender equity in education: A review oftrends and factors. Brighton, UK: Consortium for Research on Educational Access, Transitionsand Equity (CREATE). Retrieved from http://sro.sussex.ac.uk/1866/1/PTA_18.pdf.
- Bhan, G. (2001). India Gender Profile. BRIDGE (development - gender) Brighton, UK: Institute of Development Studies. Retrieved from http://www.bridge.ids.ac.uk/reports/re62.pdf.
- Government of India – Census of India 2001, New Delhi. Also available on www.censusindia.net.
- Higher education in India: Issues related to expansion, inclusiveness, quality and finance. November 2008. Secretary, University Grants Commission, New Delhi.
- Jayaram, N. (2004). Higher education in India: Massification and change in *Asian universities: Historical perspectives and contemporary challenges.* (Ed) Philip G. Altbach and Toru Umakoshi, 85-112. Baltimore and London: The Johns Hopkins Press.
- Ministry of Human Resource Development (2001). Selected Educational Statistics: 1999-2000. MHRD, New Delhi.
- Natarajan, R. (2005), The role of technical education in enabling the creation of a knowledge economy and society: The Indian experience. in G. Jones, P. McCarney, and M. Skolnik (eds.), *Creating knowledge, strengthening nations: The changing role of higher education*. University of Toronto Press. Toronto. pp. 155-66.
- National Knowledge Commission, (2009). Report to the nation. Retrieved from http://www.knowledgecommission.gov.in/downloads/report2009/eng/report09.pdf.

25 Implementation of Reservation in Higher Education: An Inclusive Approach

V. Rama Krishna
R. Shashidhar

Abstract

India was a country with highly rigid caste-based hierarchical structure, with ascending order of privileges and descending order of disabilities, which operated for about 3000 years. There was an overwhelming majority in the nation that was still backward–socially, economically, educationally, and politically. These victims of entrenched backwardness comprise the present scheduled castes (SC), scheduled tribes (ST) and other backward classes (OBC). Even though, these classes are generically the "Weaker Sections," the nature and magnitude of their backwardness are not the same. It was imperative at that point to establish a code for the political, economic, and social structure. The Constitution, established in 1950, strove to do the same. The present paper is to discuss the compression of public expenditure on higher education which has been quite sharp, if we look at the trend in per student expenditure, from the early 1990s onwards; at constant (1993-94) prices the magnitude of decline between 1990-91 and 2001-02 was almost 25 per cent and such a drastic fall has affected almost every aspect of the educational infrastructure. Also, during this period, in conformity with the structural adjustment policies, government has tried to give a big push to privatisation and a variety of mechanisms to facilitate it have been unleashed. Further the paper will review and analyse the mushrooming of private colleges and other institutions in the higher education category at an accelerated pace in the last couple of decades. Finally, the paper concludes the reservation system in higher education and quality of the education provided to weaker sections in the country where these sections are deprived socially, economically and politically since from the ages.

Introduction

On the international scene, the World Conference on "Education for

All" (UNESCO 1990) advocated that steps need be taken for education of every category of disabled person as an integral part of education system. Another UN initiative was equalisation of opportunities for persons with disabilities 1993, wherein it was proposed that members States will provide education for persons with disabilities as integral part of the education system. The Salamanca Statement and Framework for action on Special Needs Education (1994) provides for education of disabled children in nearby neighbourhood schools and recommends that children with special needs must have access to regular schools. Inclusive education for special needs students has a wider connotation than merely providing education. It includes combating discriminatory attitudes of students and teachers and creating a community that welcomes inclusive education. One of the important features of inclusive education would be to set-up a resource rooms for supporting special needs children in schools. Overall India's Vision of Education–2020 is to create a learning and knowledgeable society.

Two of the finest statements of educational vision in India must be recalled while attempting to perceive 'Vision 2020' for education in the country. The first of these was made by Gandhiji in 1931 in London in the context of universalising education in India. 'India lives in its villages. It is there that our producers live, voters live, the poor and illiterate live. It is the villages that hold the key to the country's problems. So the vision of future India can be greater than to rebuild its half a million villages. The irony is that in terms of the teaming millions inhabiting these villages our developments, our democracy, and our education have all become irrelevant. But once we decide to approach them in the right spirit they are bound to respond, and rise to end their suffering. It may be that in the first phase selected homogenous SC/ST and other backward villages may have to be taken up. In case whole villages do not come forward in the beginning, then mutual-aid teams may have to be formed. Naturally, in the whole process of rebuilding villages education will have the most vital part to play, because it alone can prepare people's mind to receive new ideas, and accept new tools, new relationships, and new forms of organisation'. The second vision statement is contained in Article 45 of the Constitution of India: The state shall endeavour to provide within a period of ten years from the commencement of this Constitution, for free and compulsory education for all cnildren until they complete the age of fourteen years. The framers of the Constitution, knowing fully well that literacy rates were only 17 per cent at that stage, had the courage and conviction coupled with confidence and self-assurance that it would be possible to universalise education within the next ten years. In fact, the mandate given in the Constitution is pregnant with 'dream' potentialities like equality of opportunity to all children in terms and participation and success. It also unfolds the possibilities for better quality of life, freedom from ignorance and obscurantism.

India after 1947 has most assuredly marched ahead as a free, democratic, secular republic. During these years education has always been considered as the engine of personal, social and economic growth. Over the years, at regular intervals, the nation has taken stock of growth and developments in education and planned activities for its future development accordingly. In 1947, 1953 and 1966 it has looked respectively at university education, at secondary education and education in its totality. The nation has made concrete formulations on educational policy in 1968, 1986 and 1992.

Education of Scheduled Castes, Scheduled Tribes and other Disadvantaged Groups

For achieving cohesive and productive society special programmes have to be launched for the Scheduled Castes, Scheduled Tribes and other disadvantaged groups. This can be done by providing positive protective discrimination and also by integrating socio-cultural and linguistic specificities into pedagogical and curricular requirements. Contextualisation of curriculum will be very important if drop-out rate of scheduled castes, scheduled tribes students is to be arrested. Facilities like mid-day meals incentive schemes and of residential schools will have to be augmented.

Literacy Rate and Higher Education

Table 1. Rural Literacy and Education Profile by Social Groups

Rural	*ST*	*SC*	*OBC*	*Others*	*UCH*[3]
Illiterate 1	578	534	452	323	183
Literate 1	422	466	548	677	817
All	1000	1000	1000	1000	1000
Dropout Rate 2	87.7	86.5	82.3	75.1	35.2
Completion Rate 2	5.0	5.2	7.1	10.8	11.4

Notes: (1) Per thousand distribution of persons aged seven and above.
(2) Percentage of literate persons aged seven and above.
(3) UCH is a subset of 'Others'.
(*Source:* Calculations on the basis of Statements three, and five-R in NSS Report No 473, Literacy and Levels of Education in India, 1999-2000 and Census 2001.)

Universities will give more attention to under-graduate teaching. By 2020 at least 50 per cent of university age learners will receive higher education. Each university will have some special programmes suited to the genius of that locality. University Education Departments will undertake more programmes relating to extension and research in school education. Links will be developed between school education and higher education. In many universities, teaching at under graduate level is not given full attention. This trend harms university education and must be checked. Most of the teaching in universities and colleges do not keep the potentialities of the learner in view. University teachers often keep only the prescribed content in focus and are unmindful of the learner's abilities to assimilate. University teachers will have to be oriented towards this through Academic Staff Colleges.

University Grants Commission (UGC)—the apex regulator for higher education in India has come out with a report and sent it to all the universities in the country stating present scenario of higher education in India. The report, (Abhay Anand, 2012) 'Higher Education in India at a Glance' prepared by the Chairman, Ved Praksah and other senior UGC members, states the vital statistics pertaining to higher education in the country in terms of number of institutions, type of degree awarding institutions and the enrollment ratio etc. in past 61 years (1950 to 2011). The report highlights encouraging figures in the growth in number of institutions and enrollment ratio but it also shows that this growth is more in professional streams. It also potrays a dismal picture on the research and development front.

As per the report, presently there are 634 degree awarding institutions in the country with Tamil Nadu leading the chart with 59, followed by 58 in Uttar Pradesh, 48 in Rajasthan, 44 in Maharashtra and Karnataka, Gujarat, Madhya Pradesh and West Bengal having 42, 36, 28 and 26 respectively. The eight states of North-East have 40 such institutions with Assam having 10, Meghalaya, 9. Rest of the six NE states Sikkim, Nagaland, Arunachal Pradesh, Mizoram, Manipur and Tripura having 5, 4, 3, 3, 3 and 3 respectively. The small number of institutions in these states can be due to the small size of these states. But we also have to admit that many students from this region move to different central universities thereby raising questions on the quality of higher education being provided by these institutions. The report also says that out of the total degree awarding institutions 47 per cent (297) are state universities followed by deemed universities with 20 per cent share (129). The central universities and institutes of national importance and other university level institutions standing at seven and 10 per cent each. Interestingly, the private universities are just 100 in number accounting for 16 per cent share.

Detailing about the growth of higher education institutions in India in past 60 years the report says that in 1950 the total number of universities were 30 (most of them government run or funded) and the number of colleges at that time were 695 which means on an average 23 colleges per university. In 2011, the numbers of universities has grown 30 folds and are 634 while the numbers of colleges are 33,023, averaging 55 colleges per university, thus putting huge pressure on the university administration in managing these institutions. It is also to be mentioned that out of these 634 universities, 100 are private. While talking about the growth in student enrollment the report states that in 1950 the total number of students enrolled in higher education institutions was 3,97,000. The growth witnessed is steady till 2001 and stood at 83,99,000 but saw an unprecedented surge in next 10 years. In 2010-11 it stands at 1,69,75,000 a figure that has almost doubled in the last decade. Representing the enrollment of girls during the same period, the report states in 1950 the figure was 43,000 and in 2001 it stood at 33,06,000 while in 2010-11 it reached 70,49,000.

India Education Review (2012) on the much debatable topic of research, the report paints a dismal picture stating that the student enrollment in this area is not encouraging. Talking about enrollment by stages, the report says that 86 per cent students complete their Graduation, while only 12 per cent opt for Post-graduate programmes and only one per cent opts for research thus making it clear that the students either do not have zeal for pursuing post-graduation and research or have better career option available after graduation. The rest one per cent go for diploma or certificate courses. The report goes in detail and states that maximum numbers of students from both the sexes choose Humanities stream followed by engineering by boys and girls choose science while management or commerce stream is still the third preference. Meanwhile, programmes in Agriculture, Education and Veterinary sciences have very few takers. Talking about the public expenditure in education the report states that in 1950 education had 7.92 per cent share of total public expenditure which was 0.64 per cent of the GDP. In 2009, it stood at 13.63 per cent of total public expenditure and 3.77 per cent of GDP. Of this the higher education got 32.3 per cent.

It can be concluded from the findings of this UGC report that despite of growth in terms of number of colleges and enrollment the numbers are not sufficient enough to cater to the education needs of increasing young population of this country. It is also evident from the above report that there is lack of interest among students to opt for research projects that could be attributed to the reason such as they prefer lucrative jobs which could fetch them more money than spending years in doing research and getting very little compensation during that period. The reason could also be that there is lack of motivation to do research and the teaching community cannot shy away from the fact that they are not able to generate that motivation and interest among their students. The onus also lies on the bodies like UGC and AICTE and the universities to provide adequate facilities to young researchers along with good compensation for them to proceed in that direction.

Reviews

Education is recognised as one of the critical elements of the national development effort and Higher education, in particular, is of vital importance for the nation, as it is a powerful tool to build knowledge-based society of the 21st century. The activities of Department of Higher Education are focussed towards developing India as a knowledgable society. The Department's constant endeavour is to improve and expand education in all sectors, with a view to eliminate disparities in access and lay greater emphasis on the improvement in the quality and relevance of education at all levels. The role of the Department, therefore, includes policy formulation, programme implementation, co-ordination with other stakeholders, knowledge management, research and innovation, creation of intellectual property, training and capacity building, reaching out to disadvantaged sections, women and minorities in the higher education sector. The Department has also established a number of premier institutions which have come to acquire a reputation for excellence and national importance. Improvement of access along with equity and excellence, the adoption of state specific strategies, enhancing the relevance of higher education through curriculum reforms, vocationalisation, information technology, quality of research, networking and distance education are some of the main policy initiatives of the higher education sector. The other important policy initiatives in higher education include programmes for general development of universities and colleges; special grants for the construction of hostels for women; scholarships to students, scheme to provide interest subsidy on educational loans for professional courses to ensure that nobody is denied professional education on account of financial wherewithal and making interventions to attract and retain talent in the teaching profession in the higher and technical education (GOI; 2011). Emphasis has been laid on expansion with equity, use of ICT in education, promotion of research and quality education.

During the last 50 years, higher education in India has made great strides leading to the Indian higher education system becoming one of the largest systems in the World. Unfortunately, it is the Indian experience that this expansion in quantity has overshadowed the quality of higher education. Access to higher education needs to be widened in the country, both within the formal system and through other effective innovative measures, such as a truly *open* system and networking of Universities. It is now imperative on the part of Indian Universities to generate their own resources to a large extent. This could be done through several methods, like raising tuition fee and collecting capitation fee, both of which having severe limitations; and others like, launching courses for foreign students, obtaining donations from philanthropists, etc., which have a good potential (UGC; 2003). In the globalised World, the State-protected educational system cannot withstand the pressure without making itself competitive. There seem to be four reasons why new policy initiatives should be taken by the Government in this connection. They are: (i) that the economic returns of primary education far exceed the returns of higher education; (ii) that the private returns on higher education far exceed the social returns; (iii) that the State funding for higher education is insufficient in countries like India; and (iv) that since private sector benefits the most from higher education, it is only just that it should make a decisive contribution. Whether or not one accepts the Government's rationale, new strategies need to be developed for the survival and well-being of the higher education system in the present scenario. Taking the problem of resource crunch in higher education at face value, some alternative ways were considered at this Seminar to combat the present situation, such as: research grants from industries, donations for admissions etc. which were found to be inadequate. It was observed that an organised structure for higher-educational fund raising and creating a culture of giving are the only possible solutions. Major recommendations of this Seminar are summarised below.

Sundaram (2006), using some basic statistics from the 55th round of NSSO data, shows that if we consider only that section of the population which is eligible for higher education (i.e., those who have passed higher secondary or equivalent examination), then the educational achievements do not vary much with their poverty levels among SCs/STs/OBCs in urban or rural areas. That means once the SC/ST/OBC groups cross the secondary education level; their decision to go for higher education is not significantly affected by their economic conditions anymore. But poverty does make a significant difference for eligible students in the general category. This implies that reservation may be helping in improving the level of enrollment, irrespective of economic status, once the threshold level of school education is crossed. However, in the absence of any econometric models predicting any causal relationship, the simple statistics presented in his analyses (Sundaram 2006 and 2007) are unable to clarify, if the differences across SRCs remain significant once differences in eligibility, economic status, regional background, etc. are also taken into account.

Partly because reservation policy had primarily focussed on SC/ST candidates till 1990, separate estimates for these categories were available from government sources. All other castes were put in the "others" category. But inclusion of OBCs for affirmative action since 1999 has resulted in the availability of some data separately for this category as well. Hence, the category of others now includes all upper castes as well as some lower castes close to SCs, and also other lower castes which are not recognised as SCs, STs or OBCs. Deshpande (2006), argues that this kind of categorisation is not appropriate for analysing the differences between the upper and lower classes in the pursuit of equitable development and prosperity. More recently, some studies have tried to combine caste and community categories to analyse its implications for affirmative action. The Sachar Committee Report on the conditions of Muslims in India (GoI 2006), defined socio-religious categories (SRCs) that distinguished between Hindus (upper castes, SCs/ STs and OBCs), Muslims (general and OBCs) and other minorities. These SRCs were further classified into economic groups (poor and non-poor). The analysis of data for these categories showed that educational and employment conditions varied across these groups.

Rakesh Basant, Gitanjali Sen (2010) in the paper said that the recent discussions on higher education in India have raised a variety of interesting policy-related issues. Unfortunately, the empirical underpinnings of this discussion have been rather weak. This is not to argue that issues of higher education can only be resolved through empirical analysis, but to suggest that a better understanding of empirical reality would facilitate a more informed debate on the relevant issues. We suggest that, in this context, a more detailed analysis on the lines of this work might be useful.

Mary E. John (2012), the current moment of higher education reforms in India has yet to receive sustained attention from scholars and activists. Historically speaking, women's education occupied a central place from the nineteenth century to the first decades of India's independence, but, curiously, lost prominence with the onset of the women's movement and the introduction of women's studies in the academy in the 1980s and since then. Although the participation of women in higher education shows steady improvement and a narrowing of the gender gap, the article examines national-level data to reveal the complex and elusive forms being currently assumed by gender discrimination. This includes recognising that disparities among women from different social groups are greater than those among men of the same groups. Secondly, many of the contexts where gender gaps have closed are also characterised by adverse child sex ratios due to practices of sex selection. Taken together, the current era of expansion in higher education demands analysis from a gendered perspective.

Mohi Kumari (2011) Reservation is such an issue regarding which everyone is quite aware and it is burning topic of our country present days. Politicians are masterminds behind the game of reservation system. Our constitutional framers put the clause of reservation for SC, ST and OBC seeing the condition of those days. That time there was caste discrimination system and people were discriminated on the basis of caste. So, to uplift these castes people, Dr. Ambedkar took this step. But focus toward the present scenario regarding reservation policy in India and you will come to know the ugly truth behind reservation game. In every field, government services, colleges etc…there is almost 50 per cent reservation for SC, ST and OBC. Do you think that this thing is fair and justice toward students? What about those students who are securing good marks in competitive exams but inspite of this cannot get into it? Now clashes started between castes to make their caste or put their caste under reserved category. We can take recent example of Rajasthan. A caste war broke out between the Meena and Gujjar communities over the issue of Scheduled Tribe status for the Gujjars when the two communities engaged in bloody battles at Lalsot town, in Rajasthan's Dausa district. Nine people were killed in the clashes on 2nd June, 2007; in this caste war to get their caste under reserve category. The Meenas, a Scheduled Tribe, do not want the Gujjars granted the same status because they fear this will eat into their share of reservations. So, you can understand the benefit of reservation for which people are fighting and killing each other. On the one side, we are talking about non-discrimination on the basis of caste, religion, sex or gender etc…should be happened but on the other hand our Constitution is discriminating on the basis of caste, sex, religion etc... How can we forget our caste and just adopt a single religion that is **humanity** when every time we are facing this worst truth?

Reservation policy is affecting Open Category Students very badly. Its not only affecting their career but creating hatredness in their mind against system and this discrimination. According to me, its really injustice toward those students who do hard labour in their study, score good but cannot get admission into college or job because 50 per cent seats are reserved and for those reserved seats people who are not at all deserving getting admission just on the basis of caste. Caste-based reservation is of no use in the changed circumstances. This is even dangerous as it will forever keep the country divided. The politicians cannot be allowed to ruin the nation, now that they have set their sights even on globally reputed IITs and IIMs. In a democratic country, the candidate who is the most worthy should get the opportunity irrespective of his caste, creed and religion. When caste becomes the criteria for selection, how can anyone expect to get suitable person for that particular job or professional courses. The government argues that it can balance the equation by increasing the number of seats in the educational institution, but then it's affecting on the quality of education. Each time before elections, new reservations start to emerge. These reservation-based admission should be totally banned because it's really injustice to Upper-Caste students and this is main obstacle in the path of success of our country. Its not the fault of that student if he took birth in higher caste and not getting admission into good colleges and good job even if meritorious because seats are reserved by some person who is not at all deserving candidate but is there due to reservation. It's seems to be curse for them. So, there is need to stop these all reservation policies and do justice with students.

Scheduled Castes and Scheduled Tribes Education Statistics

According to the Census 2001 the share of the Scheduled Tribe population in urban areas is a meager 2.4 per cent. Madhya Pradesh, Maharastra, Odisha, Gujarat, Rajasthan, Jharkhand, Chhattishgarh, Andhra Pradesh, West Bengal, and Karnataka are the State having larger number of Scheduled Tribes. These states account for 83.2 per cent of the total Scheduled Tribe population of the country. Assam, Meghalaya, Nagaland, Jammu & Kashmir, Tripura, Mizoram, Bihar, Manipur, Arunachal Pradesh, and Tamil Nadu, account for another 15.3 per cent of the total Scheduled Tribe population. The share of the remaining states/Uts is negligible. As per the Census 2001, total population of the Scheduled Castes in the country (excluding the population of Mao Maram, Paomata and Purul sub-divisions of Senapati district of Manipur) is 166,635,700 which constitute 16.2 per cent of the total population. Uttar Pradesh (35,148,377) has the largest Scheduled Caste population, followed by West Bengal (18,452,555) and Bihar (13,048,608). These states, along with Andhra Pradesh Tamil Nadu, Maharashtra, Rajasthan, Madhya Pradesh, Karnataka and Punjab comprise the group of 'top ten' states in terms of large Scheduled Caste population in the country. In Nagaland, Lakshdweep, and Andaman and Nicobar Islands, no Scheduled Caste is notified. Total population of Scheduled Tribes is 84,326,240 as per the Census 2001 which accounts for 8.2 per cent of the total population of country. Majority of the Scheduled tribe population live in rural areas and their population is 10.4 per cent of the total rural population of the country.

The share of the Scheduled Tribe population in urban areas is a meager 2.4 per cent. Madhya Pradesh, Maharashtra, Odisha, Gujarat, Rajasthan, Jharkhand, Chhattishgarh, Andhra Pradesh, West Bengal, and Karnataka are the State having larger number of Scheduled Tribes. These states account for 83.2 per cent of the total Scheduled Tribe population of the country.

Table 2. Percentage of Scheduled Castes and Scheduled Tribes Population in District, Villages, and UAs/Towns-India

	Scheduled Castes			*Scheduled Tribes*		
Proportion of SC/ST population (%)	*No. of districts*	*No. of villages*	*No. of UAs/*	*No. of districts*	*No. of villages*	*No. of UAs/*
Nil	13*	152,796	62	50**	323,487	1,090
Upto 4.9%	92	71,479	506	278	68,189	2,420
5.0%–9.9	68	61,275	1,055	56	23,742	387
10.0%–19.9%	271	110,590	1,876	69	28,662	264
20.0%–49.9%	148	153,481	856	65	44,240	160
50.0%–74.9%	1	28,672	20	35	26,788	15
75.0% or above	0	15,322	3	40	78,507	42
Total	593	593,615	4,378	593	593,615	4,378

* No SC list applicable in 11 districts.** No ST list applicable.

(Source: Primary Census Abstract, Census of India, 2001).

Assam, Meghalaya, Nagaland, Jammu & Kashmir, Tripura, Mizoram, Bihar, Manipur, Arunachal Pradesh, and Tamil Nadu, account for another 15.3 per cent of the total Scheduled Tribe population. The share of the remaining states/Union Territories is negligible. Lakshdweep, Mizoram, Nagaland, Meghalaya, Arunachal Pradesh, Dadra and Nagar Haveli, are predominantly tribal States /Union territories where Scheduled Tribes population constitutes more than 60 per cent of their total population. No Scheduled Tribes is notified in Punjab, Chandigarh, Haryana, Delhi, and Pondicherry. At the village level out of the total 5.94 lakh villages in the country 1.53 lakh or 1\4 of the villages, do not have any Scheduled Caste population. In 171,865 villages and 2,931 UAs/Towns, the proportion of the Scheduled Caste population is less than 20 per cent while in more than 20 per cent while in 154,481 villages and 856 UAs/Towns it is more than 20 per cent but less than 50 per cent. On the other hand, there are 105,295 villages and 57 UAs/ Towns which have more than 50 per cent Scheduled tribes population in the country while 3.23 lakh or half of the villages do not have any Scheduled Tribes population. It is due the fact that, while the Scheduled Castes population is more widely spread over both in rural and urban areas, the scheduled tribe population prefers to live in groups in the rural surroundings.

Literacy rate of India in 2011 is 74.04 per cent. The Male literacy rate is 82.14 per cent, and Female literacy rate is 65.46 per cent according to Census 2011 (India Facts; 2013). Among the Indian states, Kerala has the highest literacy rate•93.91 per cent and then Mizoram 91.58 per cent. Among the Union Territories, Lakshadweep has the highest literacy rate of 92.28 per cent. Bihar has the lowest literacy rate in India with 63.82 per cent.

- The Male literacy is the highest in Lakshadweep 96.11 per cent and Kerala 96.02 per cent.
- The Female literacy is the highest in Kerala 91.98 per cent and Mizoram 89.40 per cent.
- Lowest male literacy is in Bihar 73.39 per cent.
- Lowest female literacy is in Rajasthan 52.66 per cent.

Provision of Reservation was implemented for the SC/ST and OBC after the enforcement of Constitution of India. In the beginning, it was 15 per cent and 7.5 per cent for the SC and ST respectively. But in 1991 after the Mandal Commission, 27 per cent reservation was provided to the OBCs. In 1995, three per cent of reservation was allocated to the other weaker section i.e., physically disabled in jobs. After a long struggle by the teachers for SC/ST reservation in universities and colleges, the same was allowed in 1997, after 50 years of Independence. Apart from it, after the Supreme Court order, three per cent reservation in jobs of universities and colleges was provided to the physically challenged in the year 2005 and to OBCs in 2007.

Conclusion

Question arises why reservation is not provided to *dalits*, OBCs and physically disabled? In the field of education, the fact is known that the conservative casteist mindset is responsible for not implementing reservation policy even after 63 years of independence. In fact, dominant caste people are not taking sight of reservation for the exploited, deprived and marginalised section of the society-*Dalits*. What does it show? The government seems to be deceiving its people in the context of reservation in education sector. On the one hand, it is supporting the reservation policy and on the other hand, depriving *dalits* of admission through the reservation quota. The quota appears to be filled only in papers and not in reality. Even, after the Supreme Court order for SC/ST in 2000 and Physically Challenged in 2005, this quota is still incomplete.

Dominant sections and elite class live a luxurious life but *dalits* and other minorities continue their struggle in abject poverty. Cultural exploitation and atrocities on *dalits* remain same with exceeding incidents in different corners of the country. Therefore, pressure groups should work in favour of *dalits* and physically disabled. Pressure group plays an important role in the democracy and India is the largest egalitarian country in the world, so to say. Yet, the practice of casteist discrimination against *dalits* contradicts the very nature of the country. The issue of poor implementation of *dalit* quota needs to be highlighted in the print and electronic media and government's attention has to be sought on this crucial subject. The media at present is complacent to the issue; nation's political leaders indulge in party politics seeing the issue of *dalits* as just succour to their vote bank. Reservation for *dalits* appears in their election manifestos only during the elections. There is a lack of political will and no one dares to stand in opposition to the dominant caste's line of thought. Some of the *dalit* parliamentarians also ignore the issue of reservation, for sparing any risk to their political positions. The insensitive should be educated on the issue and others should be able to at least understand the *dalit* agony.

Education is getting privatised and hence expensive. Expensive education has further relegated *dalits* and other weaker sections to the periphery and they can only think of any quality higher education for themselves. Reservation in university jobs is a bit of reparation but that too is being followed in a sloppy manner. Unless *dalits* gets these reserved seats filled, the backlog will keep on escalating. Paying lip service and recruiting a miniscule number would not suffice the cause and objective behind reservation for SCs/STs. Hence, a strong movement is required and *dalits* have to be at their toes to wage this stuggle and make reservation work in their favour.

Revolution is a continuous process and needs a non-stop struggle to achieve it. To implement reservation in the education sector needs the spirit of a revolutionary. People's support has to be mobilised by making them comprehend *dalit* struggle for higher education and jobs. Maithili-Sharan Gupt, a national poet wrote–*"It is a great sin to sit by idly when you've lost your rights."* Concerted mass action is required. Today, if we are not getting reservation in the education, efforts have to be sustained to struggle for *dalit* rights in every arena, in higher education to begin with.

References

- Abhay Anand (2012), Higher Education in India at a Glance: UGC report, New Delhi.
- Census of India (2001), Scheduled Castes and Scheduled Tribes Education Census-2001.
- Deshpande (2006), "Affirmative Action in India and United States, Equity and Development", *World Development Report*, Background Paper.
- GoI (2006), "Social, Economic and Educational Status of Muslim Community of India", Sachar Committee Report presented to Prime Minister's High Level Committee, Government of India, November.

- GoI (2011), Report of the Woring Group on Higher Education for the XII Five Year Plan, Ministry of Human Resource Development, Government of India.
- India Facts (2013), Literacy Rate of India 2011, India Census 2011.
- India Education Review (2012) Retrieved from http://www.indiaeducationreview.com/features/higher-education-india-glance-ugc-report.
- Mary E. John (2012), 'Gender and Higher Education in the Time of Reforms' Contemporary Education Dialogue, Vol. 9, No. 2, pp. 197-221.
- Mohi Kumari (2011), Reservation System in Education: A Real Injustice and Curse for so-called Upper Caste Students, Giri and Giri-Advocates and Solicitors, New Delhi.
- Rakesh Basant, Gitanjali Sen (2010), Who Participates in Higher Education in India? Rethinking the Role of Affirmative Action, EPW Vol. xlv. No 39., pp. 63.
- __________ (2010), Who Participates in Higher Education in India? Rethinking the Role of Affirmative Action, EPW Vol. xlv. No 39, p. 69.
- Sundaram, Krishnamurthy (2006): "On Backwardness and Fair Access to Higher Education: Results from NSS 55th Round Surveys 1999-2000", Economic and Political Weekly, 41 (50), 16 December.
- _______ (2007), "Fair Access to Higher Education Revisited: Some Results for Social and Religious Groups from NSS 61st Round Employment and Unemployment Survey 2004-05", Working Paper No. 163, Delhi School of Economics, October.
- UGC (2003), Higher Education in India: Issues, Concerns and New Directions, Recommendations of UGC Golden Jubilee Seminars–2003, UGC, New Delhi.
- UNESCO (1990), World Conference on Education for All: Meeting Basic Learning Needs, Jomtion.
- UNESCO (1994), Final Report: World Conference on Special Needs Education: Access and Quality, Salamanca, June 7-10, Paris, UNESCO.

26 Role of NGO's in Strengthening the Quality of Higher Education in India

Dr. Shweta Deshpande

Introduction

Education is the dynamic force in the life of every individual influencing his physical, mental, emotional, social and ethical development. The educated person has a greater power of communication, critical consciousness and control over his or her environment.

Education is not for preparation of life. Education is life itself. Every individual is born with a collection of abilities and talents. Education in its many form, has the potential to help fulfill and help them in order to achieve social and economic development. It has become a common place for national development to be linked to education, with education frequently measured in terms of education.

Education, in general, and higher education in particular, plays a key role in the realisation of a nation's extra-ordinary potential and aspirations for economic and technological development. Now, it is well recognised that higher education promotes social and economic development by building human and technical capabilities of society.

Higher Education in India: A Brief Historical Insight

From time immemorial, India has been a centre for learning. Thousands of years ago, great scholars used to teach through the scriptures. A variety of subjects such as philosophy, religion, medicine, literature, drama and arts, astrology, mathematics and sociology were taught and master pieces of these subjects have been written. Under the Buddhist influence, education was available to virtually everyone, who wanted it and some world famous institutions arose out of monasteries, such as, Nalanda, Vikramshila and Takshashila.

Before independence, the first of the post secondary institutions, Calcutta *Madarasa*, was established by the British rulers in 1761. The period 1817-1852 saw the establishment of a few more colleges in engineering and medicine both by the then rulers and by various religious groups, mostly Christian missionaries. In 1857, three universities were set-up at Calcutta, Madras and Bombay. Between 1857 and 1900 a few more universities were established by law. In 1882, the government of India appointed another commission (known as Education Commission of 1882), which advocated among other things, the gradual withdrawal of the state from the direct support and management of institutions of higher education. That was the first indication of the governments resolve to leave higher education to private institutions. Based on the education policy of 1913, some universities were established both under public and private support through appropriate legislation.

After independence, the national government virtually "nationalised" all the universities and colleges and commenced funding them directly. The government approved state support of those institutions that were originally established and maintained by private philanthropies. These institutions have come to be known as grant in and institutions as against government colleges and public universities. After a certain number of years, the government encouraged the establishment of these private institutions and made them function under the academic regulations of the universities in the area.

Concept of NGO and their Contribution to the Social Welfare and Development

An NGO can be defined as a non-profit, non-government, private group that an individual joins by choice. Generally, an NGO exhibits these following features:

(a) It is an organisation which is not mainly financed by governments and not under the control of governments. It stresses on the sense of distance from the state.

(b) NGO's are non-profit making organisations, as a rule they do not generally generate their own funds completely but rely on external financial assistance from government agencies, both national and international.

(c) Programmes adopted by NGOs are welfare programmes and many a time it is government funded rural development programmes.

(d) Although NGO's are private organisations, but their nature makes them somewhat different from what one gradually refers to the private sector. Thus, they are not supposed to make any profit. An essential requirement for NGO's is they should be registered with the Central Government according to the necessary rules.

Development is a process of mutual endeavour which calls for the participation of all segments of the society. But due to the limited capability of the national government in most developing and underdeveloped countries, it has become increasingly difficult to respond effectively to the growing and diversified needs of the vast majority of population especially, at the grassroots. This has necessitated the emergence of institution which may function as a catalyst between the government and the community, but still remain independent from direct government intervention. These institutions in the present day world are being universally termed the non-governmental organisations or the NGO's.

NGO's play a crucial role in alerting states to their obligations, collaborating with states on their programmes where NGO's are better placed to forge links with communities and households, developing alternative models to state models and intervention, and monitoring state activities and their impact. Importantly, NGO's, can serve as a facilitating link with communities and individuals, and feed information to and from state institutions to citizens NGO's have always played a significant role in social welfare development. NGO's contribution to the various fields of the society has been immense and which includes health and medical services, leprosy control and rehabilitation, drug-addiction, population education and family welfare, adult education, pre-school education, housing, recreation, social welfare, disaster relief, welfare and development of children, youth, aged and infirm, welfare of the handicapped, social defense, consumer protection, rural development and agriculture extension, environment, legal aid, and training, etc. The present paper discusses the role of NGOs and how they can help in strengthening the quality of higher education in India.

Role of NGOs in Strengthening the Quality of Higher Education in India

One of the strategic factors for improving the output of educational systems is the quality of teachers. If the teacher-student rapport is at the heart of successful learning, this success cannot be attained without the knowledge of the pupils characteristics. Quality of education can only the improved only when the study programmes, text books, and instructional materials are constantly reviewed and elaborated. Infrastructure and equipments need to be changed over a period of time. The new education system also demands the usage of new information system and communication technology. Thus, there are many considerations which need to be taken into account to improve the quality of higher educations.

Universities have a major role to play in this regard co-operating closely with public institutions and civil society. However, the result can be the best achieved if there is a co-operation between Universities and NGO's.

Since education system is a part of social system it requires a concerted effort and synergy amongst all societal players, for improvement in the quality.

Generally, Universities do not recognise the need for working closely with NGO's. However, NGO's can help the Universities and also higher educational institutions in the following ways.

- Have a monitoring role and bring forward local needs to universities.
- Help in student training by bringing their expertise.
- Take initiatives in arranging campus recruitments.
- Provide their opinion on programme evaluation.
- As NGOs generally work at grassroots levels, they know the problems of the youth well sc they can participate in debates seminars, etc., organised by higher educational institutions and offer their suggestions.

Following are some of the active NGOs which are engaged in contributing to the higher education sector in India.

1. ***Atma:*** A Mumbai-based NGO, provides capacity building consulting and volunteer staff support to education organisations in India. In addition, Atma facilitates collaboration between organisations in India's education sector.
2. ***Aamir Mustafa Kidwai Trust:*** Based in New Delhi, it offers financial assistance and scholarships for pursuing higher studies to nearly and meritorious persons belonging to educationally backward minorities.
3. ***Aga Khan Foundations:*** Helps to study in UK for graduation and post-graduation programmes. It is based in New Delhi.
4. ***Dr. Ambedkar Foundation, New Delhi:*** Offers scholarship for overseas Fellowship for Post-graduates, and Doctoral Research.
5. ***Foundation for Academic Excellence and Access:*** Provides tuition fees, maintenance allowances, hostel, mess charges, up to maximum

five years for the needy under-graduates in Art/Commerce/Science/Medial/B.Ed. and other Technical Professional disciplines.

6. ***Foundation for Economic and Educational Development, Secunderabad:*** Gives scholarship for higher education.
7. ***GBK Charitable Trust, Hyderabad:*** Scholahsip for poor students studying MBBS, BDS, Pharmacy, BE. B.Tech, LL.B. MCA, MBA, M.Com. B.Ed., M.Ed. Ph.D. (for research material), nursing and polytechnic.
8. ***Hashmi Human Resources Development Society, New Delhi:*** Provides partial academic expenses to economically weaker students.
9. ***Crescent Education Foundation, Bangalore:*** Provides scholarship for higher studies for Muslim students from chanpatna city.
10. ***Muslim Social Uplift Society, Aligrah:*** Offers scholastic to students of A.M.U. Alumni organisations.
11. ***Singing Skylarks: Music for cause, Bangalore:*** Apart from providing financial assistance to deserving youth, it is also engaged in counselling students for evils of alcoholism, smoking, taking up environmental initiatives etc.
12. ***Vizuthukal:*** Offers career guidance on all possible opportunities that a student scan take up higher education, gives self-improvement training for the youth.
13. ***Jnanjyoti Sena Samiti, Tumkur:*** Promotes higher education by giving financial assistance to the poor and needy. Offers library facilities at a very nominal fee.
14. ***Stree Shakti, New Delhi:*** Offers financial aid to girls for perusing higher education. It has also associated with various organisations of different countries in the world, which provides job opportunities to women.
15. ***Vidya Poshak, Dharwad:*** Though Vidya Poshak was started with the aim supporting the students financially, through the years, many other programmes were also evolved like providing leadership development programmes, development of soft skills, giving guidance on new job opportunities, counselling the youth on the different aspects of leading a better life etc.

There are thousands of NGO's working in India helping the meritorious, deserving students to pursue higher education. Most of the times the poor once, although brilliant in studies can not take up higher education because of monetary constraints. But many NGOs through their various programmes are helping them to pursue higher education. Now-a-days, NGOs', are not only providing financial assistance, many of them also are engaged in offering career guidance, counselling, developing skills, campus recruitments etc. Thus, the quality of higher education can be strengthened if there is a mutual co-operation between NGO's and higher educational institutions. NGO's know the needs of local people and these needs can be addressed easily if both of them work together.

Conclusion

The above discussion reveals that NGO's are definitely better alternatives in taking many issues of the society including the education sector. Access to higher education and to the range of services it can provide to the society is an essential part of any sustainable development programme. The challenges and the issue relating to quality of higher education can be addressed effectively with the help of public-private partnership and with the help of mutual co-operation between higher educational institutions and NGO's.

27 Problems of Marginalised Sections in Higher Education

Mrs. P. Shailaja

Introduction

The development of any nation solelry depends on its vibrant educational system, and it is proved that education is the key to human progress and social change. Education is a powerful tool for empowerment of individual. It helps in developing confidence of any individual and community about their own capacities, inherent strengths to shape their lives and thus enhance the inner strength intellectual, political, social and economic against oppression, exclusion and discrimination.

Empowerment is the enhancement of the political, social, economic or spiritual strength of individuals and communities. Empowerment envelops developing and building capacities of individuals, communities to make them part of the mainstream society. Education is the means by which societies have been known in history, to grow out of oppression to democratic participation and involvement.

Globalisation and Higher Education

The present day Globalisation has given rise to many dichotomies in the Indian higher education system. Socially backward, obviously economically weak will be further marginalised in the market-oriented model. The private and foreign institutions may provide better quality of education, but with high costs, which is not affordable by a majority of people. No doubt, this will be an advantageous to few 'elite' in the society who comes from upper strata, who can meet the financial conditions of such education, at the same time the poor and marginalised minority groups are deprived from this benefit.

Government has set a target of increasing the Gross Enrollment Ratio (GER) from the present level of about 12 per cent to 15 per cent by the end of the Eleventh Five Year Plan, and to 30 per cent by the year 2020. Various new initiatives are being taken by the Government to increase the

GER. To measure the efforts taken by the government to increase the GER requires complete data on higher education such as number of institutions, students, teachers etc.

Marginalised Communities and Education in India

The Indian Constitution recognises socially marginalised communities based on the Caste they belong to—On the basis of caste, Scheduled Castes (SC), Scheduled Tribes (ST), Other Backward Classes (OBC) and the religious minorities, and also women are marginalised in the field of education. According to census of India 2001, the total population of SC account for 16.2 per cent of the Indian population, ST account for 8.1 per cent of the total population.

Objectives of the Study

The objectives of the study are:

1. To find out the different types of hurdles confronted by women in pursuing higher education.
2. To find out the attitude of SC, ST and Women towards higher education.
3. To see, how the SC/ST and women are motivated to participate in higher education.

Methodology

The information is collected from the Primary and Secondary data method. The primary data is collected from the field survey. The secondary data is collected from the existing data available at the records.

Constitutional Provisions

As per the Indian Constitution's Article 46 states that, *"The State shall promote, with special care, the education and economic interests of the weaker sections of the people, and, in particular of the Scheduled Castes and Scheduled Tribes, and shall protect them from social injustice and all forms of social exploitation"*.

Articles 30, 332, 335, 338 to 342 and the entire Fifth and Sixth Schedules of the Constitution with special provisions for implementation of the objectives set forth in Article 6. These provisions need to be fully utilised for the benefit of these weaker sections in our society.

Special Provisions

After independence, the Government of India has taken number of steps to strengthen the educational base of the persons belonging to the Scheduled Castes and Scheduled Tribes. Pursuant to the National Policy on Education—1986 and the Programme of Action (POA)–1992, the following special provisions for SCs and STs have been incorporated in the existing schemes of the Departments of Elementary Education and Literacy and Secondary and Higher Education: (a) relaxed norms for opening of primary/ middle schools; a primary school within one-km walking distance from habitations of population upto 200 instead of habitations of upto 300 population. (b) Abolition of tuition fee in all States in Government Schools at least upto the upper primary level. In fact, most of the states have abolished tuition fees for SC/ST students up to the senior secondary level. (c) Incentives like free textbooks, uniforms, stationery, schools bags, etc., for these students. (d) The Constitutional (86th Amendment) Bill, notified on 13th December, 2002, provides for free and compulsory elementary education as a Fundamental Right, for all children in the age group of 6-14 years. (e) *Sarva Shiksha Abhiyan* (SSA): SSA is a historic stride towards achieving the long cherished goal of Universalisation of Elementary Education (UEE) through a time-bound integrated approach, in partnership with States.

Higher Education

Enrollment situation in higher education has been captured in terms of gross enrollment ratio (GER). GER for the country in 2001 as per the Census was 12.4. It was 15.3 for males while for the females it stood at 9.2. The overall scenario of higher education in India does not match with the global Quality standards. Hence, there is enough justification for an increased assessment of the Quality of the country's educational institutions. Traditionally, these institutions assumed that Quality could be determined by their internal resources, viz., faculty with an impressive set of degrees and experience detailed at the end of the institute's admission brochure, number of books and journals in the library, an ultra-modern campus, and size of the endowment, etc., or by its definable and assessable outputs, viz., efficient use of resources, producing uniquely educated, highly satisfied and employable graduates.

As per Report of the Higher education in India, Issues Related to Expansion, Inclusiveness, Quality and Finance, the access to higher education measured in term of gross enrollment ratio increased from 0.7 per cent in 1950/51 to 1.4 per cent in 1960–61. By 2006/7 the GER increased to about 11 per cent. Notably, by 2012, it had crossed 20 per cent.

Critical appraisals undertaken by the governmental committees and independent academicians have highlighted the crisis confronting the system:

'increasing educated unemployment; weakening of student motivation; increasing unrest and indiscipline on the campuses; frequent collapse of administration; deterioration of standards; and above all, the demoralising effect of the irrelevance and purposelessness of the most of what is being done.' While the politicians and policy-makers have often spoken about the need for radical reconstruction of the system, what has been achieved in reality is only moderate reformism.

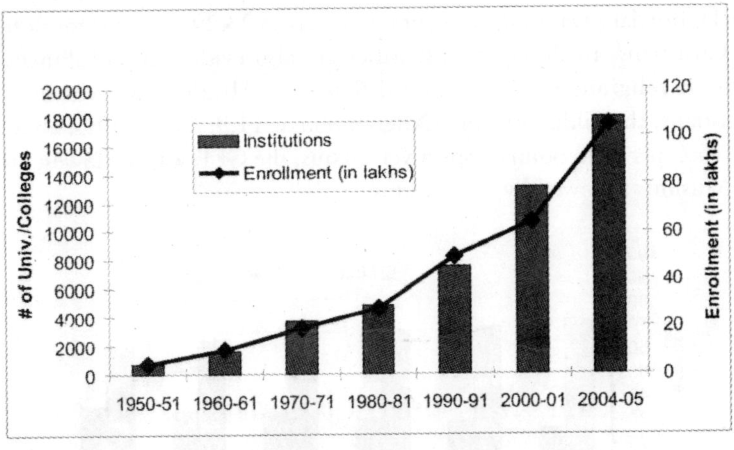

Fig. 1: Growth in Institutions and Enrollment in Higher Education in India, 1950/1-2004/5.

After recording growth rate of around nine per cent for the three consecutive years, India is now considered to be one of the most promising economies of the world. While, higher education gives India an edge in the world economy as evident from the availability of the skilled manpower, and research scholars working abroad, unemployment, illiteracy and relative poverty continue to be the major deterrents to realise her potential in human resources. The taskforce constituted by World Bank and UNESCO during 2000 has also observed that higher education helps increase wages and productivity that directly enrich individuals and society. The prospects and development in the higher education sector in India needs a critical examination in a rapidly globalising world. Expansion, inclusion and excellence were the three objectives of higher education policy of government of India. The government had taken many steps to increase student enrollment in higher education and quality improvement in higher educational institutions.

Access Enrollment

In India, the access to these social groups varies within the respective religion to which they belong. Therefore, the SCs, the STs, and the OBCs suffer unequally as religious group. In 2004-05, the GER of the OBC Muslims was six per cent as compared with 7.34 per cent for non-OBC Muslims. Similar disparities are apparent in the case of SC and the non-SC/ST Christians. In the case of the SC Sikhs, the GER was only two per cent compared with 15 per cent among non-SC Sikhs. Similarly, the GER of tribal Christians was 6.48 per cent compared to 23.29 per cent for non-SC/ST Christians. In 2004-05, disparities are also evident in enrollment rate between **religious groups**. The GER for the Hindus, the Muslims, the Christians, the Sikhs, and the Others stood at 11.9, 6.84, 16.68, about 12, and 15.4 per cent points respectively. Thus, the GER was the lowest among the Muslims followed by the Hindus.

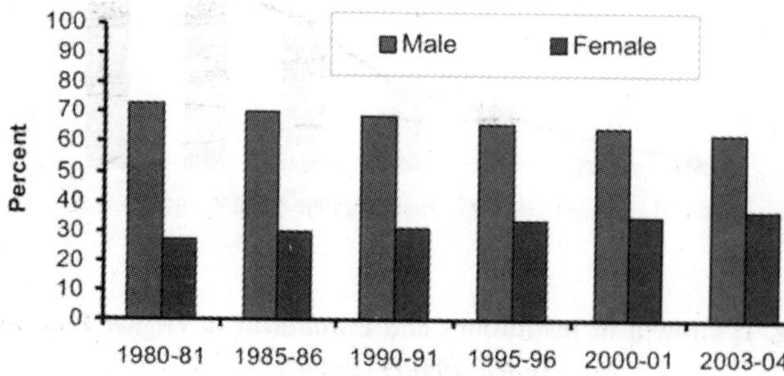

Fig. 2: Male-Female Share in Enrollment, 1980/1-2003/4.

Expansion of Women's Education

Women's access to higher education in India is an issue of women entering higher education came firmly on the global political agenda in 1998. In India, it was the Kothari Commission, which more than three decades earlier in 1964-66, had emphasised explicitly on equal educational opportunities for women and had also suggested effective steps to achieve it. Report of the Committee on the Status of Women in 1974 and women's education was placed within the broader framework of developmental issues. The National Policy of Education (1986), broadening the vision further underscored the role of education in empowering women that would overcome inequalities and disparities. The growth rate of women students in higher education between 1993-04 to 2004-05 has been 7.72 per cent as compared to 4.73 per cent for men. The census-adjusted figures for two rounds, i.e., 1993-94 and 1999-2000 (the corresponding census years 1991 and 2001), although slightly higher show similar trend, i.e., 8.77 per cent for women and 5.22 per cent for men respectively.

Gap in Enrollment

In the recent studies, it is traced that the there is a lot of gap in the enrollment rate between the male and female. As the Constitution provides the right to education to all, still we can find the difference this is due to the problems faced by the SC, ST, minorities and women in imparting higher education. We can find lot of gap in higher education in the rural areas when compared to the urban areas. The GER for poor belonging to the STs, the SCs, the OBCs, and the others stood at 1.55 per cent, 1.89 per cent, 2.30 per cent, and 3.58 per cent respectively. In the rural areas, the GER was the lowest among the STs at a marginal level of 1.11 per cent followed by the SCs at 1.35 per cent, the OBCs at 1.13 per cent, and the others at 1.66 per cent – the overall GER being 1.30 per cent. In the urban areas, the GER for the urban poor stood at 3.86, 4.78, 5.16, and seven percentage points respectively for the SCs, the STs, the OBCs, and the others – the average being 5.51 per cent.

Gender Gap and Disparity in Gross Enrollment Ratio in Higher Education

Year	*Total*			*Rural*			*Urban*		
	Male	*Female*	*Gap*	*Male*	*Female*	*Gap*	*Male*	*Female*	*Gap*
1983	10.87	4.49	6.38	6.19	1.84	4.35	22.36	12.36	9.99
1987-88	11.83	5.37	6.46	7.35	2.34	5.01	24.22	15.23	8.99
1993-94	11.66	5.88	5.78	7.22	2.01	5.21	23.05	16.89	6.16
1999-00	12.13	7.94	4.19	7.53	3.61	3.92	21.98	18.71	3.27
2004-05	14.42	10.57	3.85	9.28	5.67	3.61	24.77	22.56	2.21

Source: UGC Reports 2011.

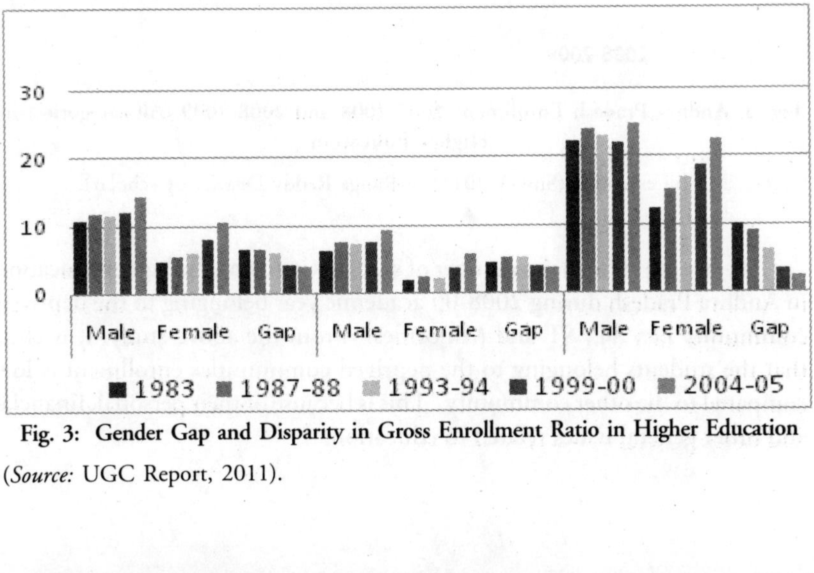

Fig. 3: Gender Gap and Disparity in Gross Enrollment Ratio in Higher Education

(*Source:* UGC Report, 2011).

Social Status (Enrollment) SC, ST, OBCs

As per the reports, the enrollment among the social status in the rural areas is very low. There is a lot of gap between the rural and urban enrollment ratios. The enrollment among the ST is very low when compared to other groups. The GER in rural area is much lower for ST, SC, and OBC as compared with others, it's being 6.43 per cent, 5.0 per cent, 7.0 per cent and 16.74 per cent respectively. Thus, GER of SC and ST of were about one-third compared with other. The GER of OBC was about half compared with others.

Andhra Pradesh Enrollment 2008-2009 (All categories)

Year	*Higher Secondary*		*Graduation (Degree)*	
	Boys	*Girls*	*Boys*	*Girls*
2008-2009	58520	52435	56152	49752

(*Source:* M.Phil Extended (Survey 2011)

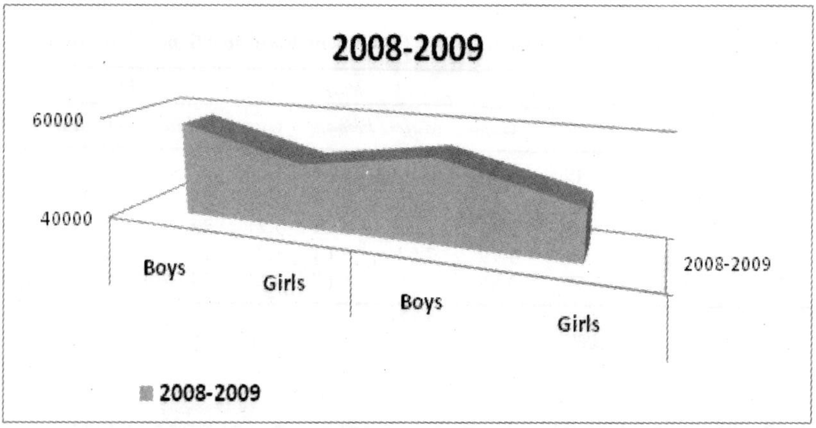

Fig. 4: Andhra Pradesh Enrollment 2007-2008 and 2008-2009 (All categories) in Higher Education

(*Source:* M.Phil extended (Survey 2011) in Ranga Reddy District by scholar).

As per the records the number of students perusing the higher education in Andhra Pradesh during 2008-09 academic year belonging to the deprived community i.e., SC, ST and Minorities. From the above study, it is clear that the students belonging to the deprived communities enrollment is low compared to the other community. This is because of their personal, financial and other general issues related to education.

Andhra Pradesh Enrollment 2007- 2008 and 2008-2009 (All, SC, ST and Minorities) in Higher Education

2008-09	*Higher Secondary (2007-08)*		*Graduation (Degree) 2008-09*	
	Boys	*Girls*	*Boys*	*Girls*
All	58520	52435	56152	49752
SC	11742	9745	10784	8745
ST	4012	3458	3984	3741
Minorities	1985	1421	1842	1154

(*Source:* Reports of State Government of A.P).

2008-09	*Higher Secondary*	*Gradguation*
All	110955	105904
SC	21487	19529
ST	7470	7725
Minorities	3406	2996

(*Source:* Reports of State Government of A.P.).

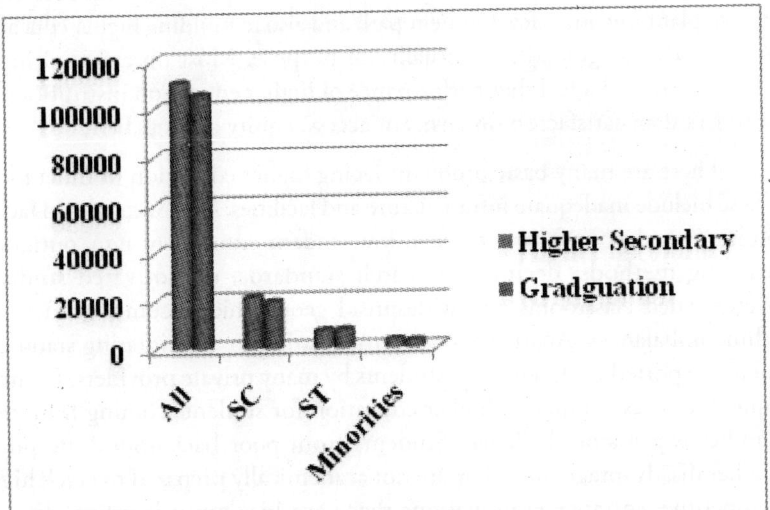

Fig. 5.

Critical Issues in Indian Higher Education

As India strives to compete in a globalised economy in areas that require highly-trained professionals, the quality of higher education becomes increasingly important. So far, India's large, educated population base and its reservoir of at least moderately well-trained university graduates have aided the country in moving ahead, but the competition is fierce; from

China in particular. Other countries are also upgrading higher education with the aim of building world class universities. Even the small top tier of higher education faces serious problems. Many IIT graduates, well-trained in technology, have chosen not to contribute their skills to the burgeoning technology sector in India; perhaps half leave the country immediately upon graduation to pursue advanced studies abroad, and most do not return. A stunning 86 per cent of Indian students in the fields of science and technology, who obtain degrees in the United States do not return home immediately following their graduation.

The present system of higher education does not serve the purpose for which it has been started. In general education itself has become so profitable a business that quality is lost in the increase of quantity of professional institutions with quota system and politicisation adding fuel to the fire of spoil system, thereby increasing unemployment of graduates without quick relief to mitigate their sufferings in the job market of the country.

The growth of higher education in India has been largely guided by the serviceable prerequisite of the economy. After independence, the role of the state in planning out a development path and also in building higher education institutions was guided by mutuality of purpose. Most observers of higher education in India feel that performance of higher education institutions has been less than satisfactory in terms of access, equity and quality.

There are many basic problems facing higher education in India today. These include inadequate infrastructure and facilities, large vacancies in faculty positions and poor faculty thereof, low student enrollment rate, outmoded teaching methods, declining research standards, unmotivated students, overcrowded classrooms and widespread geographic, income, gender, and ethnic imbalances. Apart from concerns relating to deteriorating standards, there is reported exploitation of students by many private providers. Ensuring equitable access to quality higher education for students coming from poor families is a major challenge. Students from poor background are put to further disadvantage since they are not academically prepared to crack highly competitive entrance examinations that have bias towards urban elite and rich students having access to private tuitions and coaching.

Education in basic sciences and subjects that are not market-friendly has suffered. Research in higher education institutions is at its lowest ebb. There is an inadequate and diminishing financial support for higher education from the government and from society. Many colleges established in rural areas are non-viable, are under-enrolled and have extremely poor infrastructure and facilities with just a few teachers. There is an absence of a well-informed reform agenda for higher education in the country. A few efforts made now and then are not rooted in the new global realties based on competition and increased mobility of students and workforce.

There are so many people in various parts of country which are still out of reach. This is when we have to emphasise more on our education programmes and made our system reachable to all areas. Government has to rethink on these areas to implement more on the policies. Money also plays a vital role for the education system which needs to unique for all globally recognised syllabus and curricula. Our Constitution says that this is the responsibility of central and state government to build good education system, for which we need to have funds. But despite there was a large expenditure on the funds every year on education where the fund goes and our system remains intact.

Higher Education in Andhra Pradesh

The Andhra Pradesh state have witnessed a boom in education sector in the past five years, but the number of students in the 18-23 age group enrolling for higher education in the state has not gone up. The state's gross enrollment ratio (GER) is a meagre 9.5 per cent which is the lowest among the four southern states. While the number of colleges in the state has increased by over 52 per cent from 2005 to 2009, the GER of the state is still below the national average of 13 per cent.

Further, the number of students dropping out of college every year is 20 per cent in the state i.e., an alarming two lakh students per year.

While educationists in the state attribute several reasons to the stagnant GER rates, the lack of diversity in courses offered seems to be the most important among them. There is a lack of focus on developing regular degree colleges offering interesting and up-to-date courses which can give students an edge over their counterparts in other states. Analysts point out that the only option for "good" education in the state is that of medical and engineering colleges, the quality of which is dwindling by the day. The number of engineering colleges and medical colleges in states like Karnataka and Kerala is not higher than that of the number of regular degree colleges there, Ramana points out. The ratio of professional to regular courses is maintained at 1:2, providing students with better, yet economic options for higher education. Also, AP is fast losing students to other states like Karnataka and Tamil Nadu. "To take a course in management, most students here go to Bangalore, Delhi or Mumbai where the quality of education is better.

Even though we have 894 MBA colleges, students feel that they will become employable only if they leave the state," says Professor P. Purushotham Rao, a senior professor, Osmania University. He says similar is the case with engineering and pharmacy courses in the state.

Case Study of Ranga Reddy District (A.P)

A detailed study was conducted in Ranga Reddy District of Andhra Pradesh to focus on the enrollment ratio in the district. Ranga Reddy District consists of 37 mandals including rural and urban areas. The following table represents the data on enrollment in the consequent years from 10th class enrollment to graduation level in the district.

Details of Enrollment from 2006-07 to 2008-09 (10th class to Degree) of Ranga Reddy District, A.P.

Category	*Enrollment in secondary (10th class) in 2006-07*			*Enrollment in higher Secondary (2007-08)*			*Enrollment in degree (2008-09)*		
	Boys	*Girls*	*Total*	*Boys*	*Girls*	*Total*	*Boys*	*Girls*	*Total*
All	26483	23940	50423	23471	18452	41923	21745	15328	37073
SC	3548	2874	6422	3125	2741	5866	3254	2841	6095
ST	1452	1084	2536	1041	874	1915	1142	714	1856

(*Source :* SSA and Board of Intermediate, A.P.).

Details of Enrollment from 2006-07 to 2008-09 (10th class to Degree) of Ranga Reddy District, A.P. (All, SC and ST)

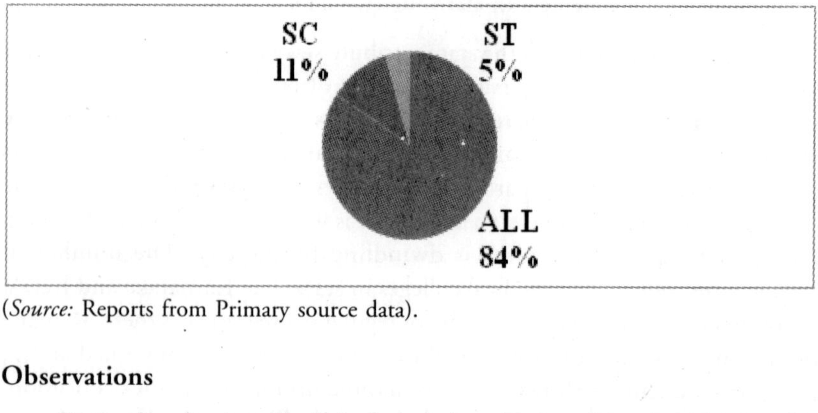

(*Source:* Reports from Primary source data).

Observations

From the above study it is found that the number of students, who enrolled in Secondary Education (10th class) are not continuing their Higher Secondary Education and Degree due to their personal and other problems.

Mostly students are dropping their studies in middle due to their financial background, employment, safety to girls, and absence of Quality Education in Government Institutions.

The Major Problems of Higher Education in India Facing by the SC/ST/OBC, Minorities and Women

In India, nearly 70 per cent of the population are residing in the rural areas. The development of the country starts from the grassroots level itself i.e., villages. Till today the rural areas are away from the basic amenities in the villages i.e., health, education, employment etc. The State and Central Government are taking many welfare programmes and implementing policies in the field of education since independence. Still the government is lagging behind in bringing equality among margnalised sections of the society especially among SC, ST and Women in the society as par with other sections. The basic problems of the SC, ST, Minorities and Women in imparting Higher Education are as follows:

1. ***Primary education:*** Primary and Secondary education is the key factor element for development of higher education in India. The quality and standards of primary education must be enhanced by improving the quality specially for the students from primary education itself belonging to SC, ST, Minorities and Girls in retention and complete their basic education upto 10th standard.
2. ***Motivation:*** Motivating the students belonging to the deprived communities in continuing higher education is the basic problem in the rural areas. Especially women students in continuing their higher education at the university levels. Due to this the enrollment of the women students at university levels is very low when compared to the men.
3. ***Infrastructure:*** Infrastructure facilities are very poor in Indian universities in imparting higher education as per the requirement of the students. Accommodation facilities must be provided to the women students in the universities with security.
4. ***Quality vs Quantity:*** In terms of quantity, India is quite impressive. Every year, India is producing 2.5 million graduates and this figure is just after US and China. However, in terms of quality India is falling behind than the developed world. *In fact, many of the graduates cannot find job as they are not up to the mark.*
5. ***Research:*** Research is the most important concept for development in the university. Indian universities are still far behind in Research

compared to other international universities standards. In fact, many of meritorious scholars from India go to US in the hope of having good research facilities. The number of SCs and STs and Women students involved in research are very less compared to the other category students.

6. *Information Technology:* The SC, ST and Women students are away from the higher education with the latest developments i.e., Information Technology (Computer) knowledge. They are notably able to get the computer education paying high fees. Due to this, they are lagging behind in getting good jobs in IT and MNC companies.

7. *Financial Problems:* Most of the students are not able to continue higher education due to the financial problems in their families. The students belonging to the SC, ST, Minorities and Women belonging to the lower sections in the society are not able to pay the fees inspite of the financial support from the government in the shape of scholarship. The scholarship released to them is not sufficient as per their requirements.

Higher education is extremely diverse and the challenges and issues faced by higher education institutions are just as diverse. The process of education is not merely digesting books. It is also about doing several co-curricular and extra-curricular activities that give a broader meaning to life in general and education in particular. I believe that opportunities for such holistic development are not enough in India. Facilities for the same are lacking or not easily accessible in India. Even where facilities exist, there is a lack of information about the same.

There is a great need to revolution in higher education. These are just some challenges which should cover all the aspect in the present scenario of education and we have to implement hard on them. Now, there is an urgent need to work for the development of the educational sector to meet the need of the emerging opportunities, increasing younger generation population and challenges of the 21st century.

Conclusion

To realise that education creates awareness at individual, family as well as social level. The role of the government plays very crucial to impart free higher education to the students, who belongs to SC/ST, women and other marginalised sections in the society. So, that their standard of living can be increased and the problem of unemployment can be solved as they will be self-employed. The following are the suggestions:

- There should be effective monitoring and control on private as well as government institutions by the government at the state and central level in imparting education.
- Policies and programmes must be taken specially for improving the enrollment in higher education in rural areas for SC, STs, women and minorities
- Research must be more encouraged among the women and students belonging to SC, ST and minorities as there contribution is very less.
- Protection and safety must be provided to the women candidates in the hostel campus.
- Reservation rules must be strictly followed to the candidates of SC, ST, OBC, women and minorities in education and employment.
- Information technology-based education must be imparted to the students of these communities as per the recent development in the education.

References

- Personal Interview to the students who discontinue the studies.
- DEPP/SSA, Andhra Pradesh.
- DPEP.SSA, Ranga Reddy District.
- UGC Report XI plan.
- MHRD (2006) Annual Report, Ministry of Human Resource Development, Department of Secondary and Higher Education. Government of India, New Delhi.
- Planning Commission (1999), Approach paper to the Tenth Five Year Plan (2002-2007). Planning Commission, New Delhi.
- UGC (2005) Research Handbook: Towards nurturing research culture in higher education institutions in India. University Grants Commission, New Delhi.

28 Empowering Women Through Higher Education in the Indian Perspective: Policies and Implementation Mechanisms

Kiran Kumar P.

Abstract

Education is the key factor for women empowerment, prosperity, development and welfare.

There is continued inequality and vulnerability of women in all sectors-Economic, Education, Social, Political, Health-Care, Nutrition, Right and Legal etc. Education is milestone of women empowerment because it enables them to respond to the challenges, to confront their traditional role and change their life, so that we can't neglect the importance of education in reference to women empowerment.

India is poised to becoming superpower, a developed country by 2020. Education also brings a reduction in inequalities and functions as a means of improving their status within the family. In order to fight against the socially constructed gender biases, women have to swim against the system that requires more strength. Such strength comes from the process of empowerment and empowerment will come from the education. This study focus on impact of education in women empowerment it also aims to find out the effect of education on women. This study also tries to find out the status of women in higher education level, literacy and also suggests some important measures for the *development of women education in the country.*

Introduction

Women constitute almost half the human race. Globalisation has presented new challenges in the realisation of the goal of empowering women and now women empowerment has become the slogan and motto of many social reformers, governmental agencies and voluntary organisations. Empowerment is a process of acquiring knowledge and awareness which enable them to move towards life with greater dignity and self-assurance. The United Nation's Organisation had declared the year 1975 as women's year and the decade 1975-1985 as women's decade on an international level. So, various studies were conducted and made a consensus that so long as women remain depressed and exploited, no nation can enjoy freedom and justice. So various steps were taken to define the concept of women empowerment and to find out ways through which women can be empowered.

Education has been recognised as an essential tool of social change and development in any society of any country. Education helps in generating awareness among women about their legal, social, political and economic rights, provisions and privileges to fight against all sorts of social discrimination. Education is considered as a potent instrument through which processes modernisation and social change come to existence. Access to education has been one of the most pressing demands of theses women's rights movements. India is poised to emerge as one of the most developed nations by 2020, more literate, knowledgeable and economically at the forefront. Though India could well become one of the largest economies in the world, it is being hindered due to a lack of women's participation. Education of women is the most effective channel for reducing the inequalities between men and women and ensuring the maximum participation of women in the developmental process.

The literature also suggests that the economic gains from women's education are generally at least as high as those from men's education. An examination of the literature on the differences in education by gender shows that the concern in most countries has to do with the low level of achievement of girls in relation to boys, the girls' lower access to education, and their lower rates of persistence to the higher levels of the educational system. There is a wide gap between male-female literacy rates in India. In order to address this problem and develop appropriate interventions, it is necessary to understand the nature and extent of the problem, as well as possible explanations for the disparity.

Development of Higher Education

Knowledge is one of the greatest human virtues has been immensely valued in Indian society and its acquisition and dissemination considered as a service of the highest order throughout the ages. During the ancient period, the saints and seers of India showed the world the path of truth, wisdom, and peace. The modern concept of a university is close to that of forest *ashram* institutions in the ancient Hindu tradition of adult learning. It is recorded that as far back as 1500 BC, Indian teachers would retire to clearings in the forests along with groups of young men who volunteered to join them in living a life of contemplation and philosophical discussion. Such *ashram* schools, when grew in number and size and attracted learners from far and wide, took the shape of corporate institutions. Buddhist centres of learning at Takshashila (5th century AD), the oldest university of the world with over 10,500 students, and Nalanda (12th century AD) with 10,000 students, and 1500 teachers are examples of ancient Indian universities (Chauhan, 2011).

The East India Company established its rule over India since 1757, which call modern period. In 1858, the British government took upon itself the direct responsibility of the administration. However women's education got importance after the country got independence in 1947 and the government has taken various measures to provide education to all Indian women. In 1904, Annie Besant established Central Hindu Girls School at Benaras. After independence, India's national government introduced some committee's and commissions for the development of women education in India. Radhakrishnan Commission or University Education Commission (1948) Smt. Durgabai Deshmukh Committee (1959), Smt. Hansa Mehta Committee (1962), to look into the causes of public support particularly in rural area for girls education and to public corporation, Kothari Commission (1964-64), Resolution on the National Policy on Education (1968), Report of the Committee on the Status of Women in India (1974), National Policy on Education (1986), etc. On the other hand, to develop the primary education and to achieve the aim of Universalisation of primary education up to age level 6-14 years, some schemes or programmes like, National Programme of Nutritional Support of Primary Education (NPNSPE) or (Mid-day Meals), RTE Act 2009 and Knowledge Commission etc. were introduced to achieve the national goal of achieving hundred per cent literacy. Despite these government efforts to the women education in India, it still generally remained unlettered and uneducated.

Need of the Study and Data Base

It is evident from the views given above that the overall outlook on women education and empowerment is a positive and optimistic one. On the basis of reviews and views of experts, it has become imperative to analyse the condition of women in education in the country. The present study entitled "Empowering Women through Education in the Indian Perspective: Policies and Implementation Mechanisms" has been undertaken in the context of these objectives:

- Firstly, to study the trends in literacy rate in the country,
- Secondly, to study the causes for low literacy among the women in the country,
- Thirdly, to examine the status of women in higher education in the country,
- Finally, to analyse the steps taken to promote women's education in the country.

The relevant secondary data have been collected from various reports and documents of Census of India Reports, UGC Annual Reports, Journals, and various Magazines. This has enabled us to analyse the impact of education on women empowerment. The findings of the study are as follows;

Need of Women Empowerment

Women must define their own needs and goals as well as strategies. A pre-requisite for women's participation in development process is their empowerment. Women must exercise full participation in decision-making process in all walks of life and fully participate with men in finding equitable and practical solution to issues both in the family and society. It also declared that human rights of women and girl child are inalienable, integral and invisible parts of universal human rights. In her message to mark the First day of the year of empowerment of women, the national commission for women chairperson Vibha Partha Sarathi said, "the year to come must see women in apex decision-making bodies, enter profession denied to them so far, recognise their contribution on important and legitimate and help them to fight against disease and deprivation, indignity and inequity".

Table 1. Literacy Rate in India

Year	*Persons*	*Male*	*Female*	*Percentage of Gap in Literacy Rate*
1951	18.33	27.16	8.86	18.30
1961	28.30	40.40	15.35	25.05
1971	34.45	45.96	21.97	23.98
1981	43.57	56.38	29.76	26.62
1991	52.21	64.13	39.29	24.84
2001	65.38	75.85	54.16	21.70
2011	74.00	82.00	65.00	17.00

(*Source:* Census of India).

Table 1 shows that at no point could the literacy rate of women match that of men. As a result, even after 65 years of independence, women occupy a secondary position in our social hierarchy. Inspire of being aware of her position, women can't transform the situation due to lack of education. Therefore, women's empowerment can't be affected unless we persuade the importance of women's education.

Another area in which women's equality has shown a major improvement as a result of adult-literacy programs is the area of enrollment of boys and girls in schools. As a result of higher participation of women in literacy campaigns, the gender gap in literacy levels is gradually getting reduced. Even more significant is the fact that disparity in enrollment of boys and girls in neo-literate households is much lowered compared to the non-literate householders.

Above data shows that the state-wise female literacy rate had an average of 65.46 per cent in all India basis in 2011 census, the high literacy rate is 92.0 per cent in Kerala and least literacy rate is 52.7 per cent in Rajasthan in 2011 census while comparing literacy rate of female 11 per cent increased in 2011 census is increased from 54.16 per cent to 65.46 per cent. Women's are growing well in the last 10 years. Government of India has been taken various steps and plans especially for women in every movement.

Causes for Low Literacy Among Women

Women education is a multi-dimensional phenomenon. No single factor or cause can be held responsible for very low literacy rate of women in India. Subsequently, it is associated with combination of many factors including social, cultural, economic, educational, demographic, political and administrative and so on. The following are the some of the important factors which could be attributed for the present poor state of affairs of womenfolk in education.

- ***The low enrollment:*** Reliable sources indicate that more than 50 per cent of the Non-Starters (those who have never been to school) are girls.
- ***Higher drop-out rate from schools:*** According to available sources, occurrence of drop-out and stagnation amongst girls is nearly twice that of boys all over India.
- ***Girl as second mothers:*** In many families girl children play the role of second mother by shouldering the responsibilities of household work such as looking after the sibling, fetching water, collecting firewood, bringing fodder for cattle, cleaning and cooking etc.
- ***Bonded labour system:*** This social evil is a quite discouraging

phenomenon which stands as barrier for girl's education in rural areas for the underprivileged families of washermen and agricultural labour, scheduled caste and scheduled tribes.

- *Dowry system:* In many families especially poor and downtrodden think that if their daughters are educated more, they have to accumulate more assets and properties to provide as dowry in large proportion at the time of marriage, so prefer rather to either stop their children with average education and so on but never higher education.
- *Existence of child labour practice:* According to UN sources India is the most child labour populous nation in the globe with more than 50 million child labourers indulged different activities. In most of these industries girl children are preferred for high productivity and low cost.
- *Early marriage:* By and large the female age at marriage of 18 (recently 21 years) as prescribed by various legislations not at all followed in India. This obnoxious practice discourages female children to continue their schooling and higher education as they enter into family life at the early age which is not advisable from the physical and mental health point of view and also of social development.
- *Poverty:* In much poverty stricken families, children especially girls are considered as economic assets as they bring income for livelihood as well to save from economic crises due to death or incapacity of parents (sick/ handicapped/aged).

Status of Women in Higher Education

Due to the efforts made by the government and the University Grants Commission over the years, women education in India has grown both in terms of number of women's colleges and proportion of women enrollment in higher education. The data relating to a number of women colleges and women enrollments are presented in Table 3.

From the above table, it is observed that the total number of women's colleges in India increased from 430 in 1970-71, to 609 in 1980-81, to 874 in 1990-91, to 1578 in 2000-01 and further increased to 2565 by 2009-10. Women enrollment as a proportion of total enrollment has witnessed a steady growth during the last four decades. The proportion of women enrollment in the total enrollment increased from 10.9 per cent in 1950-51, 16.2 per cent in 1960-61, to 22.01 per cent in 1970-71, 27.01 per cent

Table 3. Women Colleges and Women Enrollment in India

Year	*Total Enrollment*	*Women Enrollment*	*Percentage of Women*	*No. of Women's Colleges*
1950-51	396745	43126	10.9	-
1960-61	1040861	170455	16.2	-
1970-71	1292500	394594	22.0	492
1980-81	2752437	748525	27.2	649
1990-91	4425247	1436887	32.5	874
2000-01	8399443	3365410	39.4	1518
2009-10	13611008	5645002	41.4	2565

(*Source:* Sreeramamurty et al., 2012).

in 1980-81, to 32.4 per cent in 1990-91 to 39.36 per cent in 2000-01 and further increased to 41.41 per cent in 2009-10. From this it may be concluded that there has been a phenomenal growth in women enrollment in higher education particularly during the liberalisation period in India.

State-wise Distribution of Women Enrollment

Distribution of women enrollment by state shows that the percentage increase has been almost minimal in the enrollment of women as compared to the total enrollment in all the states, during the 2010-2011 over the preceding year. Among the states, Goa with 61.2 per cent topped in terms of women enrollment as a percentage of total enrollment of the state followed by Kerala (56.8 per cent), Meghalaya (51.8 per cent), Nagaland (50.5 per cent) etc. There are 17 states which had higher enrollment of women than the national percentage of 41.5 per cent. In the rest of the states, the percentage of women enrolled had been less than the national average, with Bihar recording the lowest women enrollment of 31.2 per cent only. In absolute numbers, Uttar Pradesh State had been on the top in enrolling women students (9.8 lakhs), followed by Maharashtra (8.6 lakhs) and Andhra Pradesh (7.2 lakhs) etc.

Distribution of Women Enrollment by Faculty

The faculty-wise distribution of women enrollment in higher education during 2010-2011 had been stated in the below table.

Table 4 shows that the women enrollment in the faculty of Arts had been 41.21 per cent of total women enrollment, followed by the faculty of Science (19.14 per cent), the faculty of Commerce/Management (16.12 per cent), etc., constituting 76.47 per cent in these three non-professional faculties. There is a slight change in the percentage of women enrolled in all

Table 4. Women Enrollment Faculty-wise: 2010-2011

Faculty	*Women Enrollment*	*Percentage of Total Women Enrollment*
Arts	2904596	41.21
Science	1349170	19.14
Commerce/Management	1136930	16.12
Education	323954	4.6
Engineering/Technology	800680	11.36
Medicine	330040	4.68
Agriculture	25180	0.36
Veternary Science	6926	0.10
Law	83840	1.19
Others	87372	1.24
Total	**7048688**	**100.00**

(*Source:* UGC Annual Report).

faculties as compared to the percentages in 2009-10. The faculty of Education where the percentage is 4.60 per cent in 2010-2011 as compared to 2009-2010 (3.70 per cent), Engineering Technology in 2010-11 is 11.36 per cent as compared to 7.69 per cent in 2009-10 etc. Also, double digit percentage of women enrollment is recorded only in non-professional faculties of Arts, Science, Commerce/Management and Engineering and Technology and single digit in other professional faculties. The women enrollment in the faculties of Agriculture and Veterinary Science has been a miniscule presence (UGC Annual Report 2011-12).

Women Empowerment through Education

Women Empowerment is a global issue and discussion on women political right are at the forefront of many formal and informal campaigns worldwide. The concept of women empowerment was introduced at the international women conference at Naroibi in 1985. Education is milestone of women empowerment because it enables them to responds to the challenges, to confront their traditional role and change their life. The National Commission of Women was set-up by an Act of Parliament in 1990 to safeguard the right and legal entitlements of women. If we consider the global aspect in this regard, we see that women are being given equal treatment in developed nations. It is education through which we realise this fact. For eradicating this injustice, the UNO (United Nations' Organisation) framed a Convention/ Charter which is called 'The Convention on the Elimination of all Forms of Discrimination against Women' (CEDAW), which further led to the formation of Women's Commission. Seeing all the aspects of this discussion, we will realise that education is the only means for empowerment of women. Therefore, literacy should spread amongst women. The literacy rate amongst the women in the post-Independent Era is not as per the expectations. We, as a nation, dream of becoming a Super Power by 2020. For becoming a Super Power, each element of our society, nation should contribute in the nation-building process. But women, who are a major factor of this society, aren't literate then we can't expect to become a Super Power. Therefore, it is urgent for us to know the importance of women's education, which would, in turn, give an impetus to the process of women's empowerment. Empowerment of Women in any society is an important factor to enable women to participate in the economic and political development of the society. In India, educational programmes aim at eradication of illiteracy among women for their equality in the society and to ensure their empowerment.

National Effort

The National Policy on Education (NPE) provides that education be used as a strategy for achieving a basic change in the status of women. The main features of the NPE are as follows:

(a) To gear the entire education system to plan a positive interventionist role in the empowerment of women.

(b) To promote women's studies as a part of various courses and encouragement to educational institutions to take up active programme to further women's development.

(c) To widen the access of women in programmes of vocational, technical and professional education.

(d) To create dynamic managerial structure to cope up with the targets envisaged.

The New Education Policy provides the following parameters for empowerment of women:

(a) Building a positive self-image and self-confidence,

(b) Developing ability to think critically,

(c) Building up group cohesion and fostering decision-making, and action,

(d) Ensuring equal participation in the process of bringing about social change,

(e) Providing the reasonable opportunities for economic independence.

The women's equality is essential for the overall growth of the society. Further, the women's equality can be achieved through education so that they are in a position to develop the critical understanding of all the things surrounding them.

The National Policy for Empower of Women 2001 outlines three-policy approaches;

(a) Judicial/legal empowerment by making the legal system more responsive and gender sensitive for women's need.

(b) Economic empowerment by mainstreaming gender perspectives in the development process, enhancing women's capacities and access to economic opportunities.

(c) Social empowerment through focussed efforts on education, health and nutrition.

In terms of operational strategies, the National Policy has called for gender development indices, gender disaggregated data, gender budgeting, Women's Component Plan in the Five Year Plans, so that not less than 30 per cent of benefits flow to women and gender.

Policy Measures to Improve the Women Literacy Rate in India

The following measures can be considered for bringing phenomenal change in the plight of women's education and empowerment in India:

- Since the prevailing situation of poor or less enrollment of girls in schools; closes the doors for development and prosperity of future generation of women, concerted efforts must be initiated jointly by the government, parents and civil society to achieve universal enrollment for girls without any compromise.
- The Ministry of Education both at Centre and State level should work out strategic steps to stop firmly the ongoing high drop-outs among girls especially in rural, tribal and slums areas with the serious involvement of voluntary organisations in every locality to realise zero drop-out among girls.
- The poverty-stricken families can be identified through proper research and necessary poverty alleviation services must be provided to strengthen the income thereby to enable the families to send their children to schools and colleges without much financial difficulties.

- The Mid-day meal scheme and other educational supportive services like free text books, note books, fee uniforms, free bicycles, scholarships, free bus pass and so on as done in the state of Tamil Nadu can be provided in all states and union territories to improve the literacy level among girls.
- As social evils like dowry, child marriage , caste system and other practices deprive rights of education for children belonging to poor and underprivileged families and communities, they should eliminated through well-designed packages of mass awareness programmes and social welfare measures with full support of public, political parties, NGOs and government agencies.
- Government, voluntary sector and philanthropic organisations and individuals should come forward to provide free education for poor girls and provide free hostel facilities for girls studying in schools and colleges in every state of India. This will certainly encourage children of poor families to pursue good and higher education without many impediments.

Conclusion

The analysis presented in the previous sections shows that participation of women in education at all levels is less than men, though, there has been a remarkable improvement during the last six decades after independence. Also, their participation decreases with the rise in the level of education. There are several social customs and taboos, such as child marriage and *purdah* system that restrict women's participation in education. Early marriage and subsequent migration of girls to husbands' place restricts their entry into the portals of higher-education institutions. This is true for most of the conservative societies in the world. Traditionally, and also culturally, women in India have the responsibility of managing domestic affairs. As a daughter, she has to look after younger siblings and help her mother in domestic chores. In rural areas, she has to fetch water, fuel, and fodder. As a wife, she must look after her husband and in-laws and share other family-related responsibilities with her husband. As a mother, she must discharge her motherhood-related responsibilities including rearing and looking after children, management of household, cooking and serving food for children and other members of the family.

Women empowerment is an essential element in national development. Since women constitute half of the population, there can be no development unless the needs and interests of women are fully taken into account. Women education is an important input for the economic, social and political development of the civilised society and therefore, every segment of the society; especially the institutions of learning have an important role in this venture. It is rightly believed that education of a man means education of one individual, but education of a woman means education of the entire family. To encourage the education of women at all levels and for dilution of gender bias in providing knowledge and education, established schools, colleges and universities even exclusively for women in the state. From the above analysis, it is found that modern education and facilities have influenced much in women empowerment. But still rural women are lagging behind in comparison to women living in urban areas. There is continued inequality and vulnerability of women in all sectors – Economic, Social, Political, Educational, Health-care, Nutrition, Right and Legal etc. So, education holds the key for empowerment of women.

References

- Beena Dominic and Amrita Jothi (2012): "Education- A Tool of Women Empowerment: Historical Study Based on Kerala Society", *International Journal of Scientific and Research Publications,* Vol. 2, Issue 4, April 2012 ISSN 2250-3153, www.ijsrp.org, pp. 1-4.
- Behal Anjana (2011): "Education, Women Empowerment and Related Issues", *International Educational E-Journal,* {Quarterly}, Vol. 1, Issue-1, Oct-Nov-Dec 2011, pp. 38-50.
- Chauhan, C.P.S (2011): "Participation of Women in Higher Education: The Indian Perspective", *Analytical Reports in International Education,* Vol. 4. No. 1, November 2011, ISSN-1542-3832, pp. 67-86.
- Fayaz Ahmad Bhat, Fouzia Khurshid and Nazmul Hussain (2011): "Gender Disparity and Policies of Inclusion: A Case Study of Women's Education in Jammu and Kashmir", *Researchers World, Journal of Arts, Science and Commerce,*www.researchersworld.com,Vol. 2, Issue 3, July, pp. 135-150.
- Fletcher, B. (1968): Universities in the Modern World. London: Pergamon, p. 11.
- Government of India, *Census of India 2011.*
- http://www.smeworld.org/story/focus/women-empowerment-through-sme.php.
- http://www.state.gov/p/io/rm/2010/142494.html.
- Mukut Kr. Sonowal (2013): "Impact of Education in Women Empowerment: A Case Study of SC and ST Women of Sonitpur District, Assam", *IJCAES Special Issue on Basic, Applied and Social Sciences,* Vol. 3, January, pp. 27-33.
- Narlikar, J.V. (2003): The Scientific Edge of Vedic to Modern Times. New Delhi, India: Penguin Books.

- Saraswathi Mishra (2002): "Status of Indian Women", Gyan Publishing House, New Delhi, 2002.
- Shinde Jithendra (2013): "Women's Empowerment Through Education", *ABHINAV National Monthly Refereed Journal of Reasearch in Arts and Education,*www.abhinavjournal.com Vol. 1, Issue 11 ISSN 2277-1182.
- Sreeramamurty, Sailaja and Appalanaidu (2012): "Inclusive Growth and Higher Education in India", *International Journal of Multidisciplinary Educational Research,* Vol. 1(2), June, ISSN-2277-7881.
- Suguna (2011): "Education and Women Empowerment in India", *Zenith International Journal of Multidisciplinary Research* Vol. 1 Issue 8, December, ISSN 2231 5780, pp. 198-204.
- UGC Annual Reports, www.ugc.ac.in.
- Vimala Ramachandran (1998): "Girls' and Women's Education: Policies and Implementation Mechanisms, Case Study: India", Planning and Sector Analysis Unit UNESCO, Principal Regional Office for Asia and the Pacific, Bangkok.

29 Women and Higher Education Among the Fishing Community in Puducherry Region

Sivakumar, I.
Usha V.T.

Abstract

The gender gap as regards enrollment rate increases with the level of education in all countries: the higher the level of education, the fewer the girl students. The research report indicated that direct discrimination of girls in higher education, sometimes as outright abuse, adds to the broadening gender imbalance in education, particularly in fishing community. The research finding describe that among the community, the fact that girls lower enrollment prematurely was said to be due to a lack of understanding among parents or a general depreciation of the education of girls. Discrimination in access to education does not exist and also economic progress of the family, while the boy is given the first opportunity to go to school, the girl follows the same path. Again the notion of man being the primary earner has not been dismantled and is still embedded in the cultural value system among the fishing community; in poor families women make equal or more than half contribution towards the household economy. The effect of rapid increase in the education of girls is still to be felt because of almost decade and a half of gestation period required between changes in the attitude towards education of girls and expansion of facilities for education. But increase in the number and proportion of girls at different levels of education and tremendous drop in dropout rates indicate a strong trend in education of girls not only as a social obligation, of getting educated grooms, but with a long-term need for their developing into empowered human beings.

Women's subordination to men was seen as evident in all areas of life: at home, in school, in the workplace and in society, i.e., in all kinds of human relations–as a daughter, sister, mother and wife, as a student or a teacher, as a community member and national citizen, as a government or private employee or as an informal bread-winner. The conclusion drawn in many discussions with various stakeholders was that gender awareness needs to be urgently promoted. The lack of understanding of the meaning of gender equality and of how gender inequalities are manifested in society, the ignorance of or lack of will to promote gender equality, or in short, the low-level of gender awareness in general, was considered as one of the main obstacles. Worldwide, there is abundant evidence of how education can and is effective in promoting gender equality. There was a general consensus on the need to strengthen gender equality. Mostly girls' enrollment and access were on the agenda among the fishing community. From a gender equality perspective, girls' (and boys') enrollment and retention in higher education has not received the attention and support it requires.

Introduction

Women constitute 48 per cent of the total population of India. The principle of gender equity is enshrined in Indian Constitution in its preamble, fundamental, rights, fundamental duties and directive principles and also reducing the gender gap in higher education is a focus area. The National Policy on Education, 1986 put specific emphasis on women's education. It states that: Education will be used as an agent of basic change in the status of women. In order to neutralise accumulated distortions of the past, there will be a well-conceived edge in favour of women. The National Educational system will play a positive interventionist role in the empowerment of women. The condition of marine fishing community in Puducherry region women's educational status in higher education is low. Among the community girl children and women have by far more gender roles to play than boys and men, which leave them with little time for active participation in education.

Education has a critical role to play in addressing issues of gender equality and equity in India. These issues affect individual, families, communities and society as a whole. The overall goal of this project is to promote gender equality and equity in education for economic growth and sustainable development. The strategies which have been proposed aim to reduce existing gender disparities in access, retention, transition and achievement in education. It is evident that girls and women's empowerment from socially disadvantaged places as well as vulnerable children are seriously impeded by several factors, such as cultural and religious practices, inadequate policy guidelines, poverty and lack of community awareness. These have impacted negatively on access, participation and performance at all levels in education.

The present research on women and higher education has focused on unearthing the underlying causes of gender disparities, and the factors that hinder attempts to reduce and eventually eliminate disparities. Studies reveal that key factors include social, cultural and religious beliefs, attitudes and practices, poverty, child-labour, poor learning environment, lack of role models, HIV and AIDS, pedagogy and learners attitudes, among others.

Review of Literature

The gender gap in education is more pronounced in poorer countries like South Asia and Sub-Saharan Africa (Singla, 2006). India alone has 40 per cent of the global gender lag in education. Enrollment of women in higher education in India though showing marked improvement since fifties is still lagging behind that of their male counterparts. The share of girls' enrollment in total higher education enrollment rose from a meager 10 per cent in 1950-51 to 38.3 per cent in 2005-06 (MHRD, GOI). Traditionally, not only women are less likely to continue higher education but also disproportionately registered for biological and non-quantitative social sciences as compared to mathematics and pure sciences (Chanana, 2004; Chakraborty, 2009; Dandapat and Sengupta, 2012). The under-representation of women students in science and technology is an international policy concern as well (Bebbington, 2002).

The disciplinary choices of women have been the focus of debate in the feminist discourse on education and gender (Chanana, 2004). Much has been written on the patriarchal imprint on the disciplinary choices of women in higher education and on the feminine and masculine dichotomy of disciplines (Acker, 1990; Thomas, 1994). Since masculinity and femininity are social constructions (Kellner, 1997) the underlying assumptions about subject or disciplinary choices have to be uncovered along with their close connection to women's place in society (Harding, 1986).

The perception of the importance of girls' education seems to affect enrollments (Bandopadhyay and Subramanian, 2008) and also subject choices (Bowman and Hudson, 2006). Evidence has shown that educating women can lead to improved economic and social outcomes (Wolfe and Zuvekas, 1997). Specifically, recent empirical work, which has mainly focussed on developing countries, shows that there are both positive economic consequences and social externalities arising from improving women's education. For example, increases in women's education have been associated with reductions in fertility (Subbarao and Raney, 1995; Kingdon, 2002; Osili and Long, 2008), decreases in infant mortality and increases in life expectancy (Behrman and Deolalikar, 1988; Schutlz, 1993; Dancer *et al.*, 2008), beneficial effects on children's health and nutritional status (Thomas,

1990; Mehrotra, 2006), likely to participate in political meetings (UNESCO, 2000) and greater impact of children's schooling (Filmer, 2006).

Gender disparities at higher levels of education have been limited studies in the Indian context. Vaid's (2004) analysis of trends in gender discrimination across the schooling career of children finds that transition probabilities of girls increase, relative to that of boys, at higher levels of education. Chakraborty (2009) found household economic status; educational profile and gender of the household head, potential cost of schooling, family composition in terms of the number of children and distance are the important determinants of higher education and participation in certain subjects similar to a study of Chanana (2004).

Sundaram's study (2007) of higher education focuses on disparities across social castes, but ignores gender dimensions. Thorat (2006) observed gender differences in access to higher education. But none of these works have examined that gender stereotyping as an impoitant determinant factor for accessing higher education. Overall, studies have tended to neglect the study of gender stereotyping at higher levels of education in Indian context. Chanana (2004); Chakraborty (2009); Dandapat and Sengupta, (2012) Enrollment of women in higher education in India is still lagging behind that of their male counterparts and registered disproportionately for biological and non-quantitative social sciences as compared to mathematics and pure sciences.

Indeed, gender inequality in higher education is not one homogeneous phenomenon, but a collection of disparate and interlinked problems in our society-inequalities in mortality, natality, basic facility, special opportunity, profession, ownership and household. The different forms of gender inequality can impose diverse adversities on the lives of men and boys, in addition to those of women and girls. In understanding the different aspects of the evil of gender inequality, we have to look beyond the predicament of women and examine the problems created for men as well by the asymmetric treatment of women (Sen, 2001). Gender inequalities exist because of discrimination in the family and societal institutions and social, cultural, and religious norms that perpetuate stereotypes, practices and beliefs that are detrimental to women.

Objectives of Study

1. To study the educational status of women in the community.
2. To find out the problems of women in higher education.

Research Methodology

This study used both primary and secondary data, the primary data was used questionnaire method and the secondary data collected from various published materials. The purposive sampling method used in this research study. In this study explore the possibilities Women's Studies research methodology like participatory observation and focus group discussion with girl children from the selected villages. The researcher has selected 50 girl children from Kalapet and 50 girl children from Kanagachettykulam fishing villages, thereby accounting to a total numbers of 100 respondents.

Analysis of Data

The following data were collected among the study area of Kalapet and Kanagachettykulam fishing villages in Puducherry region and the data was analysed in percentage-wise.

Table 1. Personal Profiles of Respondents

Personal profile	*Classification*	*Kalapet Girl children(%)*	*Kanagachettykulam girls children (%)*
Age	15 – 20	38	34
	20 – 25	46	56
	25 – 30	10	6
	30 – 35	6	4
Educational level	8-9	38	34
	9-10	40	50
	11-12	14	10
	UG	8	6

Note: Primary data in Puducherry region fishing villages, 2012.

Table 2. Respondents Parents Profile

		Kalapet Girl children (%)		*Kanagachettykulam Girl children (%)*	
Parents profile	*Classification*	*Mother*	*Father*	*Mother*	*Father*
Educational level	Illiterate	8	4	14	6
	Primary	40	6	36	4
	Middle	18	44	16	52
	High	26	12	24	16
Income	1000-2000	34	8	32	6
	2000-4000	40	-	38	-
	4000-6000	26	-	30	-

Note: Primary data in Puducherry region fishing villages, 2012.

Table 3. Problems in Higher Education

Problems in Education	*Classification*	*Kalapet Girl Children (%)*	*Kanagachettykulam Girl children (%)*
In Educational Institution	Fees Structure	48	58
	Lack of Female Teachers	12	8
	Co-education	30	20
	Distance	10	14
In House	Parents compulsion	60	58
	Health problem of the parents	8	4
	Marriage	22	32
	Taking care of younger siblings	10	6

Note: Primary data in Puducherry region fishing villages, 2012.

Tables (1, 2 and 3) analysis women and higher education among the marine fishing community in Puducherry region, the table (1) explains that the personal profile of the respondents; table (2) describes that the respondents parents profile and the table (3) shows that the problems of women in higher education.

Findings

The gender gap in education is unlikely to be adequately tackled by a concentration on education provision in isolation. Factors such as compulsion from parents, high fee structures, lack of female teachers, co-education, female child labour, domestic and childcare responsibilities and contraceptive provision to reduce adolescent pregnancy also need to be addressed. Early marriages, teenage pregnancy rates and high fertility rates limit the demand for female education, as school age girls are expected to care for siblings and, sometimes, their own children. Lower fertility rates have been linked to higher education levels of women.

For women, participation in higher education faces additional hurdles of culture and tradition that militate against their post-primary education opportunities. And these cultural problems are even more pronounced for rural women where the old traditions of protection of young women, subordination to their husbands and the place of women in society as focussed on the home and child rearing are the strongest and exposure to feminist reforms are the weakest.

Conclusion

Education is the primary source of human capital formation. It has also been the cornerstone of the World Bank's overall mission of helping poor and developing countries to fight poverty. In India, many commissions and committees have been appointed to consider issues of education in general and women's education in particular. In this paper, the author emphasises that women's higher education is important not only to create gender-based equal education opportunities but also for various social, economic and political returns. These gains may be in the form of higher income levels for women, better educated and healthier children, women's empowerment and economic independence, increased women's work participation in the organised sector and, above all, overall national development.

References

- Acker, J. (1990). Hierarchies, jobs, bodies: A theory of gendered organisations. Gender Sociology, 4, pp. 139–158.
- Bandopadhyay, M. and Subrahmanian, R. (2010). Gender equity in education: A study of trends and factors. Research Monograph No. 18. New Delhi: National University of Education and Planning.
- Bebbington, D. (2002). Women in science, engineering and technology: A review of the issues. Higher Education Quarterly, 56(4), pp. 360-375.
- Behrman, J. and A. Deolalikar (1988) "Health and Nutrition". In Handbook of Development Economics (1) Ed. Chenery, H. and T. Srinivasan. Amstardam, North Holland: pp. 631-704.
- Bowman, N.A., and Elizabeth, H. (2006). Gender differences and similarities in attitudes toward college access. University of Michigan.
- Chakraborty, A. (2009). Determinants of participation in higher education and choice of disciplines: Evidence from urban and rural Indian youth. South Asia Economic Journal, 10(2), pp. 371-402.
- Filmer, Deon (2000). The structure of social disparities in education: gender and wealth, Policy Research Working Paper No. 2268, World Bank Development Research Group/Poverty Reduction and Economic Management network. Washington, D.C.: World Bank.
- Kingdon, G.G. (2002). The gender gap in educational attainment in India: How much can be explained? The Journal of Development Studies, 39(2), pp. 25–53.
- Schultz, T.P. (1994). "Human capital, family planning and their effects on population growth". The American Economic Review, 84(2): pp. 255–60.
- Sen, A. (2001). Many faces of gender inequality. Frontline 18 (22, Oct. 27-Nov. 9).
- Sengupta, P and Guha, J. (2002). Enrollment, Dropout and Grade Completion of Girl Children in West Bengal, Economic and Politic Weekly, 37(17), pp. 1621-1637.

- Subbarao, K., and Laura Raney (1995). Social gains from female education. Economic Development and Cultural Change, 44 (1): pp. 105-28.
- Thomas, Duncan (1990). Intra-household allocation: an inferential approach, Journal of Human Resources, 25 (4): pp. 635-64.
- Thomas, K. (1990). Gender and subject in higher education. Buckingham. The Society for Research into Higher Education and the Open University Press, Acker, Bandra.
- Thorat, S. (2006). Higher education in India: Emerging issues related to access, inclusiveness and equity. Nehru Memorial Lecture, University of Mumbai, Mumbai.
- United Nations Educational, Scientific and Cultural Organisation (2000). Women and girls: education, not discrimination. Paris: UNESCO.
- Wolfe, B. and S. Zuvekas (1997), "Non-market Outcomes of Schooling", International Journal of Education Research 27, pp. 491-501.

30 Problems and Perspectives of Rural and Tribal People in Pursuing Higher Education in India

Vidya S. Shettemmanavar

Introduction

Education in general and higher education in particular is the strongest instrument for the development and humanisation of mankind. Higher education is very much a part of the development process. It cannot be separated from development. They are not two separate things. Education is a sense which leads to development. Apart from primary and secondary education, higher education is the most important tool for development and transformation. Higher education has the constructive role of preparing future leaders for different spheres of life i.e., social, economic, political, cultural, scientific and technological.

In the 21st century, Higher Education is the mandate to bridge the knowledge gap between countries and communities, enriching dialogues between people culture; international-linking and networking of ideas, research and technologies. The role of higher education in national development is widely recognised in the 21st century, not only in India but also in other countries as well, which is at the apex of the entire education system.

Today, Indian higher education is the world's third largest system just after U.S. and China. Indian higher education has a long tradition tracing back to several centuries with universities like Nalanda and Takshashila. It is been 155 years since the modern higher education system started in India with the establishment of three universities in Calcutta, Bombay and Madras in 1857. After the attainment of independence, India had a close look at the purpose and objectives of education to facilitate the prime objectives of national development. To eradicate prevailing systems in the pre-independence era, several committees and commissions were brought up by the Indian government starting from Radhakrishnan Commission to propose recommendations to make changes in higher education system. Considering the significance of higher education Radhakrishnan, Commission had rightly remarked—"The most important and urgent reform needed in education is to transform it, to endeavour to relate it to the life, needs and aspirations of the people and thereby make it the powerful instrument of social, economic and cultural transformation necessary for the realisation of the national goals. Thus, education should be developed so as to increase productivity, achieve social and national integration, accelerate the process of modernisation and cultivate social, moral and spiritual values". Since then the Indian government has undertaken various ethnic plans, policies, programmes to reform and reorganise the higher education system to make it relevant and resourceful.

Thus, higher education provides the competencies that are required in different spheres of human activity, ranging from administration to agriculture, business, industry, health and communication and extending to the arts and culture.

Aims of Higher Education

The aim of higher education is to enable society to make progress through an understanding of itself and its world, in short to sustain a learning society. The aims/purposes of higher education are:

(a) To educate well and aware, autonomous and responsible citizens, committed to national and universal principles, capable of dealing with the challenges of the century and of life-long learning;

(b) To provide highly-trained professionals to meet the needs of the government, the professions, and the productive and service sectors;

(c) To provide expertise to assist the economic and social development, and in scientific and technological research;

(d) To help conserve and disseminate national and regional cultures, drawing on the contributions from each generation;

(e) To undertake research and scholarship which contribute to the understanding, the anticipation and the solving of the most serious problems of the region.

Higher Education—Rural and Tribal People

The new education policy is for all Indians. It must be egalitarian. It must give equal access to every single child at every level of intelligence or proficiency in to the same type of school, but an attempt must be made to give access to the best type of education, to the most intelligent children no matter from which section of society they come, whether they are from the weakest or the most backward, they must be able to get access to the best higher education. Access to a school has been given but access to a good school has been possible only to those who have resources to meet the expenses. Access should be fair and egalitarian but there is also a material aspect in this. If India is to develop faster, if India is to harness all its resources, its resources cannot be limited to the rich or the middle class in the country. Perhaps its richest resources are people, and found amongst the poorest, the most backward areas in the country. These resources should be located in human beings, and develop them for the best benefit of our country.

The rural population accounts for a little more than 70 per cent of India's enormous population. Hence, it is extremely essential that the government takes appropriate step for the welfare and betterment of rural India.

Mahila Samakhya is one such scheme which mainly focusses on the women's literacy from rural areas. Under this scheme, the rural women are asked to attend meetings and seminars for better awareness.

Presently, the National Bal Bhavan has 10 and 68 affiliated Bal Kendra and Bhavans respectively. This scheme provides social as well as educational activities. This scheme also helps in recognising the children's talent for specific educational stream.

Another flagship scheme *'Sarva Shiksha Abhiyan'* is in process of being implemented for education in every district of India. This scheme primarily focusses in providing appropriate elementary education to all the children within the age group of 6-14 years. This programme will mainly cover educational needs for girls, and scheduled caste and scheduled tribes. Due to this programme, many new schools opened in different places but that did not have requisite facilities and proper infrastructure.

Rural people commonly suffer from unequal access to education, health-care, infrastructure, technology, institutional support and markets. It is generally inequitable and inefficient to deny basic services to rural people, in the form of education. Although over the last decade international aid has rightly stressed the importance of concentrating on the poor, it has neglected rural areas and thus the majority of disadvantaged people, a phenomenon which is particularly true for education. Basic education is a fundamental human right in itself, and essential for reducing poverty and improving the living conditions of rural populations. Yet children's access to education in rural areas is still much lower than in urban areas, where adult literacy and the quality of education are much higher. In several countries, rural illiteracy are two or three times higher than that in urban areas, and the gap is widening. Moreover, curricula and text books in primary and secondary schools often have an urban bias, are irrelevant to the needs of rural people, and seldom focus on the skills needed for life in rural areas.

There are certain sections of our society where education has not reached in the manner it is expected. They are the scheduled Castes, the Scheduled Tribes and certain other weaker sections. But, if we were to identify one section which is most deprived from the point of education, it is the women, and are the girls. Special attention must similarly be given to Scheduled Castes, Scheduled Tribes because they face countless problems. They do not have economic strength to allow the children to spend that much time in school. The problems faced by rural people are as follows:

1. ***Lesser Number of Institutes:*** In comparison to the number of higher education institution present in urban areas i.e., cities or towns, there are very few institutions in rural areas of India. Technical higher educational institutions are very rarely established in the rural areas.

2. ***Access:*** The Gross Enrollment Rate (GER), measures, the access level by taking the ratio of persons in all age groups enrolled in various programmes to total population in age group of 18 to 23. The access to higher education for all eligible in the country is a major issue before the policy-makers.

3. ***Equity:*** On one hand, GER stands low for the overall population, while on the other, there are large variations among the various categories of population based on urban or rural habitation and rich and poor. Due to regional disparity in economic development and uneven distribution of institutions of higher education, the higher education is not equally available to the different sections of the society.

4. ***Limitation of Quality:*** The higher educational institutions suffer from large quality variation in so much so that a NASSCOM-Report-2005 has said that not more than 15 per cent of graduates of general education and 25-30 per cent of Technical Education are fit for employment. First, the quality norms of which are not comparable with international standards can't be maintained by the higher educational institute of rural areas. Secondly, the enforcement process is not stringent. Further political interference and corruption

dilute the role and impact of these insuitions in ensuring the desired quality standards.

5. ***Cost of Education:*** One of the main factors of lower enrollment in rural area is the cost of education. Technical education sometimes only a dream for most of the students of rural areas where the people are mostly dependent on agriculture. Even sometimes, it is seen that normal higher education expenses cannot be afforded by some of the families coming under lower middle class tag.

6. ***Higher Teacher-student Ratio:*** Student-teacher ratio is one of the indicators used to describe the quality of education received in any education unit, be it in a city or in any rural areas of the country. UGC has recommended an ideal ratio of 1:30 for the general under-graduate courses. Unfortunately, because of lesser number of educational institutes in rural areas, more and more students are bound to enroll and the teacher-students ratio does vary to the standard so far as quality education is concerned.

7. ***Privatisation:*** In India both public and private institutions operate simultaneously. In the year 2000-01, out of 13,072 higher education institutions, 42 per cent were privately owned and run catering to 37 per cent of students enrolled into higher education. Since providing grant-in-aid to private colleges is becoming difficult, they sometimes not able to maintain the minimum standard of quality education. The quality of education in these private colleges is very uneven. Many of the colleges because of shortage of funds are not able to hire well-deserving and quality teachers which at times create a problem for the students to face. Apart from it, some institutions do not have proper infrastructure like quality laboratory, library, etc,. But on the other side of the coin, we actually could see there are some private colleges which have strived to enhance their standards and some of them rank better than many Government-run colleges today which are not accessible for all.

8. ***Misuse of Grants:*** UGC provides financial assistance to the universities and colleges for various developmental activities. But the same fund is hardly seen to be properly utilised. Specially, in rural areas where the local bodies are not so strong, the guardian of the students are not so conscious about the proper use of financial assistance, administrative bodies takes the advantage of it.

9. ***Lesser Research Activities:*** It has been seen that not more that 20 per cent of all students enrolled in a doctoral research programme

complete their work and almost 80 per cent drop out. A lack of motivation amongst university faculty to conduct and supervise research also stems from unavailability of good research students and a lack of professional incentive for research. However, to increase research output, the UGC started giving scholarships to students enrolled for a PhD in Central universities, but ignores State universities.

10. ***Poor input:*** One of the major challenges facing by the higher educational institutes in rural areas is the standard of input; i.e., students, especially in general education. So far as higher education is concerned with quality education with quality output, the biggest challenge for these institutes where minimum cut off mark is not applicable at the time of admission.

11. ***High dropout rate:*** In rural areas of India the school dropout rate is more than normal. As a result of this very few students taste the sweetness of higher education. Even during college life also because of family burden, poor infrastructural facilities, lack of monetary support, apathy towards education etc., we can see high percentage of drop out among rural students.

12. ***Lesser use of Information and Communication Technology (ICT):*** ICT can affect the delivery of education and enable wider access to the same. In addition, it increases flexibility so that learners can access the education regardless of time and geographical barriers. It can influence the way students are taught and how they learn. But in most of the rural colleges and universities, use of ICT is hardly seen while teaching. There are lots of colleges in India where electricity problem is a common phenomenon. In those institutions we can expect only the traditional method of teaching.

13. ***Inadequate physical infrastructure:*** Quality education is possible when facilities, resources and technologies are upgraded in a tandum. For this, funding is needed which has been made on the basis of grades given by NAAC on the basis of various parameters. The higher educational institution of rural areas are bound to grade in the lower side since quality of input is also very low, higher ratio of teacher-students, poor communication etc., and due to this grants are also given on the lower side which hinders improvement in physical infrastructure.

14. ***Faculty problem:*** Quality of teaching depends upon quality of teachers. Availability of adequate and qualified faculty is a prerequisite

of quality education. Quality teachers always prefer better colleges in the sense better input, standard teacher-student ratio, better communication, better physical facilities, better research facilities etc. and due to which the rural institutes has to suffer.

The Central government is actively bringing out several changes to develop higher education in rural areas. These specialised new efforts are taken with the objective of preventing the living places of Schedule Caste and Schedule Tribe, backward places and border villages from lagging behind in the field of education, as a part of the programme. UGC has planned to provide special development fund for the universities operating in these areas. This initiative facilitates to expand the earlier existing infrastructure and create new basic necessary structures. As a result, students and faculties would be provided with accommodation facilities on rental basis to pursue higher education. Apart from this, efforts are underway to provide relevant curriculum to the areas in and around this education institution and also provide transport facilities for the economically backwards students. Indira Gandhi National Tribal University in Amarkantak, Madhya Pradesh functions with great zeal to provide higher education to the people belonging to Schedule Caste and Schedule Tribe. Most of us are aware that IGNOU has established itself in providing quality higher education to almost all the places in India including the habitat of tribal people. National Mission on Education has made it possible to access higher education from anywhere and at anytime through Information and Communication Technology (ICT). Apart from this, through the 11th five year plan, there are on-going efforts to establish model degree colleges in all the 374 district that has its higher education enrollment ratio lesser than that of the Gross Enrollment Ratio. The Central government has decided to provide adequate funds to the State governments towards this endeavour.

Remedies

(a) ***Equal importance given to Rural Areas:*** To assess the availability of various policies programmes and facilities in higher education, there is an urgent need to access and find out from the students their awareness and utilisation of facilities, as also to cross-check the availability of the facilities in institutions where they are enrolled.

(b) ***Enhance Quality of Education:*** All plans for expansion must have a major thrust on enhancing quality of education. Hence, due care must be given for developing skills of teachers for enhancing teaching-learning transaction, creating conducive academic environment, improving the learning infrastructure, putting technology enabled learning into practice wherever possible.

(c) ***Establishment of research centers:*** Establishment of research centers of excellence in various areas of local relevance must be pursued and these should be affiliated with the existing universities and institutions of national importance. UGC should focus more on research-based support to the universities and colleges. It should help in developing bench-marking in teaching and research, support curricula updation, develop norms for efficient governance, establish and support large number of inter-university centre like institutions that will facilitate institutions of higher education towards quality and excellence in teaching and research. UGC should furthermore help in developing networking and electronic connectivity, besides helping institutions in optimally utilising them.

(d) ***Checking drop-out ratio:*** Higher education system should take interest in their feeder area or supply chain to improve quality and drop-out as a priority need of the community and duty of higher education system and for their own growth i.e., higher education system.

(e) ***Establishing career counseling cells:*** Special career counselling cells must be set by the government so that students can also enroll themselves in other technical and professional courses apart from other general courses. Besides, the students can select subject according to their needs and capacity.

(f) ***Adequate fund:*** To build a high quality education system, adequate funding must be made available by the Central and State governments to improve quality, at the same time, making higher education affordable to all specially for the families of rural areas where income level of the people is low and thus increasing access.

(g) ***Checking proper utilisation of grants:*** The grant provided by Central, State governments as well as other bodies to the educational institutes are how effectively utilised is a matter of doubt. Administrative bodies use the funds as per their own profitability rather than priority of the institute for greater social interests of the stakeholders. The regulatory bodies should ensure proper use of funds on the basis of priority.

Conclusion

Higher Education is a very powerful agent of social change. If the higher education system is not streamlined or improved according to the needs of the present day requirements, the primary promise of justice-social, economic and political, equality of status and of opportunity, liberty of thought, faith and worship will ever remain unfulfilled. Higher education should aim at socialisation and democratisation in true sense of the word.

Higher education has become most important and powerful economic tool in the global economy. It trains and develops skilled people required for efficient and improved production. In this way it contributes to individual and national development. So, all developed and under-developed countries accept that economic development takes place only as a result of the development of education. Education supplies required man-power to agriculture, industry and service sectors. It also creates more and more employment and income opportunities. Moreover, higher education has raised the socio-economic conditions and standards of living. It is true in Indian society, where almost all people whether rich or poor or belongs to rural or urban areas give due importance to higher education only because of its economic importance.

Thus, India needs to go a far way ensure access of higher education to all those who aspire for it.

References

- Md. Afzalur Rahman and Tarali Pathak, "Quality, Quantity and Equity in Higher Education with Special Reference to North-East Region", *University News*, 51(06), February 11-17, 2013, p. 14.
- P.K. Manoharan, *Higher Education*, New Delhi: A.P.H. Publishing Corporation, 2009, pp. 4-5.
- Nitu Konwar and Subhadeep Chakraborty "Status of Higher Education and Research in India", *International Journal of Educational Research and Technology*, Vol. 2 Issue 1 (January, 2013), pp. 6-12. www.rierc.orgaccessed on 12 June, 2013.
- Rajeev Bairathi, "Equality and Quality in Higher Education", *University News*, 51(24), June 17-23, 2013, p. 14.

31 Inter-social Groups Disparities in Access to Higher Education: A Sociological Perspectives

Usharani B.

Abstract

Access to different levels of education is a strand that runs through all considerations of inequality, poverty and poverty traps. Evidently, access to education provides opportunities for individuals in their lifetimes. It is also a primary means of intergenerational economic and social change. Disparity, measures in terms of enrollment in higher education by age group gives the representation by social group. There are intra and inter group disparities. Social groups are classified as Scheduled Caste, Scheduled Tribe and other groups. The present paper is an attempt to present various facts of the educational development of Scheduled Castes and Scheduled Tribes vis-a-vis other sections of the community and to analyse the disparity across and within higher education for a specific age group. This paper concentrates on disparities in total enrollment in higher education by different groups, disparities in different higher degree courses. In response to the ongoing societal significance of inequality in education, there is a large and growing literature in the social sciences that seeks to understand, the sources of these disparities and to identify potential solutions. The issues focusses on social group disparities in the domains of education because these disparities represent some of the most pressing societal problems today and have a vital impact on quality of life.

Introduction

Education is the most important tool for development of any society. In India, higher education has been beneficial for some but not for all streams of the society. There is a need to make the process more inclusive because some millions of people in the country have seen almost no rewards. The benefits have not reached the majority and new risks have emerged for the socially deprived and rural poor. It has also created socio-economic and cultural disparities in the society. The disparities are found in creating a gap between caste, class and communities. The present education system has failed to inclusive of equal opportunity to entire section of the society. This development has led to the unequal distribution of socio- economic standard of the society. There is a need to study inclusive of all sections of the society for providing equal standard of education and equal opportunity for the major sections of the society for the overall development of nation (Somashekar and Vinodh Kumar G.C. (2012).

Inequality of opportunities between various social groups for higher education is and has been a serious problem in India. The numbers of admissions and graduates have not been proportional to the size of population when we compare males with females, various regions, various ethnic groups, urban-rural residents, and the center with the peripheries. Usually, the males, urban residents and the center are the advantaged ones. Their participation, enrollment and graduates' rates are much higher.

In India, the hierarchical system of caste historically denied education and access to high income yielding occupation to backward caste that were kept in the lower strata of which are now called as Scheduled Caste (SC) and Scheduled Tribe (ST) of India. The marginalised sections were not only devoid of any education and decent employment, but were systematically and skilfully made dysfunctional through fear, inferiority complex, servility, hopelessness, and despair compelled to depend on the oppression for dues as to how they should view and value themselves, it is but natural for their children who constantly face a rejection, doubt that whether their families and the community really merit any more respects (Sam, 1999). The Indian social system suffers from the in flexibilities of a rigid caste system. For centuries, caste had been a determining factor in education, work and employment. Shah rightly points out, 'higher education is still mainly open to the higher castes.' (Shah 1960), Large sections of the population belonging to the lower castes were denied education and also access to high income yielding and power imparting occupations. Hence, in India, caste has been the determinant of class positions resulting in acute inequality in the distribution of wealth and incomes (Mehta and Kapoor 1998:37).

In the words of Shills, 'no other country can quite match this picture of a continuing intellectual tradition carried so long by a single section of the population.' (Shills 1961:21) The representation of the Scheduled Caste, Tribes and Other Backward Castes (OBCs) in institutions of higher learning is minuscule. (Gore *et al.* 1970:62-5) In some institutions, like the Indian Institute of Technology, during certain years, not a single Scheduled Caste/ Tribe student was enrolled. (Rajagopalan and Singh 1968:1-5) B.V. Shah found that the Hindu Gujarati male students of the University of Baroda 'largely belong to upper and middle socio-economic strata'. (Shah 1961:41) In Mysore, Siva Kumar found that under-graduate women students from the upper strata had greater opportunities for higher education than those from the middle or lower social strata (Kumar 1982:39-62).

Social Groups

Historically, the vulnerable groups of the Indian society, namely, the Scheduled Castes, the Scheduled Tribes, Other Backward Classes and women have suffered deprivation in all walks of life including education. The government in the post-independence period has been trying to promote the educational status of these groups through several measures but the progress made in their case is well below the targets envisaged. During the post-independence period, the government of India inherited the legacy of educational backwardness in addition to many other drawbacks. (Khajapeer 1996:143-52) The Constitution of India is a Magna Carta for the SCs, STs, OBCs and women in respect of the special provisions made for them, for example, reservations in jobs and educational institutions and the provisions against discrimination. (*Ibid*) Article 46, a Directive Principle of the Constitution, suggests that the state shall take special care of the educational interests of the weaker sections, particularly the SCs and STs. Even Article 15 (4) in the section on Fundamental Rights states that nothing shall prevent the state from making special provision for the socially and educationally backward classes, particularly the SCs and STs. (Choudhary 1998:437-8)

Scheduled Castes has been at the lowest end of the Hindu (social) caste hierarchy based on birth. Over long periods in the past, the social system ascribed occupations to this group which were not only low in social ordering but were also characterised by very low productivity. With ascription on the basis of birth, the system did not permit occupational mobility. Consequently, this group remained at the lowest end of the economic hierarchy as well. While the intensity of caste-based discriminatory social practices varied in different parts of the country and was partially moderated with the penetration of the impersonal market forces in varying degrees, this group remained on the fringe of the traditional village society and rural economy practising lowly occupations with little exposure to educational opportunities.

Scheduled Tribes in contrast, had not been part of the Hindu social hierarchy. Their social and economic backwardness was derived from their long time habitation in geographically isolated areas with difficult terrain and practising shifting cultivation. Lack of exposure to education and isolation from the social mainstream made them vulnerable to exploitation by the non-tribals and uprooting from their traditional habitation and occupations so that they were relegated to the lowest end of the economic hierarchy.

The remaining collection social group of "others" consisted of castes other than Scheduled Cates in the Hindu social hierarchy and non-ST members of other religious communities. This residual (non-SC/ST) group has been further sub-divided into "other backward castes" (OBC) in the Hindu social hierarchy announced by the state governments as being socially "backward" for eligibility to state-initiated programmes of affirmative action and the remaining "others".

Higher Education

After the independence there was tremendous increase in terms of the number of higher educational institutions in India, teachers and students. There after also there was big increase in the number of universities, teacher and students, but how far this jumps where distributed among all the communities and groups in India has to be examined to understand how unequal was the developments that take place in the arena of higher education. The national higher education policy adopted in 1986 has emphasised on three basic elements, Access, equal access (or equity), Quality and Excellence. But the process of development in this sector was exclusionary for the sections like scheduled tribes, scheduled casts, and other backward classes.

Through higher education has been valued and pursued even from the Vedic days in India, it was narrow in its conception in two ways. It was confined mainly to religious, grammar, logic and philosophy, only a few scholars specialised in secular subject like medicine, mathematics and astronomy. Further, higher learning was confined to a microscopic minority of the population belonging to the twice-born castes particularly to those born in to *Brahmin* caste. It was in the Buddhist era that higher education was widened in its scope and thrown open to all castes. One of the most important social objectives of education is to equalise opportunities enabling backward or under privileged classes and individuals to use education as a lever for improvement of their conditions.

Higher education clearly needs well-designed academic programmes and a clear mission. Most important to them success, however, are high-quality faculty committed and well-prepared students and sufficient resources. Despite notable excerptors', most higher education institutes in developing countries suffer severe deficiencies. As a result, few perform to a consentingly high standard. (World Bank, 2000).

Within education, higher education is considered to be important aspect of one's social and economic well-being. Recently, there has been a considerable demand for expansion and enhancement of the higher education due to growth of industries and the corresponding need of skilled manpower. As well, liberalisation of the economy led demand for new knowledge, technology and better employability directing to manpower development activities provided by higher education (Becker, 1964).

Scheduled Castes and Scheduled Tribes Enrollment in Higher Education

Total student enrollment in higher educational institutions in India has been increasing rapidly over the past half-century, from less than 2,00,000 in 1950 to almost seven million by the year 2000. During this time, the proportionate representation of scheduled caste (SC) and scheduled tribe (ST) students in total higher educational enrollment has been slowly rising. From the late 1970s to the late 1990s the SC proportion rose from 7 per cent to 7.8 per cent and the ST proportion rose from 1.6 per cent to 2.7 per cent [Rao 2002:47]. These percentage figures should be compared to the corresponding SC and ST shares of the total population of India: roughly 16 per cent and 8 per cent, respectively. Thus, by the end of the century, SC and ST student representation in higher educational institutions had reached roughly one-half and one-third of their representation in the population as a whole.

SC and ST students are distributed quite unevenly across the various degree programmes offered at Indian colleges and universities [Chanana 1993; HRD 1997]. Roughly 40 per cent of all higher education students in India are enrolled in (relatively low-prestige) arts programmes, but the corresponding figure for SC students is over 60 per cent and for ST students roughly 75 per cent. Correspondingly, the percentages of SC and ST students enrolled in the most prestigious programmes–engineering, law and medicine—are much lower than for students from the rest of the population. Not surprisingly, SC and ST students tend to be more under-represented in masters and PhD programmes than at the bachelor's degree level. There is a limited amount of evidence available on the number of Scheduled Castes and Scheduled Tribes who have graduated from higher educational institutions.

Disparities in Access to Higher Education

Sociologists see society as a stratification system that is based on a hierarchy of power (the ability to direct someone else's behaviour), privilege (honour and respect), and prestige (income, wealth, and property), which leads to patterns of social inequality. Social inequality is characterised by the existence of unequal opportunities and rewards for different social positions or statuses within a group or society. Inequality of opportunities refers to the unequal distribution of "life chances" across individuals. This is reflected in measures such as level of education, health status, and treatment by the criminal justice system.

Social and educational inequalities, continued despite the changes leaded into the Indian society before and after independence. In order to change this situation and transform the traditional social structure, new policies were formulated after independence based on a planned programme of scientific, technology, liberal and democratic frameworks of modernisation. Many steps were taken to promote social and economic equality and justice, and to provide equal educational opportunities to all, irrespective of caste and class considerations. The educational system is geared to function accordingly, but the results is not very encouraging because a great disparity in terms of educational opportunities still persists among various castes. The traditional deprivation kept SCs (Scheduled Castes) and STs (Scheduled Tribes) at the lower rung of the caste hierarchy and denied access to any form of education; with the demands of a knowledge-driven society under globalisation left them out of the mainstream as social misfits and the disposable people of society because of their lack of education. (Thorat, 2008).

Many colleges and universities were started in India for removing regional imbalances and for supporting education of weaker and disadvantaged classes. These institutions and other developmental programmes for weaker classes are still facing resource constraints, which are further aggravated by ignorance, poverty and disadvantages of the people they serve. This is resulting in widening divides and in keeping many educated from weaker and disadvantages sections outside the job and employment markets. The challenge of these marginalised and deprived to the system of education is enormous.

A number of factors contribute to these disparities. Scheduled Castes and Scheduled Tribes are poorer than others. In addition, Scheduled Castes and Scheduled Tribes students suffer from a number of other disadvantages. There are reported instances of Scheduled Castes students suffering from discrimination by teachers and other students. Scheduled Tribes, in addition to suffering from the same low expectations, face a different set of issues. They often live in hilly regions or forests that are relatively inaccessible. Demographically, tribal habitations are small and sparsely populated and hence lack many infrastructural facilities, including schools, colleges and roads. These factors are particularly constraining for tribal children, who live in isolated communities. Language poses another major challenge for tribal education. Tribes normally speak local dialects rather than the main language of the state in which they reside, and tribal students feel further alienated when the teachers are not well-trained to communicate in their tribal dialects (Sujatha 2002).

Research studies have demonstrated the low levels of participation of students from lower strata of society in the field of higher education as compared to such participation of students from middle and higher strata of society. The academic achievement of students from lower strata is lower than those who come from upper strata. Among students with comparable attainments those with high socio-economic status tend to get more opportunities to pursue higher studies than those from low socio-economic strata.

The decline in college completion among Scheduled Castes is somewhat unpredictable. Much of the social conflict surrounding positive action has cantered on Scheduled Castes and their perceived ease of gaining admission to college. Our results show that at this level, the success rates for Scheduled Castes have not improved at all. It is also important to note that although we focus on college completion rather than college entry, positive action is directed to college entrance, not graduation. However, the intent behind the programme is presumably to increase college graduation, and not just enrollment.

Unfortunately, various measures taken by the government to enhance and foster access amongst these deprived groups have not been appropriately supported by implementation and evaluation data. The Government should maintain data on transition rate, survival rate, graduation rate, drop-out and wastage. These data should be as per the sub-castes and sub-tribes amongst Indigenous. The policy framed on the basis of these data will definitely serve better results and lead to optimum utilisation of scarce resources. The issue of drop-out and wastage is prominent in technical courses, especially at graduate and higher level. The data reflection in this regard shall be useful in arriving at appropriate policy measures.

The majority of the students among these communities are unaware of future opportunities. The selection of streams and subjects in the post secondary period is also greatly influenced in ignorance. All institutions in the tribal belt should have a guidance and counselling cell. This cell is also expected to play a vital role at the time of induction of indigenous students into colleges.

Objectives of the Study

The following are the main objectives of the study:

- To observe the education inequality of social groups like SC, ST and Others.
- To find out the gaps of enrollment in various socio-economic groups in Karnataka.

Justification of the study: The concepts of caste and class aspects have led to the negative growth in higher education. The higher education system has not been reaching the general public, rural people and tribal people in Karnataka. In this regard, there is a need to study regarding the social disparities and higher education system for the better development of the society.

Methodology of the study: The study is based on secondary data collected from various sources such as, books, journals, articles, governmental reports, educational reports, newspapers and internet.

Results: When we come across the education among the socio-economic group of Karnataka, the situation is not much different by disparity. The upper caste representing seven per cent of total populations of Karnataka, 6.3 per cent are literate and among them 60 per cent are getting higher education. The OBC and SC are getting higher education 23 per cent and 16 per cent respectively, but the tribal population representing only two per cent in this regard.

In Karnataka 17 universities bring out 12 to 14 per cent graduates of total population of Karnataka state. In Karnataka, the universities giving general degree education to 4,01,548 students and 1,01,049 students are able to get professional degree education. Out of which 84,518 students are opted engineering courses. It shows that, out of every five students in Karnataka, only one student is able to get professional courses.

From this statistics majority of students are unable to get opportunity for professional degree courses. In the same way, the disparity can be found in urban and rural students. Eighty-two per cent of rural students are fall in general degree courses and 18 per cent are getting opportunity to entering to the professional courses. Out of 23 per cent of urban population only seven per cent elite, upper and upper middle class people are usurping the privileged education.

This development has created socio-economic and cultural disparities in the society. The disparities are found creating a gap between caste, class and communities. This development has also lead to unequal distribution of socio-economic standard of the society.

The literacy rate is the number of educated people in a population, over the age of fifteen who can read and write. As per Census of India statistics report, literacy rate has improved in last decade. As a result of free education system in the villages, the literacy rate has gone up tremendously, especially among females. Literacy rate has increased from 64.83 per cent in 2001 to 74.04 per cent in 2011.

Karnataka Literacy Profile 2010-2012

Community	*Literacy rate in 2001*	*Literacy rate in 2011*
Rural	59.00	68.86
Urban	81.00	86.21
Total Literacy rate	66.64	75.60

(*Source:* 2011 Census publication).

Enrollment in Collegiate Education in Karnataka (Arts, Science and Commerce) 2010-11 to 2011-12

Year	*Institutions*	*Enrollment*		
		Total	*Female*	*SC/ST*
2010-11	651	365801	186553	85941
2011-12	669	454512	228913	94239

(*Source:* Department of Collegiate Education).

Enrollment in Professional Degree Courses in Karnataka (SC/ST)

Professional degree courses	*2010-2011*	*2011-2012*
Nursing (UG)	332/89	243/69
Nursing (PG)	36/04	38/04
Ayurvedic	388	343/113
Homeopathy	52	83/67
Unani	9	1/3
Nature Cure and Yoga	19	12/5
D. Pharma	71	79
Agriculture	188	160
Horticulture	82	103
Forestry	8	9
Sericulture	7	7
Veterinary	42	73
Fisheries	15	16
Dairy Science	11	19

(*Source:* University of Agricultural Sciences, Karnataka Examination Authority, Directorate of Medical Education, (Rajiv Gandhi Medical University), Directorate of Indian System of Medicines).

Findings of the Study

- The inequalities in college education have narrowed for tribal males; but for all other groups, *dalit* males and females, and tribal females, inequality seems to be widening rather than narrowing.
- Opportunities are been held to major section of the society due to economic disability in perspective of higher education.
- Other outstanding classes of the society like rural, tribal and lower classes have seen almost no rewards.
- Tribals are more able than *dalits* to achieve the parity in college graduation with upper caste Hindus and others.
- The district-wise education reflects the serious imbalances in educational attainments across districts of Karnataka.

Conclusion

Higher education is a very powerful agent of social change. If the higher education system is not streamlined or improved according to the needs of the present day, the primary promise of justice, social, economic and political, equality of status and of opportunity, liberty of thought, faith and worship will ever remain unfulfilled. Higher education should aim at socialisation and democratisation in true sense of the word. Access to higher education has become an important component of building stable and prosperous modern societies.

Disparity in education is one of the most debated topic since it is a constitutional right of every citizen. Disparity in education will lead to disparity in human development as well as economic development and therefore, there is an urgent need for its reduction. Providing education to all is the responsibility of state. In the backdrop of inclusive growth strategy of India, it is necessary to understand the social disparity in educational development.

References

- Agarwal, P. Higher education in India: The need for change. New Delhi, *Indian Council for Research on International Economic Relations. 2006* [accessed on 23rd March, 2008] (www.icrier.org/publication/working_papers_180.html).
- Jhingran, D. and D. Sankar (2009): 'Measuring Educational Development and Disparities', in Preet Rustagi (ed) "Concerns, Conflicts and Cohesions" Universalisation of Elementary Education in India", *Oxford University Press and Institute of Human Development.*

- Karnataka human development report 2000, Government of Karnataka.
- Premakumara, G.S. (2006). Status of Women Employment in India. *Journal of Development and Social Change*. 4 (1/2), pp. 326-340.
- N. Somashekar And Vinodh Kumar G.C. (2012) Globalisation and its Dimensions of Education Inequalities: With Special Reference to Karnataka accessed on January 20, 2013 (http://iosrjournals.org/iosr-jhss/papers/Vol. 4-Issue 6/B0461117.pdf).
- Sen, Amartya, 2000, *Development as Freedom*, New Delhi: Oxford University Press.
- Sharma, Shashi. Prabha. (2007). *Basic Principles of Education* (pp. 3-4). New Delhi: Kanishka Publishers.
- Joshi, K.M. Higher education and the largest impoverished and marginalised group of the Indian population: reviewing enrollment and access to higher education among tribals in India. *Asian Social Work and Policy Review*. 2010, 4(2), pp. 57-65.
- Prakash, Ved, 2007, 'Trends in Growth and Financing of Higher Education in India', *Economic and Political Weekly*, Vol. 42 (31), August 4-10.
- Xaxa, V. Protective discrimination: Why scheduled tribes lag behind scheduled castes. *Economic and Political Weekly*. 2001, 36(29), pp. 2765-72.

32 Issues in Quality Higher Education in India

Hanumantha, G.H.

K. Vinutha Somanna

Lohith, R.

Introduction

Education is an instrument of human development and social change. In India, Nalanda and Takshasheela Universities were imparting education which had been pursued by pupils across the world. Upanishads highlighted about quality of higher Education planned, integrated, problem solving, personality development, leadership development-oriented and entrepreneurship-oriented education.

The word "education" has its root in the Latin word "exducere" which means "to bring out". True education lies in bringing forth the human values in the individuals, thus allowing the blossoming of his personality. The education is that by which character is formed, strength of mind is increased, the intellect is expanded and by which one can stand on one's own feet. The most striking problem is whether the quality education as intended by the framers of the norms and the guidelines to the education system has been a success.?

Objectives of the Study

- To examine the issues of quality higher education in India.
- To analyse the intricacies and solution there for relating to education.
- To critically focus on the current situation of higher education policies and their implementation.
- To foreground the tendency of the government in imparting education and pupils pursuing the higher education.

- To focus major anomalies of existing policies norms, schemes of governments on higher education which are needed to be addressed.
- To put forward certain standards of solution to tackle the issues involved in the quality higher education.

The present paper is based on doctrinal method. Complete study of reports of MHRD, NSSO, UGC and journals and the materials has been done.

Hypothesis

The progress of quality higher education will be hindered by the existing problems and issues. The implementation of higher education policies, rules, norms etc is not good as enshrined there in. The pupil pursuing the higher education will be far away therefrom, if the present education system continues.

Abdul Kalam has rightly observed that we are not facing problem of the employment but facing employability. Because, the present generation is suffering from lack of knowledge in subjects, communication, ICT skills due to the issues affecting the quality of education. In order to address these problems, the Nodal Agency like UGC, The Ministry of Human Resource development and the State governments have enacted and implemented several action plans, strategies, measures for streamlining higher education, policies and programmes.

The issues involved in the quality of higher education can be effectively tackled when higher education facilities would be extended to rural and tribal areas and to make them access to enjoy the higher education and establishment of new universities with innovative infrastructure, technologies and new system of syllabus. Moreover, it is necessary to have systematic and optimum utilisation of human resource.

Despite above fact that the higher education is not achieved to the maximum extent. Along with this, the higher education which we are pursuing is not a solution to address all social problems faced by vulnerable sections particularly SC, ST, Women and marginalised sections of the society.

The fruits of higher education have not equally been availed to all sections of the society, statistically speaking only 12 per cent of the country's population is getting higher education (according to NSS report).

The education being a multi-dimensional character is required to face the issues to its quality. Therefore, there is a need to create an environment in this regard. Production of policy-makers, administrators, technocrats and others could be possible if they avail the quality education.

The core idea of the paper is revolving with respect to the following issues:

- Firstly, quality: The output of education yearly pursuing is not up to the margin intended and expected.
- Secondly, no proper and effective implementation of policies and programmes existed on higher education. The implementers of the government are not ready to completely implement the schemes relating to update the quality of academic work.
- Thirdly, the efforts taken to bring other sections of the society to the main stream of the higher education are not sufficient to meet the intended goals.
- Fourthly, higher education is being the subject of the Central government; the State governments are not so serious towards imparting quality higher education (Allocation of funds 80:20 per cent respectively).
- Fifthly, the process of monitoring and evaluation higher educational service by committees like NAAC is influenced by some other facts like nepotism, political influence and so on.
- Sixthly, the syllabi prescribed by universities for academic activities and competitive examinations are outdated.
- Seventhly, there is no wider scope for healthy developments of non-academic activities which is integral part of education system.
- Eighthly, majority of the universities are governed by traditional norms and usages and we cannot expect innovativeness to maximum extent to cover all new ideas.

Higher education has immense potential to contribute to the consolidation of democracy. Such education should include all those factors which can develop the physical, mental, moral, cultural and spiritual aspects of the human personality. It should enable man to be the least dependent on others. Man should cultivate the virtues of self-dependence and cooperativeness to the highest possible degree. Education, being recognised as fundamental to all kinds of development in society, hence it is needed for planning and research in education ensuring the concentration of the quality within it. Today's institutions of higher education at large whether state supported or private non-profit faces the lack of quality. Driven by the quest for profits, these institutes do not share the ethics, the values or the concepts of what requires good higher education to the optimum level.

Growth of Higher Education System

There were **20** Universities and **500** Colleges at the time of independence. Now, the Universities and university-level institutions have raised to more than **504**, State Universities–**243**, State Private Universities–**53**, Central Universities–**40**, Deemed Universities–**130**. Institutions of national importance established under Acts of Parliament–**33**. Institutions established under various State legislations–**5**. In addition, there are **25,951** colleges including, around **2,565** Women Colleges. Out of 25,951 Colleges, **7,362** Colleges (28 per cent) have been recognised under Section 2(f) and **5,997** Colleges (23 per cent) under Section 12-B of the UGC Act, 1956.

Total Number of Students Enrolled

Total number of students enrolled in Universities and Colleges **136.42 lakhs–16.69 lakhs** (12.24 per cent) in University Departments and **119.73 lakhs** (87.76 per cent) in affiliated colleges.

The **education sphere in India** is divided into two segments.

Regulated segment—The Higher Education space falls under regulated segment comprising of degree granting universities and colleges, which are governed by UGC, AICTE, specialised professional bodies and state specific legislations. The regulated segment operates under "not for profit" model and entities allowed in this segment are trust, society or not for profit company (under section 25 of the Companies Act 1956).

The unregulated segment comprises vocational, coaching, test preparation, research, etc. and can freely operate under 'for-profit' model. Higher education is a social aspiration and instrument of nation development. The former president APJ Abdul Kalam quoted *"For achieving the status of developed nation by 2020, there is no chance but to significantly increase the access with quality in higher education for generating the Ignited minds".*

The systematic problem of the higher education system is its overall coherence, rationality and appropriateness, in relation to the socio-economic development needs. It also relates to the size of the system (overall enrollments, participation rates and number of institutions), the shape of the system (the nature of institutions, their mandates and focus). The levels and range of their programme offering, their field/disciplinary orientations and modes of educational delivery.

Indian higher education has been developed from access and equality to the qualitative measure. Within the equity and access framework, facilities for higher education expanded significantly during the post independence period. The present approach of the government is required and necessary to face the global challenge under the WTO and GATT regime which highly focusses on emergence of foreign universities across the world.

In order to improve and increase the quality education public and private collaboration and private initiative and participation in higher education have to be coined as a complimentary mechanism.

Promotion and Preservation of Indian Culture and Values

The nodal agency UGC continued to provide assistance for promotion of thoughts of Gandhian, Buddhist and Ambedkar studies. The assistance is provided for setting up centres for these studies, conducting programmes to acquaint teachers and students with their philosophy and ideas. It has also been providing assistance for value-oriented education in order to foster among students and teachers alike such values are necessary for retaining the national identity and sustaining a peaceful and harmonious society.

Recently, Human rights scheme has been introduced for upgrading values o f human being by respecting and promoting human rights through set up of Human rights Branches.

According to the Education for All: Global Report 2005: The imperative two principles characterise most attempts to define quality in Education as follows.

- The first identifies learner's cognitive development as the major explicit objective of all education systems.
- The second emphasises education's role in promoting values and attitudes of responsible citizenship and in nurturing creative and emotional development.

Although there is no hard and fast rule to determine the quality education, still it can be examined in terms of:

(1) The intention and objective that lie behind individual policies or whole projects, schemes.

(2) The administrative and financial arrangements that are used to deliver policies.

(3) The outcome of policies, particularly in terms depends on the success rate.

Changes and challenges in the provision of higher education are as follows. The promotion of trade in education services is directly linked to a number of significant trends in higher education. These include:

(1) The emergence of new for-profit education providers,

(2) The growth of alternate electronic delivery modes both domestically and internationally,

(3) The responses to the labour market,

(4) The increase in international academic mobility of students, professors and programmes, and

(5) The limited budget capacity or political will of government to meet the increasing domestic demand for higher education.

Educational Outreach Activities Undertaken

The five year plans particularly the 9th, 11th and 12th advocated guidelines to be observed by the higher educational institutions for following programmes:

- Vocational/career-oriented programmes
- Equivalency programme
- Quality of life improvement programme
- Leadership and human resource development programmes
- Social and citizenship role awareness programme
- Individual interest programme.

Major Issues Involved

Quality—The output of education yearly pursuing is not upto the margin intended and expected

In spite of several programmes and policies initiated by apex authorities, governments and MHRD particularly research-oriented programmes, innovative schemes, area studies programmes, initiated towards establishment of autonomous colleges, new recruitment methods and standards for appointment of teachers and their training, facilities for improvement in efficiency, development of engineering/technology and management education, innovative standards to compete with international level of education, facilities and welfare programmes for weaker sections, SCs/STs, the outcome or net result of the qualitative higher education is not to the optimum level which so essential to the movement of educational status.

India is not completely free from this situation therefore it has been lagging behind in achieving the standards, excellence required in the qualitative education.

Secondly, no proper and effective implementation of policies and programmes existed on higher education

To achieve the qualitative education, the task of implementation of the programmes and policies on higher education is received paramount status. It is essential that we get the policies and architecture right as far as the educational sector is concerned. It will be necessary to have a proper set-up of the administration which can absorb the change-over to higher education and necessary steps will enable the higher education to develop efficiently and extensively in the context of quality. The implementing agencies like universities at the stage of execution of policies and programmes do not have complete willingness towards comprehensive implementation of them. This would be major hindrances and hurdle in the path of qualitative higher education that needs effective and comprehensive implementation through various agencies and branches set-up for this purpose.

Thirdly, the efforts taken to bring other sections of the society to the mainstream of the higher education are not sufficient to meet the intended goals

As a matter of reservation and social justice in higher education, government through its specialised agencies has been implementing reservation policies for the benefit of economically, socially and educationally disadvantaged groups and weaker sections namely SC/STs. Moreover, initiatives in the form of financial assistance, fellowships for research work, establishment of SC/STs cells, remedial coaching centres and skills and proficiency development centres, coaching facilities for computer literacy, strengthening the knowledge of English.

However, there is a lack of communication between these centres and prospective benefitted groups (needy students, educationally backward students and so on) this results into excluding them from availing those kind of facilities.

Fourthly, higher education is being the subject of the Union; the state governments are not so serious towards imparting quality higher education

Though the Constitution of India contemplates that education is the subject of concurrent list, the subject of higher education is enumerated in Central government list. As a result of which, only it is the responsibility of Central

Government to take any initiative programmes and policies for qualitative higher education through various Nodal Agencies but the State Governments do not come forward to achieve the above said goal.

Fifthly, the process of monitoring and evaluation of higher educational service by committees like NAAC is influenced by some other facts like nepotism, political influence and so on

The standards and measures of quality higher education has to be assessed periodically by some committees namely NAAC, BCI the Karnataka State Higher Education Council, MCI, and others in order to check the existing flaws in the educational system and suggest the remedial measures to cure them.

But in reality, they are not working towards progressive of quality higher education in the process of accreditation and assessment. It affects directly on education system in the country. In the process of assessment, they have not been influenced by educational standards and policies and programmes rather than other adverse matters on education.

Sixthly, the syllabi prescribed by universities for academic activities and competitive examinations are outdated

In order to compete in the competitive world, the universities are required to update their syllabus in accordance with innovative standards which enhance the interest of the students in gaining the ocean knowledge of new areas.

Most of the conventional universities have been suffering from qualitativeness in the educational system with that of the most forward universities in the area of academic especially updated syllabus, the relations between the pupils and the teachers, no exposure to the development of the student's personality, integrity, competitiveness, lack of healthy environment for studying including writing research articles, presentation of papers in the seminars, lack of study materials etc.

Seventhly, there is no wider scope for healthy developments of non-academic activities which is integral part of education system

For success of the educational system, the combination of academic and extracurricular activities is essential and extracurricular activities are necessary for physical and mental development of the students. Unfortunately, majority of the universities imparting higher education are concentrating only on academic performance of the students partially and on self development of the authorities. Therefore, these universities are not in the position to compete with other universities.

The examination system adopted by these universities may increase passing percentage of the students but they will be a failure in getting suitable jobs according to their qualification. These kinds of problems have not been identified and addressed by conventional universities. The present era is highly requiring the students with competitiveness whose production is the major obligation of the educational institutions committed for higher education with quality. If they fail in this task, there is a possibility of students unemployed involving in anti-social activities.

Eighthly, majority of the universities are governed by traditional norms and usages and we cannot expect innovativeness to maximum extent to cover all new ideas

The traditional norms and usage like conventional methods in obtaining admission, examination process, and teaching coupled with the convention methods, assessment mechanisms of pupils and in other fields have been acquiring dominant status in conventional universities. The adoption of these means and modes affect innovativeness which is essential for progress and improvement of higher education system.

Recommendations and Suggestions

1. It is suitable time to incorporate the regime of human values in academic work of universities like honour living human beings, respect the nation, women, to extend help to the needy groups, upgrade cultural integrity and traditions of the motherland, exchange views about knowledge and skill among learning groups, to co-operate with policies and programmes initiated by the government for well being of all aspects including qualitative education.
2. For successful completion of higher education the foundation is comprehensive of primary and secondary education which the students have been nurtured and nourished with all characteristics and qualitative of ability and standard and integrity that are so much required in order to get the quality higher education. In this way, to build strong system of higher education there is need to focus on quality primary and secondary education. After pursuing secondary education, the students enrolled in higher education become less, in this stage and circumstances the effective mechanisms to be developed by concerned authorities to access the facilities of higher education to the excluded groups.
3. In countries like India, the education system (primary and secondary) covering the pattern the exam is that no student shall be held back of expelled from school till completion of elementary education as

per Section 8 of Free and Compulsory Education Act, 2009. Of course, undoubtedly this provision helps the students but it reduces the number of quality students and the students benefitted from this kind of provision, fail to to make their mark in higher education.

4. To envisage education with morality and quality, the universities are mandated to adopt subjects like moral education along with the regular subjects.

5. To enhance the innovative and inventions in their specified field relating to academic particularly production of new formulas, recognition of copyright works, generation of new ideas, designs, artistic works etc., there is a need to establish patent and copyright offices for legal recognition of their intellectual works.

6. Students need a consistent level of basic information about the content and expectations for each course they have enrolled. Along with all updated information, the opportunities must be announced and made available for all students. Each syllabus must include two types of information, first information must include information related to specific course such as its title, goals, readings, assignments. Second information must include university policies that may have an impact on their participation in the course. This information includes the university grading system, disabilities statement and how to resolve problems between students and instructor.

7. In accordance with the guidelines and suggestions of UGC, every university in its each department, it is essential to establish centre for excellence to enrich the knowledge and skill of students in all aspects including academic and extra-curricular activities. Moreover, the said centre has to work for benefit of teachers in accessing update information.

8. For effective implementation of the educational policies and programmes to the all sects of students, the implementing authorities who fail in the task of implementation shall be punished in the form of withdrawing the incentives, benefits like delay in promotions, increments and such other facilities.

9. Table of academic events of particular year has to be specified and intimated to the students well in advance to have proper time management to the students and smooth administration to the departments which helps both the students and teaching faculty to be free from all kinds of burdens, tensions.

10. The students who are the output and suffered from lack of employability are required the facilities of placements and jobs. In order to meet the current demands, proficiency development imparting training skills has to be given to them.

Conclusion

The key policy objective that must define the overall capacity of the higher education system is the need to develop the high-level and varied intellectual conceptual knowledge, abilities and skills needed to meet the local, regional, national and international requirements of a developing democracy. These capabilities must not confined to simply economic goals but must address the needs of social, intellectual and cultural developments. The intellectual and conceptual knowledge at the levels of knowledge production and dissemination as well as ongoing development of professionals at difference levels, different economic and social sectors in different fields and disciplines must be given much importance. The higher education sector owing to its huge, potential holds very promising aspects, it is, thus called as "sun rise sector". The collaboration across sectors, strong partnerships between campuses and industry, meaningful engagement from the civic leaders and better communication with the policy-makers for elementary and secondary schools are all the necessary approaches to recast today's higher education.

References

- John Baldock, Nick Manning, Sarah Vickerstaff (2008)—*Social policy, Education and training*. IInd Edition, Oxford University Press.
- Kishore Singh, (2009). *Non-discrimination and Equality of Opportunity in Education and UNESCO's Convention Against Discrimination in Education: Recent Developments in International Law, with Reference to India,* Vol. 49, p. 213, Indian Journal of international Law.
- Manoj Kumar Singh (2005)—"*Right to Education: National and International Perspectives*" Indian Journal of International Law, Vol. 48, pp. 188-207.
- Amit Banerjee (Jan 2013), *Educational intervention for the marginalised group-A critical Appraisal-* All India Reporter.
- *World Education Report 2000–Right to education – Towards education for all throughout life.* UNESCO Publishing 2000.
- *Convention on technical and vocational education 1989,* Paris.
- Prof. Ramesh Chandra, (2005) *Virtual Education and Educational Futures,* Kalpaz Publications, Delhi.
- *Education For All Global Monitoring Report 2005* by United Nations Educational Scientific and Cultural Organisation.

- Pavan Agarwal (2009), *Indian Higher Education; Envisioning the Future*-I edition Sage Publications.
- Dr. N.K. Sharma, Dr. Prem Sunder, I edition, *Educational Encyclopaedia*, edited and compiled by KSK Publishers and Distributors, New Delhi.
- Professor Ruhela. S.P., (2000) *Indian society and education in 2010* (Futurist Perceptions of Indian Colleges Youth), Indian publishers distributors.
- Dr. R.L. Nikose, (2012), *Teacher Education-Issue and Challenges,* A.P.H. Publishing Corporation.
- *UGC Annual Report,* 2010-2011- DGET; *Ministry of Human Resource Development (HRD) Annual Report* 2011.
- B.N. Dash, (2004), *Education and society*, Dominant Publishers and Distributors, New Delhi.

Abbreviation

HRD - Human Resource Development

WTO - World Trade Organisation

GATT - General Agreement on Tariffs and Trade

MHRD - Ministry of Human Resource Development

UGC - University Grant Commission

AICTE - All India Council for Technical Education

MCI - Medical Council of India

NAAC - National Assessment and Accreditation Council

33 Impact of Reservation Policies on SC and ST Students: Enrollment in Higher Education

Sri. Nandeesh C.

Dr. Kotreshwaraswamy A. Surapuramath

Abstract

There can be no doubt that a substantial share of SC and ST student enrollments in Indian higher educational institutions is attributable to India's reservation policies. It is very difficult, however, to estimate just how much difference these policies have made. The difficulty of such estimation is due not only the scarcity of detailed data on the composition of higher Educational enrollments. Very few SC and ST students can succeed in open competition for general entry seats at prestigious institutions because they rarely have access to high-quality secondary education, or to privately-funded preparatory workshops and tutorials, all of which contribute to the substantial competitive edge enjoyed by students from relatively well-to-do families. In order to get a sense of the overall quantitative significance of India's reservation policies in higher education.

Introduction

The government is making a lot of efforts for the betterment of the weaker sections of the society. A number of schemes have been floated for the benefit of the SC/ST students with the ultimate aim of providing them better education and better career opportunities so that they may come up in life.

There can be no doubt that a substantial share of SC and ST student enrollments in Indian higher educational institutions is attributable to India's reservation policies. It is very difficult, however, to estimate just how much difference these policies have made. The difficulty of such estimation is due not only the scarcity of detailed data on the composition of higher educational enrollments. It is also due to the complexity of the way in which India's reservation policies in the educational sphere are structured and administered.

First of all, the policies apply only to public institutions. The majority of Indian higher educational institutions are indeed under central or state-level government control; but the number of private institutions has been growing rapidly since the early 1990s.

In virtually all centrally-controlled higher educational institutions,15 per cent of the seats are reserved for SC members and 7.5 per cent for ST members; these ratios were established to reflect the corresponding shares of *dalits* and advises in the national population. Although the reservation of seats at higher educational institutions for SC and ST students was established as a national policy in the early 1950s, its actual implementation was delayed by a decade or two in various regions and institutions, and even now it is not fully established everywhere in India. In the case of higher educational institutions controlled at the state level, the percentages of SC and ST reserved seats are determinedly the (approximate) proportions of these groups in the state population. Some states also have a percentage of seats reserved for other backward castes (OBCs).

General entry seats are filled first, with applicants from the top score downward in the relevant examination. Where OBC seats are reserved, these too are almost always filled with applicants from the top down to a somewhat lower cut-off point score. In the case of SC and ST reserved seats, minimum qualifying scores are set well below the cut-off point for general entry applicants, and some schools do not require any minimum exam score; age limits are also often waived for SC and ST students. Even so, SC and ST reserved seats often go unfilled–especially at the more selective schools– because there are not enough applicants from these groups who have completed secondary education and otherwise met the requirements for admission.

What can we conclude about the overall impact of reservation policies on the representation of SC and ST students in Indian higher educational institutions? First of all, we can be quite confident that virtually all SC and ST students' at the most elite Indian universities and institutions for professional and technical training (most of which are centrally-controlled) would not have been admitted in the absence of reserved seats. Very few SC and ST students can succeed in open competition for general entry seats at prestigious institutions because they rarely have access to high-quality secondary education, or to privately-funded preparatory workshops and tutorials, all of which contribute to the substantial competitive edge enjoyed by students from relatively well-to-do families. Even with lower cut-off points for admission, SC and ST students typically do not come close to filling the available reserved seats at such institutions.

It is much harder to estimate the number of SC and ST enrollments attributable to reservation policies in the vast majority of Indian higher educational institutions, where admissions requirements are much less demanding than at elite schools.

A considerable number of SC and ST applicants score high enough on the relevant examinations to qualify for general entry admission to some non-elite institution. In many cases, the effect of reservation policies is simply to redistribute beneficiary students upward in the hierarchy of institutional selectivity and quality.

Without reserved seats, however, the appeal of a higher educational institution for SC and ST potential students is likely to be substantially diminished. For one thing, the availability of reserved seats improves the quality of the school that an SC or ST student can enter–and hence the value of a higher educational degree in the job market. Second, admission to a reserved seat enhances the ability of an SC or ST student to gain access to financial and other forms of government aid, without which staying in school may prove very difficult. Government provision of scholarships, special hostels, meals, supplies and book loans have enabled many SC and ST students to enter and persist in higher education; even though such support is usually inadequate to meet all the economic and social needs of such students, it often makes the difference as to whether such a student decides to continue his/her education.

In order to get a sense of the overall quantitative significance of India's reservation policies in higher education, I will estimate how many SC and ST students have been enabled by reservation policies to enroll in 'desirable' higher educational programmes.

As a rough approximation, one may consider all programmes other than the low-prestige arts programmes to be relatively) desirable. According to Rao (2002: 47, Table 1), a total of roughly 5,10,000 SC students and 180,000 ST students were enrolled in Indian universities in 1996-97. In the previous section, I cited estimates that roughly 60 per cent of SC students and 75 per cent of ST students were enrolled in arts programmes. These figures imply that roughly 2,00,000 SC students and 45,000 ST students were enrolled in the remaining programmes–commerce, science, engineering, etc. A non-negligible fraction of these students would surely have qualified for admission to some–the relatively less demanding – of these programmes; so a very rough estimate of the total number of SC and ST students enabled by reservation policies to attend desirable programmes is 2,00,000.

In sum, it seems reasonable to conclude that about a third of the SC and ST students enrolled in Indian higher educational institutions in the late 1990s were pursuing higher education in a relatively desirable programme because of the existence of reservation policies in admissions.

Suggestions from Teachers

- To Improve Participation in Admission to Institutions the teachers contacted were requested to give their valuable suggestions to improve the participation level of SC, ST students in admission to institutions of higher learning.
- Various suggestions have come up. A consolidated list of such suggestions are indicated below.
- We should provide all facilities to SC/ST community to compete with other including relaxation in standards or eligibility criteria.
- Provide the opportunity of special guidance, coaching camps or consultancy camps. Before admission season starts.
- The weaker sections among the SC/ST should be given better attention and more facilities.
- Arrangement of special guidance/coaching to be provided free of cost.
- The students should be made strong in basics while at primary and secondary level of education.
- Scholarship/extra career coaching/financial supports are to be provided on a larger scale.
- Coaching for development of their skills, language, communication capability etc., are to be arranged in a broad-based manner. Capability building camps have to be organised periodically and the SC/ST student's capability should be improved through them.
- Reservation should be properly implemented.
- Reservation should be scrapped. Students should work hard and face competition.

To Improve the Participation in Job Opportunities

- The teachers contacted were also requested to give their valuable suggestions to improve the participation level of SC, ST students in job opportunities. Various suggestions have come up a consolidated list of such suggestions are indicated below:

- Students should be more focussed regarding the job opportunities, according to their education.
- Provide better facilities for their education at and outside the home/ State/Country so that they may be able to compete for better jobs.
- Awareness to among SC/ST category should be increased through different programmes by showing example of the man who has been benefitted by the reservation–success cases.
- Give free education at high secondary level and give training free at different technical training institution. Special training programme and aptitude development programme should be conducted for the SC/ST students by appropriate authorities. Better advertisement and publicity of information regarding job opportunities is to be done. Reservation should be properly implemented in letter and spirit.
- Reservation should be given only at first entry to the job and performance-based promotions are to be given and SC/ST students must be encouraged to perform well. All efforts should be made to make SC/ST students capable by giving all concessions and assistance before they enter the job market. Once they are made capable they should be asked to compete with others in the job market.
- There should not be again reservation in the job market.

On Solutions Apart from Reservation for Betterment of SC/ST Students

The teachers were further requested to give any other possible solutions apart from reservation quota that can be taken up for betterment of SC, ST category students in achieving responsible position in their career. Their responses from them are given below:

- Separate College/Hostels are to be established for the benefit of SC, ST Students in a wide spread manner.
- There should be a survey in different areas to find out the exact needs of persons and then action should be taken to fulfill those needs. (Some may need financial assistance, some may need extra coaching, some may need nutritious food etc.).
- Government should take care of the families of SC/ST community, so that their spouses and children should get proper food, refreshment, health-care, educational facilities etc. They should be

provided all the opportunities/facilities available to others. If they grow well like other children of upper classes they can compete with them. Equally.

Create better awareness of the various opportunities available special efforts are to be taken to improve their communication skill and skill for speaking and writing in English.

Recommendations

Based on the above mentioned findings in each section of the study, the suggestions either as offered by the respective respondents or that emerged from the findings are described below:

- For improving the level of competence of SC/ST students and bring them at par with general category it is suggested to hold special classes for training fundamentals on the subjects/courses, aptitude development programme and have regular contacts with faculty members after classes.
- In order to improve participation level of SC/ST students in admission to Institutions of Higher Learning emphasis should be laid on primary and secondary level education and basics should be strong.
- Among the SC/ST students who are actually socially and economically backward should be given adequate facilities (including scholarship and financial support) to compete with others.
- Special coaching for development of communications skills should be provided to SC/ST students.

Conclusion

Reservation policies at all levels of higher education both redistribute SC and ST students upward in the university quality hierarchy and attract into universities significant numbers of SC and ST students, who would not otherwise pursue higher education. My very rough estimate is that reservation policies enabled about half of the 7,00,000 SC and ST students attending Indian universities in the late 1990s either to gain access to a relatively desirable institution or programme, rather than settle for a relatively mediocre one, or to enroll in a university at all, rather than abandon any possibility of pursuing higher education. The vast majority of SC and ST beneficiaries of reservation policies enter university programmes with poorer preparation and lower academic qualifications than their peers and, not surprisingly, they tend not to perform as well in their studies. There is evidence, however, that the entry-test-score gap between SC and ST and other students has been narrowing over the past few decades.

References

- Aikara, J. (1980): 'Scheduled Castes and Higher Education: A Study of College Students in Mumbai', Dastane, Pune.
- Anderson, E. (2000): 'From Normative to Empirical Sociology in the Affirmative Action Debate: Bowen and Book's 'The Shape of the River',' *Journal of Legal Education*, 50, pp. 284-305.
- Chanana, K. (1993): 'Accessing Higher Education–The Dilemma of Schooling: Women, Minorities, Scheduled Castes and Scheduled Tribes in Contemporary India' in S. Chitnis and P. Altbach (eds.), *Higher Education Reform in India*, Sage Publications, New Delhi, India.
- Chitnis, S. (1981): A Long Way to Go: Report on a Survey of Scheduled Caste High School and College Students in Fifteen States of India, Allied, New Delhi.
- Galanter, M (1984): *Competing Equalities: Law and the Backward Classes in India*, Oxford University Press, Delhi.
- Henriques, J. and J.J. Wankhede (1985): *One Step Forward, Yet Two Steps Behind: A Study of Wastage and Stagnation in Education of SC-ST in Maharashtra*, Report submitted to Ministry of Education, Government of India, New Delhi.
- HRD (1997): *Selected Educational Statistics, 1996-97,* Ministry of Human Resources Development, Government of India, New Delhi.
- Karlekar, M. (1975): 'Higher Education and the Scheduled Castes', *Journal of Higher Education*, 1, pp. 178-87.
- Kirpal, V. (1978): 'Higher Education for the Scheduled Castes and Scheduled Tribes', *Economic and Political Weekly*, Vol. 13, pp. 165-69.
- Kirpal, V. and M. Gupta (1999): *Equality Through Reservations*, Rawat Publications, Jaipur.
- Kirpal, V.N. Swamidasan, A. Gupta and R.K. Gupta (1985a): 'Scheduled Caste and Tribe Students in Higher Education: A Study of an IIT', *Economic and Political Weekly*, 20: 1238-48.

34 Higher Education Challenges: A Language Debate

Archana M.

Abstract

Language is one of the most debated topics in Indian education. Being a democratic, multilingual country, India is constantly grappling with the issue of what languages should be the medium of instruction. Language has been and continues to be a barrier to access and success in Higher Education. Since the language for Higher Education in India is English, all students irrespective of their backgrounds have to study their subjects in English. The quality of education has comparatively gone down in many institutes of higher learning due to many such factors. The challenge facing higher education is to ensure the simultaneous development of a multilingual environment. Educational policy-makers have difficult decisions to make with regard to languages. The key objectives of this paper will be to establish links between excellence in quality of higher education and the language factor as a challenge to students, and also to develop suggestions for policy to promote bilingual and multilingual education as a way of improvements in educational attainments. This paper is based on an extensive review of secondary literature. It will be presented analysing the role of language in education, India as a multilingual country and the problems faced by students in the context of language, the interpretation of language policy confusions in India, the specific issues which are hindering quality higher education, the Government policies and programmes regarding the issue and finally a way forward. This paper concludes with a strong argument for selective bilingualism and multilingualism in education.

Introduction

Role of Language in Education

The method of human communication either spoken or written, consisting of the use of words in a structured and conventional way is

Language. Language is fundamental to learning. Language is a medium of communication and plays a central role in the migrant integration process and educational attainment. In other words, language of instruction in school is the medium of communication for the transmission of knowledge. Proficiency in the language of instruction is a vital condition for success at school. Language is a key to integration and inclusion. Language and, in particular choice of language of instruction in education is important, especially for basic education, because it is the basis for all further learning. The language of instruction in or out of school refers to the language used for teaching the basic curriculum of the educational system. The choice of the language or indeed the languages of instruction is a recurrent challenge in the development of quality education. While some countries opt for one language of instruction, often the official or majority language, others have chosen to use educational strategies that give national or local languages an important place in schooling. Speakers of mother tongues, which are not the same as the national or local language, are often at a considerable disadvantage in the educational system similar to the disadvantage in receiving instruction in a foreign official language.

Language is a private good, a public good and also a social good. Language has both *Intrinsic* as well as *Instrumental value*. It contributes to both individual development, human capabilities and also to a knowledge society. Then the other public good dimension is means of communication, education, social advancement and so forth. Therefore, same kind of decisions that we need to make about transport, public health, environment, are the same class of decisions which deal with the question of language. Even in those areas we are not clear about our policies of equity, inclusive development.

Indian Scenario

In a country like India, where the population is **1,220,200,000** (1.22 billion), 1,652 languages and dialects spoken as per 1961 census, has four major families of languages (Indo-European, Dravidian, Austro-Asiatic and Tibeto-Burman languages). The 1991 Census had 10,400 raw returns of mother tongues and they were rationalised into **1576** mother tongues. They are further rationalised into 216 mother tongues, and grouped under 114 languages, 29 languages have more than one million native speakers (0.1 per cent of total population) according to 2001 census. There are 216 languages with more than 10,000 native speakers. The largest of these is Hindi with some 337 million (the second largest being Bengali with some 207 million). Twenty-two languages are recognised as official languages.

Thirty languages are spoken by more than a million native speakers, 122 by more than 10,000. Further, in India, the scheduled languages are spoken by 10 to 80 millions of people. Each of the scheduled languages has about 10 to 97 recognisable dialects. The number of mother tongues in States varies between 58 (Orissa) and 454 (Maharashtra), and in Union Territories between 14 (Lakshadeep, Minicoy and Aminidivi islands) and 210 (Himachal Pradesh). Out of the 1,652 mother tongues approximately 400 are tribal mother tongues, most of which are unwritten. Therefore, in designing elementary education all these factors have to be taken into account; and the language or dialect of early childhood experience of the learners would have to be determined for the purpose of elementary education and teaching English at the primary level not only undermines the culture of all groups, but by weakening the mother tongue base, it builds disabilities in the system which undermines education itself.

With 5.04 lakhs of primary schools, having over 1213 lakhs of students and about 40 lakhs of teachers, it is inconceivable that English could be taught to all at any time and also India has to cope with 1652 mother tongues, between 200 and 700 languages belonging to four or five language families, written in 10 major script systems and a host of minor ones, presents the biggest challenge of language management. There are some states where the majority language is spoken by between 85 to 95 per cent of the population and on the other hand there are some states, where no language is spoken by more than 20 per cent of the population. Therefore, with such varied nature of the country it is a herculean task of framing a uniform language policy all over the states and one national language policy. India which has 19 official languages, 17 of them regionally and two nationally used in education, administration and mass communication, pursues a deliberate policy of multilingualism. Karnataka state offers primary education in eight languages. The country's educational programmes are so designed that by the end of the school stage all children are supposed to have learnt three languages. But the pattern of education is still diverse. Though there is a constitutional obligation to give primary education in the mother tongue of the child, only 58 mother tongues are used as the medium of instruction in schools at the present time. When we come to the context of higher education, India has one of the largest higher education systems in the world, with 25.9 million students enrolled in more than 45,000 degree and diploma institutions in the country. It has witnessed particularly high growth in the last decade, with enrollment of students increasing at a Compound Annual Growth Rate (CAGR) of 10.8 per cent and institutions at a CAGR of nine per cent. We should analyse the problem of language in the growing higher education sector, which can cause a lot of damage and at the cost of quality.

Review of Literature

Jayaram N. (1993), "The language question in higher education: trends and issues"—This paper argues, nowhere is the language scenario and the problems associated with it as complex and controversial as in a multicultural and linguistically diverse country like India. Since language is the medium through which educational transactions take place, the vicissitudes of language and the language controversies have had a significant bearing on the structure, process, and outcome of her educational endeavour. This article examines the various issues and trends in the language conundrum vis-à-vis education in general and higher education in particular. Broadly, it is divided into four parts. The first part provides a brief sketch of the background and context in which the linguistic imbroglio in higher education becomes meaningful. The next two parts deal respectively with the twin aspects of the language problem in relation to education, namely, language instruction and language as a medium of instruction. The concluding part recapitulates the scenario and delineates the dilemmas of policy perspective.

Evan, Stephen (2002) "Macaulay's Minute Revisited: Colonial Language Policy in nineteenth-century India"—This paper examines a crucial episode in the history of language policy in British colonial education: the controversy of the 1830s over the content and medium of government education in India. The bitter dispute over colonial language-in-education policy during this period raised fundamental questions about the roles and status of the English language and the Indian vernacular and classical languages in the diffusion of Western knowledge and ideas on the sub-continent. This paper reassesses Macaulay's influence on British language policy in 19th century India. The second part examines the short-term and long-term consequences of Macaulay's scheme in India and in other British colonial contexts.

Barla, Venkateswarlu December (2012) "Issues in the Development of English Language for the Engineering Students—A Classroom Experiment"—This study involved an experiment for development of English language for the first year Engineering students at Visakhapatanam, India on a sample of 108 students out of 120 students.

Jain, Tarun (2012) "Common tongue: The impact of language on economic performance"—Language is an important social institution that has potentially large impact on economic performance. Reorganisation of Indian states on linguistic lines is a natural experiment to estimate the impact of speaking the majority language on educational and occupational outcomes. Evidence present that these benefits accrue through the channel of lower transaction costs, as evidenced by higher educational achievement and employment in communication intensive sectors. After reorganisation, historically minority language districts experience greater growth in educational achievement compared to previously majority language districts, indicating that reassignment could reverse the impact of history.

Language as an Input to Development

Any development that takes place in any nation is executed with language. It is the tool of communication and business. Having acquired a language, the individual enters the university and other institutions to read all kinds of academic disciplines and begin to contribute their quota to national development. Economic development is based on specialisation and trade. Individuals who specialise and trade must develop common means of communication. This in turn leads to the use of a common language. Thus as countries move on the ladder of economic development and increase the network of trade both within and outside the country, a common language will impose itself and will be used by an increasing number of individuals. This then puts pressure on the local languages, and in the long run will push many of these into extinction. Thus in the long run economic development will lead to a decline in the number of languages and in language diversity. As one language increases in size, its communication value increases. As a result, the incentives to switch to its use by those who do not speak that language, increases. The results confirm the existence of a causal link from common language to trade, i.e., countries that speak the same language tend to trade more with each other than countries without a common language. To the extent that international trade promotes economic growth and development one can conclude that a common language also leads to more growth and development

Language Policy in India

The Language Policy of India relating to the use of languages in administration, education, judiciary, legislature, mass communication, etc., is pluralistic in its scope. It is both language-development oriented and language-survival oriented. The policy is intended to encourage the citizens to use their mother tongue in certain delineated levels and domains through some gradual processes, but the stated goal of the policy is to help all languages to develop into fit vehicles of communication at their designated areas of use, irrespective of their nature or status like major, minor, or tribal languages. The policy is accommodative and ever-evolving, through mutual adjustment, consensus, and judicial processes. Evolving and monitoring implementation of language policy is a major endeavour of the Language Bureau of the

Ministry of Human Resource Development, Government of India. This is done by the Bureau through language institutions set-up for the purpose under its aegis: Central Hindi Directorate, Centre for Scientific and Technical Terminology, Central Hindi Institute, Central Institute of Indian Languages, National Council for Promotion of Sindhi Language, National Council for Promotion of Urdu Language, *Rashtriya Sanskrit Sansthan* (RSKS), *Maharishi Sandipani Rashtriya Vedavidya Pratishthan* (MSRVVP), Central Institute of English and Foreign Languages. Another recent initiative of the government in addressing the language factor is Technology Development for Indian Languages (TDIL) Programme initiated by the Department of Electronics and Information Technology (DEIT), Ministry of Communication and Information Technology (MC&IT), Government of India has the objective of developing Information Processing Tools and Techniques to facilitate human-machine interaction without language barrier; creating and accessing multilingual knowledge resources; and integrating them to develop innovative user products and services.

India adopted the three language formulae for education in schools. Language is not just an issue in India, it is a matter of emotional concern to the people of India. When there is a preference given to one language, the other language people take it personal and start to fight for their own rights and preference. Agitations start to build up. This created a wide incompatibility between languages used for state administration and education in India. This led to a linguistic movement against retaining Sanskrit as the first language in school education. This made the government rethink about the language policy for school. The context for the debate on language instruction at the school is provided by the "Three Language Formulae" which was first suggested by Central Advisory Board of Education in 1957, endorsed by the National Integration Council in 1968.

Despite many efforts done by the government to address the issue, even to this day, language agitations in favour of regional language as the sole medium of instruction or in favour of retaining English as an important alternative medium still continues.

Role of English in Higher Education

The system of education that the British introduced was modelled after the system prevalent in their mother country. This was particularly so as regards higher education. The striking feature of this educational transplantation was English, which was not only taught as a language but also became the medium of instruction. In India, English is more often the second language in many states and the honour of first language is occupied by the regional languages. Even though the status of English in India as a second or foreign language is debatable, nevertheless, it enjoys the privilege of being an associate official language along with Hindi in Devanagiri script. In India, the introduction of English at school varies from state to state. English is only a subject in many of the government aided schools and not the medium of instruction. When these students pass out from schools and enroll in colleges and universities, they find it difficult to compete with the students who have come from English medium schools. Since the language for Higher Education (in Universities, and in some colleges) in India is English, all students irrespective of their backgrounds have to study their subjects in English. Thus some students are privileged, whereas others have to suffer due to their schooling in regional language as the medium of instruction. Therefore, the students with good command over English get an edge over the ordinary students because they have an access to more information and knowledge. The government, whether state or central, spends a lot of money in the name of Higher Education. But the quality of education has comparatively gone down in many institutes of higher learning due to many such factors. The output of the colleges or universities in the matter of quality of students is very poor. Therefore, the importance of English in the present scenario cannot be denied.

The shift towards using English as the language of instruction has been seen as a natural and positive development for many reasons, for example; in a number of disciplines, the publication of academic papers takes place almost exclusively in English. Teaching in English is therefore seen as necessary in order to prepare students for an academic career. In many disciplines the majority of textbooks used are written in English and therefore the step to teaching in English may not be seen as a large one. The use of English develops the language skills and confidence of Indian lecturers and can be seen as promoting movement/exchange of ideas in the academic world. Using English as the language of instruction allows the use of visiting researchers in undergraduate and post-graduate teaching. Teaching in English allows exchange students to follow courses at Indian universities. Indian students can be prepared for their own studies abroad. A sound knowledge of English has become a strong asset in the job market

Problems of Language in Current Context

When there are arguments for the Mother Tongue education for children in schools, globalisation and information technology have created a greater demand for English education, and education through English. The state governments are vying with each other, taking steps to cope up with the demands for English education. Gradually, the number of students opting for regional language medium is fast decreasing. The social and educational system, as already illustrated through various statistics, has covertly designated English medium for the elite and the regional language medium for others. The changing equations in the society are clear for everyone to see. English education bestows an advantage on those who adopt it. Naturally, the poor people also desire to somehow improve their lot by opting for the English medium education for their children. When the elite social groups do not care for their language and culture, why should others bother about the mother tongue, and education through that language? The fear is that if the present trend continues, the market forces will convert the regional and other Indian languages only as subjects of study and eliminate them as medium of instruction. This is an unfortunate and retrograde step for any society. But a multilingual state like Karnataka, populates with other mother tongues and borders many other languages. While the majority of children in each speak the medium of instruction, all have at least some second-language learners. So should the government allow other languages as the medium of instruction in schools? Which language children are supposed to learn in or which language has to be taught as a medium of instruction in schools? It is a chaotic situation of language policy and therefore the development of the state through education and a confused language policy needs an immediate attention.

A significant problem in using the regional languages as media of instruction is the acute paucity of better quality reading material. And often this along with the inadequate development of the regional languages and their lack of an adequate technical terminology are advanced as arguments against their use as media of instruction. The inability of the students to use language effectively as a means of communication is a major problem and prime failing of university education. The poor linguistic skills of the college students seem to be having a bearing on the method of instruction as well as the nature of material used by them. Teaching at the undergraduate level and in some universities even at the post-graduate level is almost entirely identified with the delivery of lecturers and the dictation of "notes". By and large, notes and "guides" (written in question-paper format in simple and often in bad English) have almost eclipsed students in the subject, have boiled down to summarising the prescribed textbooks or just the clarification of the notes which are dictated. Naturally, all these reflected in the examination system not only in the kind of questions that are set but also in the evaluation.

Language Policy Confusions

After independence the government of India appointed the University

Education Commission (1948-49) under the Chairmanship of Dr. S. Radhakrishnan. The Commission observed that "no other problem has caused greater controversy among educationists and evoked more contradictory views from our witnesses than the language problem", and recommended that "higher education be imparted through the instrumentality of the regional language with the option to use the federal language as the medium of instruction either for some subjects or for all subjects" (Ministry of Education 1962, pp. 304-26). The National Integration Council as well as the Emotional Integration Committee endorsed this recommended in 1962.

Perhaps the most important landmark in the matter of the medium of instruction at the higher levels of education in the post-independence period is the policy-making process set in motion after the 1967 general elections. The framework for the policy statements in this phase was provided by the recommendations of the Report of the Education Commission (1964-66). This report emphasised the need "to move energetically in the direction of adopting the regional languages as media of education at the university stage" (Ministry of Education 1971, p. 527).

The then Union Minister of Education, Dr. Triguna Sen, announced in July 1967, the Government of India's resolve to accept in principle that the regional languages would become the media of instruction "at all stages and in all subjects, including agriculture, engineering, law, medicine and technology." Later, addressing the Vice Chancellors' conference in September 1967, he advocated a general flexibility in approach to the changeover of the medium of instruction. There has however hardly been any systematic review of the extent and nature of this changeover and the implementation of the Education Commission (1964-66) in this regard.

In India language policy has followed a pattern of evolution toward languages lower in the prestige hierarchy which gain more valued roles in the educational system by weakening the exclusive role of the prestige language while the non-prestige languages have begun to gain status as a medium of instruction first at the elementary and secondary levels, then in early childhood education and finally in higher education.

The question as to which language should be used as a medium of instruction in schools in multilingual societies is a controversial one. Should the medium of instruction be a familiar local language or wider communication like English? Using mother tongue of a child as the medium of instruction has been a debate when English language is spreading everywhere. In multilingual societies, where the medium of instruction chosen is that of the majority, the needs of other language speakers are also an issue. Countries have to consider at what point or whether to introduce other national, regional and international languages into their educational systems. Their decisions will determine who has access to education, the quality of that education and whether minorities are treated equitably. Language choice is important, especially for basic education, because it is the basis for all further learning. Indian linguistic situation is altogether different from rest of the world. India is a multilingual and multicultural country. Education to the children in different Indian socio-economic condition is varied based on rich, poor, tribal non-tribal, urban rural and such dichotomy. Indian educational system is always grappled with using English from Class I which is most unfortunate. Research says that, a child strong in mother tongue can be stronger in other tongues.

The poor quality of school and the knowledge that is imparted to the children in an alien language, imagine the child's learning. For any meaningful education, mother tongue or first language of the child is pre-requisite, rather non-negotiable but on the other hand, English education-rewards are linked to opportunities in the global marketplace for higher education and jobs, including the export-oriented service industries in India. English is necessary for a wider world, but not at the cost of mother tongue or the state language and not at the cost of children's linguistic human rights.

The Persistence of the Problem in Higher Education

The question that the present language policy poses is whether Indian students involved in higher education receive sufficient linguistic support in Hindi, English, or their mother tongue. This question is a complex one and has to be addressed by not only examining the present language situation in higher education in India but also against the backdrop of the dilemma that faces India like other former British colonies, which is whether to promote its national language (Hindi) for ideological purposes, or English in keeping with the demands of the emerging global market where English is seen as a tool of progress and success. The significance of the learner's mother tongue in imparting education especially in the initial years of schooling is also an important factor that cannot be put aside. The choice of a language to be the medium of instruction or a language to be studied is a complex matter. It involves various factors including the aims of the language planners, language needs of learners, parental and teachers' attitudes. In addition, there are practical factors involved, like available economic resources to implement the policy in terms of training of teachers, as well as development of materials in the language so selected. One major problem is the lack of research in the areas of language planning in education in India.

English is a compulsory subject, failure in English means failure in the entire university examination. This attributes the failure in English examinations mainly to flawed pedagogy and material design and concludes that perhaps the teaching of English is not necessary for all levels of the population. The weak proficiency of emerging graduates has led to a lowering of standards of performance at the graduate and postgraduate and equivalent levels where English is the official medium of instruction and assessment. "High rate of failure affects students in two ways: it destroys their opportunities for white collared jobs in the country and also destroys their morale".

The full implications of this spread of English in the field of education is best understood in terms of second or foreign language instruction. Research into English in primary and secondary education and the use of English as a medium of instruction as well as the teaching of English as an additional language shows that there is little doubt that at present there is a great demand for English language instruction, and this demand will continue to grow in the future. The highest number of courses offered in second or foreign languages around the world are in English. In many parts of the world, English is regarded as the language of power, success, and prestige. In many countries English has become implicated in social and economic mechanisms that structure inequality, linking poverty not only with region, class, gender and ethnicity but also with access to the lingua-franca of the global elite. Parents and children in these countries often see English medium education as a means to economic success. It is also argued that where teachers themselves are not fully proficient in the English language and are not aware of the full implications of teaching English as a second language, there is a danger of students being condemned to a second rate education. An important educational trend world-wide is the teaching of a growing number of courses in universities through the medium of English

Conclusion

- One way to overcome this situation and comparatively the best way is to adapt to multilingual education and also to reinvent learning English following the same method or process of acquiring the mother tongue.
- The foregoing analysis seems to suggest that there has been a shift from monolingual medium of instruction towards bilingual and even multilingual media of instruction and this shift is away from English medium and towards Hindi and other regional media of instruction. However, a closer examination about the medium of instruction in different courses and levels (under-graduate and post-graduate) of

university education reveals that the shift is more apparent than real.

- English as the exclusive medium of instruction in almost all the courses is prevalent more at the post-graduate than at the under-graduate level. English is still the predominant medium of instruction in all courses of higher education. It is invariably offered as a medium of instruction, either exclusively or as one of the alternative media.
- Thus a complete switchover to the regional languages as media of instruction at all levels and in all courses is not a possibility in the foreseeable future. Therefore, what appears to be the only feasible course at this juncture is **"selective bilingualism"** the introduction of the regional languages as alternative media of instruction along with English in selected courses and levels of education.
- There should also be a good number of initiatives by the government of the Central and State in this matter to give it a more weightage. And there should be a proper blend of education and language policies which can support the bilingualism and multilingualism point of view.

References

- Jayaram N. (1993), "The language question in higher education: trends and issues." Journal of Higher Education – Vol. 26, No. 1, pp. 93-114.
- Evan, Stephen (2002), "Macaulay's Minute Revisited: Colonial Language Policy in Nineteenth-century India" Journal of Multilingual and Multicultural Development Vol. 23, No. 4.
- Grin, Francois- (2003), "Language Planning and Economics" Journal- Current Issues in Language Planning Vol. 4, No. 1.
- Vinoba Gautam (2003), "Education of tribal children in India and the issue of Medium of Instruction: A Janshala experience."
- UNESCO position paper (2003), "Education in a Multilingual World", Communication and Information-Resources-Publication and Communication Material- Publications.
- Spolsky, Bernard (2007), "Towards a Theory of Language Policy."
- Biswas, Debajyoti, November (2009), "Role of English in Higher Education" Academy Vol. XIII, No. 1.
- Desai, Zubeida Khatoom March (2012)—"A Case for Mother Tongue Education?".
- Marginson, Simon July (2012), "The Problem of Public Good(s) in Higher Education".

- Barla, Venkateswarlu December (2012), "Issues in the Development of English Language for the Engineering Students—A Classroom Experiment".
- Jain, Tarun (2012), "Common tongue: The Impact of Language on Economic Performance".
- Chakrabarti, Raj and Sengupta, Shil, June (2012), "Globalisation of Indian Higher Education: Public and Private Innovations" Journal of the World Universities Forum, Vol. 2, Issue 6, pp. 23-32.
- Meyer, Stephan and Gekeler, Petra, June (2013), "Plurilingualism, Multilingualism and Internationalisation in the European Higher Education Area: Challenges and Perspectives at a Swiss University" Journal—Language Learning in Higher Education, Vol. 2, Issue 2, pp. 405-425.

35 Higher Education in New Era Issues and Challenges in India

Ravi, P.

Dr. R. Gopalaraju

Introduction

Education in India has always been valued more than mere considering it as a means towards earning a good living. Right from pre-historic days, education, especially higher education has been given a predominant position in the Indian society.

Higher education is of vital important for the country, as it is a powerful tool to build knowledge-based society of the 21st century. Improvement of access and quality, the adoption of state-specific strategies, enhancing the relevance of higher education through curriculum reform, vocationalisation, Networking and Information Technology and distance education are the main policy initiatives of the higher education sector. The other important policy initiatives in higher education are the main policy initiatives of the higher education sector. The other important policy initiatives in higher education are programmes for general development of universities and colleges.

Goals of Higher Education

It is necessary to recognised that the present approach towards higher education is governed by the "National Policy on Education" of 1986 and Programme of Action of 1992. The 1986 policy and Action Plan of 1992 was based on the two landmarks report namely, the "University Education Commission" of 1948-49 (popularly known as Radhakrishna Commission), and the "Education Commission" of 1964-66, (popularly known as Kothari Commission Report).

The period ranges from 1857 to 1917, accepting the recommendations of Woods Dispatch of 1855, the Universities of Calcutta, Bombay and Madras were established in 1857 on the model of London University. In 1882 to

1887 Punjab and Allahabad University were also established under the leadership of Lord Curzon who was the Viceroy of India. The progress of higher education developed rapidly. However, British to create a socio-cultural base for recruitment and training of administrative functionaries enabled Indians to become civilising mission of British rule.

After independence early in 1950s higher education has been diversified and extended its reach and coverage quite significantly. The number of universities has increased from 20 in 1947, to about 357 in 2005, there are now 20 Central universities, 217 State universities, 106 Deemed to be universities, and 13 institute of national importance established through central legislation and 05 institutions established through state legislation. We have higher education institution under the category of institution of national importance like IITs, IIMs, AIIMs and the Central universities. All funded cent per cent by the Central government, however, some marginal financial supports are provided by the Central government as plant grants through various schemes of the UGC. The numbers of the universities up to the year 2010 has been reported to be 518 by the UGC. 12.3 millions Students enrollment under these institutions. The number of universities in year 2000 to 266 and there is almost 100 per cent growth in less than Eight years.

Growth of Higher Education Institutions and Enrollment in India

Year	*Universities*	*Colleges*	*Total*	*Enrollment (Lakhs)*
1947-48	20	496	516	2
1950-51	28	578	606	2
1960-61	45	1819	1864	6
1970-71	93	3277	3370	20
1980-81	123	4738	4861	28
1990-91	184	5748	5932	44
2000-01	266	11146	11412	88
2005-06	348	17625	17973	105

(*Source:* www.ugc.an.com).

Includes Central, State, Private and Deemed-to-be Universities as also institutions of national importance established both by the Central and the State legislatures.

Today Higher Education system is geared up for the mass catering to meet the demands of a vibrant democracy committed to the principles of equity. India today's takes the pride for its best of the institutions and products. Yet, it is not happy with its institutions that are not of that quality and hence the produces are of the same quality.

The World Bank report of 1994 highlights the worth of higher education wherein it is considered that institutes of higher learning benefit state and society in several ways; they equip individuals with advanced knowledge and skills to discharge responsibility in government, business and professions; produce new knowledge through research and at least serve as conduct for the transfer, adaptation and dissemination of knowledge generated elsewhere in the world.

The task force constituted by World Bank and UNESCO during 2000 has also observed that higher education helps increase wages and productivity that directly enrich individuals and society. As against these world opinions in its paper on government subsidies (1997) that higher education as 'non-merit' good-based on the reasoning that it benefitted individuals more than the society. The Birla Ambani reports on the policy framework for Educational Reform too suggested that the government subsidies on higher education should be minimum it should concentrate on Primary Education sector as per constitutional guarantees and perhaps focus Secondary Education area too. They felt private universities by legislation is perhaps the answer to the malady.

The Present Scenario

The University sector in India has grown significantly over the year after independence as of 2009, India had 20 Central university's 215, State universities, 100 deemed universities, five institution established and functioning under the state act, and 33 institutes which are national importance other institution include 16000 colleges, including 1800 exclusive Women's Colleges functioning under this universities and institutions the emphasis in the tertiary level of education lies on Science and Technology, Indian Educational Institution by 2004, consisted of a large number of technology institutes.

At present the number of university had gone upto 513 universities (44 central, 299 state, 140 private, 130 deemed to be universities) and 33023 colleges in the higher education sector, which are affiliated to different state (provisional) authorities, beside enhancing number of autonomous higher education institution such as Indian institution and Indian institutes of technology and Indian institute of Management that are labelled as institutes of national importance.

Differences between the Central and State Universities Perspectives

Over these years the Central universities in India relative to State universities, have been better endowed financially, have enjoyed better governance and have taken the lead in research and development activities. But as State universities was fly outnumber their central counterparts issues of poor governance and narrow outlook that arises out of provinciality remains key issues for the university sector in India. The prospective needs to be modernised and should match international standards which will help the higher education aspirants to stand at par with world class counterparts, a unified reformation needs to be done and a unified prospective needs to be designed so that both the Central and State universities enjoy better governance and contribute to research and development activates.

Issues Pertaining to Autonomy

Autonomy is also a major issue which impacts the smooth functioning of the higher education system. Governance of state universities is carried out through a separation of duties between State and Central government while U.G.C which is a central body is responsible for grants-in-aid from public funds to central and state universities (including deemed universities) and also for maintenance of standards, the state are in-charge of operations of the state universities including appointment of administrative and academic staff setting up of curriculum, direction of R and D activities and interaction with industry. It is imperative to solve the issues pertaining autonomy to ensure that the benefits of higher education to all.

Financial changes pose a major threat in the growth and promotion of higher education. Despite an impressive economic growth that India has register in the last two decades, it still remains largely an agrarian economy with 50 per cent of the work-force employed in the agricultural sector adult literacy rate is only at 65 per cent (2011 censes puts it at an increased 74 per cent) and gross enrollment ratio in higher education stand at 13 per cent (economy that is comparable to India in terms of population).

Status of Higher Education in 21st Century

Status of higher education in India is the 3rd largest in world, but has many issues like:

- Access to the higher education system is currently restricted to a small portion of the society.

- Low enrollment in vocational education.
- Low public expenditure on higher education as a percentage of GDP comparable to other countries.
- Large rural-urban divide in access, gender inequity and large differences in GER various communities.
- Shortage of faculty and poor infrastructure.

India GER is higher education is about 12.6 per cent other countries such as the USA 82 per cent, 23 per cent, China 75 per cent in Brazil have much enrollment rate in expenditure on higher education for also not satisfactory, where as 3.1 per cent, USA, 1.3 per cent, 1.5 per cent China and one per cent in India of GDP on higher education. Vocational training is viewed as an important source of imparting skills, but existing training capacity is insufficient in India. The existing training capacity in India is just 3.1 million, but 12.8 million new entrants into the work-force one every year, only eight per cent of the young Indian labour force receive vocational training, whereas industrialised country 60 to 80 per cent. Urban population is around 20 per cent in the GER, but for rural area it is only six per cent, the given below chart indicates the wide gap between the GER higher education in rural and urban areas. Also GER for SC/ST/OBC varies between 6-8 per cent. It shows that rural sector and some backward communities requires a lot of improvement to increase the overall GER in higher education in India.

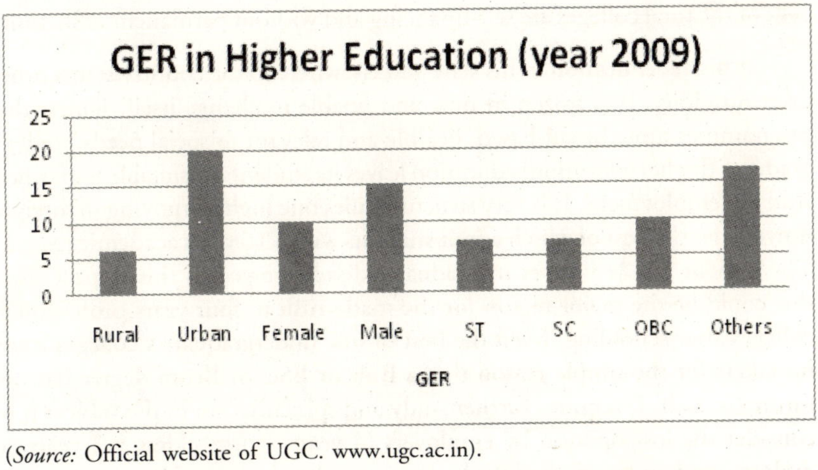

(*Source:* Official website of UGC. www.ugc.ac.in).

Higher Education in India is evident that there is a very serious effort required in terms of creating new channels of education, developing. A standard delivery system of education, generating funds to support the universalisation of primary education and other level, increasing the vocational training at all levels to create able man power in the society.

University Grants Commission had put together a report to a higher education in the country. Higher education in India issues and challenges and expectations as also basically stands on:

- Lower access to higher education.
- Inter-state and inter-district disparities and rural-urban differences in the access to higher education.
- Issues of quality in higher education, relevant education.
- Academic reforms and reform of governance in higher education.
- Issues related to education and collaboration towards the regulation of private sector in higher education.

The above mention issues shift can occur only through a systematic approach to change as also the development of its human resources and networking the system through information and communication technology. Relates to the quality of higher education recognise that a substantial portion of colleges and universities are not assessed for quality and therefore we don't have total picture of the quality and excellence of university and college sector engaged in higher education. The 40 per cent and 38 per cent have been brought which satisfies some minimum educational standards. Only 20 per cent of the total colleges are self-financing and without permanent affiliation.

A higher education in his state and elsewhere in the country status from extermirigidity. It is frozen in time and unable to change itself. Unless the programmes more broad-based, flexible and relevant to social needs, under-graduate (higher education) education leaves its students unsuitable for farther study or employment. It is very structure rules one higher studying in foreign universities the best of which admit students with a 16 years academic record. The present 10+2+3 leaves its graduates disadvantaged in this respect also, this could be the major region for the made-rush to four years professional colleges after schooling. Even the best of one undergraduate's colleges have no takers for the simple reason that a B.A. or BSc. or Bcom degree has no future by itself. It requires further study and specialisation in the subject it is consider the lost opinion by employers (4 years course--eldest 2-3 years, a diploma student has studied the basic science, humanity and long nags could lead to jobs that require just these qualification).

What is wrong with a programme that offers so much flexibility and freedom? Without going into the details of study patterns, under-graduates' educations soundly impart knowledge as it should make the acquisition of that knowledge interesting and challenging. Why do we think that education should always be a serious, pompous activity, devoid of the fun and joy of learning? Why can't are the students enjoy what their study take pleasure while acquiring information and turnout better candidates for further education or employment? When India's favourite writer R.K. Narayan, was given the responsibility of teaching English literature in an American-I view league college he deserted classroom with its stuffy atmosphere, and instead, read out interesting stories to his pupil, instead of taking the tress in the campus, he felt that enthusing students to read and enjoy a good book was also education. It was the better way to insist a love of literature, the same principle holds good for any subject of study. It is time that ours "educationist" understood this plain truth. At a same time, there is an urgent need to improve physical and academic infrastructure if these institution thus call for a "revival of college and state university sector".

Lastly we re-call the statement of **Rabindra Nath Tagore** that is ***"the highest education is that which does not merely give us information but makes our life in harmony with all existence".***

Conclusion

Observations made about are not something new being discussed in this country. A lot of commissions and committees appointed by the government for suggesting reforms have also pinned upon same obstacles in the Indian higher education. They have also advocated for a system which rises above the wastages of British legacy, a system which take into account an ever-growing innovation demand in the country being asked for but there has been sheer dearth of courage and a political will, the way attempts have been made to reform secondary level education in schools, higher education needs to be referred too its high-time that universities cater to the growing demand of students or else this human resource boon will soon prove to be population ban for the economy.

References

- Alstele. J.W. (1995), Bench Marking in Higher Education Adopting but Practices to Improve Quality. Ashe-Eriche: Report. No. 5. The George Washington University, Washington.
- Balasuramanyam. S., Jayanti. S. Ravi and Others: Improving The Quality of Higher Education Model. Vikalpa, 37(3).

- India department of higher education ministry of HRD Govt of India Web site http//murd.gov.in.overviewh, viewed on. 15 October, 2012.
- Inclusive Education: The Way of the Future: Indian Education System.
- Pavan Agarval, Higher Education in India, the Need for a Change, ICRIER, Working Paper No. 179, May-2006.
- Power, K.B. (2005), Quality in Higher Education Edupro Publishers, New Delhi. (Report of the Indian Universities Commission, 1902), Report p. 1.
- Rona Tas, A., 1992, A New Approach to Quality Assurance in Higher Education, pp. 94-100, 2001. Inqaahe, Banglour.
- Sudha Rao, K. Dr. Mithilesh K.R. Singh:150 Years of University Education in India: Challenges Ahead.
- UGC, www.ugc.ac.in.
- Vinudhar Bhatt: Higher Education in India-Issues, Challenges and Expectations.

36 An Overview of the Potentials of *Rashtriya Uchchatara Shiksha Abhiyan* in Enhancing Higher Education of Marginalised Groups in India

Dr. H.R. Uma
Madhu, G.R.
Pushpa Nanaiah K.

Introduction

Education plays a vital role in the development of an individual, society, nation and country, as it is a powerful tool to build knowledge-based society of the 21st century. The Indian higher education system is one of the largest such systems in the World. India possesses a highly developed higher education system which offers facility of education and training in almost all aspects of human creative and intellectual endeavours. The spread of education is very wide in recent years. The awareness level among people has increased. The expansion in institutional capacity in terms of number of universities/colleges and teachers has provided greater access to the students to post higher secondary education. The sphere of higher education has still not seen any concerted efforts for improvement in access or quality. An educated and productive workforce is what needed to achieve through a concerted effort to improve quality and relevance of higher education. Greater emphasis has to be laid on the improvement of the quality of teaching-learning processes in order to produce employable and competitive graduates, post-graduates and PhDs. In recent, 12th five year plan, government of India put more emphasis on higher education and set target of 30 per cent in 2020. Keeping in view the recommendations of the Planning Commission, the need for reforms in state higher education sector, using central funds in a strategic manner to ensure holistic planning at the state level and enhancement of allocations for the state institutions, a new centrally sponsored scheme is proposed. The scheme would be spread over the two plan periods (XII and XIII), and would be an over-reaching scheme for funding the state universities and colleges to achieve the aims of equity, access and excellence. This scheme is called *Rashtriya Uchchatar Shiksha Abhiyan* (RUSA).

Definitions

Educationists should build the capacities of the spirit of inquiry, creativity, entrepreneurial and moral leadership among students and become their role model, says Dr. A.P.J. Abdul Kalam.

Higher Education

Higher education refers the study beyond the level of secondary education. Institutions of higher education include not only colleges and universities but also professional schools in such fields as law, theology, medicine, business, music, and art. They also include teacher-training schools, community colleges, and institutes of technology. At the end of a prescribed course of study, a degree, diploma, or certificate is awarded.

Marginalised Group

The process whereby something or someone is pushed to the edge of a group and accorded lesser importance. This is predominantly a social phenomenon by which a minority or sub-group is excluded, and their needs or desires ignored.

Education is the most powerful instrument for empowering the socially disadvantaged groups. If look back in to the history of India, education was never in reach of its entire people. Unequal access to education has been rampant in India. Discriminatory order in the caste system has been instrumental in perpetuating this. Over the generations one section of the society were enjoyed the fruits of the education and remaining majority of Indian communities particularly marginalised sections like Scheduled Castes (SC), Scheduled Tribes (ST), Other Backward Classes (OBC), Religious Minorities and Women were denied the opportunity.

Objectives of the Paper

(1) To study the aims and objectives of the *Rashtriya Uchchatara Shiksha Abhiyan.*

(2) To analyse the need of *Rashtriya Uchchatara Shiksha Abhiyan* in reducing inequalities in higher education among marginalised groups in India.

Methodology

This paper is based on secondary data. Secondary data collected from journals, government of India reports and programme document of *Rashtriya Uchchatara Shiksha Abhiyan.* Excel is used for tabulation and construction of chart.

Objectives of *Rashtriya Uchchatara Shiksha Abhiyan*

The objectives of RUSA would be to achieve the target of GER of 30 per cent, which the Central government has set for itself, by the year 2020. Government of India aims to improve the quality of state universities and colleges and enhance existing capacities of the institutions to become dynamic, demand-driven, quality conscious, efficient and forward looking, responsive to rapid economic and technological developments occurring at the local, state, national and international levels.

The salient objectives of the scheme can be enumerated as follows:

- Improve the overall quality of existing state institutions by ensuring that all Institutions conform to prescribed norms and standards and adopt accreditation as a mandatory quality assurance framework.
- Usher transformative reforms in the state higher education system by creating a facilitating institutional structure for planning and monitoring at state level, promoting autonomy in state universities and improving governance in institutions.
- Ensure academic and examination reforms in the higher educational institutions.
- Enable conversion of some of the universities into institutions of excellence at par with the best in the world.
- Create opportunities for states to undertake reforms in the affiliating system in order to ensure that the reforms and resource requirements of affiliated colleges are adequately met.
- Ensure adequate availability of quality faculty in all higher educational institutions and ensure capacity building at all levels of employment.
- Create an enabling atmosphere in the higher educational institutions to devote themselves to research and innovations.
- Expand the institutional base by creating additional capacity in existing institutions and establishing new institutions, to achieve enrollment targets.
- Correct regional imbalances in access to higher education by facilitating access to high quality institutions in urban and semi-urban areas, creating opportunities for students from rural areas to

get access to better quality institutions and setting up institutions in unserved and underserved areas.

- Improve equity in higher education by providing adequate opportunities of higher education to socially deprived communities; promote inclusion of women, minorities, SC/STs and differently abled persons.

Strategic Framework for Enhancing Higher Education

Excellence: Institutional differentiation by creation of multi-disciplinary research universities, teaching institutions, vocational education institutes, etc.

Equity: Revamping and integration of schemes targeted at underserved areas, and vulnerable and deprived communities.

Expansion: Scaling up of capacity in existing institutes rather than adding new institutes.

Governance

- Enhancement of institutional autonomy and transparency
- Co-ordination of regulatory Reforms

Financing

- Increased public and private funding
- Linking of funding with outcomes

Implementation and Monitoring

- Enhanced co-ordination across ministries and agencies
- Greater flexibility provided for implementing agencies

Above chart 1 shows the colleges of the particular year from 1950-to 2011, the chart clearly shows that tremendous increase in establishment of universities from decade to decade. In 1950, India had only 30 universities, it increased to 133 in 1980s and in another two decades 126 universities were established in India. It is little lower compare to previous two decades, but in the year 2001 to 2011 establishment of universities increased three-fold, below chart-2 refers to the total universities in the India. During the period of independence, the number of college were very low but after 1970-71, the number of colleges increased at very high rate. In 1980's total number of colleges increased to 4722 from 3604 in 1970. In 1990s the total number of college increased to 7346 and during 2001 to 2011 there is four-fold

Chart 1

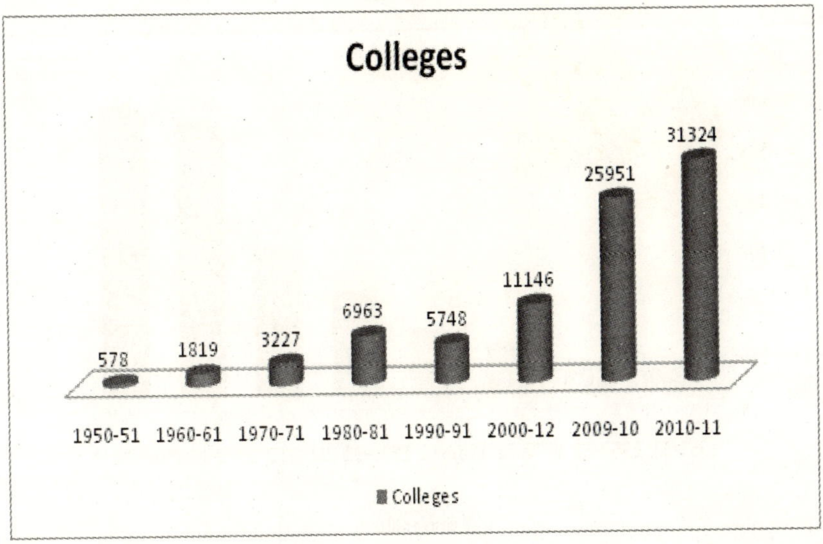

Table 1

Year	*Total enrollment*	*Per year increase*	*Percentage*
1984-85	3404096	96447	2.9
1989-90	4602680	317191	7.4
1994-95	6113929	296680	5.1
1999-00	8050607	345087	4.5
2004-05	11038543	836562	8.2
2009-10	17243352	1474935	9.4
2010-11	18670050	1426698	8.3
2011-12	20327478	1657428	8.9

Source: All India survey on higher education 2010-11.

increase from 7346 to 33023. Over the last decade, the number of universities in the country has grown at CAGR of 7.5 per cent as against the 4.7 per cent growth observed from 1951-2001. The number of colleges has grown at CAGR of 11 per cent in the period 2001-2011 as against 6.1 per cent in the period 1951-2001. More than 5,000 colleges have been added in the last one year alone.The number of universities has grown more than six times in the last four decades; India has more than 33,000 colleges with one-third of the colleges having been set-up in the last five years.

Table 1 shows the gross enrollment ratio from 1984-85 to 2011-12. The table contains the total enrollment, increase of enrollment per year and

Chart 2

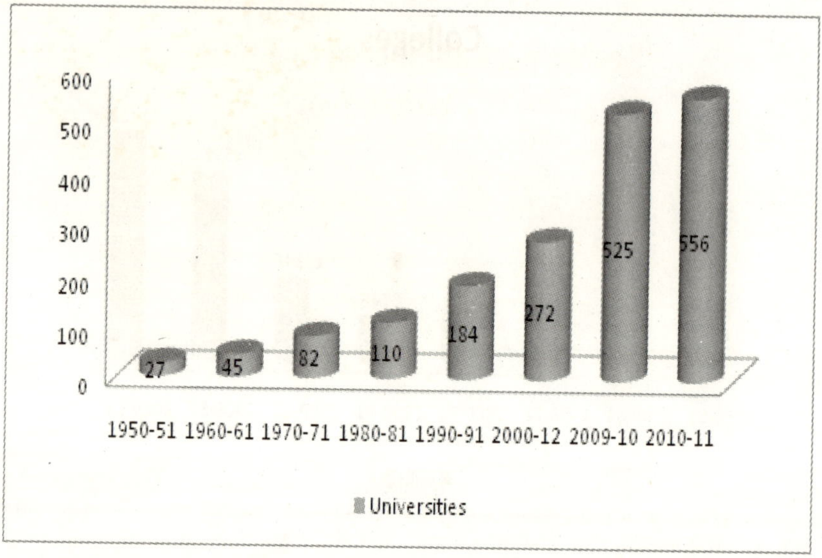

percentage increase per year. Here, we observe that enrollment in higher education increased to 8.9 per cent from 2.9 per cent in 1984-85. There is a considerable increase in the enrollment ratio up to 9.4 in 2009-10 but it decreased to 8.3 and 8.9 in 2010 and 2011-12 respectively. Here we notice that we fail to reach world GER's average rate of 29 per cent also. India aims to reach 30 per cent of the gross enrollment ratio in 2020. Due to this reason, we need the programme like RUSA.

Above chart shows the region-wise number of institutions and enrollment in higher education. Currently, North India has 9,834 institutions (31 per cent), South has 9,970 (32 per cent), West has 4,307 (14 per cent), East has 2,946 (9 per cent) and Central has 4,261 institutions (14 per cent), Central India recorded the highest growth in number of institutions an 18.7 per cent year by year growth. However, enrollment over the same period increased by only 3.7 per cent, while South India added about 800 colleges from 2009 to 2010 (10.5 per cent year by year growth), enrollment increased by 15.5 per cent, the highest amongst the regions. This table clearly shows the deficiencies in accessibility.

Above chart 4 and chart 5 shows clearly the disparity in gender basis and area basis. It clearly shows that there is significant difference in male and female, urban and rural enrollment. Male has higher enrollment rate, when compare to rural population; urban population has higher enrollment.

Chart 3

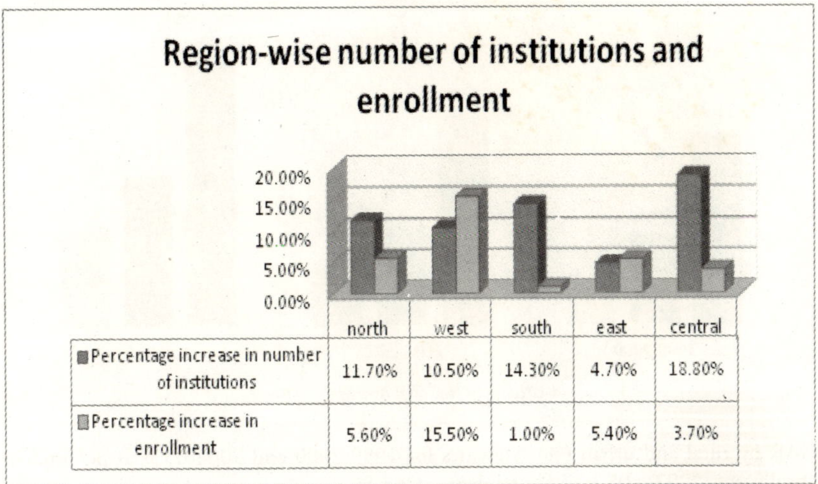

Sources: UNESCO Global Education Digest 2010, 2009; Eleventh Five Year Plan, 2007-12, Vol. II Social Sector.

Chart 4

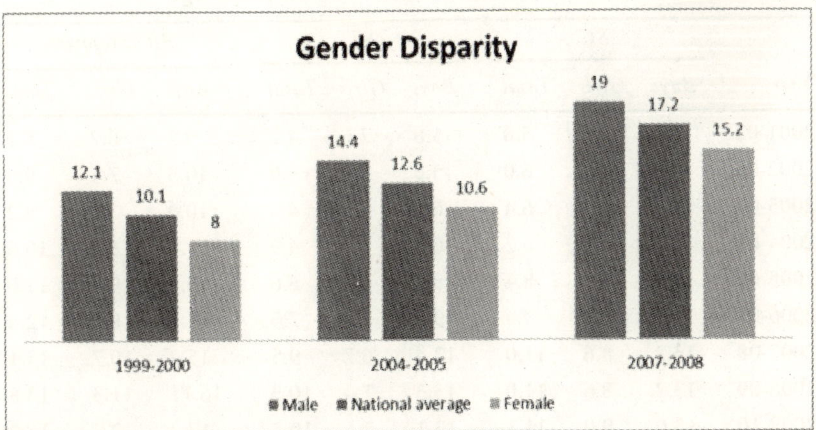

GAR by gender (%) *statistics for 1999-2000 and 2004-05 is as per student enrollment, 2007—08 is as per student attendance.

Source: Eleventh Five Year Plan: Chapter on Higher and Technical Education, Twelfth Five Year Plan: Chapter on higher education, UGC report: Issues related to expansion, inclusiveness, quality and finance, November 2008.

Chart 5: Urban and Rural Disparity

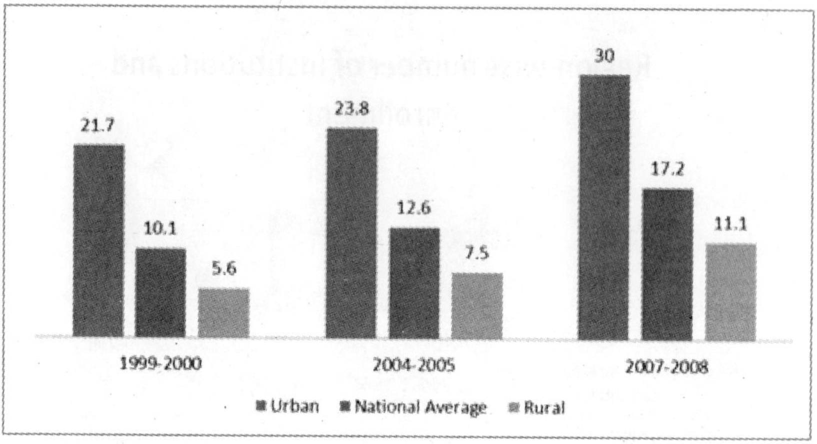

GAR by rural and urban (%) *statistics for 1999-2000 and 2004-05 is as per student enrollment, 2007—08 is as per student attendance.

Source: Eleventh Five Year Plan: Chapter on Higher and Technical Education, Twelfth Five Year Plan: Chapter on higher education, UGC report: Issues related to expansion, inclusiveness, quality and finance November 2008.

Table 3: Gross Enrollment Ratio (In percentage)

	SC			*ST*			*All categories*		
Year	*Boys*	*Girls*	*Total*	*Boys*	*Girls*	*Total*	*Boys*	*Girls*	*Total*
2001-02	7.7	3.6	5.8	5.8	2.6	4.2	9.7	6.7	8.1
2002-03	8.0	3.7	6.0	5.6	2.4	4.0	10.3	7.5	9.0
2003-04	8.3	4.3	6.4	6.2	3.1	4.7	10.6	7.7	9.2
2004-05	8.1	5.2	6.7	6.3	3.5	4.9	11.6	8.2	10.0
2005-06	10.1	6.4	8.4	8.6	4.7	6.6	13.5	9.4	11.6
2006-07	11.5	6.9	9.4	9.5	5.5	7.5	14.5	10.0	12.4
2007-08	13.2	8.6	11.0	12.4	6.7	9.5	15.2	10.7	13.1
2008-09	13.2	8.6	11.0	13.3	7.4	10.3	16.11	11.3	13.8
2009-10	13.0	9.0	11.1	13.1	7.5	10.3	17.2	12.7	15.0
2010-11	NA	NA	NA	NA	NA	NA	20.9	16.5	18.8

(*Source:* Education statistics glance, 2012).

Table 3 shows the gross enrollment ratio among the SCs, STs and other categories from the year 2001 to 2011 here clearly shows the disparity in the GER in higher education from 2001 to 2011, all the years GER of the SCs and STs are very low compare to the other category, national average 17 per cent and world average of 28 per cent. This clearly shows that improvement in higher education GER but it fail to reach the targetted rate of enrollment in higher education and reduce the inequalities in higher education. This clearly shows the need of the programme like RUSA.

Above chart 6 refers the enrollment differences in marginalised groups, here compare to national average all mentioned groups has lower enrollment rate, it shows the clear disparity in higher education.

Chart 6: Enrollment Disparities among Marginalised Groups

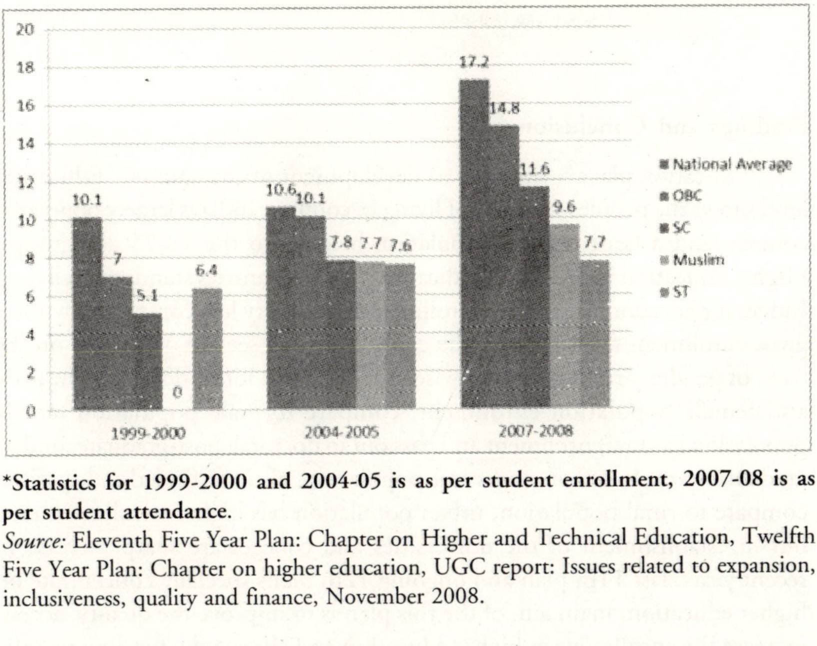

***Statistics for 1999-2000 and 2004-05 is as per student enrollment, 2007-08 is as per student attendance.**

Source: Eleventh Five Year Plan: Chapter on Higher and Technical Education, Twelfth Five Year Plan: Chapter on higher education, UGC report: Issues related to expansion, inclusiveness, quality and finance, November 2008.

Above chart refers the Actual/Projected GER and Target GER India's performance on GER is expected to fall short of targets unless the CAGR is more than doubled from the current 3.3 per cent to eight per cent. The Planning Commission has set a target of achieving a GER of 15 per cent by 2011-12 (end of the 11th five year Plan) and 21 per cent by 2016-17 (end of 12th five year Plan). The Ministry of Human Resource Development has set a target of achieving 30 per cent GER by 2020. However, at the current growth rate (3.3 per cent over 2000-10), the GER is projected to fall short of all the targets. To achieve the 30 per cent target GER by 2020, the CAGR needs to be pushed up from the current 3.3 per cent to eight per cent.

Chart 7: Actual/Projected GER and Target GER

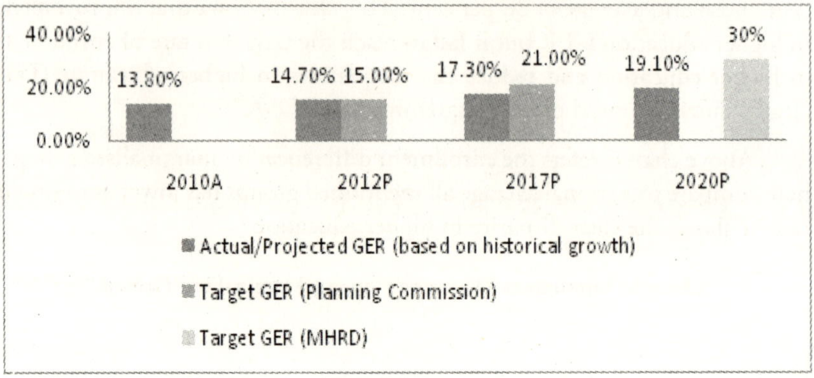

Findings and Conclusion

Education plays a vital role in development of the country. Education level shows the peoples standard of living in country. India is largely populated country and a large part of population belongs to the 18-25 age groups. Higher education is one of the indicators for the countries standard on living. Indian higher education, gross enrollment ratio is very low compare to world's gross enrollment ratio. Within the country we can see the disparities on the basis of gender, area and region-wise. We find that lot of disparities in male and female population enrollment, compare to male population female population has low enrollment and pass out in doctoral, post-graduate, under-graduate level. In urban and rural population, also we find the disparities compare to rural population, urban population has higher enrollment rate, but in establishment of the universities and colleges are sharp increase in recent years, last 11th plan and ongoing 12th plans specially concentrate on higher education, main aim of the this plan is to improve the quality, access, increase the enrollment in higher education and change the funding to State and Central government institution. 11th five year plan gave special provision to higher education and set the higher enrollment target but fail to reach that target. Therefore, in 12th plan, government India again set target in enrollment of 30 per cent in 2020. Due to this reason, GOI launches the programme named *Rashtriya Uchchatara Shiksha Abhiyan*. RUSA is umbrella programme it includes whole things about higher education in the country, and all higher education related institution working under this programme. GOI try to reach targetted enrollment rate and inclusive growth in higher education as well as inclusive growth of the country.

References

- Jandhayala B.G. et.al., (1991), Financing Higher Education in India, Higher Education, Vol. 21, No. 1, Springer.
- Dana Dunn (1993), Gender Inequality in Education and Employment in the Scheduled Castes and Tribes of India, Population Research and Policy review, Vol. 12, No. 1, Springer.
- Anne Moursund and Oystein Kravdal (2003), Individual and Community Effects of Women's Education and Autonomy on Contraceptive Use in India, Population Studies, Vol. 57, No. 3, Taylor and Francis Ltd.
- Pawan Agarwal (2006) Higher Education in India: The Need for Change, Indian Council for Research on International Economic Relations, WP-180.
- P. Nair and Deepak Kumar (2004), The Financing of Higher Education–A Broader View, The ICFAI University Press.
- Education statistics at a glance 2012. Published by Government of India, Union Ministry of Human Resource Development, New Delhi.

37 Constitutional Dimensions of Marginalised Sections and Inclusive Policies in India—A Study

Dr. N. Mudduraju

Abstract

The Right to Education received considerable impetus during the last decade. As a result of the concerted effort of many groups and agencies that made determined efforts to ensure that all children in India receive at least minimum education irrespective of their socio-economic status and their ability to pay for education in a situation of continuous impoverishment and erosion of basic needs.

Introduction

Education is the most important tool for a civilized society. For the effective and smooth functioning of a democracy education is a *sine qua non*. In this context, words quoted by Indira Gandhi is relevant even now i.e., "education is a liberating force, and in our age it is also a democratising force, cutting across the barriers of caste and class, smoothening out inequalities imposed by birth and other circumstances". India is a land of diversities and education is necessary in order to surpass the differences in caste, colour, religion and culture and for attaining the fruits of democracy. Illiteracy and poverty are the two stumbling blocks which come in the way of attaining absolute justice in India. Besides this there are neo-liberalisation trends which have come into limelight in the recent past and it has its impact on the educational policies of not only India but also almost all developing countries across the globe. In this paper, I have tried to analyse the plight of educational system that has existed in India prior to independence and post-independence in the background of neo-liberalisation trends, also I have attempted to detail Constitutional provisions dealing with right to education, major provisions of Right to Education Free and Compulsory Act, 2009 and a critical analysis of the same.

Education–Historical Perspective

India is a country where existed one of the world's oldest system of education i.e., *Gurukul* system of education wherein teacher becomes the second father for the student and guides the student on how to achieve ultimate success in life. Ancient transcripts of India has better emphasised on the importance of value education. Rajadharma says, a man who makes his study complete and acquires knowledge, develops good understanding and shines bright. Great Sanskrit poet Bhartruhari stressed on the importance of pious obligation of every individual to acquire knowledge (*Rishiruna*) and to spread knowledge to the next generation (*Manavruna*). During those days imparting education was considered as a sacred affair. Despite the influence of caste system which was prevalent those days, our learning centres like Nalanda, Takshashila etc were considered to be the prominent centers of learning. These seats of learning were responsible for developing the higher mind of the country, its conscience and its ideals. Later Buddhist and Jainist philosophies made its imprint in Indian educational system of those days by spreading the importance of democratic education throughout the country. Subsequently, with the advent of Britishers to India traditional Indian system of learning started deteriorating. Mahatma Gandhi described traditional educational system as a beautiful tree that was destroyed during the British rule. With the advent of Britishers to India, English education was established for the first time in the country. Though Christian missionaries established schools and universities in India there had been a widespread discrimination and as observed by Hunter Commission in 1882, "during those times British governments' funding of education tended to benefit *Brahmins* a higher class while leaving masses wallowing in ignorance and poverty".

Methodology

For the methodological purposes of examining the educational status among the Marginalised sections, and the non-marginalised sections under the Constitution of India, the working paper aligns with data from the Annual Reports of various Ministries of Government of India for different time periods. It is important to conceptually clarify at the outset that for the purposes of this research paper.

The objectives of this study are as follows:

(a) To assess the state of special needs and inclusive education in the country in terms of policies, resources and practices.

(b) To identify and document the experiences of 'good practice models' of special needs and inclusive education for children with disabilities.

(c) To provide recommendations to strengthen the capacity of the government and other partners in the country to bring about policy reforms and promote programmes that support inclusive education.

Education–Post Independence Era

After independence Ministry of education under the Chairmanship of Dr. S. Radhakrishnan took initiative to remodel the prevailing system of education in India in 1948 but emphasis was given only for higher education. Later in 1964 the Government of India set up Kothari Commission, and the commission advocated the concept of free and compulsory education in India. It also introduced the notion of neighborhood schools with the aim of providing 'good education' to all children irrespective of the differences in caste, creed, community etc. According to the report all children in a given neighbourhood, drawn from diverse backgrounds, should be able to study and socialise together in a common public space. This has been the organising principle of school education in G-8 countries like the USA, Canada, France, Germany and Japan. The Commission set the target of accomplishing free and compulsory education before 1986. But the then government did not successfully implement the Kothari Commission Report.

Later in 1986 National Policy on Education was formulated and it marked the onset of neo-liberal framework in education in India. In 1985-86, the Ministry of Education was renamed as Ministry of Human Resource Development. The policy of 1986 introduced non-formal education along with the establishment of Navodaya Vidyalayas meant for a handful of children. If we compare the Kothari Commission Report 1968 and National Policy on Education 1986 we can see that when Kothari Commission tried to narrow down the wide discrepancy between the children of rich and privileged groups, the latter policy widened the gap by creating parallel layers of education. In 1990 India signed 'World Declaration on Education For All and Framework for Acton to Meet Basic Learning Needs' adopted at World Conference on Education for All: Meeting Basic Leaning Needs' held at Jomtien, Thailand under the Joint sponsorship of UNDP, UNESCO, UNICEF and World Bank. The Convention indirectly laid down the foundation for World Bank intervention in educational policies of India and with that started the World Bank providing assistance for implementing educational policies of India. Further in 1990 the concept of Minimum Levels of Learning was introduced and in 1993 government introduced DPEP and SSA. With this the number of enrollment of students to the government schools decreased considerably. Besides, there is also a considerable reduction in the budgetary allocation towards education. If we compare India with other Asian countries like China, Japan, South Korea we can see that with somewhat of the same expenditure on mass education those countries have achieved maximum literacy rates. And India sets the record as the State with the largest single producer of the world's illiterates. One of the reasons behind this is India's educational policies underlying the design to push down primary education to the state of indignity.

Right to Education under the Indian Constitution

In India until 2002 right to education was given emphasis only in the Directive Principles of State Policy under Article 45. The Constitutional mandate to the state under Article 45 was to provide free and compulsory education to every children upto the age of 14. It also mandated that this must be ensured within 10 years from the commencement of the Constitution. After forty three years, the Supreme Court in its verdict in the case of *Unnikrishnan v. State of Andhra Pradesh* declared that *"the right to education up to the age of 14 years is a fundamental right within the meaning of Article 21 of our Constitution."* This judgment was much in consonance with the spirit of the Constitution-makers. Later right to free and compulsory education was elevated as a fundamental right under the Constitution through the 86th Amendment Act of 2002. Article 21A reads;

> *"The State shall provide free and compulsory education of the age of six to 14 years in such manner as the state may by law determine".*

The preamble of our Constitution establishes a sovereign, socialist, secular, democratic, republic. Preamble further envisages social, economic and political justice to the masses, the main aim of which is the establishment of an egalitarian society, wherein everyone will have equal opportunities for self-realisation which is again not possible without proper education. Thus preamble to our constitutional envisages the need for a well-informed, educated society for ensuring social, political and economic justice. Further Article 21 protects right to life of which even right to education forms a part as an unenumerated fundamental right which has become a fundamental right now. As held by the Supreme Court in Unnikrishnan's case "right to education flows directly from right to life". Article 21A inserted through 93rd Amendment Act, 2002 guarantees free and compulsory education to all children of the age 6 to 14 years.

Article 14 and 15 is also relevant for education; the education which is granted must be in consonance with Article 14, 15, 16 (1) of Part III which guarantee equality before law, prohibit the state from discriminating against citizens on grounds only of religion, race, caste, sex, place of birth or any of them and equality of opportunity in matters of public employment respectively. In view of the second aspect of Article 14 there is a positive duty on the state to ensure equal protection of laws by bringing in necessary social and economic changes so that everyone may enjoy equal protection of laws. Further 15 (3) enables the government to make special provisions in favour of women and children.

Article 24 prevents employing children below 14 years of age in hazardous industries. The Supreme Court in *M.C. Mehta v. State of Tamil Nadu* issued broad directions to give effect to this article.

Under Part IV, there are three main articles that deals with the educational rights of the children i.e., Article 41, 45 and 46. Article 41 directs the state to ensure to the people within the limit of its economic capacity and development: (a) employment (b) education. Article 45 enjoins the state to make provisions within 10 years for free and compulsory education for all children until they complete the age of 14 years. Article 46 requires the state to promote with special care educational and economic interest of the weaker sections of the people, and in particular of the Scheduled Caste and Scheduled Tribe.

Right to education is also recognised as a basic human right under the International Charter on Human Rights–Universal Declaration on Human Rights (Art 26), International Covenant on Civil and Political Rights (Article 13), International Covenant on Educational, Social and Cultural Rights. Convention on the Rights of Child also provides for the right to education (Article 28). Apart from these there are a number of international and regional agreements that supports the cause of right to education worldwide.

Right to (free and compulsory) Education Act, 2009

It was in pursuance of the judicial pronouncements in *Mohini Jain v. State of Karnataka* and *Unnikrishnan v. State of U.P.,* that the government passed Right to Education Act in the year 2009. In Mohini Jain's case the Apex Court held that,

> "Unless the 'right to education' mentioned in Article 41 is made a reality, the fundamental rights in Part III will remain beyond the reach of the illiterate majority".

The following are some of the important features of the Act.

1. The Act provides for free and compulsory education to every child of the age of six to fourteen years.

2. Establishment of neighborhood school within such area and limits of neighbourhood in the prescribed area and limits within three years from the commencement of the Act.
3. The government shall ensure that weaker and disadvantaged children is not discriminated and prevented against pursuing and completing elementary education on any grounds.
4. The Act imposes a duty on the parent to cause or to be admitted his or her child or ward for elementary education to the neighborhood school.
5. Section 12 provides for reimbursement of the money which the private school has incurred for giving effect to the provisions of the Act.
6. The Act makes it penal collection of capitation fee and subjecting the child, his or her parent or guardian to any screening procedure for the purpose of admission.
7. The Act prevents expelling of students from the schools until completion of elementary education.
8. The Act prevents imposing physical and mental punishment on the students.
9. The Act provides for norms and conditions for private schools subject to which recognition shall be granted.
10. The Act establishes a School Management Committee.
11. The Act mandates National Commission for Protection of Child to examine the protection of rights provided under the Education Act. The Commission can inquire into complaints relating to child's right to free and compulsory education.
12. The Act establishes a National Advisory Council for its effective implementation.

Right to Education–A critique

Though the Act seems to be a comprehensive code assuring education to all there are loopholes. Following points give a testimony to that effect.

Free and Compulsory Education

The Act guarantees free and compulsory education to children between the age of 6-14 years. But with 8th standard education a child will not be able to find any job or a vocation suitable to his age as the minimum qualification required for a job in India is 12th standard education. So even after his/her getting elementary education the child will go for working in any industry, hotel etc. So the Act cannot improve the conditions of child labour existing today. Also the Act undermined the decision of Supreme Court in Unnikrishnan's case wherein Court held education upto 14 years to be made compulsory. The Act is silent about the educational rights of the child upto six years. So, the Act has evaded the right given by the Supreme Court.

Privatisation of Education

Justice Jeevan Reddy in Unnikrishnan's case stated that privatisation is an outcome of the government's failure in providing necessary support to in the higher education. This is equally applicable in the field of primary education as well. The Act seeks to establish private participation in the field of education. For implementing the provisions of the Act the government is planning to make 25 per cent reservation in private schools in favour of disadvantaged, disabled, weaker sections of the society and government will be providing financial assistance to those private schools for improving its infrastructure, teaching requirements and for other facilities etc. We can say that through this government is shifting its fundamental responsibility of providing education and is giving it in private hands. If we look at the budgetary allocation toward education we can find that over years the allocation is coming down. The reason given by the government is lack of financial incapacity of the state to provide education to the masses. In this context it is worth quoting the words of Amartya Sen, "To say that India does not have the money for education (and health-care) is absolute, utter unmitigated nonsense." In fact, it is the neo-liberalist principle which the state is paying heed to.

Concept of Neighborhood Schools

The Act once again introduced the concept of neighbourhood school after Kothari Commission Report. Section 6 of the Act reads as follows:

> "For carrying out the provisions of this Act, the appropriate Government and the local authority shall establish, within such area or limits of neighbourhood, as may be prescribed, a school, where it is not so established, within a period of three years from the commencement of this Act."

As the responsibility of providing education lies with the private schools, the practicality of this section is doubtful. Private management may not be willing to establish its schools in village hamlet and remote areas wherein there is not much scope for getting students and returns. If this is the case then Article 46 which makes state responsible for promoting educational interest of SC's and ST's will be destabilised as a large population of them dwells in remote areas and in villages. Moreover, the Act left undefined the term 'neighbourhood school'.

Rich-poor Gap

The Act provides for a fertile ground for the growth of neo-liberalisation agenda which commenced in India with National Policy on Education 1986. The policy introduced non-formal education (primarily meant for government schools) and a layer of expensive residential Navodaya Vidyalayas for a handfull of students (about 80 children per district per year). These schools are named as 'Specified Schools' under the Act as per Section 2 (p) and Section 5 (1) says that a child cannot seek transfer to the specified category schools and unaided schools defined under Section 2 (iv) in any case. This provision further widens the gap between rich and poor in India which has its foundation on principles of equality, liberty and fraternity.

Reluctance of Private Schools

Private schools are reluctant to admit children to their schools and in Delhi this has lead to filing of Public Interest Litigation by Socio Jurist Forum. In most of the schools, authorities deny admission saying "admissions were shut", "no vacancies" etc. Following the judgement the Government passed an Order directing the private schools in Delhi to admit students from weaker sections etc and to give them seats on the basis of reservation as is mentioned under the Right to Education Act, 2008.

In contrast to this situation sometimes even after getting admission the parents may not be able to send the children to the school because of the incidental expenses attached with educational expenses. Apart from this there are also instances were in the school authorities put the children under harassment. In the capital city harassment for non-payment of school fee made a 14-year-old student to commit suicide. Thus, we can say that there are blatant violations of the provisions of Right to Education Act.

Closing of Government Schools

Even before the introduction of the Act, privatisation in education was rampant. A survey conducted by Annual Survey of Education Report (ASER) 2008 revealed that there was a 37 per cent increase in private school enrollment just between 2005 and 2008. Indirectly it is the impact of introduction of Minimum Levels of Learning implemented through schemes like District

Primary Education Programme (DPEP), *Sarva Shiksha Abhiyan* (SSA) funded by World Bank and IMF.

In *PUCL v. Union of India* the Supreme Court directed all states and Union Territories to implement the mid-day meal scheme in every Government and Government Aided Primary Schools as a means to control the drop-out rates in those schools. But there is absenteeism of teachers, lack of infrastructure which will ultimately result in closing down of government schools. The impracticality of the provisions of 2009 Act and the above mentioned problems will ultimately favour commercialisation of education in India consequently will result in denial of education to poorer and weaker sections of society.

Violations of Constitutional Provisions

Right to Education Act does violate the provisions of the Constitution. The Bill perpetuates a multi-layer discriminating school system. It categorises the schools in India into government schools, aided private schools, special category schools and non-aided private schools. As per the Act, if any child is not in a position to complete his/her elementary education in the school where he/she was studying there is a right of seeking admission in any other school but in such a case the child is statutorily prohibited from getting admission in any specified category schools or in non-aided private schools. Thus, we can say that there is violation of the equality clause as is enshrined in the Constitution and it is also against the concept of common school system given under Kothari Commission Report. Besides the Act does not have any strict stipulation about medium of instruction. It says that the medium of instruction as far as possible be in the child's mother tongue. In the absence of a strict language policy normally the private educational institutions may adopt English as the medium of instruction. In such a case the Act will undermine children's mother tongue and it constitutes violation of Article 350 A of the Constitution and also it amounts to defiance of right to freedom of speech and expression under Article 19 (a). Further the Act violates Article 45 of the Constitution and the guarantee given by the Supreme Court in Unnikrishnan's case, i.e., free and compulsory education upto the age of 14 years.

Suggestions

The government should undertake the responsibility of providing education to the masses through sufficient budgetary allocation instead of privatising education in India and thereby it should try to alleviate the class disparity in education.

- The government should give sufficient infrastructure and training for the teachers in government schools. Under the Act a teacher can be deployed for non-educational purposes like population census, disaster relief duties or duties relating to local authority, State Legislatures or Parliament. This is not a welcoming trend and there should be an alternative for this.
- Compulsory education must be given for every 'child' till 12th standard or until 18 years of age which is in conformity with the standard set by Convention on the Rights of Child. (A child means every human being below the age of 18 years).
- Apart from providing education at free of cost government should also take steps to 'mitigate the household expenditure of acquiring elementary education atleast of the poorer and other marginalised sections of the society. The Act makes compromise of the tuition fee of the child but the Act is silent about the incidental expense that has to be incurred for uniform, travelling etc which is a heavy burden on the parents of those children's.

Conclusion

In April 1, 2010, Prime Minister Manmohan Singh addressed the nation on the occasion of the coming into force of the Right of Children to Free and Compulsory Education Act 2009. To some the day marked a historic day for the children of 'India' and a bad day for the children of '*Bharat*, as the Act has taken double standards in promoting education. There are widespread sentiments against the provisions contained in this Act. It is opined that the new Bill seeks to put the constitutional promise of free and quality education for all at the mercy of market forces. Education means giving education to the Indian masses, providing education to a particular class is not a herculean task and is being done by large number of private educational institutions. But the state is not giving attention to the tribulations of weaker sections of the society as far as their educational interests are concerned, rather it is trying to evade from the responsibility of educating the masses. The following are some of the suggestions which can improve the alarming state of affairs of elementary education in India.

References

- Verse IV-20 Manusmriti.
- Bhartruhari was a poet, philosopher and king of Ujjain during the First Century B.C.

- See Justice M. Rama Jois, Human Rights and Indian Values, NCTE Monograph Series, New Delhi, 1998 p. 20.
- See Justice M. Rama Jois, Human Rights and Indian Values, NCTE Monograph Series, New Delhi, 1998 p. 20.
- S. Radhakrishnan, The Foundation of Civilisation: Ideas and Ideals, 3rd Edn. 1997, p. 9.
- Dharmapal Collected Writings, The Beautiful Tree: Indigenous Indian Education in the Eighteenth Century, Volume III, Other India Press, 2010. The phrase 'the beautiful tree' was used by Mahatma Gandhi in a speech in England to describe traditional Indian education.
- See supra 39.
- Available at www.unesco.org/education/pdf/JOMTIE_E.PDF - France.
- See supra 23.
- The Hindu, March 22, 1994, 26.
- AIR 1993 SC 2178.
- During the Constituent Assembly Debates in 1948-49 it was contended by one of the members that 14 years must be reduced to 11 years but it was Dr. B.R. Ambedkar who vehemently argued for raising age upto 14 years.
- AIR 1997 SC 699.
- Article 26 (1) Everyone has the right to education. Education shall be free, at least in the elementary and fundamental stages. Elementary education shall be compulsory. Technical and professional education shall be made generally available and higher education shall be equally accessible to all on the basis of merit.
- Article 13 (1) The States Parties to the present Covenant recognise the right of everyone to education. They agree that education shall be directed to the full development of the human personality and the sense of its dignity, and shall strengthen the respect for human rights and fundamental freedoms. They further agree that education shall enable all persons to participate effectively in a free society, promote understanding, tolerance and friendship among all nations and all racial, ethnic or religious groups, and further the activities of the United Nations for the maintenance of peace. The States Parties to the present Covenant recognise that, with a view to achieving the full realisation of this right:

  (a) Primary education shall be compulsory and available free to all…
- Article 28 (1) States Parties recognise the right of the child to education, and with a view to achieving this right progressively and on the basis of equal opportunity, they shall, in particular:

  (a) Make primary education compulsory and available free to all;

(b) Encourage the development of different forms of secondary education, including general and vocational education, make them available and accessible to every child, and take appropriate measures such as the introduction of free education and offering financial assistance in case of need;

(c) Make higher education accessible to all on the basis of capacity by every appropriate means;

(d) Make educational and vocational information and guidance available and accessible to all children;

(e) Take measures to encourage regular attendance at schools and the reduction of drop-out rates.

- Article 5 of Convention on All Forms of Racial Discrimination, Article 6 of United Nations Declaration of Rights of Disabled Persons, Article 3 of Convention Against Discrimination in Education, International Convention on the Rights of the Child, International Conventions on the Protection of the Rights of All Migrant Workers and Members of their Families.
- See Article 14 (1) of Charter of Fundamental Rights of European Union, Article 34 of Arab Charter on Human Rights, Article 2 to First Protocol to the European Convention, Article 17 to African Charter on Human Rights and Peoples Rights, Article 18 to Additional Protocol to the American Convention on Human Rights in the Area of Economic, Social and Cultural Rights, Article 11 of African Charter on the Rights and Welfare of the Child, Article 12 of American Declaration of the Rights and Duties of Man.
- AIR 1992 SC 1858 Court held that the State is under a constitutional mandate to provide educational institutions at all levels for the benefit of the citizen.
- AIR 1993 SC 2178.
- Even before these judgements there happened to be a few judgements wherein the Courts have appreciated right to education as a fundamental and basic right viz; *Anand Vardhan Chand* v. *University of Delhi* AIR 1978 Del. 308, *Francis Coraile* v. *Administrator, Union Territory of Delhi* AIR 1981 SC 746 *Banhua Mukti Morcha* v. *Union of India* AIR 1984 SC 802.
- *Ibid.,* 667-78.
- Section 3.
- Section 6.
- Section 9.
- Section 10.
- Section 12.
- Section 13.
- Section 16.

- Section 17.
- Sections 19 and 20.
- Sections 21 and 22.
- Section 31.
- Section 33.
- Deccan Herald, Monday, April 4, 2011, 5.
- Social Jurist, A *Civil Rights Group* vs *Gnct and Ors* 2008.
- Mallica, 'Poor' Children in 'Rich' Schools, Working Paper Series available at www.iist-india.org.
- http://www.ndtv.com/article/cities/delhi-unable-to-go-to-school-14-yr-old-commits-suicide-86965 (02/05/11).
- Frontline, Vol. 21, Issue 01, January 02-15, 2010.
- Writ Petition No. 196 of 2001.
- Section 2 (n) (i).
- Section 2 (n) (ii).
- Section 2 (n) (iii).
- Section 2(n) (iv).
- Section 2 (p).
- Section 5 (i).
- Section 29 (f).
- Article 350 A—It shall be the endeavour of every State and of every local authority within the State to provide adequate facilities for instruction in the mother tongue at the primary stage of education to children belonging to linguistic minority groups; and the President may issue such directions to any State as he considers necessary or proper for securing the provisions of such facilities.
- Gladson Dung Dung, 'Ensuring Right to Education in the Red Corridor', Mainstream, Vol. XLVIII, No. 45, October 30, 2010.
- See Anil Sadgopal, *C for Commerce*, Tehelka Magazine, Vol. 5, Issue 23, Dated June 14, 2008.

38

A Study on Marginalised Section and Higher Education: With Special Reference to Gadag and Dharwad Districts in Karnataka State

Dr. H.H. Bharadi

Abstract

The beginning of the 21st century is witnessing a great thrust in the development of the social sector and education sector in particular has been assigned the top priority. The inclusive growths for all social groups have equal access to the services provided by the State and equal opportunity for upward economic and social mobility. In India, certain deprived social groups like SCs, STs, OBCs and Minorities and women have historically been disadvantaged and vulnerable. Constitution of India contains various provisions for the development of such marginalised groups, and their individual and collective growth. The SCs constitute 16.23 per cent of India's population. The gross enrollment ratio for the country as a whole in 2000 was about 10 per cent. For the SCs, however, it was significantly lower at 6.4 per cent. STs constitute 8.2 per cent of the total population of the country with 91.7 per cent of them living in rural areas and 8.3 per cent in urban areas. The 11th and 12th plan emphasised on inclusive education, it means increased access to deprived groups, the enrollment rate is much lower among the SC, ST, Minorities such as Muslim, and female. Inclusive policy to be effective would demands measures to improved access to these social, religious, female and economic groups. UGC has proposed schemes for these groups, which will include scholarships, hostel and other schemes at university and college level. The increase in the enrollment rate among this group will help to boast up the overall enrollment ratio. So inclusiveness is a main source for increasing overall enrollment rate. Therefore, the present study focussed on the issues like the gross enrollment, gross enrollment ratio by sex, dropout position and ratio of girl's enrollment, combination-wise distribution of students and the UGC schemes for these groups. Therefore, there is a need to study on Marginalised Section and Higher Education: with Special Reference to Gadag, and Dharwad Districts in Karnataka State at the micro-level. The study is mainly based on both primary and secondary data and used simple percentage and average method. Further, simple random sampling technique is used in the present study.

Introduction

The role of higher education in human resource development in India is well-recognised and the higher education system is one of the largest in the world, the Gross Enrollment Ratio (GER) is low at about 10 per cent. Accelerated globalisation is remaking the prospects and potentials of higher education, higher education institutions play a distinctive role in the social and economic life of a country. Higher Education is the ultimate aim of every parent, who has a child in secondary school today in India. The wells to do are always a step ahead of the poor and therefore, tend to disproportionately benefit from any quantitative expansion in higher education.

People belonging to SC communities are spread all over the country, with 80 per cent of them living in the rural areas. The SCs constitute 16.23 per cent of India's population. The drop-out rate is a crucial indicator of lack of educational development. The drop-out rates for SC students are still very high. The population of STs in India stood at 84.33 million. STs constitute 8.2 per cent of the total population of the country with 91.7 per cent of them living in rural areas and 8.3 per cent in urban areas. The literacy rates for Muslim girl students are particularly low. This can be attributed to a number of reasons. Many parents do not send their girls to the colleges as they feel unsafe, especially in view of the growing communalism, lack of basic infrastructure, marriages of women. Further, as the dependency ratio for the young is high among Muslims, older siblings often have to stay home and provide care. Given the high levels of poverty and self-employment, children also provide much needed labour. Finally, many SC/ST and Muslim girls and boys are first generation learners. Therefore, the present paper on Marginalised Section and Higher Education: with Special Reference to Gadag, and Dharwad Districts in Karnataka State on the various issues like gross enrollment, drop-out position, combination-wise distribution of students at the micro-level.

Methodology

The whole discussion of the paper has been made on the basis of both primary and secondary sources. The primary data were collected through the structured schedule from the selected colleges. The different sources of secondary data like books, journals, related websites and annual reports of the UGC have been consulted in this regard. The two districts, two government and two unaided colleges have been selected. The Gadag GFGC and unaided colleges are situated in the Gadag district headquarter, the other GFGC of Annigeri and unaided colleges are comes under rural area. Dharwad district is educationally forward and Gadag is backward districts. The random sample method is adopted to select four colleges in both the district. Further, the study used simple percentage and average method. The period of the study is 2011-12 and 2013-14 academic years have been selected. The students of deprived classes like SC/ST/OBC/2B/ male and other category have been selected for the present study.

Objectives of the Study

The main objectives of the study are as follows:

1. To study the gross enrollment of category-wise students in different colleges.
2. To examine the drop-out positions of the different colleges in selected district.
3. To know the combination-wise distribution of students.
4. To know the main findings of the study.
5. To suggest a suitable recommendations.

Analysis and Interpretation

Gross Enrollment of SC/ST/OBC and Women Students in the UG Classes

The student's enrollment in higher educational institutions in India has been increasing rapidly over the past half-century, from less than 2,00,000 in 1950 to almost seven million by the year 20002. During this time, the proportionate representation of Scheduled Caste (SC) and Scheduled Tribe (ST) students in total higher educational enrollment has been slowly rising. The SC proportion rose from 7 per cent to 7.8 per cent and the ST proportion rose from 1.6 per cent to 2.7 per cent. The 11th Plan that recognised the increase in enrollment rate from 10 per cent to 15 per cent will involve inclusiveness. Increase in the enrollment rate will have to come from those social groups and regions whose access to higher education is lower than the other groups. The 11th Plan also recognised the inter-regional; inter-social groups and male female imbalances. The inclusive education focus on these aspects, Technical education has grown at 12.7 per cent as compared to 2.6 per cent for general graduate education during the period 2000-01 to 2003-04. Enrolled technical graduates are 11.1 lakhs as opposed to 80.1 lakh general in 2003-4. Therefore, this section examined the enrollment position of two

Table 1. Total No. of Students Enrolled for the Academic Year 2013-14 in Govt. First Grade Colleges

Categories	*BA Gadag*		*BA Annigeri*		*B.Com Gadag*		*B.Com Annigeri*		*B.Sc. Gadag*		*B.Sc. Annigeri*	
	Boys	*Girls*	*Boys*	*Girls*	*Boys*	*Girls*	*Boys*	*Girls*	*Boys*	*Girls*	*Boys*	*Girls*
SC	26	10	8	11	9	7	1	1	3	1	—	1
ST	8	7	7	5	4	3	2	3	—	1	—	—
OBC	52	34	60	81	62	24	56	72	16	3	4	8
2B	10	11	11	22	11	1	4	22	—	2	2	4
Others	7	89	1	3	1	63	6	2	—	12	—	—
Total	103	151	87	122	87	98	69	100	19	19	6	13
Grand Total	254	209	185	169	38	19						

(*Sources:* Compiled from the primary data).

government and two unaided colleges in Gadag and Dharwad districts in north-Karnataka. The tables 1 and 2 explain the enrollment of students in all the four colleges.

The selected four colleges appellated to the Karnatak University, Dharwad. Further, The HCES College is accredited by the NAAC, but the other three colleges have not been accredited by the NAAC. The total strength of the Government First Grade College, Gadag is 477 in all BA, BCom and BSc courses; out of this the total female strength is 268 and worked out that almost 56.18 per cent of the female students pursuing their higher education in Gadag Government College. Regarding the SC students, the 38 male and 18 female students are studying in all courses, whereas the 12 male and 11 female ST students pursuing their degree course. As for as OBC students are concerned the 128 male and 61 female students, and 21 male and 18 female 2B categories students studying in Gadag Government College. On the other hand, the total enrollment in HCES Unaided private college in Gadag is 697 in BA and Bcom courses only, out of which the female strength is 366 and it is higher than that of the Gadag Government College. The 63 male and 35 female SC students and the 14 male and 22 ST female students are enrolled for BA and Bcom degree courses in the same unaided college. Regarding the OBC students the 221 male and 281 female students studying in both the courses, it shows that in all categories, the enrollment in un-aided college is in better progress that too female students, it is because of the well-equipped buildings and the college is situated in the heart of the city and very near to the central bus-stand compare to the government college. The 30 male and 24 female 2B students enrolled for their BA and Bcom courses, it is also more in number when compared to the government college.

Table 2. Total No. of Students Enrolled for the Academic Year 2013-14 in Unaided Colleges

Categories	*BA HCES college Gadag*		*BA Amrutheshwar College Annigeri*		*B.Com. HCES College Gadag*		*B.Com. Amrutheshwar College Annigeri*	
	Boys	*Girls*	*Boys*	*Girls*	*Boys*	*Girls*	*Boys*	*Girls*
SC	52	25	14	15	11	10	7	—
ST	12	15	7	6	2	7	1	—
OBC	104	198	78	120	117	83	35	7
2B	13	16	25	29	17	8	10	—
Others	—	1	5	3	3	3	—	—
Total	181	255	129	173	150	111	53	7
Grand Total	436	302	261	60				

Sources: Compiled from the primary data.

Similarly, while looking into the Government First Grade College Annigeri, the total students enrolled for pursuing their degree is 397, out of this the total female students are 235 (59.19 per cent), it means almost more than 50 per cent of the students are pursuing their degree in all the four colleges except Amrutheshwar unaided college in Annigeri, where in BCom courses was started just two years ago. The 12 male and 13 female SC students, the nine male and eight female ST students are studying in the Annigeri government college. The counterpart unaided college got admitted 21 male, 15 female SC students and seven male and six female ST students. The 281 OBC students enrolled in the Government College, out of which 161 female students are studying in all the courses. Similarly, the 240 OBC students are admitted in unaided college in Annigeri, out of which 127 female students are got admitted for BA and B.Com. courses and is comparatively less in number when compared to the government college, Gadag. Regarding the OBC students the enrollment is more are less same. Finally, it is concluded that in all the colleges female enrollment is greater than male students, particularly in both the unaided colleges. The 184 SC/ST students enrolled in both the unaided colleges is greater than that of the 118 SC/ST students in both the Government colleges. Similarly, the 742 more OBC students took their admissions in unaided colleges than that of the 472 in both government colleges. Therefore, it is suggested to improve the infrastructure facilities like buildings, recruitment of full-time teachers and other basic amenities in the government colleges.

Drop-out Positions of the Different Colleges

The drop-out position is a crucial indicator of the lack of educational development. The drop-out rates for SC/ST and other categories students are higher in general UG courses at the micro-level as it is in the macro-level in India. The tables 3 and 4 explain the drop-out position of the government and unaided colleges in Gadag and Dharwad district. The Annigeri GFGC and Amrutheshwar unaided colleges have been selected since they are in rural and remote area in Dharwad district. The GFGC Gadag and HCES Colleges in Gadag town have been selected to know the drop-out positions. The drop-out rate of GFGC Gadag is 46 per cent, 22 per cent of Annigeri GFGC when compared to the 15 per cent of an unaided college in Gadag town and six per cent of unaided college in Annigeri respectively. Though there are many incentives have been given by the government in the name of different scholarships, books, and hostel facilities, etc., to increase the enrollment rate as laid down in the 11th and the 12th plan.

Drop-out rate of SC/ST and other categories is too high in both the government colleges and Gadag unaided colleges. However, it is little less in

Table 3. Comparative Drop-out Positions of GFGC and Unaided College in Gadag District

Categories	*GFGC Gadag 2011-12*		*Total*	*GFGC Gadag 2013-14*		*Drop Out Percentage*	*HCES College Gadag 2011-12*		*Total*	*HCES College Gadag 2013-14*		*Drop Out percen-tage*
	Boys	*Girls*		*Boys*	*Girls*		*Boys*	*Girls*		*Boys*	*Girls*	
SC	28	7	35	15	2	18(51)	17	9	26	16	8	2(8)
ST	2	—	2	1	—	1 (50)	6	4	10	4	4	2(4)
OBC	43	20	63	41	16	6(10)	80	81	161	65	77	19(12)
2B	12	4	16	7	8	1 (6)	15	10	25	8	7	10(40)
Others	7	46	53	4	29	20(38)	—	—	—	—	—	—
Total	92	77	169	68	55	46(27)	118	104	222	93	96	33(15)
Grand Total	169		123		222		189					

Sources: Compiled from the primary data.

Annigeri unaided college. It is observed that the drop-out rate of SC 51 per cent, ST 50 per cent, others 38 per cent and OBC 10 per cent respectively in GFGC Gadag. In contrast to this the drop-out is 40 per cent of 2B categories, 12 per cent of OBC and very least of other categories in HCES unaided college. To prevent the overall drop-out and encourage the Muslims students, the HCES societies have been giving the Rs 4000 scholarships to all the students and it also maintain the own hostel. The same trend is continued in the Annigeri GFGC, where also the 2B categories is 42 per cent, others 40 per cent, SC 37 per cent, ST 15 per cent and OBC 15 per cent. However, there is a negative drop-out rate found in SC/ST/OBC categories in Annigeri unaided college. It is inferred from the table that the female dropout rate is more in all the colleges.

The main reasons for the drop-out rate is poverty, lack of knowledge about the higher education, marriages of women, dowry problem, lack of basic infrastructure facilities available for female students in the colleges that too in the government colleges. Therefore, it is suggested to encourage the poor students, female students, Muslims and other OBC students to continue their education. It is also better to advise the parents about the dowry and marriage of their daughters. The SC/ST/OBC students also need to be encouraged to prepare for various competitive examinations.

Distribution of Students by the Combination-wise

The subjects elected by the students are also an indicator through which they have a vision in their mind to get the jobs in the job market. Some students are interested in pursuing their PG education at the university level. It also indicates that students chosen the subjects for a competitive examinations like UPSC and KPSC and scoring more marks. So that the table five is explained the distribution of students according to the combination in all the four colleges, there are as many as seven optional subjects. The GFGC gadag introduced five optinal for BA and two combinations for BSc courses; whereas GFGC Annigeri has introduced only two and one combination for BA and BSc courses respectively. In contrast to this the seven and five groups have been introduced by the Gadag and Annigeri unaided colleges respectively. Both the unaided colleges do not introduced the BSc courses.

Most of the students in GFGC Gadag took the combinations like HKP 98 (Kan), HEP 82 (Eng), HES 40 and HEP 39, but they have least bothered about the remaining subjects. But on the other hand only 15 students opted the PCM combination and 18 students took PMCS combinations. However, during the academic year 2013-14, they have not introduced the PCM combination, due to the full time faculty, lack of laboratory facilities and

Table 4. Comparative Drop-out Positions of GFGC and Unaided Colleges in Dharwad District

Categories	*GFGC Annigeri 2011-12*		*Total*	*GFGC Annigeri 2013-14*		*Drop-out percentage*	*Amrutheshwar College Annigeri*		*Total*	*Amrutheshwar College Annigeri*		*Drop-out percentage*
	Boys	*Girls*		*Boys*	*Girls*		*Boys*	*Girls*		*Boys*	*Girls*	
SC	4	4	8	2	3	3 (37)	2	2	4	5	6	+7
ST	4	2	6	4	1	1(17)	1	—	1	3	1	+3
OBC	44	46	90	36	40	14(15)	51	27	78	39	44	+5
2B	10	9	19	3	8	8(42)	11	8	19	8	9	2(11)
Others	3	2	5	3	—	2(40)	2	3	5	1	1	3(60)
Total	65	63	128	48	52	**28**(22)	67	40	107	56	61	5(6)
Grand Total	128		100		107		117					

(*Sources:* Compiled from the primary data).

Table 5: The Combination-wise Distribution of Students in all semi for BA and BSc Streams

Name College % Combination	*GFGC Gadag*		*Total*	*GFGC Annigeri*		*Total*	*HCESC Gadag (unaided)*		*Total*	*Amru-theshwar Annigeri (unaided)*		*Total*
	B	*G*		*B*	*G*		*B*	*G*		*B*	*G*	
HEP	21	18	39	51	43	94	92	94	186	18	57	75
HES	12	28	40	—	—	—	96	72	168	19	52	71
HEP (Eng)	33	49	82	—	—	—	127	174	301	84	111	195
HKP (Kan)	34	43	98	—	—	—	118	138	256	16	25	41
HKS	1	9	10	36	87	123	110	111	221	40	64	104
HGE (Edn)	—	—	—	—	—	—	94	62	156	—	—	—
HGE (Hin)							49	55	104	—	—	—
PCM	6	9	15	—	—	—	—	—	—	—	—	—
PMCS	12	6	18	6	13	19	—	—	—	—	—	—

Sources: Compiled from the primary data.

lack of interest of the students. similarly, GFGC Annigery provide an opportunity to take only two optional HKS 123, HEP 94 students in BA section and only 19 students in PMCS combination, because it is purely a rural college, they have lack of knowledge about the importance of the subjects and the language. In contrast to this the unaided college of Gadag and Annigeri are introduced the BA and Bcom course alone and have not introduced the science courses. The HCES College introduced the seven groups for its students, where as Annigeri Amrutheshwar unaided college introduced only five optional subjects. In both the college, HEP (Eng) group is opted by the most of the students. When compare to all the colleges, HCES unaided college admitted more students. HKS, HKP and HEP subjects are also demanded by the students. Therefore, the privatisation of higher education is one of the striking features of the development of higher education in India over the last few decades has been the extent to which private institutions have entered the scene and attempted to respond to the massive demand for education at the post-secondary level. This is particularly true in the fields of higher educational unaided institutions.

Main Findings of the Study

India is well-recognised and the higher education system is one of the largest in the world, the GER is low at about 10 per cent. Higher education institutions play a distinctive role in the social and economic life of a country.

The SCs constitute 16.23 per cent of India's population; the drop-out rates for SC students in higher education are still very high. The population of STs in India stood at 84.33 million. STs constitute 8.2 per cent of the total population of the country with 91.7 per cent of them living in rural areas and 8.3 per cent in urban areas. The literacy rates for Muslim girl students are also low.

The 11th Plan that recognised the increase in enrollment rate from 10 per cent to 15 per cent will involve the inclusiveness. Increase in the enrollment rate will have to come from those social groups and regions whose access to higher education is lower than the other groups. The Plan also recognised the inter-regional; inter-social groups and male female imbalances.

It is found from the analysis that four colleges have been selected from the two district, two government and two unaided colleges and one is forward and another is backward district. The total strength of the GFGC Gadag is 477, the GFGC Annigeri is 397, the unaided college of Gadag is 697, and another unaided college in Annigeri is 362, the female enrollment is 268, 235, 366 and 180 in all the respective colleges and courses.

It is observed that more than 50 per cent of the female students pursuing their higher education in all the government and unaided colleges. It is worked out that the proportion of SC 11.74 per cent, ST 4.82 per cent, OBC 39.62 per cent and 8.17 per cent of 2B category students are admitted for their degree courses in GFGC Gadag. Similarly, the proportion of SC 6.30 per cent, ST 4.28 per cent, and OBC 70.78 per cent and 16.37 per cent of 2B category students are admitted for their degree courses in GFGC Annigeri. Against to this, the proportion of SC 14.04 per cent, ST 5.16 per cent, and OBC 72.02 per cent and 7.74 per cent of 2B category students are admitted for their degree courses in HCES unaided college in Gadag. In the same way, the Amrutheshwar unaided college in Annigeri 9.94 per cent of SC, 3.59 per cent of ST, 66.29 per cent of OBC and 17.68 per cent of 2B students got enrolled.

It is observed that the drop-out rate of SC, 51 per cent, ST 50 per cent, others 38 per cent and OBC 10 per cent respectively in GFGC Gadag. In contrast to this the dropout is 40 per cent of 2B categories, 12 per cent of OBC and very least of other categories in HCES unaided college.

The same trend is continued in the Annigeri GFGC, where also the 2B categories is 42 per cent, others 40 per cent, SC 37 per cent, ST 15 per cent and OBC 15 per cent. However, there is a negative drop-out rate found in SC/ST/OBC categories in Annigeri unaided college. Most of the students in GFGC Gadag took the combinations like HKP 98 (Kan), HEP 82 (Eng), HES 40 and HEP 39, but they have least bothered about the remaining subjects. But on the other hand, only 15 students opted for the PCM combination and 18 students took PMCS combinations.

GFGC Annigery introduced only two optional like HKS 123, HEP 94 students in BA section and only 19 students in PMCS combination

The HCES College introduced the seven groups for its students, whereas annigeri Amrutheshwar un-aided college introduced only five optional subjects. In both the college HEP (Eng) group is opted by the most of the students. When compare to all the colleges, HCES unaided college admitted more students. HKS, HKP and HEP subjects are also demanded by the students.

Recommendations

1. The government colleges should have their own buildings, full-time faculty, ICT, students supporting schemes and basic information facilities to raise overall enrollment in the government colleges compare to that of the unaided colleges.
2. The separate category-wise cells should be open in the government college to look upon the welfare of the students of each category (including female students).
3. The counselling is essential for female students and their parents by that some sort of female drop-out can be prevented.
4. There is a need to introduce the choice-based subjects, more optional, and employment-oriented subjects.

Conclusion

The study covered the enrollment of the students in category-wise, course-wise, college-wise, sex-wise and subject-wise, the drop-out rate in the same manner and the distribution of students according to their combination-wise. Therefore, there is a variation found on the enrollment and drop-out of students in certain categories, so it is a serious issue and policy has to be framed to increase the inclusiveness of the higher education

References

- Aikara, J. (1980): 'Scheduled Castes and Higher Education: A Study of College Students in Mumbai', Dastane, Pune.
- Annual Reports of UGC, Various issues.
- Bowen, William G. (2005): Equity and Excellence in American Higher Education (Thomas).

- Jefferson Foundation Distinguished Lecture Series. University Press of Virginia.
- Burke, Joseph C. (Editor) (2004): Achieving Accountability in Higher Education: Balancing.
- Public, Academic, and Market Demands. Jossey-Bass.
- Chanana, K. (1993): 'Accessing Higher Education—The Dilemma of Schooling: Women, Minorities, Scheduled Castes and Scheduled Tribes in Contemporary India' in S. Chitnis and P. Altbach (eds), Higher Education Reform in India, Sage Publications, New Delhi, India.
- Devasia M.D. (2008). 'Pricing Higher Education: *Equity* vs *Profit*', in Meera Bai ed., Kerala Economy: Slumber to Performance, New Delhi: Serial Publications.
- Duraisamy, (2008) 'Enrolment Forecast of Higher Education for Inclusive Growth in the 11th Five Year Plan', in UGC Report on Higher Education in India.
- Expansion, Inclusiveness, Quality and Finance, New Delhi: University Grants Commission, pp. 27-50.
- Government of India, (2007) Selected Educational Statistics 2010-11, Abstracts, (Provisional), New Delhi: Department of Higher Education, Ministry of Human Resources Development.

39 A Critique on Oversight Committee Relation to Implementation of the New Reservation Policy in Higher Education

Ramesha, K.

Prakruthi, A.R.

Abstract

India is a country with a very rigid caste-based hierarchical struture, where the highest caste enjoyed most of the benefits while the lower caste. The majority of the papulation was backward in socialy, economically, educationally and politically. The backward classes were classified as the Scheduled Caste (SC), Scheduled Tribes (ST) and Other Backward Classes (OBC). Article 46 of the Indian Constitution stated that the state should promote with special care, the education and economical interest of the weaker section of the people, also protecting them from social injustice and all forms of exploitation. Although the reservation policy in higher education is an exception to the equality rule it is still considered as an essential element of equality. Reservation in higher education its support and financial aid to the backward caste people to seek higher education accessible through the reservation. An overall purpose is to develop education opportunities as a means for individual member to reach education, cultural, economic and social success and contribute protecting and advancing the sovereignity and way of life of people.

Accordingly, in the Eleventh Five Year Plan (2007-12), which was described as an Educational Plan, allocation to higher education was scaled up and major expansion was planned. As many as 30 new Central universities were to be set-up, of which 15 have been opened in the last two to three years. At the commencement of the Eleventh Plan, only 20 such universities existed. Plans for expansion also included setting up six new Indian Institutes of Management, seven Indian Institutes of Technology, 20 National Institutes of Technology, four Indian Institutes of Information Technology, nearly 2,000 colleges of engineering and technology, 1,300 polytechnics, 400 under-graduate colleges and many other institutions.

In 2005, the Central Educational Institution (Reservation in Admission) Act which was enacted by Central government, it provides the reservation in admission of students belonging to the scheduled castes, the scheduled tribes and the other backward classes of citizens. On 27th May, 2006 the Act was established Oversight Committee relates to Implementation of the New Reservation Policy of Higher Education, under chairmanship of the Mr N. Veerappa Moily and others 13-member for the purpose of implementation of reservation in higher education, this committee conduct the five preliminary and submit the interim reports on 31st August 2006, and ultimately this committee submitted the final report submitted on 31st September, 2006.

The present study focuses on reservation in higher education relates to Central Educational Institution (Reservation in Admission) Act, 2006 and to make a study on recommendation given by the oversight committee in 2006 for implementation of new reservation policy in 2006.

Introduction

Education is the fulcrum of life, for peace, progress and development. It provides seedlings for culture and civilisation. The higher education in India was started in 1857 with the inception of universities in the three presidency towns. At present, India possesses a highly developed higher education system which offers facility of education and training in almost all aspects of human's creative and intellectual endeavours such as arts and humanities, natural, mathematical and social sciences, engineering; medicine, dentistry, agriculture, education, law, commerce and management, music and performing arts, national and foreign languages, culture, communications etc.

The expansion in the field of reservation in higher education provides the best way to empower the inclusive growth in some section of the society. According to Plato—"Education enables us to prepare a citizen, by the light of knowledge and not by rule of custom, to perform the duties of his station and further the education seeks to turn in the feeling and imaginative of youth as one mould tune a layer with many vibrating strings. So finally higher education enables us to bring the individual to resonate in unison with society. Reservation in higher education has been a long standing policy concern in India and it has to be considered based on the social groups at the Central and the State levels policies of the higher education, the implementation of reservation for Schedule Caste, Schedule Tribe and Other Backward Castes (OBCs) in the centrally-aided higher education institutions effectively from the year 2006. In pursuance of the 93rd Amendment to the Constitution of

India, The Central Educational Institutions (Reservation in Admission) Act 2006, was enacted and has been notified in January 2007 and the main objectives of the Act is providing statutory reservations to SCs, STs and OBCs in Central Educational Institutions and to give necessary resources to the Central Educational Institutions, and the act ensuring that reservations would not lead to any reduction in the seats as were available to unreserved categories before coming into force of this Enactment. The Central Educational Institutions (Reservation in Admission) Act, 2006, the Act under which the following scheme of reservation has been provided: (i) SC - 15 per cent, (ii) ST - 7.5 per cent, and (iii) OBC - 27 per cent. As a result of this, about 50 per cent of the seats have now come under reservation in all central educational institutions including institutions of higher learning and professional institutes like IITs (Indian Institute of Technology), IIMs (Indian Institute of Managements) and government medical and engineering colleges. On May 27, 2006 the Act was established Oversight Committee relates to Implementation of the New Reservation Policy of Higher Education, under chairmanship of the Mr N. Veerappa Moily and others 13-member for the purpose of implementation of reservation in higher education, this committee conduct the five preliminary and, *inter alia* look into the following aspects, the committee submit its interim report on 31st August, 2006 and ultimately this committee submitted the final report on September 31, 2006.

(1) Implementation of 27 per cent reservation for the OBCs in institutes of higher learning, and

(2) Assessment of additional infrastructure and other requirements for increasing the overall availability of seats to a level so that the present level of seats available to the general category students does not decline.

Objectives of the Study

The present study is consisting of following objectives:

1. To study the salient features of the Central Educational Institutions (Reservation in Admission) Act 2006.
2. To study on report of the Oversight Committee relates to Implementation of the New Reservation Policy in Higher Education.
3. To examine the implementation of reservation policy in higher education.

Research Methodology

The present paper is based upon doctrinal work. The study basically employs the analytical, critical view concern to reservation in higher education system in India and also studies the final report on the Oversight Committee. In doctrinal work, Text books, Journals, Legislative materials, various reports to concern of reservation in higher education in India to be used.

Concept of Education and Higher Education

Education is difficult to define because the concept entails varied aspects of knowledge, which can be passed on in various forms, including oral, written or behavioural. It also includes various forms of passing on information. However, education has been defined as, "training and instruction designed to give knowledge and develop skills. United Nations Economic Social and Cultural Organisation (UNESCO), Convention against Discrimination in Education, adopted on December 14, 1960, has given a comprehensive definition of the term higher education. UNESCO notes that higher education includes, "all types of studies, training, and training for research at the post-secondary level, provided by universities or other educational establishments that are approved as institutions of higher education by the competent State Authorities." The present university and higher education system comprises 504 universities of which 243 are State universities, 40 are Central Universities while 130 are Deemed Universities and five institutions have been established under State legislation. There are 53 State Private Universities and 33 Institutes of national importance established by Central legislation. In addition, there are 25,951 colleges including 2,565 women's colleges in India. Reservation in Higher education, also sometimes denoted as "affirmative action" or "positive discrimination", it refers to a policy or programme, of giving certain preferences to certain groups over the others. Certain objectives to achieve to the purpose of giving reservation in the higher education system those are:

- Uplift lower strata of society.
- Reservation in higher education its support and finacial aid to the backward castes peoples.
- The mian purpose to devolop education opportunities as a means for individual member to reach education, cultural, economic and social success and contribute protecting and advancing the sovereignity and way of life of people.

- Promotion of reservation in higher education is to create equal opportunity to all sections of the society.

Salient Features of Central Educational Institutions (Reservation in Admission) Act, 2006

The Rationale

Part IV of the Constitution containing the Directive Principles of State Policy, in **Article 46**, lays down that the State shall promote with special care the educational and economic interests of the weaker sections of the people, and, in particular, of the Scheduled Castes and the Scheduled Tribes, and shall protect them from social injustice. Access to education is of utmost importance in ensuring advancement of persons belonging to the Scheduled Castes, the Scheduled Tribes, and the socially and educationally backward classes of citizens, who is also referred to as the Other Backward Classes (OBCs).

The Constitution (93rd Amendment) Act, 2005, inserted clause (5) in Article 15 of the Constitution, with a view to promote the educational advancement of the socially and educationally backward classes of citizens, the Scheduled Castes and the Scheduled Tribes through special provisions relating to admission of students belonging to these categories in all educational institutions, including private educational institutions, whether aided or unaided by the State. In terms of this provision, Parliament as well as the State Legislatures are empowered to make appropriate laws for the educational advancement of the weaker sections of the people. With a view to give effect to the Constitutional provisions, it was thought expedient and necessary to make statutory provisions in the proposed Bill for reservation in matters of admissions for the students belonging to the Scheduled Castes (SCs), the Scheduled Tribes (STs) and the socially and educationally backward classes of citizens (OBCs) in the Central Educational Institutions, including Institutions deemed to be Universities established, maintained or aided by the Central Government. The provisions of the proposed Bill, *inter alia,* would not apply to the minority educational institutions referred to in Clause (1) of Article 30.

The Central Educational Institutions (Reservation in Admission) Act, 2006 was challenged in the famous case *Ashok Kumar Thakur* v. *Union of India* (2008) 6 SCC 1. The Supreme Court, in its decision, upheld the validity of the Constitutional Amendment Act. The Court has failed to take notice of the fact that reservation is not the only prescribed means for ensuring development of SC/ST/OBC and that such high percentage of reservation in higher education could not have been the dream of the founding fathers of our Constitution. Mediocrity over meritocracy, in this twenty-first century, will not only hamper the quality of education but will also retard the progress of the nation as a whole. Instead of finding out other suitable methods for the development of backward classes, simply giving reservation is nothing but a fraud on the Constitution. In fact, after six decades of the commencement of the Constitution, the time has come to impartially review the entire reservation system and ensure that only the best talents get place in educational institutions, irrespective of his caste or class.

Composition, Principles and Objectives of the Oversight Committee

The Oversight Committee, under the chairmanship of Mr M.Veerappa Moily held four plenary meetings and separate discussions with the group heads. Defining the scope and ambit of the report, it was agreed that the Oversight Committee would cover such institutions of higher learning which have already implemented reservations for SCs/STs. Institutions primarily engaged in R&D will not fall within this ambit. The programme and guidelines drawn up by the Oversight Committee, with the help of the Groups, would act as a point of reference and help the other Ministries of the Government of India to take such measures to introduce reservations in institutions of higher learning from the academic year 2007-08. The Oversight Committee has been set-up to monitor the implementation of the decision to introduce reservations in higher educational institutions.

The fundamental princles of the committee is seeks to expand the provision of Higher Education while at the same time ensuring social inclusion and academic excellence, because a society which excludes a significant section of its population from access to higher education cannot be said to be providing equality of opportunity, along with that, academic excellence also get compromised in the process of expansion, it would lose its competitive edge in the emerging knowledge society–an edge which can propel India to a position of global leadership. While making its recommendations, the Oversight Committee had guided by the following three major principles:

1. ***Expansion:*** Planning for expansion of higher educational opportunities and infrastructure it includes, (a) Physical Infrastructure requirement, availability and utilisation, (b) Strategies of faculty recruitment and remuneration etc., (c) Reorientation of relevant courses, (d) Ways of strengthening research capacity of institutions, (e) Social profile of existing and potential students.

2. ***Inclusion:*** Making higher education inclusive and equitable by designing a scheme that is transparent, fine-tuned and effective, and
3. ***Excellence:*** Maintaining and adding to the excellence of the institutions of higher learning and building a global brand equity for institutions of national importance.

The main objectives of the oversight committee as follows:

1. To identify in each of the Institutions/Universities, the courses at Under-graduate and Post-graduate level and student intake for the academic session 2007-08: Interim report of the oversight committee on the implementation of the new reservation policy in higher educational Institutions.
2. To identify in each course the total number of seats for OBCs and consequently to other categories.
3. To identify for each course the increase in the total number of seats so as to maintain the total availability of seats in the unreserved category.
4. To determine the requirement of faculty and other infrastructure for the enhanced intake and to determine the additional requirement of recurring and non-recurring expenditure for the same.
5. To suggest phasing of expenditure both recurring and non-recurring.
6. To suggest measures, in short term to be taken by each institute for the enhanced intake from the academic session 2007-08.
7. To suggest any other preparatory or consequential steps and required to be taken in order to implement the policy of reservation.

For achieving the above objectives the theme of the oversight committee recognised several critical constraints on capacity enhancement (within a period of one year) and discussed different strategies to tackle them. It also noted that the programmes in IIMs and NITIE relevant to the OBC Quota are all Post Graduate Programmes. Apart from two years PG Diploma programmes, IIMs also have other programmes like Fellow Programmes, Executive Development Programmes, and Faculty Development Programmes etc. Except for the two-year PG Diploma Programme, the other programmes may require work experience, sponsorship, etc. The existing reservations for SC and ST are in the two years PG Diploma and equivalent Programmes only. Therefore, the reservations for OBCs should also be extended only to these.

Recommendations of the Oversight Committee

For achieving the objectives of the committee, it recommended that the prescribed increase in intake in all Central Government institutions will be 54 per cent. The Committee has largely concentrated its deliberations on institutions of Higher Learning under the Ministries of Human Resource Development, Agricultural Research and Education and the Health Ministry. While making recommendations the committee has been guided by the principle that in matters relating to academic and faculty related issues, and infrastructural and development issues, it should be ensured that the existing infrastructure and faculty in the institutions of higher learning are optimally used before considering creation of additional infrastructure and faculty.

Recommendations on Academic and Faculty Related Issues

(a) The institution and universities department must be filling up the existing vacancies or otherwise for retaining or re-engaging the existing personnel, particularly, those who have either superannuated during recent years or those who are likely to superannuate during the next three years. So this would be in addition to making optimal use of the existing faculty.

(b) The institutions of higher learning should keep these three principles in view, while determining threshold marks for admission to OBC students. While expanding the intake, due care should be taken to ensure that capacities are expanded in subjects or areas in which there are opportunities on account of employability.

(c) The committee recommends that the threshold for admission should be determined by the respective institutions alone, as is done today, commensurate with the level of its excellence.

(d) As regards 'cut-offs' in institutions may be placed somewhere midway between those for SC/ST and the unreserved category, carefully calibrated so that the principles of both equity and excellence can be maintained.

(e) The Committee strongly feels that the students, who currently tend to get excluded, must be given every single opportunity to raise their own levels of attainment, so that they can reach their true potential. The Government should invest heavily in creating powerful, well-designed and executed remedial preparatory measures to achieve this objective fully.

(f) Engaging visiting or adjunct faculty, assigning additional workload to existing faculty, within reasonable limits so that there is no dilution. For motivating the existing faculty additional compensation may be contemplated.

(g) Amendment in eligibility criteria for faculty recruitment. The requirement of a Ph.D qualification could be considered for waiver by the concerned academic authority where a faculty member has enough relevant experience, like a practising manager and autonomy will also have to be given in respect of the compensation packages to be offered in contractual engagements. Here, providing residential facilities to faculty.

(h) The Committee shares that Group's proposal for developing an action plan for Quality Improvement and upgrading the skills of the existing faculty. The establishment of a National Centre for Faculty Development and also conducting sequential summer programmes for faculty development would provide affirmative action with long-term benefits.

(i) The Committee shares that Group's proposal for developing an action plan for Quality Improvement and upgrading the skills of the existing faculty. The establishment of a National Centre for Faculty Development and also conducting sequential summer programmes for faculty development would provide affirmative action with long term benefits.

(j) The teacher student ratio (TSR) varies from Group to Group and the Committee would like to categorically state that enhancement of faculty should be based on a rational and viable teacher student ratio. An unreasonable and non-viable teacher student ratio would impede the process of implementing the reservation policy.

(k) Suitable policy changes to be make for the purpose of enhancement of the retirement age, contractual appointments, modifications in eligibility conditions for faculty, lifting of the ban on recruitment of non-academic staff, provision for adequate support staff will have to be effected immediately so that the special recruitment process can be set in motion.

Recommendations on Infrastructural and Developmental Issues

In order to ensure that the additional student intake will be matched by commensurate infrastructural facilities, a plan for developmental expansion has been improved by the institution, the Committee makes the following recommendations relating to infrastructure:

1. In general, all institutions will need additional physical space, construction of new college and hostel buildings, additional laboratories, library facilities, books, furniture and equipment, computer laboratories, campus wireless connectivity, video-conferencing and IT enabled classrooms. Optimal use should also be made of the existing infrastructure.

2. The other major elements of the capital cost would be relating to residential accommodation for teaching staff and in some special cases non-teaching staff.

3. The procedures involved in setting up additional infrastructure especially civil works and procurement of furniture and equipment, have laid down administrative procedures.

4. Necessary delegation of powers and increased autonomy will have to be provided so as to ensure that the necessary infrastructure will be put in position at the earliest.

5. The Committee recommends the setting up of an **Empowered Committee** in each institution and Ministry, which will give the necessary approvals and sanctions.
   - This Empowered Committee can be constituted in each institution as per their relevant governing norms. The Empowered Committee should be given clear cut terms of reference with appropriate powers of delegation.
   - The delegation must ensure that the local unit will have the powers to issue necessary administrative orders for undertaking civil works and procurement of furniture and equipment.
   - The Empowered Committee will also supervise the implementation of the development plan, observance of timelines and quality aspects of the projects' execution.
   - Suitable policies will have to be notified for establishment of the Empowered Committee and also for delegation of financial and administrative powers.

6. Each Group has broadly laid down the infrastructural requirements. However, the specific requirements institution-wise will also have to be taken into account, which would figure in the final report. The Groups should attempt preparation of institution-wise DPRs.

7. There will be an Implementation Monitoring Committee in the

Planning Commission, which will review the progress in the implementation of the OBC reservation plan and the execution of DPRs.

8. Wherever land acquisition is necessary for setting up the infrastructure, appropriate administrative orders will have to be issued for removing any bottlenecks and for placing the process on a fast track.

9. In order to ensure that the process of expansion commences immediately, release of adequate proportionate funds will have to be effected. This is essential for timely implementation.

10. The additional infrastructure will involve sizeable non-recurring capital costs and also recurring costs, which are being projected separately.

11. Each group will have to submit an institution-wise detailed project report drawing up the master plan for expansion.

Implementations of Reservation on Admissions to Higher Education

The expansion in the field of reservation in higher education provided great access to all sections of the society. However, owing to a number of constraints, and socio-economic factors, the benefits of expansion of educational facilities have not fully reach to all the communities specifically among the Scheduled Castes (SC) and Scheduled Tribes (ST). In 2004-05, the GER (Gross Enrollment Rate) in higher education was about 10.84 per cent at overall levels, the GER among the SC's (6.30 per cent), the ST's (6.33 per cent), and the OBC (16.60 per cent). Thus, the GER for the SC/STs was three times and that of the OBCs was about two times lower as compared with the others. Between the SC/ST's and the OBC's, however the GER was lower among the former by two per cent points. As per the annual publication "Statistics of Higher and Technical Education" of the Ministry of Human Resource Development, the Gross Enrollment Ratio (GER) of Female (All Categories), SC students and ST students enrolled in higher education as a percentage of the respective population in the age group of 18-23 years in the country during 2008-09 and 2009-10 (Provisional) is given below.

Year/Category	*2008-09*	*2009-10*
Female	11.4	12.7
SC	10.5	11.1
ST	9.2	10.3

Source: Ministry of Human Resource Development, 2008-10.

The GER of female students in the country is estimated to be 16.5 in 2010-11, as per the provisional report on the All India Survey on Higher Education-based on data collected up to 31st July, 2012. Data on OBC students in higher education is not available till 2009-10. However, in the All India Survey on Higher Education, provision has been made for the collection of data on the enrollment of OBC students from 2010-11 onwards.

The Tata Institute of Social Sciences (TISS) conduct a report on the 'Impact of Reservation Policy in Higher Education in India' on May 24, 2009, it stated that to some centrally funded institutions, namely the IITs, AIIMS and TISS, the percentage of SC/STs preparing for the IIT-JEE through self-study is much higher than for other groups and the sharp urban/rural and CBSE/state board divides probably affect the success rate based on the adverse impact they have on these sections. They speculate that disparities in parents' educational status as well as household income are other important factors affecting the performance of SC/STs. A similarly high rate of failure of SC/STs in the AIIMS entrance exam is also noted. As for enrollment at TISS, it is stated that SC/STs have surpassed their respective quota shares and while the numbers are only rough estimates, a significant number of OBCs (10 per cent) are believed to be getting in through merit although their percentage is still less in proportion to their eligible population, therefore through this reservation in higher and technical education we can ensure higher education to this people.

In Uttar Pradesh, OBC applicants to professional courses were fewer than their proportion in the overall population and filled fewer slots in medical colleges than the allotted quota but exceeded the stipulated 27 per cent in engineering colleges. Performance-wise (as determined by pass percentages), there is something of a surprise: OBCs fared the worst, SC/STs the best with general category students in between. Reserved seats were not filled in post-graduate engineering courses and an inverse correlation was found between demand for a course and the number of SC/ST/OBCs enrolled in it.

In Tamil Nadu, backward class (BC as distinguished from Most Backward Class, MBC) students out-performed the open category (OC) students in qualifying for medical admission and very nearly matched the open category for engineering admission. The report notes that even while engineering education in the state is highly privatised (96.7 per cent of all engineering colleges are self-financing), BCs and MBCs were adequately represented whereas SC/ST numbers are low. Also 27 per cent reserved category candidates who are selected for MBBS in Tamil Nadu take admission without any reservation. The majority of these (25 per cent) are from BC and MBC categories. It also states that at the exit level of professional courses, no marked difference exists between the performance of reserved category students vis-à-vis the general category is noted and hence quotas have not diluted merit in engineering institutions. The last finding is erroneous as the conclusion can only be asserted with confidence with respect to BCs and MBCs, not SC/STs.

Conclusion

To sum up, disadvantages among groups and individuals need to be minimised, but not all forms of prevailing disadvantages justify the same solution or policy prescription. The problem posed by the Indian government's decision to extend reservations and quotas in higher education to SC, ST and OBC is that it ignores this dimension and focuses only on existing differences of end results. This shortcoming is further accentuated by the government's decision to reserve seats in higher education without creating opportunities for disadvantaged groups at an early level, so that talents can be nurtured from a younger age and differences arising from background conditions minimised over the years. The merit of the capability approach is that, while it emphasises the need to make basic social goods available to everyone, it underlines the value of creating an environment in which individuals can develop their talents and capabilities and act as free agents. If we are to shift away from the politics of identity and patronage, then this is surely a better way of minimising disadvantages and nurturing the democratic ethos.

References

- Akash Shah (2013), Critical Analysis on Reservation Policy in India Published in the online, web address is http://www.legalservicesindia.com/article/.
- Asha Gupta (2006), Affirmative action in higher education in India and the USA: a study in contrasts, Research and Occasional paper series: CSHE - 10.06, Centre for studies in Higher Education, University of California, and Berkeley.
- Final Report of The Oversight Committee on the Implementation of The New reservation Policy in Higher Education in India, Government of India, September, 2006.
- Higher Education in India: Twelfth Five Year Plan (2012–2017) and beyond, FICCI Higher Education Summit 2012 by Planning Commission Government of India.
- Interim report of the oversight committee on the implementation of the new reservation policy in higher educational Institutions, 2006.

- Jandhyala B.G. Tilak (2012) Higher Education Policy in India in Transition, Economic and Political Weekly, Vol. XLVII, March 31st, pp. 36-40.
- K. Samu (2012) 'Reservation-2012', Human Rights Documentation, Indian Social Institute, Lodi Road, New Delhi, India.
- Mehbubul Hassan Laska (2010) Rethinking Reservation in Higher Education in India, Indian Law Review, New Delhi, pp. 25-53.
- National Knowledge Commission , Note on higher education, 29th November 2006, published by National Knowledge Commission, Government of India, Dharma Marg, Chanakyapuri, New Delhi-21.
- Pawan Agarwal (2006), Higher Education in India: the need for change, India Council for Research on International Economic Relations, working paper no. 180.
- Rakesh Basant and Gitanjali Sen (2009), Who Participates in Higher Education in India? Rethinking the Role of Affirmative Action, Economic and Political Weekly, September 25, 2010 Vol. xlv. No. 39. pp. 62-70.
- Report of the Committee on India Vision 2020, Planning Commission, Government of India, New Delhi, December 2002, p. 47.
- Report of the National Commission for Religious and Linguistic Minorities April 2010, pp. 13-22.
- Thomas E. Weisskopf (2004), Impact of Reservation on Admissions to Higher Education India Economic and Political Weekly, September 25, 2004, pp. 4339-4349.

40 Pattern in Growth and Financing of Higher Education in India: Does Quality Responding to It?

Dr. Nanjunda
S. Jyothi Lakshmi

Concept

After the Globalisation, the demand for higher education has been growing rapidly with both enrollment and new institutions perspectives. However, causality of all these is undermining equity a quality of higher education. The number of students entering into higher education after completing lower education has in recent years grown irrespective of socio-economic background. Some institutions of India, such as the Indian Institutes of Technology (IITs), have been globally acclaimed for their standard of education. In the same way Government expenditure is also growing fast like anything where shortage for social welfare programme. Experts opined India's higher education system can be predictable to be improved associated to private sector and be more crystal clear and inclusive as soon as possible provided the government should intensely focus on implementation, monitoring and quality assurance mechanisms. The present paper is an effort to scrutinise financing of higher education in India in the last previous two decades, sources for funding, scholarships, bank loan, functioning of private sector and self-financing courses in the public higher educational institutions.

Background

"Since budget resources are limited, and such resources as are available, need to be allocated to expanding primary education, it is important to recognise that the universities must make greater efforts to supplement resources from the government", (Government of India, 2001, 2002-2007).

As we are aware educational influences and is also influenced by rapid economic growth and the social changes that accompany it. Education by itself is not sufficient for economic growth that preceded the take off by

India was built on the foundation of educational achievement. Human capital acquired through education influences economic growth by increasing adoption of new technologies and the productivity of the labour force. It also influences the evolution of politico-economic institution and the anticipation of future economic growth and affects enrollment decisions and attainment through changes in the rate of return to education (James Antony and S. Saravanan, 2012). In this paper, an attempt is made to analyses the broad trend in the public expenditure on education of India. This analysis was done using 17 years data over the period from 1990-91 to 2006-07 (Aggarwal, 2000).

However, there are certain critiques that In India, the priority has been on secondary and higher education. In most Indian states, the share of secondary education is higher than that in Latin American middle income countries. Although they have secondary enrollments higher than those in most Indian states. Due to the public subsidisation of secondary and higher education, the children coming from poor socio-economic backgrounds not benefitted, and they constitute the bulk of school students who do not pursue higher education in India. They are in no position to gain anything from the public spending on secondary and higher education. Every country which has achieved universal elementary education has done so through public intervention; the experiences of the developed and high achieving developing countries were markedly similar; and the private sector's role was limited at the elementary level. It is concluded that additional public spending should concentrate mainly on elementary rather than secondary education and should go to government schools (Dev and Mooij, 2002). General scenario of higher education in India does not compete with the world Quality standards. Therefore, there is enough rationalisation for an augmented appraisal of the excellence of the country's educational institutions.

Some Facts about Highest Education India

India's GER of 16 per cent was much below the world average of 27 per cent, as well as that of other emerging countries such as China (26 per cent) and Brazil (36 per cent) in 2010.

Excellence

1. *Faculty shortage*—There is 40 per cent and 35 per cent shortage of faculty in state and central universities, respectively.
2. *Quality institutions*—Sixty two per cent of universities and 90 per cent of colleges were average or below average in 2010, on the basis of their NAAC accreditation.

3. *Low citation impact*—India's relative citation impact is half the world average.

(*Sources:* Higher Education in India Twelfth Five Year Plan (2012–2017) and beyond).

Table 1. Growth of Public Expenditure on University/High Level Education in India during 1990-91 to 2006-07 (Rs in crores)

Year	*Expenditure on Higher Level Education*	*Index No.*	*Annual Growth Rate*
1990-91	3956.09	100	—
1991-92	4396.78	111.4	11.14
1992-93	4922.91	124.44	11.97
1993-94	5557.2	140.47	12.88
1994-95	6299.53	159.24	13.36
1995-96	6954.07	175.78	10.39
1996-97	7983.11	201.18	14.79
1997-98	8595.67	217.28	7.67
1998-99	11097.42	280.51	29.10
1999-2000	15112.89	382.02	36.18
2000-01	16928.21	427.90	12.01
2001-02	14323.32	362.06	-15.39
2002-03	17099.87	432.24	19.38
2003-04	17114.54	457.89	5.93
2004-05	20174.23	509.95	11.37
2005-06	23588.78	596.26	16.93
2006-07	26878.81	679.43	13.95

(*Source:* Educational Statistics of India).

The public expenditure on university/high education in India, during the period from 1990-91 to 2006-07 has a witnessed a sizeable increase. The value of public expenditure on university/high education has increased from Rs 3956.09 crore in 1990-91 to Rs 26878.81 crore in 2006-07. The index number has increased from 100 in 1990-91 to 679.43 in 2006-07 with fluctuations. The linear growth rate is 36.21 per cent. The lowest annual growth rate was -15.39 in 2001-02 and the highest annual growth rate was 36.18 in 1999-2000.

Conclusion

It is found that a recent assessment of universities and research institutes all over the world, conducted by a private agency, no single Indian university

Graph 1. Picture of Student's Enrollment

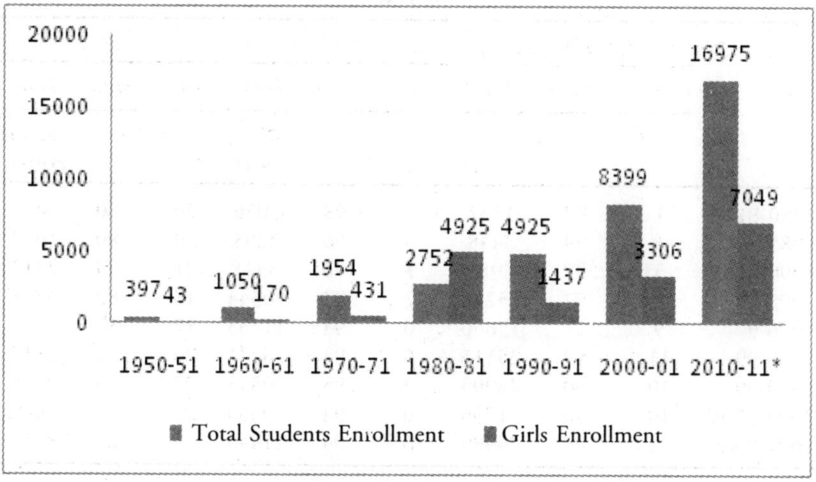

Table 2. Public Higher Education Institutions and Students Enrolled Therein in India

	Institutions			*Enrollment (in lakhs)*		
	Colleges	*Univ. and Research*	*Higher Education*	*Colleges*	*Research and PG*	*Higher Education*
1980-81	4152	206	4358	21.25	3.17	27.59
1985-86	4815	228	5043	29.66	3.56	33.22
1990-91	6008	281	6289	39.21	4.12	43.33
1993-94	6764	309	7073	42.07	3.95	46.02
1996-97	8529	327	8856	54.37	5.01	59.38
1999-00	9906	349	10255	71.31	5.95	77.26

Source: Based on Selected Educational Statistics, various issues.

Table 3. Share of Education Expenditures in GDP and Revenue Expenditure

	1981-82	*1985-86*	*1990-91*	*1995-96*	*1999-00*	*2001-02(B)*
			Percentage of GDP in			
Total education	2.49	3.00	3.59	3.60	4.22	4.18
Elementary	1.09	1.39	1.58	1.44	1.58	1.66
Secondary	0.81	0.92	1.10	0.98	0.94	0.98
Higher	0.38	0.42	0.36	0.37	0.47	0.43
			Percentage of Revenue Expenditure in			
Total education	9.09	11.11	9.23	13.34	17.01	14.46
Elementary	3.98	5.14	4.06	5.32	5.44	5.34
Secondary	2.94	3.42	2.82	3.61	3.80	3.40
Higher	1.39	1.56	0.94	1.35	1.88	1.49

Source: Analysis of Budgeted Expenditure on Education, various issues.

Table 4. Role of Center-States in Financing Different Levels of Education (Total Expenditures)

	Elementary			*Secondary*			*Higher*		
	Center	*States*	*Total*	*Center*	*States*	*Total*	*Center*	*States*	*Total*
	(in %)		*(Rs in crores*	*(in %)*		*(Rs in crores*	*(in %)*		*(Rs in crores*
1980-81	1	99	1537	2	98	1036	20	80	484
1985-86	1	99	3448	4	96	2293	20	80	1047
1990-91	3	97	7956	7	93	5531	21	79	2312
1995-96	8	92	15218	7	93	10344	18	82	3871
1996-97	9	91	17850	6	94	11735	17	83	4288
1998-99	11	89	25115	6	94	16721	26	74	6117
1999-00	10	90	27905	5	95	20845	27	73	8248
2000-01(R)	10	90	31756	6	94	20489	25	75	10342
2001-02(B)	11	89	34489	6	94	21444	19	81	8577

Source: Analysis of Budget Expenditure, various issue.

Table 5. Sources of Income for Higher Education

	Government	*Fees*	*Others*	*Rs in crores*
1950-51	49.4	26.8	13.8	114.38
1960-61	53.5	34.8	11.7	344.38
1970-71	61.0	25.5	13.5	1118.28
1980-81	72.8	17.4	108	3766.71
1986-87	75.9	12.6	11.5	9011.98

Source: Education in India Vol. II (S).

in the world's top 300 while China has six. Our Prime Minister Manmohan Singh in 2007 opined "Our university system is, in many parts, in a state of disrepair... In almost half the districts in the country, higher education enrollments are abysmally low, almost two-third of our universities and 90 per cent of our colleges are rated as below average on quality parameters... I am concerned that in many states university appointments, including that of vice-chancellors, have been politicised and have become subject to caste and communal considerations, there are complaints of favouritism and corruption". It is the time to focus on merit-based student financing and we need to work on Internationalisation of education also. Moreover this is the time to enabling a research environment in higher education sector. High quality faculty, improved technology for teaching delivery will be an edge in dealing with both access and quality of higher education.

References

- Aggarwal, Ya. (2000), Public and private partnership in primary education in india—a study of unrecognised schools in Haryana. Operations Research and System management Unit, NIEPA.
- Bashir, S. (2000), Government expenditure on elementary education in the nineties. New Delhi: European Commission.
- Cordella, T. and G.D. Ariccia (1988). Budget support versus project aid. (IMF Working Paper, WP/03/88). Washington: International Monetary Fund.
- Dev, M. and Mooij, J. (2002). Social Sector Expenditures in the 1990s: Analysis of Centre and State Budgets. *Economic and Political Weekly,* Vol. No. 27 (9), 2002.
- James Antony and S. Saravanan growth of public expenditure on education in India IJSERC Vol. 3 No. 1 2012.
- Prakash, V. (2007), Trends in growth and financing of higher education in India. *Economic and Political Weekly,* Vol. No. 39.6, 2007.
- Ramji, V., Sujatha, S. and V.K. Srinivasan (2001), A Study on Management of Public Expenditure by State Governments in India, Indian Institute of Economics, New Delhi.

41 Higher Education Through Distance Education: A Review of Karnataka State Open University

Mr. Harisha N.
Dr. Jayasheela

Introduction

Open learning system has true influence to impart education globally and reach out to hitherto uncovered segments of Indian population in remote and far off areas. Meeting the challenge of reaching millions of unreached people in the country with an effective multi-media package, the system of distance education could be the chosen mode for such programmes of education and training. Distance Education, or earning a degree online is a rapidly growing industry already slated to be worth billions. Distance learning is a field of education that focusses on the pedagogy, technology, and instructional system designs that aim to deliver education to those students who are not physically "on site" like in a traditional classroom or campus. Although India is the third largest country in the world in terms of higher education, after China and the United States, India still has a current ratio of enrollment in the educational institution below nine per cent which is less than the average of lower-middle-income countries in the world. In this context, distance and open learning open up the door of higher education due to its flexible and innovative as well as low cost characteristic.

Objectives of the Present Paper

The main objective of this paper is to provide an overview of the role and developments of distance education in India and to review the expansion of higher education through Karnataka state Open University. This study is based on secondary data from university annual reports from last five years and based on literatures from different journals and online sources.

Role and Growth of Distance Education in India

With growing social aspiration for education and massive expansion of secondary education in the post-independence era, the pressure for places in higher education grew significantly. The states did not have enough resources to laterally expand collegiate education. On the other hand, millions who aspired for higher education were not able to access formal time-bound education, even if access were available. There had to be a search for alternative mode of education.

The Education Commission (1964-66) recommended introduction of correspondence education so that larger number of aspirants find educational opportunities at the university level. This was also reflected in the first National Policy on Education, 1968. The University of Delhi was the pioneer to introduce correspondence courses as a pilot project in 1962. Subsequently, the University of Delhi appointed a sub-committee to recommend different courses at the first-degree level. The success of Delhi University's endeavour in distance education motivated other universities to introduce several kinds of programmes through correspondence courses.

In 1970, the Ministry of Education and Social Welfare, in collaboration with the Ministry of Information and Broadcasting, the University Grants Commission (UGC) and the Indian National Commission for Cooperation with UNESCO organised a seminar on Open University. The seminar recommended the establishment of an open university in India on an experimental basis. Subsequently, the Government of India appointed an eight-member working group under the Chairmanship of G. Parthasarthy to consider the establishment of Open University. The group opined that the University should have jurisdiction over the entire country so that when it is fully developed; students even in the remotest corner of the country can have access to its instruction and degrees. In 1982, an expert committee under the chairmanship of Professor G. Ram Reddy prepared a project proposal on an Open University in Andhra Pradesh. The committee stressed that the provision of access to higher education could be enlarged by action on a variety of fronts; its greater accessibility, course structure, organisation of learning activities, new teaching.

Methodologies, transferability between institution and courses, the flow of publicity material, student finances and the availability of the new technologies like radio, television, audio visual-aids and effective and efficient organisation of regional and study centers (Government of Andhra Pradesh, 1982). On the basis of the recommendation of the expert committee, the Government of Andhra Pradesh established Andhra Pradesh Open University (later renamed as Dr. B.R. Ambedkar Open University in 1991) in 1982; Professor G. Ram Reddy led the first Indian Open University as its vice-chancellor.

In 1985, a committee was constituted by the Ministry of Education to develop a project report on Indira Gandhi National Open University. Professor G. Ram Reddy was called upon to develop the project document. On the basis of that project report, the Union Government introduced a bill in the Parliament in 1985, and the National Open University came into existence in September 1985. Encouraged by the success of IGNOU and BRAOU, many other states established State Open Universities. Presently, there are one National Open University and thirteen State Open Universities.

Expansion of Higher Education through Karnataka State Open University Brief Review about University

Established on 1st June 1996, vide Government Notification No EDI/UOV/95 dated, 12th February 1996–KSOU Act 1992, keeping in view the education needs of country in general and state in particular. KSOU has a rich and long experience in the field of Distance Education as this was carved out of the erstwhile Institute of Correspondence Courses and continuing Education of University of Mysore.

The university is situated at the North-Western end of the Manasagangotri campus. The campus, which is about five kms, from the city centre, has a serene atmosphere ideally situated for academic pursuits. Distance Education is perhaps the only way to meet the increasing demand for higher education especially in a developing country like India. Distance education programme at KSOU are specially designed for:

(a) Students who discontinue their formal education owing to pecuniary or other circumstances.

(b) Students residing in geographically remote areas.

(c) Students who cannot get admission to a regular college/post graduate department.

(d) Employed persons who cannot pursue their study as full-time students, and

(e) Individuals who wish to pursue learning for knowledge sake.

The Karnataka State Open University came into being to achieve the following objectives.

1. To provide access and equity through open flexible learning, this is relevant to the learners, at their doorsteps.
2. To create individualised virtual learning spaces to the needs of the new-age learners.

3. To enable universal knowledge resource sharing through innovative pedagogy.
4. To assure better quality and excellence through institutional collaboration and accessibility.
5. To ensure institutional determination towards emancipator learning.
6. To widen students access through innovative technology for life-long learning.
7. To create learning environment and knowledge media of first choice for learners and professional worldwide.
8. To keep pace with the new-age requirement and encourage proactive convergence of media and technology for teaching and learning.
9. To innovate, explore and practice new avenues in knowledge management and sharing, for positive social intervention.
10. To ensure sustained efforts to interpret and operational learners need to develop new skills through collaborative and interactive learning.

Growing Student Enrollment

The correspondence courses institutions are offering more than 400 programmes in India, about 50 per cent of which are professional in nature. The enrollment in these institutions is of the order of 9,00,000 in year 1999, which forms 11.64 per cent of the total enrollment in higher education in the country. An important point to be noted here is that the growth rate of enrollment in correspondence and distance education mode has been higher than that of higher education in general (Period, 1990-2000, *Source:* UGC Reports).

The same trend of rapid growing enrollment for different post-graduation courses and diploma courses we can see at Karnataka State Open University also.

Table 1, provides the information relating to the students enrollment at Karnataka State Open University for different post-graduation courses and diploma and certificate courses in the year 2006-2007 and 2011-2012. The data indicate that the enrollment for both post-graduate courses and diploma courses increased significantly from 49504 to 113220 during the period of 2006 to 2012. This shows that the Karnataka State Open University contributes a lot to expand the higher education throughout Karnataka and other parts of the country.

Table 1. Student Enrollment for Different Post-graduation Courses and Diploma Courses at KSOU

Sl. No.	*Courses offered*	*2006-07*	*2011-2012*
1.	B.A.	13938	49102
2.	B.Com	3069	6856
3.	B.Ed	1000	1988
4.	B.Sc	4368	
5.	B.L.I.Sc	492	459
6.	M.A.	14323	35574
7.	M.Com	3409	11485
8.	MBA	3634	2719
9.	M.Ed	950	950
10.	M.Sc	2600	897
11.	I.L.L.M.		228
12.	MLSc	175	217
13.	PG Diploma and Certificate	1546	2745
	Total	49504	113220

Source: Annual Report 2007-08 and 2011-2012, KSOU.

Major Finding

The major findings of the study:

1. The number of State Open Universities is increasing rapidly. In the year 1982 first Open University started in the state of Andhra Pradesh in the name of Andhra Pradesh Open University. Now the number of State Open Universities is increased to 13.

2. Distance education system made a greater accessibly to higher education throughout the country.

3. The another major findings of the study is that, the number of student enrollment for both post-graduate courses and diploma courses increased significantly from 49504 to 113220 during the period of 2006 to 2012 in Karnataka state Open University. Which clearly indicates that the expansion of higher education increasing rapidly through distance education.

Suggestions

The National Knowledge Commission (NKC) believes that a radical reform of the system of open and distance education is imperative to achieve the objectives of expansion, inclusion and excellence in higher education. Distance education has an enormous potential to spread higher education opportunities beyond the brick and mortar world. But there are reasons for concern. They are:

1. The Quality of Higher Education need to be Improved

The distance education universities are provides educational opportunities not only to those who discontinue formal education on account of economic or social compulsions, but also to young school drop-outs who are simply unable to secure admission in the formal stream at universities. There is a clear need to improve the quality of distance education and to make it more appropriate to the needs of society.

2. Innovative Practices—The New Technologies to be Adopted

Distance education institutions should adopt new innovative practices in their teaching and learning business. In this regard, we recommend that the digital broadband Knowledge Network proposed by National Knowledge Commission should have provision for inter-connecting the major distance education institutions and their study centers. A national information and communication technology backbone should be adopted to enhance access and *e*-governance in distance education, and enable the dissemination of knowledge across all modes, that is, print, audio-visual and internet-based multimedia.

Conclusion

So, we can say that distance education mode has become very popular and common in India, because it is catering to a wide range of aspirants (students), who are willing to upgrade their educational qualifications for various reasons. The Distance education system provides opportunities not only to younger students but also to those from the older age groups. The main reasons for increasing interest in distance education lies in the need for continuing education in today's competitive world. Every people always try to add value to their competence in their bid to advance their carrier further. Distance Education is also very cheaper to compare with regular mode of education. Distance education has greatly reduced the wall of distance between education and a normal student beyond the long distance of home or work place to university. Now just a little need to increase the need to make it professional and employability part of education community.

The globalisation of distance learning allows institutions to reach new audience and widens consumers' choice. Learners will be able to hook-up to the net and search the best buy they can get from around the world. Educational service is an emerging area of *e*-commerce. To the institutions, it is a challenge and an opportunity, challenge because of keener competition and opportunity because of a much bigger market. To the learners, there are more choices and better programmes. So the future has never been brighter for the distance education institutions. But at the end of the day, it is quality and quality alone that determines.

References

- Annual Report (2006-2007), Karnataka State Open University, Mukthagangotri Mysore.
- Annual Report (2007-2008), Karnataka State Open University, Mukthagangotri Mysore.
- Annual Report (2008-2009), Karnataka State Open University, Mukthagangotri Mysore.
- Annual Report (2009-2010), Karnataka State Open University, Mukthagangotri Mysore.
- Annual Report (2010-2011), Karnataka State Open University, Mukthagangotri Mysore.
- Annual Report (2011-2012), Karnataka State Open University, Mukthagangotri Mysore.
- Dipankar Saikia (2011), The Role of ODL in Assam State India, Asian Journal of Distance Education, Vol. 2, pp. 72-75.
- Kamlesh Gupta and Manjiri Damele (2013), Contemporary Challenges in Higher Education, University News, Vol. 32, August 12-18-2013.
- Online edition of India's National Newspaper, Tuesday, August 7, 2001.

Index

G

I

O

P